D0630650

Unpopular Privacy

Studies in Feminist Philosophy is designed to showcase cutting-edge monographs and collections that display the full range of feminist approaches to philosophy, that push feminist thought in important new directions, and that display the outstanding quality of feminist philosophical thought.

STUDIES IN FEMINIST PHILOSOPHY
Cheshire Calhoun, Series Editor

Published in the Series:

Abortion and Social Responsibility: Depolarizing the Debate
Laurie Shrage

Gender in the Mirror: Confounding Imagery
Diana Tietjens Meyers

Autonomy, Gender, Politics
Marilyn Friedman

Setting the Moral Compass: Essays by Women Philosophers
Edited by Cheshire Calhoun

Burdened Virtues: Virtue Ethics for Liberatory Struggles
Lisa Tessman

On Female Body Experience: "Throwing Like a Girl" and Other Essays
Iris Marion Young

Visible Identities: Race, Gender and the Self
Linda Martín Alcoff Women and CitizenshipEdited by Marilyn

Friedman Women's Liberation and the Sublime: Feminism, Postmodernism, Environment
Bonnie Mann

Analyzing Oppression
Ann E. Cudd

Self Transformations: Foucault, Ethics, and Normalized Bodies
Cressida J. Heyes

Family Bonds: Genealogies of Race and Gender
Ellen K. Feder

Moral Understandings: A Feminist Study in Ethics, Second Edition
Margaret Urban Walker

The Moral Skeptic
Anita M. Superson

"You've Changed": Sex Reassignment and Personal Identity
Edited by Laurie J. Shrage

Dancing with Iris: The Philosophy of Iris Marion Young
Edited by Ann Ferguson and Mechthild Nagel

Philosophy of Science after Feminism
Janet A. Kourany

Shifting Ground: Knowledge and Reality, Transgression and Trustworthiness
Naomi Scheman

The Metaphysics of Gender
Charlotte Witt

Unpopular Privacy: What Must We Hide?
Anita L. Allen

Unpopular Privacy

What Must We Hide?

Anita L. Allen

OXFORD
UNIVERSITY PRESS

Oxford University Press, Inc., publishes works that further
Oxford University's objective of excellence
in research, scholarship, and education.

Oxford New York
Auckland Cape Town Dar es Salaam Hong Kong Karachi
Kuala Lumpur Madrid Melbourne Mexico City Nairobi
New Delhi Shanghai Taipei Toronto

With offices in
Argentina Austria Brazil Chile Czech Republic France Greece
Guatemala Hungary Italy Japan Poland Portugal Singapore
South Korea Switzerland Thailand Turkey Ukraine Vietnam

Published by Oxford University Press, Inc.
198 Madison Avenue, New York, New York 10016

www.oup.com

Oxford is a registered trademark of Oxford University Press

Library of Congress Cataloging-in-Publication Data
Allen, Anita L., 1953–
Unpopular privacy : what must we hide? / Anita L. Allen.
p. cm.
(Studies in feminist philosophy)
ISBN 978-0-19-514137-5 (alk. paper)
1. Privacy, Right of. 2. Privacy, Right of—United States.
3. Women's rights. I. Title.
JC596.A44 2011
323.44'80973—dc22 2010046920

1 3 5 7 9 8 6 4 2

Printed in the United States of America
on acid-free paper

CONTENTS

PREFACE

I first began writing this book a dozen years ago.[1] My plan was to use diverse examples, drawn from contemporary US privacy and data protection law, to raise philosophical questions about legal coercion and paternalism under liberalism. In a liberal society, "freedom is normatively basic, and so the onus of justification is on those who would limit freedom, especially through coercive means"; moreover, "political authority and law must be justified, as they limit the liberty of citizens."[2] But around that time privacy law in North America and Europe was entering an uncertain, rapid-growth phase.[3] In the United States, major federal Internet, financial, and medical privacy laws were on the horizon, including the Children's Online Privacy Protection Act, the Gramm-Leach-Bliley Financial Services Modernization Act, and the Health Insurance Portability and Accountability Act. The European Union had enacted its historic data directive in 1995, dictating a harmonized set of legal reforms within member states.[4] It was widely anticipated that the directive would transform information privacy practices far beyond European borders. The European Union expanded its data protection policymaking in succeeding years, with additional directives concerning telecommunications, electronic data transmission, and data retention. In light of all of these developments, I decided to set my manuscript aside and wait for the legal dust to settle. In the meantime, I published short papers exploring topics I wanted to treat more extensively as essays in this book.[5]

The terrorist attacks of September 11, 2001 kicked up legal dust, too. The feeling in the United States was that the world had been remade and needed a reinvigorated regime of security and law enforcement. Even before September 11, some commentators were concluding that the United States had become a Kafkaesque bureaucracy evoking "impotence, anger, and anxiety"; or, worse, a surveillance society seemingly modeled on Jeremy Bentham's panopticon or torn from the pages of George Orwell's novel *1984*.[6] Hastily enacted and reauthorized with modest amendments a few years later, the USA PATRIOT Act permitted new levels of government surveillance.[7] Now government was expressly asking members of the public, especially when they traveled, placed phone calls, or used the Internet, to give up previously fostered expectations of physical and informational privacy. Since the late nineteenth century, fear of potentially invasive technologies, from cameras to telephones and computers, had been major factors prompting growth in privacy law. After 2001, privacy advocates and civil libertarians stepped up their watchdog functions, as a worried, patriotic public seemed willing to accept technology as an appropriate vehicle for surveillance by government and its private sector partners, waging an international "war against terrorism." Yet, skepticism about the war on terrorism set in as the public tried to make sense of racial profiling, indefinite detention, torture, and executive power-grabbing. In 2005 President George W. Bush acknowledged secretly authorizing the National Security Agency to eavesdrop on US residents in the United States, side-stepping the constitution and the special judicial process established by the Foreign Intelligence Surveillance Act (FISA). Amendments to the FISA passed by Congress in 2008 authorized certain warrantless searches outside the jurisdiction of the FISA court and also made it easier for telecommunications companies to escape liability for handing over customer data to top-secret federal investigators.

Awaiting the passage of time seemed to make sense for another reason as well. Dramatic changes in attitudes about privacy were afoot, wholly unrelated to terrorism or state surveillance. The United States seemed to be in the midst of a revolution in the nature of the public's moral attachment to privacy. The attachment to decisional privacy concerning sexuality, health, family, and religion appeared fairly stable; though the public seemed to tolerate increasingly more restrictions on abortion and fewer on homosexuality than twenty years earlier. But the attachment to physical and informational privacy was not stable. Emergent electronic lifestyles told an intriguing story about informational privacy. There appeared to be a general relaxation of concern about privacy, an abandonment, a waiver of privacy rights. There was nothing new about "Americans . . . willing to give up a certain amount of privacy in exchange for the fun and convenience" of novel inventions, including the Kodak camera, the telegram, and the postcard, for example.[8] But the great twenty-first century give-away far eclipsed its nineteenth and twentieth century predecessors. No device on the planet in 1925 could access and store the amount of information that the ordinary personal computer or cheap cell phone in common use today can. Moreover, nothing could compete with the data access and storage potential of cloud computing.

Although opinion polls indicated that most Americans highly valued informational privacy and welcomed laws protecting it, people appeared open to readily disclosing personal matters and identifiers in everyday life.[9] Americans in love with "connectivity" freely disclosed intimacies in phone calls in public places, on the Internet, in print media, and as guests on television and radio. Market incentives for voluntary intimate disclosure and self-disclosure multiplied; fleeting fame and fast money proved effective lures. Ideals of convenience, friendship, accountability, and peer and professional networking seemed to be other, equally effective lures. Disclosures of personal data of all sorts, not just intimacies, were becoming a way of life. Privacy advocates and civil libertarians in the United States decried disrespect for privacy, yet the general public seemed to tolerate requests from businesses and government for personal identifiers—names, addresses, social security numbers, driver's license numbers—as well as personal information about family, friends, health, and finances. Now some of this may have been premised on a mistaken belief that government surely adhered to the fair information practices it espoused and that businesses with written privacy policies surely adhered to generally accepted privacy principles.[10] Could adult Americans be so trusting and oblivious? In 2007, the Samuelson Clinic at the University of California at Berkeley and the Annenberg Public Policy Center released a report showing that "most consumers think privacy policies prohibit common online advertising practices" and that most adults "do not understand the basics and legality of information collection techniques."[11]

Enough of the social and legal dust finally settled to allow me to move forward with this book, reasonably confident of the terrain on which I tread. This is not to say that the social and political contexts of privacy or privacy law have become wholly static or unambiguous. In 2009, with President Barack Obama in the White House, the Federal Trade Commission and other federal agencies in Washington entrusted with privacy protection powers began rethinking the optimal balance between self-regulation and government regulation, on the one hand, and freedom of choice and paternalistic consumer protection, on the other.[12] By 2010, Internet commerce, political action, and education, along with web-based social networking, were integral parts of everyday life for individuals, organizations, and affinity groups. In 2011, social media had progressed to the point of playing a critical role in efforts to topple longstanding regimes in Tunisia, Egypt, and Libya, and in how those efforts are reported in the United States and around the world. But the moment will never come for a study of privacy mandates if either policymaking or culture must stand utterly still for a snapshot. And, perhaps I need not have delayed at all, since it was always the case that my ultimate concern is an enduring one of inherent and practical value—namely the just limits of choice, intervention, and coercion.

I do not for a moment think it is a small or easy task persuasively to deliver the central argument of this book, my third on the subject of privacy. In *Uneasy Access: Privacy for Women in a Free Society* (1988), I stressed the importance of privacy and private choice for women. In *Why Privacy Isn't Everything: Feminist Reflections on Personal Accountability* (2003), I stressed the need to acknowledge accountability as a moral counterweight to privacy demands. In this book I again stress the importance of privacy, but physical and informational privacy and for everyone; and here I offer up a difficult, contentious claim that places me out on a limb: privacy is so important and so neglected in contemporary life that democratic states, though liberal and feminist, could be justified in undertaking a rescue mission that includes enacting paternalistic privacy laws for the benefit of uneager beneficiaries.

Focusing on physical and informational privacies, I want to urge that some forms of privacy are extremely important human goods—I will say "foundational" human goods—on which access to many other goods rests. Government should take a special interest in securing these privacies, including through the creation of positive rights of privacy. The protection of privacy rights, I want further to urge, should not be thought of as something that can be waived by intended beneficiaries at will. I suggest that in free societies there is a place for freedom of choice about privacy, a place for nudging and persuasion about privacy, and a place for coercing privacy. Demanding, imposing and coercing privacy which is unpopular—that is, unwanted and even resented—need not be acts of political domination of the sort against which feminists and libertarians famously caution. While liberal societies properly constrain government coercion, they also properly constrain individual choice to prevent serious harm and preserve foundational goods, including essential privacies. A degree of paternalism in public policies aimed at harm prevention is warranted when it comes to foundational liberty (hence the ban on voluntary slavery), and, I argue, foundational privacy. This principle explains the rules enacted by the US Congress through the Children's Online Privacy Protection Act. The 1998 Act was designed to prevent children under thirteen from disclosing personal information to website operators. Whether similar privacy-protecting paternalism is warranted in the case of adults is a question well worth considering, as I do here.

Part I, chapter 1, introduces the main themes of the book. It provides a brief description of the expanding and increasingly salient corpus of US privacy law. Using legal examples, the chapter then identifies values ascribed to physical and informational privacies and how those values relate to liberal ways of life. The heart of the chapter is my argument that in an egalitarian liberal democracy, particularly if justified on broadly dignitarian grounds, legal policy makers (1) must create strong privacy rights, of course; but, moreover, (2) must be open, in principle, to coercive privacy mandates that impose unpopular privacies on intended targets and beneficiaries. Part II, consisting of chapters 2, 3, and 4, reflects on themes of freedom and coercion in relation to privacies of place and body. Chapter 2 broadly explores physical privacies of space (seclusion, solitude, and isolation). Here, with freedom and coercion in mind, I deal in some of the root ideas of modern privacy. I approach privacies of seclusion, solitude, and isolation in relation to several very different contexts: the adventurous retreat, the home, the prison, the hospital, and sites of quarantine. I contrast voluntary privacies and public policies that facilitate them, with nonvoluntary privacies (one resists dignifying them as privacies!) and the public policies that facilitate them. When unwanted and unremitting, "privacies" of seclusion, solitude, and isolation threaten rather than enhance productive personality. In connection with the privacy of the home, I consider US regulations that created a popular national "do not call" registry aimed at enhancing privacy by reducing the number of unsolicited telephone calls. The policy choice implicit in the National Do Not Call Registry program reflects what is arguably a characteristic US bias against paternalistic protection of adults. The registry rules gave people with telephones the option of enhancing their privacy by signing up to receive fewer telephone calls from telemarketers. A government persuaded of the vital importance of domestic privacy might have pursued a course of banning telemarketing calls to private homes and cell phones altogether, forcing phone customers to do without them. But, by proud design, the telemarketing call-limiting program made it possible for consumers to protect their domestic privacy without cutting off for anyone the option of living with the status quo ante of frequent unsolicited calls.

Chapters 3 and 4 explore physical privacies of the body, examining legal approaches to bodily dress and undress. In chapter 3, I draw comparisons between French and American responses to the hijab. In 2006 in France, girls were asked to attend public schools without the hijab, to cultivate a uniform atmosphere of secular individualism. Then, in 2010, the French Parliament banned facial concealment in public places, effectively criminalizing the niqab. In the United States, authorities have demanded that women remove the niqab in courtrooms, airports, and motor vehicle bureaus, but the right to wear hijab or niqab in daily life and in public schools is often deemed a basic constitutional right of individuals. The virtue of Islamic modesty is neglected by the French law requiring a peculiar kind of reserve of religious minorities: namely, that they hold back from publicly displaying "conspicuous" symbols of their creeds and cultures. Although bodily concealment is voluntarily chosen—most of us choose a degree of it all the time—concealment has also been mandated by anti-nudity laws. To get at the heart of the justice of mandating bodily concealment, I assess in chapter 4 the constitutional arguments used in the United States and Canada to defend and strike down laws against nude entertainment. The stated aim of imposing cover-ups on erotic performers has been to promote a mishmash of interests in public morals, public health, and crime control. I consider in detail whether proffered rationales adequately support coercion.

Part III, consisting of chapters 5, 6, 7 and 8 take on privacies of information—confidentiality, informational privacy, and data protection. Chapter 5 explores a domain of well-accepted mandatory privacy, compelled occupational silence. I start with the premise that asking people to be silent about what they know is a substantial burden on freedom. Lawyers cannot freely publicize their conversations with interesting clients, even if there are profits to be earned by doing so. Doctors, lawyers, therapists, and several other categories of professional service providers are bound by law to maintain the confidentiality of information disclosed in private, professional encounters with clients. Silence is imposed on professionals to protect the privacy and other interests of the people they are hired to serve. Sometimes occupational confidentiality entails silence practices for others. Intimate family confidants of the people US securities laws term "insiders" privy to undisclosed corporate information breach confidentiality expectations at their peril—confidants may prompt third parties to trade securities unlawfully. Sometimes occupational silence entails keeping secrets only about oneself. A professional might be asked to keep her sex life or compensation package a secret from coworkers.

Privacy is sufficiently important that we should not view rights of waiver as inevitable features of privacy protections. Some privacy rights should not be waived. Yet I maintain that in behavioral health contexts, the reasons that confidentiality combined with rights of voluntary waiver are the rule are sound. It makes sense that the law permits beneficiaries of professional medical and psychiatric silence to waive the requirement. Secrets may need to be disclosed as an antidote to victimization.[13] Truly voluntary waiver can put an end to dysfunctional secrecies and further public education about interpersonal abuse.

Chapter 6 explores the concept of racial privacy, a concept not at home in public discourse in the United States. Indeed, we might ask how there could be something called "racial" privacy in a country which, following George Yancy, has demanded hypervisibility of nonwhite populations, especially African Americans.[14] In the United States a person's race is generally treated as public information. Some isolated courts have characterized information about race as private and refused to order or permit its disclosure. But there is no racial privacy statute or constitutional prohibition on collecting and disclosing race data in the United States.

The European Union's data protection standards regard racial data as a form of sensitive data that should not be collected, if it can be avoided, and should not be shared for most commercial purposes, even with consent. I consider whether "racial privacy" mandates proposed for the United States would be more liberating than subordinating. Is racial privacy a largely indifferent or unpopular form of privacy whose time has come? Defeated at the polls in 2003, the memorable California referendum Proposition 54 afforded one democratic polity an opportunity to embrace coerced privacy. Opponents of "Prop 54" feared that a ban on race disclosure would make California's vulnerable minority groups, some recovering from histories of state-backed inequality and discrimination, even worse off. Expressing skepticism about the wisdom of racial privacy statutes for the United States, I offer by way of contrast the principle of associational privacy derived from interpretations of the First Amendment. The jurisprudence of the First Amendment provides a welcome legal vehicle for protecting the interests of racial minorities who wish to keep information about their race and race-related affiliations confidential.

Chapters 7 and 8 tackle electronic privacy laws, actual, projected and imagined. I begin with the existing regime of federal privacy statutes and the values they seek to further. I then describe what I characterize as the great "privacy give-away." Conducting life on the web comes with inherent informational privacy and data security risks many adults do not take care to avoid. Personal information freely posted on social networking sites quickly moves beyond individuals' control. The privacy give-away problem will get worse before it gets better. In the future, convenient, attractively packaged lifelogging technologies will allow users to record and archive their entire lives. The consequences for social and legal accountability will be staggering. Could the law have a beneficial, coercive role in helping us avoid injuries to reputation risked by personal archiving and subscribing to third-party data retention services to cache our lives?

Chapter 8 offers a detailed examination of the overtly paternalistic Children's Online Privacy Protection Act (COPPA), enacted by the United States Congress in 1998 and enforced by the Federal Trade Commission.[15] The law requires in the first instance that transactions between website operators and children under thirteen be anonymous. Yet with parental approval, a child may disclose personal identifiers to site operators. COPPA is a paternalistic law that seeks to protect family privacy by imposing duties of self-care. Young children would prefer to win treats and toys playing games on the Internet without Mom or Dad lording over them. The law mildly frustrates the desire of precocious preteen children for independent access to websites that collect personal data. Does an abhorrence of paternalism counsel against it in this domain?

If paternalism is justified for children, perhaps it is justified for vulnerable adult Internet and web users engaging in online transactions. Is a degree of paternalism on behalf of adults justified by intractable problems of data-mining, identity theft, phishing, pretexting, or data breaches? Do harassment, defamation, and bullying on the web suggest a role for paternalistic regulation? Consumer education and "nudging," may be as far as a seriously liberal democracy should go.[16] But given the ascribed value of privacy, given its claim to status as a special, foundational good, it is not self-evident that the United States should pass up policy options that limit the capacity to choose giving away sensitive personal data. What might those options be? Are any workable? More questions can be raised than easily answered. In chapter 8, as elsewhere in this book, I consider the competing demands of private and public, liberty and coercion, risk and precaution.

Unpopular Privacy

PART ONE

Normative Foundations

1
PRIVACIES NOT WANTED

A man heard rumors around town that his young daughter was living with his ex-wife and her new lover, another woman. Hoping to win legal custody of his daughter, the man sneaked up to his ex-wife's bedroom window under cover of night with a camera to take photographs of what he deemed "illicit" sex. Needless to say, he violated the lovers' expectations of privacy, here the physical privacy of the two women's intimate seclusion. He got sued for it.[1]

In another case, a physician was approached by an adult adoptee who wanted help finding her biological mother. Knowing that the state would unseal the woman's official adoption records only if there were a serious reason, the physician armed the woman with a bogus medical excuse. The state accordingly unsealed the records. When identified and located, the adopted woman's biological mother was not pleased. She had moved on in her life, relying on promises of professional secrecy. The physician violated the birth mother's expectations of privacy, specifically the informational privacy of traditional, undisclosed adoption. Like the peeping tom ex-husband, the confidentiality breaching doctor got sued.[2]

The general subject of the essays that comprise this book is what I refer to as *physical* and *informational* privacy. My opening examples illustrate real-world invasions of privacy of just these two sorts. Physical privacy is illustrated by the case of the photographed lovers, and informational privacy is illustrated by the case of the uncloaked birth mother. Other examples of physical and informational privacy disputes would call attention to the privacy implications of the World Wide Web and social networking: Google was sued by homeowners who complained that unauthorized vehicles entered a private road to take photographs of their homes that wound up on Google Street View; a medical facility was sued when confidential health information about a patient tested for a sexually transmitted infection after commencing an extramarital affair wound up on a MySpace page where the patient was dubbed "Rotten Candy" and a cheater.[3]

The law imposes obligations, of course, including obligations to respect others' privacy. I will try in this book to illuminate the normative bases of lawmaking aimed at promoting and protecting a wide variety of physical and informational privacies, from seclusion and bodily modesty, to confidentiality and electronic data protection. But there is a twist. The central theme of this book, the theme that separates it from most books about physical and informational privacy, is what I call "unpopular" privacies. Some forms of physical and informational privacy that could be promoted, protected, or required by law are unpopular. By "unpopular" I mean unwanted, disliked, not preferred, and resented privacies. Is it just for government to stick us with these?

EVERYDAY MEANINGS OF PRIVACY

Privacy means many things to many people, of course. Yet the concept itself is not as difficult to get a grip on as it was a short half century ago, when the right to privacy was seldom in the news and academics paid it no mind.[4] Today, laypersons, lawyers, and judges refer to a predictable range of conditions and liberties when they speak of "privacy." Moreover, in everyday parlance, "invasion of privacy" refers to real and imagined violations that fall into a handful of easily illustrated categories.

"Physical" privacy, sometimes called "spatial" privacy, is disturbed when a person's efforts to seclude or conceal himself or herself are frustrated; "informational" privacy is disturbed when data, facts, or conversations that a person wishes to secret or anonymize are nonetheless acquired or disclosed. What is sometimes referred to as "locational" privacy is a hybrid: the privacy of information about a person's physical—that is, geographical—whereabouts. I began this chapter with examples of physical privacy (violation by a peeping tom) and informational privacy (violation by a confidentiality breaching physician), but we can also speak of "decisional," "proprietary," "associational," and "intellectual" privacy.

States' refusals to condone assisted suicide or same-sex marriage are condemned by many liberals and celebrated by many conservatives as denials of "decisional" privacy.[5] The publisher who used a large family's portrait without permission, to illustrate an amusing story about experiments using caffeine to enhance sperm motility, breached expectations of reputational "proprietary" privacy.[6] The gay man who unsuccessfully sought membership in the Boy Scouts, along with the gays and lesbians who sought to march in Boston's St. Patrick's Day Parade, ran up against heterosexuals' "associational" privacy claims.[7] What Neil Richards dubs "intellectual" privacy is another, complex hybrid: the marriage of "associational" and "informational" privacies.[8] The book seller who intercepted customers' e-mail en route to rival Amazon.com, like the Internet service provider who turned over a customer's e-mail in response to a crafty lawyer's overly broad subpoena, compromised the privacy of his customers' intellectual activities. He compromised what customers read, thought, planned and discussed with their personal and business associates.[9]

PRIVACY LAW

Privacy law consists of diverse mandates—set by courts, legislators, agency regulators, and other officials—with a common feature. They take the protection of what are thought to be legitimate privacy interests as their main purpose. So conceived, privacy law includes criminal and civil remedies for egregious intrusions, searches, publications, and appropriations of identity; regulations requiring that firms and professionals who collect personal information protect it from nonconsensual disclosure to third parties; and limits on state interference with family, healthcare, and sex life. Privacy law, a portion of which is both highly coercive and unpopular, has emerged as an important field of legal practice at a time when theorists still engage in lively debates about the value, utility, and taxonomy of what is or should be referred to as "privacy" or the right to it.[10]

Contemporary US privacy law is found in the common law, in constitutional law, and in statutes. In a nutshell, US privacy law includes the four common law invasion of privacy torts recognized in most states and by the American Law Institute's *Restatement of (Second) of Torts*: intrusion upon seclusion, publication given to private facts, false light publicity, and misappropriation of identity. Privacy law includes the common law of publicity and confidentiality, in so far as they protect privacy interests. Next, privacy law includes provisions and interpretations of the federal constitution. Although the word "privacy" does not appear in the US Constitution, a cherished part of the document, the Bill of Rights, has spawned a mountain of privacy protection requirements. The First and Fourth Amendments' jurisprudence of associational, physical, and informational privacy are notable in this regard.[11] The controversial Fourteenth Amendment equal protection and substantive due process decisional privacy jurisprudence is part of privacy law, too.[12] The Third, Fifth, Eighth, and Ninth Amendments have been held to protect privacy interests.[13] Think broadly enough to construe personal lifestyle preferences as privacy interests and even the Second Amendment "right to bear arms" and the Twenty-First Amendment ending national alcohol prohibition start to look like branches of privacy law. Returning from the fringe to the center, privacy law includes state constitutions. State courts have repeatedly held that state constitutions, some with explicit privacy protection provisions, significantly expand privacy protection beyond federal limits.[14] The final major dimension of privacy law consists of the federal and state statutes that protect privacy interests.[15] Dozens of federal privacy statutes and agency rules (many enacted in the 1970s and 1980s, but many after 1996 and as recently as 2009) regulate (1) government record management, (2) health, education, and financial data, (3) video rentals, (4) cable and telecommunications customer data, (5) computers, the Internet, and the World Wide Web and (6) surveillance.

Lawyers know some of these sector-specific regulations by common nicknames: Title III, HIPAA, FERPA, COPPA, and GLB.[16] The fifty states have privacy protection statutes of their own, governing everything from medical records and library records, to adoption records, state tax returns, and data breach policies.

Privacy law in the United States promotes, requires, and enforces both popular and unpopular privacy. Popular privacy is the physical, informational, proprietary, decisional, associational, and intellectual privacy that people in the United States and similar liberal nations tend to want, believe they have a right to, and expect government to secure. For example, typical adults very much want privacy protection for the content of their telephone calls, e-mail, tax filings, health records, academic transcripts, and bank transactions. Most books about privacy law focus on measures that mandate—or that should be enacted so as to mandate—protection of popular forms of the privacy. This book will focus on the normative underpinnings of laws that promote, require, and enforce two forms of privacy—physical and informational privacy—but that are unpopular with intended beneficiaries and targets.

ARE PATERNALISTIC PRIVACY POLICIES JUSTIFIABLE?

One of the questions I consider in this book is when government is justified in mandating unpopular privacy by law. A privacy mandate can be unpopular with, first, intended beneficiaries and, second, intended targets of compliance.

By "intended beneficiaries," I mean members of the class of people for whose sake courts, legislatures, or agencies have established particular privacy protection standards. Medical patients are the intended beneficiaries of federal health privacy statutes, for example. I am especially interested here in the justification of laws that are unpopular with intended beneficiaries, and that therefore raise questions about choice, freedom, and government paternalism. Now, a great many privacy laws are popular with intended beneficiaries and I do not mean to suggest otherwise. For example, most homeowners enthusiastically embrace common law physical privacy rules that deter peering into bedroom windows. Homeowners understand the value of their own privacy. They praise obedience to such laws, not because they fear the consequences of their own indifference or disobedience, but because they possess (to adapt a concept from H.L.A. Hart) "internalized" respect for laws against trespass and peeping.[17] Indeed, homeowners who filed an invasion of privacy lawsuit against Google for entering a private road and driveway to take pictures of their house and yard for Google Street View were undoubtedly disappointed that the court held that no wrongful "intrusion upon seclusion" had occurred.[18]

Public policies aimed at privacy protection commonly require specific behavior and behavioral constraints of persons other than the intended beneficiaries of the policy. These persons I call the "intended targets." The intended targets are the class of people whose conduct is directly regulated by particular privacy protection standards. Physicians, nurses, and hospitals are among the intended targets of US federal health privacy statutes. A privacy law can be unpopular with its intended targets. Intended targets may resent the burden on their freedom and financial costs associated with compliance with privacy protection laws designed to benefit others. Consider the phlebotomist sanctioned because she mentioned a patient's pregnancy to the patient's own twin sister in good faith, but in violation of categorical privacy rules.[19] Yet plenty of intended targets do not resent the burdens privacy laws impose. For example, in my experience many physicians and medical researchers embrace information privacy rules that deter breach of medical confidentiality. These physicians understand why the law targets them for confidentiality mandates, despite the costs and inconveniences, and accept the law as sound policy legitimately imposed for the benefit of their patients. Physicians know that many of their patients trust them with knowledge of embarrassing symptoms only because a regime of custom backed by law reduces fear of undue publicity. Moreover, there is a plain respect in which the privacy laws that target healthcare practitioners primarily to bestow a benefit on patients also bestow an indirect, incidental benefit on health practitioners by enhancing their stature and business.

The classes of beneficiaries and targets are not mutually exclusive, for another reason. If a privacy protection standard requires that its intended beneficiaries behave in a certain way or refrain from acting in a certain way, then the standard's intended beneficiaries can also be described as its intended targets. But consider the potential affront to a freedom loving person of being subjected (as one of its beneficiaries) to an unwanted, paternalistic law that also requires (as one of its targets) unwanted and perhaps costly limits on conduct. Some actual and potential privacy laws are unpopular in this way; their intended combined beneficiaries/targets fail to embrace the conditions of privacy that government prescribes for them.[20]

For example, suppose the federal government enacted a strict privacy protection statute prohibiting websites from collecting personal information from any person under the age of eighteen, no exceptions.[21] The purpose of my hypothetical "Youth Right to Privacy Online Act" would be to force young people, for their own long-term good, to keep sensitive personal data out of the market until government presumes them mature enough to make responsible, fully informed choices. Website operators, the primary targets of the act, would not like it because of concerns about their bottom lines. But neither would the act's intended young beneficiaries/targets, forbidden to give up personal data and barred from websites that require personal data disclosures.

"That law treats us like babies!" they would complain. More than a few brave teens would say "Act be damned!" and try to circumvent it.

Focusing not on the website operators, but on affected youth, how might one describe this hypothetical state of affairs? Using the vocabulary of this book, one might say that "government-mandated Internet privacy is unpopular with young adults." One might also say that Internet privacy is "unwanted," "imposed," or "coerced" privacy. Finally, one might even say that Internet privacy laws make online privacy a youth's "duty," "obligation," or "responsibility." In a free society, autonomy-loving individuals—including my imagined mature adolescents prepared to thwart a regime of Internet data protection—may believe that they are morally entitled to freedom from unwanted, imposed, or coerced privacies. From a philosophical perspective, they may be right; but then again, they may be wrong. Given the level of Internet complexity and fraud, perhaps paternalism in the case of young adults could be justified. Sigal R. Ben-Porath has argued that "paternalist policies are justified when they advance the public good of civic equality, as related to the private good of enhanced well-being and expanded opportunity."[22]

A RIGHT TO WAIVE PRIVACY PROTECTION?

Another question I explore in the chapters of this book is whether individuals should always have a right voluntarily to waive privacy, and if so, why. Individuals in the United States commonly waive the physical and informational privacy rights they possess under the law. Could certain privacies be so important that they should be legally protected and the legal protections not subject to voluntary waiver by their intended beneficiaries?

A common law informational privacy tort recognized in many US states makes a person or the press liable for publication of private facts. This tort aims to deter private individuals and the media from highly offensive publication of true but sensitive personal information about others without consent, with exceptions for publications about public officials, celebrities, and ordinary people caught up in newsworthy events. The law constraining publication of private facts is popular with intended beneficiaries, but unpopular with targeted tabloid newspapers, magazines, and websites, who stand to profit from the right to publish sensational stories about private life. Though popular as a rule with intended beneficiaries, the private fact tort's protections can be voluntarily waived and frequently are.

Joyce Maynard waived her rights against publication of private facts. When she was only eighteen, she had an intimate affair with famed writer J. D. Salinger. He was fifty-three. For a short while, the mismatched lovers lived together. In 2006, long after the affair, Maynard announced she would sell the fourteen unpublished love letters that the author wrote to her from his New Hampshire hideaway between April 25, 1972 and August 17, 1973. Maynard knew how greatly Salinger valued his privacy and that he would be offended by her decision. But she did not much care. Maynard said that the letters belonged to her; they were her property, and she needed money to send her children to college.[23] She felt she herself had nothing to hide, since she had published *At Home in the World*, a memoir of the fascinating affair.[24] Sotheby's auction house agreed to manage the sale. Like it or not, the rules of privacy law allocated Maynard, one of the intended beneficiaries, along with Salinger, the right to waive her own privacy interests in intimate correspondence. The rules of property law allocated Maynard the right to profit from ownership of intimate papers. I suspect few would think that the privacy of someone in Maynard's position should be legally coerced for her own sake. She is, after all, a sane adult. But the matter is not beyond philosophical dispute and merits query. Maynard may not have been seriously or irrevocably harmed by self-disclosure through publication of her memoir and the sale of the Salinger letters; but someone in her situation could in principle suffer, for example, nontrivial dignitary, emotional, and reputational harms. It is not self-evident that the law should be indifferent to such a possibility and allow people unbridled freedom of self-disclosure. We might imagine a legal regime that valued informational privacy so greatly that it paternalistically mandated waiting periods or informed consent procedures in advance of major acts of self-disclosure.

It is worth adding that one might wish for privacy (or intellectual property) laws that give a former lover, even a celebrity, the right during his lifetime to enjoin sale or publication of purely personal correspondence. Interestingly, in an earlier episode, Salinger successfully appealed to US copyright law to prevent the use of his private correspondence in an unauthorized biography. But when it came to the Maynard letters, the law was apparently of no avail. The legal owner of the letters was allowed to sell them, despite the disclosures the sale entailed. Maynard capitalized on the alienability of her common law right to be free of public disclosures of private fact. Salinger was an unfortunate victim of misplaced trust. Maynard's property rights trumped Salinger's privacy interests and, for that matter, by her choice, her own. The reclusive Salinger was lucky: Peter Norton, a software entrepreneur and art collector, paid $156,500 at auction for the letters in 1999, and said he would return them to the author.[25]

WHY IMPOSE UNPOPULAR PRIVACY?

Government can protect and promote physical and informational privacies; it can even mandate them. It can impose unpopular privacy on supposed beneficiaries and prohibit waiver. When and why should it do these things? I believe it can be legitimate for liberal, egalitarian governments to mandate physical and informational privacy even when the privacy in question is unpopular—unwanted, resented, not preferred, or despised by intended beneficiaries or targets. Few readers will disagree with me that liberal governments can, do, and should mandate at least some privacies. Surely government can insist that our neighbors do not peer into our bedroom windows, tap our phones, or hack into our investment accounts. Government can surely legitimately mandate health record privacy and limit access to tax records. Government can surely require lawyers and corporate insiders to keep professional secrets, even though some lawyers and corporate insiders will disagree that limiting their freedom to speak what they know is warranted and will view compliance as unwelcome sacrifices.

But I expect some readers will be concerned about the specter I pose of government turning privacies into duties—especially, duties of self-care. Should youthful Internet users really be blocked from websites that collect sensitive personal information, for their own good? (My hypothetical law affected children and youth under the age of 18, but an existing paternalistic US law, the Children's Online Privacy Protection Act, applies to children under 13.) Should the law obliged us to forego Amazon.com because the giant consumer goods seller keeps track of our purchases and makes recommendations, or Gmail because it pitches ads to us based on words that appear in our private messages to family and friends?[26] Should adults with intimate secrets be banned from publishing them? Should authorities have forced Joyce Maynard to keep her intimate letters from Salinger to herself for her own good, if not for his? Is there a possible justification, paternalistic or otherwise, for laws that deny homosexuals the right to disclose their sexual orientations or minority group members the right to disclose their races?

Just a few scholars have raised the general questions I explore at length about unpopular privacy mandates and waivers. Sociologist Amitai Etzioni broached it in relation to a vision of the common good.[27] Political theorist Jean Cohen thoughtfully explored it, in relation to fair treatment of homosexuals in the military.[28] Legal theorist Ian Ayres considered versions of my question in relation to telemarketing and campaign finance disclosures. He expressly rejected coerced privacy in the telemarketing context.[29] But he provocatively defended the utility and constitutionality of a proposed law requiring that people who make donations to candidates for public office do so privately, on a strictly anonymous basis.[30] Such a law targeting donors and coercing privacy constrains freedom, to be sure. Strict libertarians could oppose a donor privacy law merely on that basis. However, as Ayres demonstrates, mandated donor privacy would further collective goals fit for a liberal democracy, including reducing political corruption, while enabling donors both freely to vote for and freely to give money to whomever they pleased, without accountability to others.

I will consider a range of proposed and actual government policies and practices that in one respect or another impose privacy and constrain freedom, sometimes paternalistically. In the pages ahead I will claim that some of these are defensible for reasons lovers of freedom and equality, including those who characterize themselves as libertarians or feminists, can endorse. Persuading libertarians and feminists to endorse regimes of imposed privacy is a significant challenge. I identify with libertarian liberalism and liberal feminism, recognizing that both in their own ways caution against unpopular, imposed privacies.

FEMINIST SKEPTICISM

The assessment of social norms and legal rules that disadvantage women was a core task of nineteenth- and twentieth-century feminist philosophy.[31] Receiving the most scholarly attention were the discriminatory norms and laws governing family caretaking, education, violence, wages, and political participation.[32] But norms and laws governing privacy have received a share of the attention, in my work and the work of others, too.[33] Indeed, that a life of liberty properly includes both privacy and freedom from privacy stands as a central insight of feminism. Feminist philosophy, with its characteristic emphasis on problems of domination, subordinating paternalism, unequal opportunities, and second-class citizenship, has helped to illuminate the justice and injustice of popular and unpopular privacy mandates targeting women.[34] Card-carrying feminist philosophers have not been alone in this task. Gerald N. Rosenberg pointed to the "danger of privacy to autonomy, communication, and responsive democracy . . . clearly illustrated by the treatment of women, particularly in the 'sheltered haven' of the family."[35] Michel Foucault's *The History of Sexuality* chronicled compelled privacies, especially silence about sex; he exposed the ability to demand self-serving practices of disclosure and nondisclosure as exercises of power. "What is peculiar to modern societies," Foucault wrote, "is not that they consigned sex to a shadow existence, but that they dedicated themselves to speaking of it ad infinitum, while exploiting it as *the* secret."[36]

History shows that women have fought against lives in the shadows, kept there by privacy-related expectations that they dress modestly, stay inside the home, and keep their mouths shut. Unsurprisingly, the problem of unwanted, unpopular privacy that is mandated, imposed, or coerced has constituted a major theme within feminist thought.[37] In the nineteenth century, the utopian feminist Charlotte Perkins Gilman argued against one form of unpopular privacy, seclusion in and about family homes.[38] In the twentieth century, Catherine McKinnon argued against another form of unpopular privacy—namely, interpersonal relationships in which men dominated women's decision making and turned their wives' and lovers' constitutional abortion rights into male privileges.[39] Now, in the early twenty-first century, feminists eager to understand forms of sociality and self-revelation unique to life on the World Wide Web have a beef with privacy, too.

Cyberfeminists say the "privacy" of offline life is as isolating as great-grandma's root cellar; online self-disclosures can be fun, creative, educational, and politically empowering. They warn, though, that the anonymity available on the Internet can diminish accountability that serves women's interests in civility, honesty, and safety.[40] Fortunately, American courts recognize First Amendment interests in online anonymity, but do not treat them as absolute rights. This point is well-illustrated by the well-publicized case in which a female Yale Law School student was offended and defamed by an anonymous individual (calling himself AK47) who posted vicious messages about her on Autoadmit.com. The law student successfully fought a motion to quash a subpoena requiring AT&T to reveal the identity of the person from whose IP address the postings had been made accusing her of sexually transmitted diseases, numerous gay lovers, harboring rape and incest fantasies, and abusing heroin.[41]

Feminism provides no categorical case against coercing unwanted privacy. (There is certainly no generic feminist case to be made in favor of always coercing desirable forms of privacy.) This book stands opposed to the proposition that there is generic liberal or liberal feminist case against all coercive privacy mandates, and explains why. I offer contextually specific assessments of a variety of unpopular privacy requirements, informed by liberal feminist conceptions of freedom and equality.[42] The tie between feminism and liberalism is not accidental since, in the words of Martha Nussbaum, "liberal individualism, consistently followed through, entails a *radical feminist program*."[43]

LIBERTARIAN SKEPTICISM

People give away their privacy all the time. They load personal facts onto unprotected websites, tell all and bare all on social networks and in memoirs; they tweet, text, send instant messages, phone, and e-mail constantly. They crave celebrity and sensationalize their own intimacies and disasters. They expose themselves via GPS, cell phones, cloud computing and, potentially, digital lifelogs and nanotechnology-based tracking devices. Should we care? Should government step in to do something about this indifference to privacy, this preference for publicity and accessibility? Cato Institute fellow Julian Sanchez has argued that while privacy paternalism premised on assumptions of consumer irrationality or indifference is not warranted, government regulation in response to the "prisoner's dilemma" view of privacy might be. On this view, government may step in when "there are systematic consequences to information sharing, such that we each get some benefit from participating in certain systems of disclosure, but would all be better off if nobody did."[44]

In a 2008 book called *Nudge*, Cass Sunstein and Richard Thaler argue that paternalism is not utterly inconsistent with the strong, freedom-emphatic version of liberalism often termed "libertarianism." They mark out a principled stance to guide policymaking that they call "libertarian paternalism," described as "a relatively weak, soft, and nonintrusive type of paternalism" that self-consciously attempts "to move people in directions that will make their lives better" without blocking, fencing off or significantly burdening choice.[45] Libertarians—whether, in the US context, Democrats or Republicans—can and should support government action aimed at furthering the best interest of its subjects. Specifically, it is acceptable for government to function self-consciously as what Thaler and Sunstein call a "choice architect." Current research has "raised serious questions about the rationality of many judgments and decisions people make."[46] Government should not mandate, block self-injurious choices, or significantly change economic incentives; but it should "nudge." That is, using cheap and easy strategies—such as manipulating default rules that apply to employer subsidized health insurance and retirement savings plans or placing the healthiest food choices in the cafeteria first and at eye level—government should intervene to make it easier for people to make the most rational choices. In the absence of such intervention by government or the private sector, it is predictable that people will fall prey to the perils of procrastination, lack of, self-control, information deficits, overreliance on rules of thumb, and cognitive biases familiar to behavioral economists. These include framing biases, status quo biases, loss aversion biases, and overconfidence.[47]

Like Sunstein and Thaler, I defend a brand of state paternalism that does not amount to a wholesale invitation to a "Nanny State" in which government "wardens of well-being" enact oppressive laws that make it impossible for people to harm themselves.[48] Toward addressing concerns about unjust and excessive paternalism, I will take a different tack, however, urging that we think of some forms of privacy as what might be called "foundational" human goods. The foundational goods are the sorts of resources liberal philosophers and political theorists since John Rawls have often referred to as "primary goods." Rawls's own long list of primary goods featured the following: basic rights and liberties; freedom of movement and free choice of occupation against a background of diverse opportunities; powers and prerogatives of office and positions of responsibility; income and wealth; and the social bases of self-respect.[49] My view is that for the sake of foundational human goods, liberal societies properly constrain both government coercion and individual choice, including the choice to forgo privacies we will typically need for a lifetime of self-respect, trusting relationships, positions of responsibility, and other forms of flourishing.

THE CONTEXT

Assuming the standard broad contrasts between comprehensive and political liberalism, and between deontic and consequentialist ethics, the implicit philosophical foundation of my arguments is a comprehensive deontic liberalism committed to toleration, religious diversity, and gender and race equality, understanding tensions implicit therein.[50] I focus on privacy protection in a particular setting. I could describe the setting as "contemporary America" or "North America and Western Europe," since these are the regions whose laws and values I principally discuss in the pages ahead.

But in writing concretely about these familiar regions, I mean to talk, aspirationally, about all societies similarly structured as mixed regulated free market economies dependent upon consumerism and technology.[51] I am talking, then, about all societies in which individuals are aspirationally ascribed equal human worth and are known to share many identical wants and general values, despite varied priorities, languages, religions, subcultures, ethnicities, colors, sexualities, and affiliations. I am talking about societies committed to surviving as constitutionally ordered egalitarian democracies. It does not matter, for present purposes, whether that optimal democracy is understood as one in which policies are the result of procedures that mostly aggregate raw preferences—think of Bruce Ackerman's quip that "a liberal does not insist that each individual go through some form of talk therapy before he commits himself to a set of personal ideals"—or one in which policies are the result of procedures that meaningfully invite rational deliberation about raw preferences.[52] I am also talking about societies constitutionally committed to individual freedom; but freedom bounded by a rule of law designed to constrain selfish and dishonest tendencies that stand as ethical barriers to the care, concern, and cooperation that are hallmarks of flourishing communities of respected individuals, groups, and associations. In short, I am talking, aspirationally about egalitarian liberal democracy and concretely about its imperfect manifestations in my own American society.

The kind of society I have in mind will and ought to regard certain privacies as foundational moral and political goods. "Secrecy and confidentiality," according to the philosopher S. I. Benn, are "closely bound to the liberal ideal."[53] The liberal demands privacy, but the "totalitarian claims that everything a person is and does has significance for society at large."[54] In the mind of the totalitarian "the public or political universe is all-inclusive: all roles are public, and every function whether political, economic, scholarly or artistic, can be interpreted as creating public responsibility for and in its performance."[55] The liberal disagrees with the totalitarian, but why? Why does the liberal believe in physical and informational privacy and why does she think it fair to ask people to hold back from going where they are not wanted and saying what they know to be true?

Benn made a compelling, nonutilitarian case for the kinds of privacy I place at center stage in this book. Benn's case was premised on the concept of respect for persons. Respect for persons, he argued, demands respect for freedom, but it also requires us to refrain from insult and injury. Even when they cause no physical or emotional injuries, invasions of privacy are insults to personality that signal a lack of respect and undermine self-respect. The peeping tom offends because his "spying...deliberately deceives[s] the person about his world: it thwarts, on the basis of reasons that are not his own, the agent's attempt to make rational choices."[56] The intruder makes a fool of her victim if intrusion is covert, and if the intrusion is open, the intruder insults, still. By accessing the unguarded self, intruders and data snatchers can form humiliating, despicable pictures of their victims that interfere with their victims' self-concepts and self-esteem, making them doubt they are the people they have worked to be. Invasions of privacy allow others to form an impression "which, even though accurate and detailed, still permits him to interpret it in ways the subject finds humiliating, and is powerless to influence, because it is done without his knowledge, let alone his consent." Managing and controlling identities is hard work; privacy invaders make the work for naught. This is a point of view Jeffrey Rosen (citing Erving Goffman rather than Benn) picked up on and advanced in his work characterizing privacy as a right to go "backstage" and not be construed out of context.[57]

To grasp the full story of dignitarian harm caused by invasions of informational and physical privacy and to understand which invasions violate what is properly regarded as a sphere of privacy, one has to study particular contexts in detail, as I endeavor to do in chapters to come. This is because "the liberal cannot give absolute specifications...for what is private and what is not, because privacy is...relative to the social nexus in which it is embedded."[58] But already one can see the general kinds of reasons that are likely to emerge on a dignitarian liberal account for imposing privacy. Imposing privacy is disallowing people to demean their self-worth by yielding appropriate concern for the formation of reputation and self-concept. It may not be enough that they are well paid for it, as Maynard was paid for her letters from Salinger. (Although in Maynard's case, it is not clear the intimate letters in question reveal as much about her as they reveal about Salinger, their author.)

A liberal society concerned with treating persons with respect will want to arm its members with strategic advantages that affirm their human worth. In a discussion of law and social norms, Eric A. Posner characterized privacy in this way: "To say that a person values privacy is the same thing as saying that he fears the enforcement of social norms."[59] Caught on camera, a man with concerns about his reputation in the community might be driven to suicide. Rutgers University freshman Tyler Clementi jumped off the George Washington Bridge after his roommate activated a webcam that broadcast live video of him necking with a male friend. An assistant district attorney in Texas, Louis William Conradt Jr., shot himself in the head when he learned he was about to be arrested for soliciting a minor online as a result of a sting operation by the NBC Universal news program *To Catch a Predator*. Both men had good reason to fear the enforcement of social norms, although only young Clementi had the law of privacy solidly on his side.

By extrapolation from Posner, saying that a society values privacy is the same thing as saying that a society fears the enforcement of social norms. Privacy rules adopted by a liberal society could be viewed, following Posner, as a way of addressing "the pathologies of nonlegal mechanisms of enforcement." By deterring peeping toms—and webcam wielding roommates—with criminal and tort law, we protect house dwellers from the social sanctions that would follow if the community at large knew what went on behind closed doors. By deterring breach of medical confidentiality, we protect patients from the social sanctions that would follow if the community at large possessed information it needed to inflict sanctions such as shaming and discrimination. Physical and informational privacy mandates, like decisional privacy mandates, enhance liberty.[60] They enhance the liberty to live secretly in accord with nonconforming preferences. And they also enhance the liberty of seeking the help of experts, friends, and family with whom one can trust sensitive information, thoughts, and feelings. A liberal society might regard relationships of trust as so critical that it imposed silence on professionals and spouses, as indeed US law importantly does in its procedural and substantive law of confidentiality and privilege (discussed in chapter 5).

In describing the virtues of the republican ideal of a government marked by nondomination, Philip Pettit puzzled over the role that trust of officials and trust of fellow citizens should play. He confronted a dilemma. "Much of what is best in life," he wrote, "comes from overtures of personal trust, as when we initiate relationships of love and friendship by risking ourselves in such acts: by showing that we confidently put ourselves at the mercy of the other person."[61] And yet, the republican ideal calls for citizens' "eternal vigilance," he argues, a watchfulness over officials and fellow citizens that imposes a high degree of accountability that reads as incivility. Now accountability is at odds with privacy. We may want to limit government secrecy, but we do not want to obliterate the privacy that enables citizens to hold their heads up high and practice virtue. As Robert Post and others have emphasized, in Goffman's vein, privacy laws against intrusion upon seclusion can be interpreted as rules of deference and demeanor that are hallmarks of civility.[62] The civility case for informational privacy was subtly advanced by Pettit. Pettit responded to his dilemma of vigilance and trust by arguing that the two *desiderata* are consistent. Republican vigilance is consistent with endorsing a civility regime of personal trust. The republican goal of promoting nondomination requires civility and concomitant trust: "consistently with endorsing the republican theory of freedom and government, we can see sense and value in people's reliance on overtures of personal trust to build up a world of supportive relationships around them."[63] There is a message here for liberal, no less than republican, political theory. To the extent that physical and informational privacy are dimensions of civility and interpersonal trust on which a free and egalitarian society depends, they should be understood as foundational goods. The laws that mandate such privacies are laws that understand the value of independence, nondomination, in a context of supportive interpersonal relationships.[64]

Returning to Posner, he seems to have missed a point. Privacy protection law functions to shelter legal noncompliance. Persons and societies value privacy out of fear of the enforcement of legal mandates as well as social norms. Some of the conduct that can be observed when others enter our secluded spaces, and some of the information others come to know when it is disclosed by our confidantes, bears the taint of illegality rather than mere social disapproval. Peep in the window, and you might discover someone bagging crack cocaine; bug a psychiatrist's office and you might hear that a man has assaulted his wife. As the courts have often pointed out in Fourth Amendment cases, criminal suspects have a right to privacy too; the fact that someone is secretly committing crimes is no reason to deny him the protection of the Fourth Amendment warrant requirement. The Supreme Court in *Katz v. United States* (1967) held that a man in a phone booth making illegal bets has a legitimate subjective expectation of privacy that the government is not tapping the phone and recording his conversations.[65] He may deserve the disapproval of fellow citizens and criminal prosecution, to boot, but to prevent the law from over enforcement of its rules, the constitution disallows intrusions without a judicial warrant issued on the basis of probable cause.

Bruce Ackerman's unique take on the liberal case for privacy construes privacy as a way of affording persons what he calls "transactional flexibility" to live as they like, while allowing others to similarly live as they like.[66] Denying that liberals have any special fondness for such things as intimacy or nudity, Ackerman argued that liberals will strategically prefer an arrangement, such as rules of seclusion and concealment that allow people to behave as they wish behind closed doors without imposing any costs on others who might find their conduct disagreeable. Liberalism cannot ban morally offensive conduct, but it can compartmentalize it. A dignitarian like Benn would agree with compartmentalization, but on other grounds; it allows moral agents freedom to live by their own lights as required by their worth, without denying other moral agents similar freedom. Diana T. Meyers explains in common terms that, "A moral agent is an individual who is capable of choosing and acting in accordance with judgments about what is right, wrong, good, bad, worthy, or unworthy. Such individuals are thought to be free and hence responsible for what they do."[67] Creating physical sanctuaries and data protection by law is a way to give moral agents added opportunities make choices, and act on them without fear of recrimination, even to the point of breaking the law. The permissive ideal is reflected in judicial determinations that people can use illegal drugs in their homes, but not sell them, or view legally obscene films (featuring adults) in their homes, but not market them.[68]

I am not centrally concerned with decisional privacy here, but it is worth noting that there is a dignitarian case for decisional privacy as a foundational good, too. Decisional privacies limit the extent to which the moral agency of individuals can be supplanted by government agency. If there are not limits to state power to control of the details of individual lives, there can be no meaningful political freedom at all, hence Jed Rubenfeld's notion that decisional privacy critically checks totalitarianism.[69] Some philosophers have maintained that extremes of state control over the details of individual lives interferes with the formation of autonomous personality and therefore with meaningful citizenship and democracy. Democracy is attractive precisely because it regards individuals as distinct moral personalities; and liberal democracy is attractive precisely because it understands individuals as capable free agents. Privacy institutions and practices play a role in creating and sustaining the capable free agents presupposed by liberal democracy, and for that reason are properly deemed foundational. Moreover, the subjective happiness of individuals often depends upon the sense of liberty and the availability of choices that matter in daily life. Orwellian totalitarian control over a person's life is outside the frame of liberal democracy, as are unrestrained, intolerant moralism and theocracy. David A. J. Richards identified respect for tolerance as a principled basis for legal, constitutional protection of decisional privacy.[70] Yet within the frame of plausible liberal egalitarian regimes of choice and coercion, there are bound to be debates about precisely which decisions should be deemed "private" and to what precise extent. There will be reasonable restrictions on marriages, religions, and sexual expression in liberal egalitarian societies, even though these are without question among the most intimate areas of life. There will be reasonable restrictions on travel, parenting, and education, even though these are among the most personal areas of life, too. Drawing lines in principled and politically acceptable ways is a policymaking task sure to leave some members of society dissatisfied. The ongoing debates in the United States over abortion privacy, marriage privacy, and the privacy of refusing medical care reveal just the policymaking challenge to which I am alluding.

NEGLECTED RIGHTS, FORGOTTEN DUTIES

In 1906, the Supreme Court of Georgia became the first US state high court to recognize the right to privacy. An Atlanta man sued because his photograph had been used in an advertisement for insurance without his prior knowledge or consent. The court likened invasions of privacy to slavery—a discredited institution, well-remembered in the heartland of the former Confederacy. The discovery that privacy has been invaded, said the court in *Pavesich v. New England Life Insurance Co.*, brings "not only the person of an extremely sensitive nature, but even the individual of ordinary sensibility, to a realization that his liberty has been taken away from him" and that for the time being "he is no longer free, and that he is in reality a slave without hope of freedom, held to service by a merciless master."[71]

Hyperbolic, perhaps, but if invasions of privacy (in *Pavesich*, reputational, proprietary privacy) are like slavery, could impositions of privacy be like slavery, too? In particular, are impositions of unwanted privacy slavery-like deprivations of freedom? Charlotte Bronte's fiction helps us imagine how they could. She created a poor, female heroine who lived a prescribed, secluded life of home, church, and school. Jane Eyre likened her housebound childhood among uncaring kin to "slavery" and her life as a governess in a great house as a lonely "servitude." There was an oppressive aspect to the privacy demanded of Jane, who, as one commentator observes, became "addicted" to the diet of dutiful concealment and confinement with which she was force-fed.[72]

Political theorist Jean Cohen has insightfully argued that the law includes "duties" of privacy as well as "rights" of privacy.[73] Take, for example, the US federal government's "Don't Ask, Don't Tell" policy, her central concern.[74] This regulation—finally repealed by the US Senate in December of 2010 after years of debate—required that homosexuals keep their sexual orientation private, as a duty and condition of military service. "Don't Ask, Don't Tell" was wildly unpopular with homosexuals who rejected the closet, but desired careers in the military and a chance to serve their country. How a society should balance interests in freedom from privacy with interests in mandating unpopular privacy is a topic that demands greater attention from social, political and legal theorists interested in the just bounds of individual freedom and coercion.

The American right to privacy has enjoyed wide appeal for several decades now. Legions of philosophers, lawyers, judges, policy makers, and journalists have made the compelling case for privacy rights protecting personal spaces, personal information, and personal choices. It is generally agreed that privacy rights, even if understood to be fundamental or human rights, are not absolute. Accordingly, scholars have extensively aired the case for limiting the right to privacy for the greater good. We have heard the argument that robust privacy rights can slow down the efficient collection and flow of data preferred by many businesses and officials charged with responsibility for law enforcement, public health, and national security. We have also heard the argument that robust privacy rights tolerating diverse lifestyles and intimate choices negate a common, shared morality. The question of how to reconcile the ideal of privacy rights with the need for information, surveillance, and social cohesion is an unquestionably important one, the subject of frequent debates. Yet debates over how to reconcile privacy with data accessibility, privacy with security, or privacy with responsible community are not the only ones that deserve a forum. As this book is designed to show, we need to extend debates—common in feminist literatures—about balancing freedom from unwanted privacy rights, on the one hand, with duties of privacy, on the other. Following the lead of feminists, all privacy theorists must add to their routine agendas explorations, in practical contexts, of the extent to which varied forms of privacy may be imposed by law, even in the face of an unwelcoming target or beneficiary.

OPPORTUNITY IMPERATIVE OR EXPERIENCE IMPERATIVE?

"One must, if one values the individual as an agent of self-determination and community building," wrote Julie E. Cohen, "take seriously a conception of data privacy that returns control over much personal data to the individual."[75] Privacy is so often coupled in this way with the libertarian concepts of "choice" and "individual rights" that it is easy to overlook or underplay the fact that many individuals do not freely elect the privacies that are their lot in life. Many people would prefer to be free of the burden of one form of privacy or another. And although privacy is often depicted, monolithically, as a basic good that rational people naturally want and demand of good government, the reality is that plenty of people, young and old, will give up seemingly beneficial privacy when allowed or encouraged to do so. This is one of the reasons some philosophers of privacy doubt that consent to divulge personal information should be a "discussion stopper" for public policy makers.[76]

Liberalism posits individuals as rational moral agents fit for autonomous decision making and self-government. Liberals believe social benefits flow from a rule of law that ascribes adult individuals the right to run their own lives. Under principles of liberalism defended for nearly two hundred years by John Stuart Mill, Joel Feinberg, and like-minded thinkers of varied fame and influence, state coercion requires special justification.[77] State coerced privacy requires special justification, too. We must thus consider what justifications for coercing unpopular privacy have been offered, and what further justifications could and should be.

Now, if privacy were just a routine good, like hot bagels and fast cars, the case for coercing it would not have particular weight. But philosophers continue to maintain that privacy is of special value. Privacy, they say, is key to personality development and moral autonomy; personal honor, dignity, identity, creativity, and innovation; psychological well-being, intimacy, and family; civic association, religious expression, and ideals of a limited, tolerant government.[78] These are weighty claims, amenable to serious defense, whether the "privacy" one has in mind is freedom from eavesdropping, medical confidentiality, or access to safe abortions. If privacy is an aspect of freedom and moral autonomy, should government shove it down our indifferent or rebellious throats?

Not necessarily. We should perhaps be free to abandon some of the privacy to which we are entitled. In free societies, the state permits individuals to make choices about which of their legally cognizable interests they will favor. The law allows for tradeoffs that can result in privacy interests taking a back seat to other personal interests. Law in the United States often permits individuals the latitude to choose whether to prefer their property rights to their privacy rights. This is what happened in the Joyce Maynard case: she preferred to sacrifice her privacy and advance her property rights. Was this a good thing? Benn did not seem to doubt at all that privacy rights can be consensually surrendered, though he labored over the question of the scope and duration of waivers.[79] He seemed persuaded that candidates for public office and celebrities implicitly waive some of the law's privacy protection.

There is an ambiguity in the philosophical literature defending privacy. The ambiguity concerns whether it is the *opportunity* to choose the experience of privacy that is supposed to be vitally important, or is it the actual *experience* of privacy. Privacy conceived as a kind of "self-sovereignty" might suggest that the key is the opportunity, not the experience.[80] I believe *both* opportunities for privacy and private choice *and* the actual experience of privacy and private choice importantly enhance typical human lives. If the experience of privacy is as important as I (and many liberal, libertarian, republican and communitarian philosophers alike) believe that it is, then parents, teachers, and clergy should teach the value of privacy with gusto. Assuming the wisdom of private sector educational efforts aimed at cultivating a taste for privacy and habits of respect for privacy, it is worth considering whether there is a role for the public sector to play. Should government, like parents, shore up the preference for privacy? Should the state, moreover, enact or enforce coercive privacy laws that affected individuals may not welcome? How can government action in this domain of "choice" and "individual rights" be justified and constrained?

JUSTIFICATION AND PRACTICAL LIMITS

Foundational political goods are those without which a nation state fails to be good and just. Privacy, I maintain, is a foundational good in the liberal west, to which the United States and similar nations should have a substantive commitment, as they do to personal freedom, and race and gender equality. People should be taught to value others' privacy and their own. Government will sometimes be entitled or even required to reinforce privacy practices.

Coercion is not always a way or the best way to get the job of privacy protection done. Liberalism typically proceeds from a utilitarian or deontic presumption against government coercion. In the pages ahead I will defend some forms of government coercion aimed at privacy promotion in particular contexts, but I will not maintain that government coercion is always necessary or effective. One can readily see the limits and risks of state coercion aimed at privacy protection in an illustration from Germany at the dawn of reality television.

In early 2000, German regulators considered forcing the nightly televised game show "Big Brother" off the air to protect the privacy of its contestants. Modeled after a Dutch predecessor, the adult contestants on the show agreed to live in isolation on a stage designed to look like a house. Contestants were not allowed television sets, the Internet, phone calls, or newspapers. Every aspect of their lives on the set was recorded on camera, including trips to the toilet, hygiene, and intimacy. Each week the viewing public voted a contestant off the program, until a final contestant was declared the winner and presented a large sum of prize money.

Interior Minister Otto Schilly raised the possibility that the television program violated the German constitution. The German constitution provides for an inalienable right to human dignity: "Human dignity shall be inviolable. To respect and protect it shall be the duty of all state authority."[81] Not all Germans were troubled by the show. A fan of "Big Brother" from Berlin urged fellow Germans to "just have fun and relax, and not to spend all their time worrying and discussing everything."[82] Under the pressure of opposition from prominent officials like Schilly and public figures, the producers of "Big Brother" voluntarily made changes in the show's format to address concerns about dignity. The producers created a camera-free room to which contestants could retreat for one hour of privacy a day. In a free society, moral appeal to the spirit of the laws can sometimes achieve goals otherwise sought through outright coercion.

To mandate privacy more forcibly by taking "Big Brother" off the air would have required lawmakers to risk a wave of political disapproval. Many Germans enjoyed watching the show, and many more disapproved of government meddling with the arts and entertainment media in principle. Moreover, there was a certain futility for government regulators to implement a ban. The television show was actually a compilation of highlights from "Big Brother" the twenty-four-hour, seven days a week webcast. Had the forty-five-minute nightly television show been cancelled by a privacy mandating government, "Big Brother" would have continued on the Internet. Pragmatically speaking, banning the television show would have been a symbolic expression of privacy values rather than a concrete method for directly increasing contestants' privacy.[83] The point I wish to make is that despite privacy's importance, coercive interventions may not be possible, necessary, or worthwhile in some instances.

CONSTRAINING STATE DOMINATION

Certain conditions of privacy are felt burdens and wrongfully imposed. At the same time, the actual, reliable experience of privacy is a moral imperative and can be a requirement of social justice. The importance of privacy cannot be reduced to the importance of the legal right to opportunities for privacy, with its built-in assumptions of at-will alienability. Liberal democracies must not only champion certain privacy rights as protected options; they must also treat some privacy as vital enough to be imposed on the uncaring and resentful. Too much free choice, including choice about privacy, can be a kind of tyranny.[84] A central question for privacy scholars then is this: when is coercing privacy by state mandate on its supposed beneficiaries required by background political ideals, and when does coercing privacy contradict background ideals?

Government can turn privacy into a weapon against its own citizens and charges. Government can coerce privacy to reduce the transparency of its operations and the accountability of officials. A problem arises when government seeks to avoid transparency by imposing privacy, using individual privacy rights as pretextual grounds for withholding information the public or its representatives have a right to know.[85]

In 2008, the American Civil Liberties Union won a victory from the Second Circuit Court of Appeals, which held that the government could not use prisoner privacy as a rationale for refusing to release photographs of US military personnel allegedly abusing prisoners in Iraq and Afghanistan.[86] The Freedom of Information Act (FOIA), the main federal open-records statute in the United States, requires the government to disclose records sought by citizens; however, the act expressly allows the government to withhold records whose release would constitute an "unwarranted invasion of privacy" or that are "medical, personnel or similar" files.[87] The court noted in ruling against the government in the case that there was a considerable public interest in the release of the shocking photographs, and that the government's concerns about privacy could be met by simple partial redactions of those images in which a specific person's identity was clearly ascertainable. Celebrating a "resounding victory for the public's right to hold the government accountable," in an official press release, ACLU attorney Amrit Singh proclaimed that "these photographs demonstrate that the abuse of prisoners held in US custody abroad was not aberrational and not confined to Abu Ghraib."[88]

Consider, though, government efforts during the second George W. Bush administration to keep secret the names of post-9/11 detainees. After September 2001 terrorist attacks in the United States, the federal government detained hundreds of individuals believed to have a connection to terrorism. Media and civil liberties groups attempted to use FOIA to get the names and other information about the detainees, suspecting that a number were being held on legally inadequate grounds. However, the government asserted that FOIA contained exceptions for information whose disclosure might jeopardize privacy, law enforcement, or national security. Ironically, in this instance, many of the detainees would have preferred ready disclosure of their names over bureaucratically vaunted privacy rights. Hence, the privacy protection the government asserted on their behalf was received as an unwanted privacy mandate. Critics of the government claimed that by essentially coercing detainee privacy, the government was really trying to protect state secrecy and avoid accountability for overly broad national origin, religion and ethnicity-based roundups. The Court of Appeals for the District of Columbia sided with the government in a 2003 decision, *Center for National Security Studies v. US Department of Justice*.[89] The Court of Appeals for the Second Circuit sided with the government in a 2009 decision, *Associated Press v. Department of Defense*.[90] The privacy concerns raised in the Associated Press case were wide-ranging. The Associated Press for years sought documents relevant to the issue of whether terrorism-related detainees at the Guantanamo Bay Naval Base were being mistreated. (Within days of taking office, President Barak Obama moved without success to close the Guantanamo prison, stymied by political opposition to transferring prisoners to locations on the US mainland or abroad.[91]) The government asserted that FOIA exemptions allowed it to protect the privacy of Guantanamo naval base detainees, their personal correspondence, and their families. Reversing a district court finding to the contrary, the Court of Appeals found that the Associated Press had failed to establish that it needed those portions of government-held documents that would reveal the identities of the detainees and their families. We can imagine that while detainees seeking legal assistance and public outrage might want their names and stories shared with the public, detainees might not wish intimate correspondence with family members about their plight to be made public.

It is not in principle out of order for the government to mandate unpopular privacy for the sake of good government. Nor is it out of order for government to concern itself with the privacy of officials. A Secret Service agent assigned to protect the life of the Secretary of State has a duty of privacy (confidentiality) respecting the details of intimate life and sensitive government business. Civil servants understand that their jobs come at the price of silence concerning confidential records and government secrets. The unauthorized release of US State Department diplomatic cables to WikiLeaks was a rare exception. In 2009, former federal employees with access to passport records pled guilty to charges they had unlawfully accessed personal data concerning then-future President Barak Obama and his 2008 campaign rivals.

Government must have the power to coerce privacy, both to protect itself and its employees, prominent persons, and to protect ordinary men, women, and children.

Yet this power, like all state power, is subject to abuse. Governments may coerce privacy as a tool of social control, depriving individuals of socioeconomic opportunity, sexual identity, due process, and freedoms of expression and association. Thus, while coercing privacy is highly desirable from a liberal democratic point of view, it is also potentially dangerous from a liberal democratic point of view. Ultimately, society must constrain the power to mandate privacy not only to promote ideals of responsible freedom, but also to promote ideals of responsible government.

CONCLUSION

Privacy protection can be popular with its intended targets and beneficiaries or it can be unpopular. Here, I consider diverse unpopular physical and informational privacies. I explore the case within liberal political and moral theory for imposing unwelcome duties of privacy and limiting the alienability of privacy rights. The inspiration for my inquiry is, broadly speaking, feminist. My text is American law. My context is an exhilarating era in which "privacy" simultaneously evokes the nineteenth century's confidence in traditions of hearth and home, the twentieth century's promise of personal freedom backed by limited government, and the twenty-first century's barely hesitant embrace of technologies of surveillance, mobile communication, and social networking.

Once, ideal women were modest in speech and dress, and lived lives centered on family caretaking. Women made the most of their lives by developing meaningful capacities for care, intimacy, reflection and artistry. But the regime of state-mandated privacy feminists call "patriarchy" was decidedly coercive. Recalling legal efforts to regulate the conduct of women flags broader tendencies of paternalism and subordination in the law, at odds with liberal aspirations. Good government will ideally coercively mandate only essential privacies, and only essential privacies that are unobtainable through other, practical, noncoercive measures. Among the government privacy mandates that I treat in the pages ahead, some are weakly coercive and others are strongly coercive. Weak privacy mandates are those that mildly constrain freedom to speak, act, or choose. Weak mandates include mechanisms for opting out of otherwise required privacy protections. Strongly coercive privacy mandates are those that extensively constrain freedom and do not provide ready mechanisms of lawful circumvention. In practice, because individual and market freedoms are dear in the United States, both weakly and strongly coercive privacy mandates spawn normative controversy. The strong and unpopular privacy mandates are among the most controversial.

It was ethically problematic for Joyce Maynard to sell Salinger's letters during his lifetime, knowing her ex-lover's views about his privacy. She took heat for it. But the law allowed her to betray a moral confidence. And what of Maynard's own privacy, and her own moral stake in the matter? The damage was done; she had published a tell-all memoir, even though for forty years she had feared Salinger's "disapproval and wrath" for speaking with "true honesty" about her own history.[92] Middle-aged men who initiate relationships with teenagers should not, perhaps, expect the same degree of privacy they rightfully expect when dealing with undominated equals. Yet, privacy is so valuable that individuals must sometimes be guided—and if necessary and potentially effective, forced—to accept it for the good it does them or others. For this reason, government, even a liberal one, may justifiably mandate unpopular privacy. In the right situations, government can make privacy a duty, a responsibility of self-care. I shall try, throughout the subsequent chapters of this book, to further advance these philosophical perspectives on mandating unpopular privacy.

PART TWO

Physical Privacies: Seclusion and Concealment

2
SECLUSION

Seclusion is perhaps the most basic, tangible notion of privacy—a physical separation from others. It is a state people crave at times, but can also dread. Alone at home with a good book is one thing; being quarantined on an island or tossed into a supermaximum security prison cell, another. Seclusion can be chosen, freely and autonomously, or it can be mandated and imposed. Where mandated, seclusion can be embraced or it can be despised. Faced with felt threats of violent crime, political terrorism, dangerous insanity, and public health pandemics, liberal societies may wish to put people away for the common good. But when is coercive separation from society an acceptable deprivation? What norms of solitude, isolation, and confinement make sense to us, and why?

SOLITUDE

Known as a philosopher of the politics and morality of the public sphere, Hannah Arendt was also a subtle philosopher of the politics and morality of privacy. Arendt offered evocative phenomenologies of solitude, loneliness, and isolation. She characterized solitude as a "silent dialogue of myself with myself."[1] For Arendt, "solitude means that though alone, I am together with somebody (myself, that is)."[2] The company of oneself can lead to boredom and loneliness, she noted, but solitude is not the same thing as loneliness. We can enjoy solitude; whereas loneliness is typically a pain. Arendt understood that a person may be lonelier in a crowd than while alone, because the company of oneself can be such a pleasure. Loneliness, she suggests, can be tolerable if it "is transformed into solitude," a state of mind in which a person takes pleasure in her singularity and self-accompaniment.[3] Physical privacy that leads to solitude without loneliness is a blessing.

Arendt distinguished solitude from loneliness and loneliness from isolation. Being alone amounts to isolation, she offered, "when I am neither together with myself nor in the company of others but concerned with the things of the world." The work I perform can be isolating if I am "so concentrated on what I am doing that the presence of others, including myself, can only disturb me." Isolation is a "negative phenomenon" where "others with whom I share a certain concern for the world may desert me."[4] Isolation connotes desertion. Prisons isolate. Hospitals isolate. Bad marriages isolate. Seclusion anywhere is experienced as isolation, rather than one of the positive forms of privacy, when it brings on feelings of having been abandoned, shut off, put away.

With Arendt's distinctions in view, one sees that privacy, the physical separation of one body from others, potentially spawns disparate states of mind, some blissful, some wretched: solitude, loneliness, or isolation. But there are other ways to look at and describe these things. Philosophers do not use privacy-related concepts in uniform ways. There is no definitive taxonomy. Some philosophers marshal the concept of solitude to represent an objective subtype of privacy itself. Israeli philosopher Ruth Gavison understood solitude as a form of privacy in this way. Privacy is limited access to people and information; and one subtype of privacy, so conceived, is solitude, limited access to a person who is alone. Competing taxonomies aside, Arendt and Gavison would agree, though, that being utterly alone and inaccessible is a rare experience for human beings, and an emotionally risky one. Under the typical conditions of life experienced in the twentieth century by Arendt and Gavison on three continents, achieving solitude was so unusual that extraordinarily spirited people went away to find it, and then wrote books about what they found.

GETTING AWAY, HIDING OUT

Richard E. Byrd traveled to the South Pole to find solitude. As he would later explain in a published memoir, he wanted to satisfy "one man's desire to . . . be by himself for a while and to taste peace and quiet and solitude long enough to find out how good they really are."[5] All alone, the adventurous Admiral Bryd operated the Bolling Advance Weather Base on the icy continent of Antarctica through the winter of 1934. Barely accessible to others at one frigid end of the earth, Byrd experienced a nearly total privacy of thought and action. Writer May Sarton, an adventurer of another sort, chose to search for solitude in a country house. The "chief benefit of the house," according to Gaston Bachelard, is that "the house shelters daydreaming, the house protects the dreamer, the house allows one to dream in peace."[6] An American country house shares some of the romance of the hut—a place of refuge and freedom.[7] Sarton hoped solitude would stimulate her creativity as a writer. In a popular memoir, Sarton exalted her aloneness (an atypical state for anyone, and especially a woman of her generation) as her "real" life.[8] By herself in her garden or at her desk, Sarton enjoyed an unusually rich and artistic privacy. Both Sarton and Byrd discovered that companionless existence is a mixed blessing. Sarton interrupted her seclusion by welcoming visitors to her house when she felt lonely. For months, cut off from society by the limits of technology and brutal nature, Byrd could not entertain company at will. He consequently became melancholy, longing for his wife and the comforts of their home. Lucky for him, his unique isolation was of his own design and temporary.

STUCK AT HOME: FLANEUR AND HAUSFRAU

Solitude is not always temporary and a choice of one's own doing. It can be mandated. If home is where you truly want to be, there is no place better. But what if home is a house you long to escape? What if home is a series of dreary tasks that isolate you from participation in civic life, industry, or the professions? What if your seclusion and solitude constitute a servitude, and your very intimacies are blatant dictates of custom, backed by law? Being stuck at home was a mode of mandated seclusion problematized by creative nineteenth-century minds, male and female. Charles Baudelaire had his idealized Parisian poet longing for the streets, Brontë her English governess, longing for the world, too.

Baudelaire's flaneur is an independent male artist, whose "passion and his profession is to merge with the crowd."[9] As described by Keith Tester, the flaneur is a figure native to nineteenth-century French literature, of a man who is "existentially at home only when he is not physically at home." For such a man, "the private sphere is the home of an existence devoid of an almost orgiastic pleasure," namely the sublime joy of losing oneself in a crowd. For such a man freedom is the capacity to roam the city, the love of roaming the city, the flights of mind inspired by public spaces, chance meetings, collisions among the anonymous. For such a man, his personal identity is not fixed, not known, not remembered. He is unconfined.

Charlotte Brontë's heroine, the narrator of *Jane Eyre*, is confined. Brontë's 1847 novel can be read as a study of an imposed privacy, household seclusion. Jane is an independent-minded female governess who cannot safely roam at will, even within the confines of her own residences. Danger and madness haunt the attics. Jane's identity is fixed, settled for all time. She is expected to domesticate her passions in undertakings that keep her close to home: reading, drawing, teaching, marriage. Jane Eyre's confinement to what Italians refer to as the prescribed routine of "casa, chiesa, schola" is a product of her gender, class, and a legal system favoring male heirs. Her confinement is secured by norms of silence and restraint.[10]

Readers accompany Jane Eyre as she moves through six residential venues: a great house, a large boarding school, another great house, a modest house, a school with a room out back for teacher, and another modest house. The change in her life is change within a cloister and Jane knows it. When the fictional autobiography opens, the orphaned heroine is only ten. Her deceased parents were a poor clergyman and a disinherited gentlewoman. Jane lives unhappily at Gateshead Hall. Mrs. Reed, the head of the Gateshead Hall household, is Jane's aunt, the widow of Jane's well-to-do maternal uncle. Jane is barely tolerated by her cold aunt's three taunting children, cousins near Jane in age, but inferior to her in intelligence and character. As a poor girl with no prospects, Jane is morally and legally powerless. Stuck in an inhospitable home, she imagines herself a rebel slave, her bullying, violent cousin John Reed a murderous slave-driver. Well aware of his contingent rights at law as male heir to inherit the house in which they all lived, John Reed abuses his doting mother and demands "habitual obedience" to his rules. John reminds Jane with his fists that she "ought to beg" for a living.

Jane achieves modicums of freedom through acquiring new servitudes. When Mrs. Reed gets rid of Jane by handing her over to Mr. Brocklehurst, head of a sickening, charitable boarding school, Jane feels a bit of freedom. "Even for me," Jane recalls, "life had its gleams of sunshine." There would always be gleams of sunshine in her walled life, but cruel and arbitrary limits on her freedom. At eighteen, Jane sought what she termed "at least a new servitude" and wound up at Mr. Edward Rochester's Thornfield Hall, where she worked with restless ambivalence as governess. She nearly committed adultery with the duplicitous Mr. Rochester, who marched to his own drummer and kept a mad wife Bertha locked in an attic. Jane eventually got her man, though, when Bertha committed suicide.

In every home in which she lived, Jane was victimized by men who disregarded her feelings in the name of discipline, charity, husbandly love, or God. Coerced by custom and law to a woman's life, Jane could never satisfy her desire for travel, variety, and experience. A man with a "restless" nature like her own could seek "action," Jane observed. A man could envision for himself a life in "the busy world, towns, regions full of life." A man would have access to "more practical experience" and "acquaintance with variety of character." As Jane matures in the novel she comes to understand that this is not a life she can hope to live, and she abandons dreams of that sort. She becomes resigned to live a life committed to rules and principles, a "respectable, proper, en regle" existence.

The love of Mr. Rochester quells Jane's inward complaints of the tedium of her female roles, "the viewless fetters of an uniform and too still existence." Jane finds happiness in loving a husband, and in knowing for sure that her own powers of reason and judgment are equal to those of her social and legal superiors. Though a physically and socially inferior woman, she is blessed with the endowment of moral autonomy—the ability to reason and do what is right. Is this a happy ending? Subjectively, perhaps; objectively, no.

Jane chose geographical confinement and marriage over freedom. Under the English legal system presupposed by Brontë and her novel, legal sovereignty over the household normally belonged to a man. Feminists of Brontë's time argued that married women were nothing short of slaves. Husbands controlled their own property as well as any the wife brought into the family. Men had the authority to decide matters of domicile and child-rearing. A married woman needed the permission of her husband to sue and enter contracts. A man could physically chastise his wife. Before 1857, divorce was nearly impossible.[11] When the possibility of an independent life is opened up for Jane through an unexpected inheritance, she gives away a full 75 percent of her new wealth. She marries Rochester, subjugating herself in the eyes of the law to a helplessly blind amputee, mutilated while trying in vain to prevent the suicide of the wife he had stowed away upstairs.

The notion that women can be passionate made *Jane Eyre* something of a shocking and radical novel for its time. Yet ultimately the novel embraces formal education, religion, hard work, sacrifice, marriage, and family responsibility as its messages—conventional by any measure. Women will be secluded and mastered; it's only a choice of masters.[12] The point is not new; *Jane Eyre* titillated nineteenth-century patriarchy while offering it a kind of reassurance Mary Wollstinecraft's and Harriet Taylor's feminist writings did not—that women free to choose would ultimately choose to sustain business as usual.[13] Rochester's spare house and loyal servants at Ferndean became Jane Eyre's haven. In more banal terms, Jane winds up stuck at home, a contented hausfrau.

SANCTUARY

Perhaps the spacious, well-appointed manse idealized by the nineteenth-century European and American intelligentsia promised the inner flaneur some of variety, anonymity and surprise of the city. The romance of the home played a pivotal role in the conceptualization of the right to privacy. The idea that there should be a legal right of privacy was set out systematically for the first time in 1890 in an article penned by Boston Brahman Samuel D. Warren and Louis D. Brandeis for the *Harvard Law Review*.[14] A legal right of privacy, they asserted, could protect "the sacred precincts of private and domestic life." E. L. Godkin, a fellow high-toned intellectual of their day, was not persuaded that the law could do much to enhance privacy, but he believed steadfastly in the power of domestic architecture to create the proper haven. In an 1890 article in *Scribner's Magazine* and in another in *The Nation* the same year, Godkin argued that civilized people need private houses with rooms of their own; women's household responsibilities rule out optimal privacy, making separate withdrawing rooms essential.[15] The vision of Warren and Brandeis won out in the American judiciary, where the "cases show, all details are intimate details, because the entire area is held safe from prying government eyes."[16] (Unless the home is a low-income housing project, in which case there are plenty of governmental eyes prying.[17])

"Having to stay home" has been an important sort of unwanted seclusion for women, for teenagers, and for men who are disabled, jobless, or superannuated. At the same time, "getting to stay at home" (even if you work from home) has come to signify a luxury, a treat of convenience and informality. For the majority of contemporary Americans home stands counter to work, however, symbolizing an escape, a respite from the "tribulations of their daily pursuits."[18] The law valorizes home, not the hospital, as "the last citadel of the tired, the weary, and the sick."[19]

American judges and policymakers in the United States encourage the public to think of homes as havens, putting on convenient blinders to realities that make homes among the most dangerous places for women and children on earth. But, even setting aside the risk of domestic violence, homes are not simple sanctuaries. At home we face intrusions, interruptions, and distractions. We face everything from abortion protesters picketing on our front lawns to funeral parlors telephoning us with the latest deal on their "most sensitive product."[20]

INTERRUPTED: DO NOT CALL

Telephone calls from politicians, charities, and businesses who want our money are a characteristic disturbance in the US home. What is the role of the state in protecting against telephonic disturbances? May the state remove these interruptions even if the callers believe they have a right to reach us and a percentage of householders do not mind picking up the phone? If the question seems too mundane for philosophy consider this: "the State's interest in protecting the well-being, tranquility, and privacy of the home is certainly of the highest order in a free and civilized society."[21]

In 2002 a typical residential homeowner in the United States might receive dozens of telemarketing calls a week on landline telephones. These calls disturbed home life and whatever hope of solitude and intimate repose it otherwise carried. Unsolicited calls frequently came in the early evenings when they were likely to interrupt rest, meals, homework, religious observances, bathing, sex, bill-paying, housework, or child and elder care. Calls came in by cellular telephone, too. The profitable, $150 billion telemarketing industry tried to minimize the seriousness of the disturbances caused by their calls to private homes. The industry argued that people did not have to answer the phone, could turn their phones off, or could use caller I.D. to sceen calls. Call recipients could also request that individual callers not call back, and report those who ignored such requests to federal authorities for prosecution under telecommunications laws.

During the first administration of President George W. Bush, the US Federal Trade Commission (FTC) identified telemarketing calls as a major source of unwanted invasions of privacy and sought to do something about it. The FTC argued that the number of calls was overwhelming, and the procedures for blocking and screening calls were inconvenient, impractical, and expensive for phone customers. No one had the time to keep track of the names of the telemarketers who made repeated calls and then to pursue legal action against them.

The FTC could have moved to ban all telemarketing calls for all residential phone customers. This would have mandated privacy even for home dwellers who did not want more privacy. (Some states, including Indiana, have stricter do not call laws, so the idea is not unprecedented.[22]) The FTC settled on a weakly coercive approach to addressing the problem of privacy-invading telemarketing calls. Instead of banning calls, it decided to give individuals the ability to "opt out" of accessibility to most telemarketers, simply by notifying the FTC that they wanted their phone numbers to be included on new National Do Not Call (DNC) Registry list.[23] People who valued their privacy and knew of the registry could opt in; people who did not particularly value their privacy could live with the status quo.

Under the program, most commercial telemarketers were prohibited from calling landline phone numbers and cell phone numbers that individuals with telephone service chose to place on the government-managed DNC list. Politicians seeking votes, researchers, and charities were permitted to continue making unsolicited calls, but only businesses with a prior relationship to a residential phone customer could place unsolicited calls to registered numbers. Telemarketers who broke the rules by calling numbers on the registry faced fines, which in 2008 were increased from a maximum of $11,000 to $18,000 per call. Other rule violations exposed telemarketers to sanctions as well, violations such as not limiting calls to the 8 A.M. to 9 P.M. timeframe, not allowing numbers to be captured on caller ID, unlawful automated dialing and faxing, and perpetrating scams and fraud. In 2005, the satellite television firm DIRECTV paid $5,335,000 to settle FTC charges that a telemarketing firm working on its behalf placed calls to phone numbers that appeared on the DNC Registry. DIRECTV's telemarketers also violated the "abandoned call" rule by failing to put a live sales representative on the line within two seconds after the consumer answers her phone.

The National DNC Registry was a hit with the general public. As the program prepared to go live, people signed up by the millions. Naturally, the lucrative telemarketing industry was not pleased. A successful suit was filed in Oklahoma District court by the Direct Marketing Association and three others claiming that the FTC lacked the legal authority from Congress to regulate access to phone customers. The telemarketing industry plaintiffs persuaded the court that the Federal Communications Commission (FCC) has responsibility for phone matters, not the FTC. The FTC believed that it created the registry pursuant to its authority to fight unethical and deceptive trade practices, of which it believed the telemarketing industry was often guilty. The original national registry rules were teamwork, enacted with the nod of the FCC pursuant to the Telephone Consumer Protection Act of 1991 and by the FTC pursuant to the Telemarketing and Consumer Fraud and Abuse Prevention Act of 1994. Congress quickly responded to the telemarketer's suit with legislation to make the FTC's uncertain authority, certain, and the president signed on. Even before the suit, Congress had appropriated funding for the FTC to implement the registry program, implicitly granting the agency regulatory authority.

A second lawsuit filed in federal court in Colorado by Mainstream Marketing Services Inc. and two other firms attacked the registry on broad constitutional grounds.[24] The claim was that the right to commercial free speech was violated by the program. The FTC was guilty of "content discrimination" because it singled out commercial telemarketers, excepting politicians and charities from the registry. If the ballet and the Republican Party can disturb diaper-changing with cold calls to a household, why can't a commercial telemarketer?

The federal appeals court in Colorado sided with the FTC, emphasizing the constitutional importance of the privacy of the home. The First Amendment does not give commercial entities the right to impose their messages on a captive audience of unwilling listeners, and thus an opt-in Do Not Call Registry is constitutional. As for banning some unwanted calls but not others, the court argued that government is free to fix part of a problem by singling out what it reasonably believes are the worst offenders. After the government's complete victory in 10th Circuit, the National Do Not Call Registry program went on line in 2003.

Why did the FTC, which endorsed the idea that "the privacy of the home is of the highest order in a free and civilized society," not take a more strongly coercive approach to resolving the telemarketing problem?[25] One more strongly coercive approach would have been for the FTC to categorically ban all telemarketing calls. This move would have denied freedom of choice to both telemarketers and residential phone owners, some of whom apparently want marketing calls more than they want additional privacy at home. Another more strongly coercive approach would have required phone owners wishing to receive telemarketing calls to opt in to a national "calls permitted" registry. The weakly coercive approach the FTC in fact took recognized the significance of freedom of choice, leaving telephonic access to all landlines by telemarketers as the default rule.

Ian Ayres and coauthors proposed an approach to the problem that that would have recognized the significance of freedom of choice and the commercial value of private time. Rather than foist unwanted privacy on phone customers, they suggested, let them get paid for giving it up. Ayres proposed that the government institute a system whereby telemarketers would pay phone customers for each telemarketing call placed and answered.[26] The requirement of payment would force telemarketers to make fewer calls, better tailoring the number of calls placed to the expected profits earned by placing calls.

The severity of the problem of interrupted lives was sufficiently great in my view to warrant a categorical ban on telemarketing calls or an opt-in "calls permitted" registry. One argument for strongly coercing privacy policy in this context is frankly paternalistic: some people may not realize the importance of the privacy they are losing as a result of constantly responding to telemarketing calls. But another argument for coercion could be based on a subtler reading of the significance of liberalism's bias against coercion. Liberalism is a prejudice against public and private coercion that interferes with essential freedoms and equalities. A default rule that frees us from the need to attend to outsiders' commercial projects when we retreat to our homes might be a truer requirement of liberalism's bias against coercion, than the default rule Congress and the FTC left in place that makes us free game. It is liberating to be free of the option continuously to make routine and unimportant choices. That a certain number of outsiders' commercial projects are fraudulent strengthens the case for protectionism. An Illinois fundraiser actually pocketed 85 percent of the proceeds earned by telemarketing on behalf of a charity.[27] Government could spare the people the need to make continuous routine and important choices.

PUT AWAY: IMPRISONMENT

Being at home feels good, if that is where you want to be—and home can be precisely where you want most to be when the risk of violence is low and interruptions minimal. But being stuck at home, like being put away in jail or prison, is very often experienced as a burden on freedom. Being stuck at home and put away in prison come together in the method of penal control known as "house arrest." In 2008 a judge ordered $10 million in bail and house arrest for the notorious investment advisor Bernard Madoff, whose "house" happened to be a luxury penthouse apartment in New York City. Madoff admitted to a gargantuan Ponzi scheme that robbed myriad individual and institutional investors of an estimated $50 billion. House arrest is mainly reserved for low-risk nonviolent offenders and suspects in the United States, who are on parole or, like Madoff at the time, awaiting trial or sentencing. (In 2009 Madoff pled guilty to numerous felonies and was sentenced to 150 years in federal prison.) House arrest tethers arrestees to their homes and circumscribes routine obligations outside the home by means of "electronic bracelet" monitoring technology locked onto their ankles (the most common part of the body to encase). Law enforcement authorities receive instant electronic notification when arrestees travel outside their authorized ranges.

Confinement of people who break the law (or are suspected of doing so) in jails, prisons, and detention centers is a large, important class of mandated seclusion. Confinement within the walls of a prison—like public health quarantines and involuntary mental health commitments—can entail privacies of seclusion that are not much valued at all by the people who must endure them. This is a sort of seclusion Arendt would term isolating and lonely, despite the presence of others.

One might refuse to refer the condition of coerced, unwanted confinement as privacy, on the ground that "privacy" should be reserved as a valorific, a term for something normal human beings will seek and enjoy. Privacy, on this view, is wanted privacy, popular privacy. Moreover, for all of the aloneness and loneliness experienced in prisons, they are not, on balance, especially private places.

Jail or prison is the home of one in one hundred US men and women.[28] It is a place in which the men and women we call "inmates" are accommodated in rooms we call "cells". They have few privacy rights, as a matter of law, and even fewer opportunities for the beneficial modes of privacy. The partly panoptic design of historic Eastern State Penitentiary in Philadelphia assured that the cellblocks could be closely monitored by armed guards. In contemporary US prisons, men and women occupy cells that resemble barred cages or boxes. Prisoners can be compelled to share their cells, empty their bladders and bowels into open toilets, submit to cell and body cavity searches at will, and undergo blood and urine testing on demand. Sexual intimacy is treated as a disciplinary infraction, a punishable offense. Administrative segregation for prisoners deemed "disruptive and unable to live peacefully in the general population" and disciplinary segregation for those who have broken the rules can extend for many months, and indeed years.[29]

According to Carol S. Steiker, punishment is the power to blame, ideally bounded by just and humane criminal procedures.[30] The survival of cruel methods of punishment that wound the body and destroy the mind has been helped along by the notion that punishment is autonomy—the autonomy of accepting blame, of being held accountable for one's conduct. Punishment has been characterized as a right to be corrected and perhaps improved, earned by knowing nonconformity to the law.[31]

Amenable to theoretical construction as freedom, incarceration lends itself to the quite different construction as slavery and civil death. Joan Dayan has argued that American-style incarceration in which prisoners, especially blacks in the post-Civil War South, were forced to work in ball and chain, functioned as a new slavery—"a new servitude," to borrow Brontë's phrase. "Confinement of prisoners in the United States . . . became an alternative to slavery, another kind of receptacle for imperfect creatures whose civil disease justified containment," Dayan wrote. The disproportionate number of African American men subsisting in prison today lends more than a patina of plausibility to her claim. Dayan argued that "once convicted of crime, the criminal can be reduced—not by a master but by the state—into a condition sustained under the sign of death." Slavery was the jural equivalent death; prison became the jural equivalent of death, even more so because of techniques of solitary confinement capable of turning "humans into the living dead."[32]

The Eastern State Penitentiary opened in Philadelphia in 1829, with an innovative design by British architect John Haviland. The philosophy behind the institution, pressed by Dr. Benjamin Rush and Benjamin Franklin, was that men who broke the law should repent of their wrongdoing through earnest thought and reflection. To achieve this end, Eastern State both secluded its prisoners from society, and, for the first time in the history of punishment in the United States, imposed a life of quiet, morally uplifting solitude. Situated on a hill outside the city's center when built, the structure—now a conserved ruin—haunts the expanded city's vibrant museum district.

When the prison opened, its policy was to confine each inmate to a separate cell, containing a bed, a toilet, a sink, and a skylight. Inmates were to spend virtually all their time in their individual cells, performing assigned work, or out of doors in the personal walled yards adjacent each ground level cell. Inmates were not allowed to speak to one another; and when they left their cells, their heads were covered to preserve anonymity. The experience of Eastern State Penitentiary was supposed to change the criminal wrongdoer, to guide him to become a better person, then release him back into the world untainted, to rebuild his life. Solitary was supposed to be more humane than corporal punishments and public shaming, the methods it supplanted.[33]

Over time, prisoners developed ways of communicating with one another by tapping out codes on metal pipes. No doubt the solitude and silence at Eastern Penitentiary constituted a desperately lonely privacy for its inmates. No matter that the Philadelphia prison replaced, with relative Quaker humanity, the regimes of filth, crowding, and violence found in typical period jails.[34]

Eastern State Penitentiary emphasized moral reform, but the US prison system has been more greatly influenced by Auburn Prison in New York.[35] Completed in 1821, a few years before the opening of Eastern State, Auburn Prison confined inmates to "solitary cells and dungeons" without much concern for their reformation. The Auburn system of incarceration emphasized punishment and deterrence. Private seclusion in prisons was supposed to be an improvement over the chaos of open jails, and the shame and humiliation of public spectacles of beatings, burnings, and the pillory. Yet isolation carries its own cruelties.[36] In the early years before conditions were improved, Auburn prisoners intentionally injured and mutilated themselves, pathological responses to the trauma of their lonely isolation.

According to Martin I. Meskell, "the conclusion that solitary confinement without labor causes mental breakdown and sanity has never been seriously questioned." If his assessment is even partly correct, why does the number and variety of solitary confinements in the world of American prisons continue to grow?[37] The answer appears to be that US policy makers regard efficiency and retaliation more highly than other goals that could be sought after in dealing with noncompliant populations. Forcing someone into a realm in which he or she is untouched and untouchable relieves the prison of financial costs associated with managing groups, many of whose members struggle with moral self-control. But evidence suggests the cost to the individual placed in segregation for the convenience of the system is extremely high. "The threat of substantial, serious and possibly irreversible . . . psychological illness," argues one critic, would ideally "increase the burden on prison authorities to explore feasible alternative custodial arrangements."[38] Yet lengthy solitary confinement is a normal practice, alternatives to which are not widely explored. Affected inmates have felt unjustly treated, but a year or more in solitary confinement does not appear to violate constitutional standards against cruel and unusual punishment embraced by American courts.[39] In a Colorado facility, teenagers as young as fourteen were subjected to solitary confinement for weeks.[40]

"Supermax" is the nickname commonly given for the highly restrictive conditions found in super-maximum security prisons or the disciplinary or administrative areas of modern American prisons since 1984. Supermax confinement segregates dangerous gang members and behaviorally difficult inmates.[41] Supermax houses inmates in small solitary units with no view onto the world outside, twenty-three hours a day. Inmates in Supermax-style confinement are deprived of company and most diversions. Describing the Supermax facility at an Ohio prison (OSP), Supreme Court Justice Anthony Kennedy wrote that conditions "are more restrictive than any other form of incarceration in Ohio, including conditions on its death row or in its administrative control units."[42] At the Ohio prison, he continued:

> almost every aspect of an inmate's life is controlled and monitored. Inmates must remain in their cells, which measure 7 by 14 feet, for 23 hours per day. A light remains on in the cell at all times, though it is sometimes dimmed, and an inmate who attempts to shield the light to sleep is subject to further discipline. During the one hour per day that an inmate may leave his cell, access is limited to one of two indoor recreation cells. . . . Incarceration at OSP is synonymous with extreme isolation. In contrast to any other Ohio prison, including any segregation unit, OSP cells have solid metal doors with metal strips along their sides and bottoms which prevent conversation or communication with other inmates. All meals are taken alone in the inmate's cell instead of in a common eating area. Opportunities for visitation are rare and in all events are conducted through glass walls. It is fair to say OSP inmates are deprived of almost any environmental or sensory stimuli and of almost all human contact.[43]

By 1997, thirty-six states had already adopted some sort of heightened lockdown for prisoners deemed difficult to manage or keep safe. By 2009, the Supermax prison phenomenon was pervasive enough and thrilling enough to have warranted prime-time MSNBC cable television reality shows.

Many experts believe confinement in Supermax does more harm than good. They say it harms inmates by destroying their fragile ties to society, exacerbating their pre-existing mental health problems, and causing a long list of cognitive, sensory, and psychiatric problems: hypersensitivity, perceptual disturbances, problems thinking, difficulty concentrating and remembering, severe anxiety, agitation, paranoia, and outright psychosis. The public might care more about the wretched fates of secluded convicts, if they thought they deserved humane alternatives. But the larger problem with public understanding may be a matter of framing—are we talking about "nearly complete isolation and deprivation of environmental stimuli" or "merely 'secure control of inmates' or 'limited direct access to staff and other inmates'"?[44]

Inmates confined to Supermax prisons have frequently sued the government. They have sued complaining about the unfairness of the procedures that landed them in Supermax, and they have sued complaining about the substantive conditions of confinement Supermax imposes indefinitely—in some cases, for a lifetime. The Eighth Amendment prohibits cruel and unusual punishment, but Supermax has not been found to be cruel and unusual by the Supreme Court. The Supreme Court has ruled that Supermax prison conditions impose an "atypical and significant hardship" which may only be imposed on the basis of a fair set of procedural safeguards.[45] In short, while confinement in the extreme conditions of Supermax is not unconstitutional, Fourteenth Amendment liberty requires significant procedural safeguards. That said, the inmates in the Ohio prison described by Justice Kennedy lost their bid in the Supreme Court for additional safeguards.

SHUT AWAY: QUARANTINE

The sick are shut away, sometimes unwillingly and by means of force. After a period of unwanted seclusion and treatment, the sick may improve. The coercion will have been temporary, perhaps a case of "infringing autonomy to create autonomy."[46] Hospital patients feel lonely, but not because they are alone. Hospital rooms are likely shared, and may bustle with the intrusions of doctors, nurses, social workers, technicians, cafeteria workers, cleaners, medical students, and clergy. Patients feel lonely because sickness and dying are existentially isolating experiences, and also because they miss ordinary associations with friends, coworkers, and family. They feel deserted in the way Arendt describes: abandoned by the more fortunate, healthy world. McLean Hospital, a Boston-area psychiatric hospital affiliated today with Harvard

Medical School, was once open to the "gracefully insane," wealthy patients shut away with many of the comforts of home—an exception to the rule of institutionalized care.[47]

Quarantine is a preventative, not a treatment or cure.[48] For this reason, compulsory quarantine has been imposed on the healthy to prevent the spread of diseases known or feared, as well as on the ill. In Italian, the word for the numeral 40 is "quaranta." The original quarantine was the forty-day period set by a fifteenth-century Venetian statute for keeping a "suspected plaque ship... anchored offshore before being allowed to dock."[49] It has been documented that between 1918 in 1920, more than 18,000 women were confined for far longer than forty days in institutions protected with armed guards and barbed wire to prevent them from spreading sexually transmitted diseases among American military troops.[50] In the 1980s, children with acquired immune deficiency syndrome (AIDS)—symbolized by Ryan White—were sometimes excluded from school, effectively quarantined in their homes. Forcing people into quarantine, even in their own homes or the equivalent, does not create for them a welcome haven. It is unlikely that "Typhoid Mary," the poor Irish American cook who became New York City's most infamous quarantine, regarded her exile to an islet in the Bronx River as a haven of privacy of any kind.

In the United States, federal public health officials are armed with constitutionally designated police powers. Officials can inoculate a person against her will, and may quarantine a person against her will. The availability of vaccines and antibiotics has reduced the perceived need for quarantine, but it has not eliminated it. Citizens of the United States and immigrants entering the country against may be quarantined against their wills for suspected exposure to any one of a long list of contagious diseases. The list of diseases for which a person might be involuntarily detained, hospitalized, or kept home includes tuberculosis, smallpox, cholera, leprosy, the Ebola virus, and severe acute respiratory syndrome (SARS).

Federal officials share the power to quarantine with uncertain combinations of local, state, and international authorities. Modern quarantine laws in the United States include procedural safeguards permitting a person segregated for quarantine to appeal quarantine orders and rules of immunity. The immunity rules protect officials who order reasonable and necessary quarantine from prosecution in civil suits. Concern is growing about the potential for serious conflicts between the protection of civil liberties, on the one hand, and effective government responses to a public health emergency, on the other. The anthrax bioterrorism scares of 2001, the SARS epidemic scares of 2003, and subsequent avian flu scares have put the problem of the politics of quarantine squarely on the public agenda. What would we do in the (unlikely) case of an outbreak of smallpox caused by bioterrorism? What should a free state to do? Most experts would agree that intervention should be prompt, should include vaccination, and should include quarantine.[51] Sociologist Amitai Etzioni has argued that we must be ready and willing to "call a state of emergency and do whatever needs [to be done to save lives]."[52]

Lawrence O. Gostin suggests that it is jejune to think that "you can have all your civil liberties and all your public health"; he charges that "in the modern United States, we are so focused on the salience of autonomy that we forgot the tradition of the common good."[53] A leading public health lawyer and prominent civil libertarian, Gostin has been far from unconcerned, however, about the civil liberties issues and others justice issues raised by communicable and transmittable disease law practices. He has urged the adoption of measured guidelines that include a better definition of the mission of public health authorities, equal application of public health laws, voluntary cooperation as the primary way to obtain compliance with public health measures, and the use of compulsory powers only where there is a demonstrable threat of significant risk.[54] Yet guidelines Gostin drafted in collaboration with the Centers for Disease Control and Prevention, Johns Hopkins University, and the Center for Law and Public Health at Georgetown University were controversial. They granted the government what bioethicist George Annas described as "unprecedented and, I think, unconstitutional power."[55]

The World Health Organization recognizes that extreme responses to public health threats provide a false sense of security and can backfire. During the 1950s, the era of a great polio epidemic, American children were placed in isolation wards. The sickest ones might spend months in an iron lung. Fear of the crippling contagion led most people to voluntarily cooperate with authorities. In the late 1980s, when AIDS was first recognized as "a truly international phenomenon" and it seemed that the course of the disease was "invariably fatal," officials debated quarantine and travel restrictions to limit the spread of the disease.[56] Travel had led to the spread of cholera, plague, and flu in the past, and it was feared travel might easily lead to the rapid spread of AIDS as well. Widespread quarantine and travel restrictions were not in the end determined to be effective and appropriate means to address the AIDS virus.

The Canadian government resorted to quarantine to help manage an outbreak of severe acute respiratory syndrome (SARS). Canadian officials found that most people were willing voluntarily to quarantine themselves in their homes. But a few of the uncooperative were placed in involuntary quarantine. In 2003 Singapore reportedly "quarantined thousands of people in their homes... for coming anywhere near SARS patients or for visiting a hospital where such patients were treated."[57] In Hong Kong the same year, many people were required to report for health exams and many required to stay at home; fearful of the results of noncompliance, officials announced plans for police to make unannounced visits to deter people exposed to SARS from leaving their residences.[58] Quarantine by electronic tether could be a trend of the future.

From a civil liberties perspective it is assumed that self-quarantine in the home is far better, where effective, than compulsory quarantine by government away from home. Yet both forms of mandated seclusion have moral costs. Both can be lonely and isolating: again, desertedness. Both are and can feel like servitudes. Michael Davis argued that simple confinement for treatment is morally permissible because the only alternative is to allow the person confined to engage in reckless endangerment of others.[59] Davis raised the question of whether civil confinement, like a public health quarantine, is less burdensome than criminal confinement, such as a prison term. I should think whether civil confinement is less burdensome on the individual depends upon a variety of contextual factors: how long the civil confinement, what happens during the civil confinement, and where it takes place. One of the burdens of nonvoluntary mental health confinements is that patients are asked to submit to unwanted pharmaceutical treatment. Treatment demands place the body at the mercy of medical professionals and officials. For patients in any number of American state psychiatric hospitals in the 1940s, the age of Walter Jackson Freeman's transorbital lobotomy, an involuntary civil commitment on account of mental illness could have led to having ice picks pounded into your eye sockets by a vainglorious self-promoter.[60]

We must be mindful of the medical ethics of mandatory, coercive treatment, and explore equally important concerns about the overall quality of a life during unwanted confinements. Unwanted confinement can devolve into a kind of servitude both because unwanted treatments are required (say electroconvulsive shock therapy, lobotomies, or psychoactive drugs) but also because of unmet material needs and unremitting feelings of loneliness and isolation.

"Typhoid" Mary Mallon, a perfectly healthy carrier of typhoid who infected more than a dozen well-to-do New Yorkers, was shut away to North Brother Island off the Bronx for life.[61] Smallpox Hospital on Roosevelt Island in the East River opened in 1856. Its purpose was less to care for the sick than to quarantine them: "patients and their families resorted to bribes to get nursing care, milk for sick children, coffins for the dead."[62] In the late 1800s the sick smallpox suffers of San Francisco might have wound up on Angel Island in San Francisco Bay. Baltimore arrivals marked with signs or suspicions of cholera, yellow fever, smallpox, plague, typhus, anthrax, and leprosy might be confined at the public health service Quarantine Station located at Leading Point.[63]

While rich and poor have been quarantined for a variety of illnesses and conditions, the rich have sometimes been allowed to stay at home. Official decisions about who should be placed in quarantine have had class and ethnic dimensions, reflecting the prejudices and biases of power holders in the society. According to Sherwin Nuland, anti-Semitism played a role in explaining why Russian Jews arriving in New York in steerage aboard the French steam ship S.S. *Massilia* were herded into quarantine on North Brother Island. The proffered reason was to prevent a possible outbreak of typhus infection. But there was obvious bias in the interpretation of risk. The four hundred non-Jewish passengers aboard the *Massilia* were allowed freely to disembark.[64]

CONCLUSION

I have launched a wide-ranging account of unpopular privacy by identifying a particularly salient form of it: unwanted seclusion. I have juxtaposed familiar but disparate contexts in which varieties of unwanted seclusion once were or still are routinely imposed. Government imposes seclusion on men, women, and children. People are stuck at home or put away because they have broken the law, contracted or spread an infectious disease, or become dangerously mentally ill. The state of "being let alone"—to borrow a phrase from the nineteenth century popularized by lawyers Samuel D. Warren and Louis D. Brandeis—has the ring of a good; but some of the neglectful, isolating practices built around the idea have very little to recommend them.[65]

Americans do not seem to take the consequences of sustained coercive seclusion seriously enough. Approaches to penal incarceration in the United States suggest remarkable public and official acceptance of the harmful consequences of extremes of lonely isolation. Incarceration is but a single example of seclusion with dangerous consequences. One is struck by news stories of forgotten children confined in residential facilities for juvenile justice, behavioral, or family problems who have been beaten, crushed, suffocated, and killed by supposed caretakers.[66] And what of the ways in which getting laid off from work, sinking into depression or succumbing to social anxiety and agoraphobia effectively isolate people to their detriment? Unwanted seclusion can be lonely and isolating in ways philosophers like Arendt helped us understand, cruel and inhumane in ways countless lawyers and many psychologists have begun to illuminate.

Social forces in western societies once imposed unwanted seclusion on modern women, trapping them at home in domestic caretaking roles. The situation of choice and opportunity has improved on the whole for women in North America and Europe. The traditional feminist critique of domestic seclusion invites the discourse of "freedom and servitude" into the assessment of unpopular seclusion of all sorts. It counsels scrutiny of personal choices that lead to voluntary seclusion for signs of self-slavery, self-endangerment, and harm to others. It demands penetrating supposed havens (like homes and hospitals) for signs of hell, whose tortures of violence, degraded autonomy, or merely incessant interruption government (or someone) may have the capacity and authority to abate. And lastly, it calls for honest reevaluation by policy makers of what might first appear to be necessary and inevitable coercive segregation demanded by public health and safety.

3
MODESTY

Walls and distance separate. They can hide a person from other people. So, in a way, can clothing. Clothing can conceal the precise look and contours of a person's body. Clothing can render age, sex, or race invisible. Clothing can be a shelter, a cocoon, an emblem of reserve. But clothing can as easily work like a flag, announcing who one is and what one believes. The style, color, and fit of clothing can make a person more visible to others, disclosing social status, membership in an ethnic group, and conformity or nonconformity to cultural norms.

Dressing oneself is an act of concealment, like stepping inside a closet. Dressing cannot be reduced to the act of self-concealment, though, because clothing furthers aims of exhibition and adornment as well as self-concealment. How a person covers up will determine whether he attracts or deflects attention. A person who does not wish to be noticed as she moves about the world will have to dress so as to blend in, donning the "uniform" worn by other women in her milieu, whether that is a burqa or pair of blue jeans. Not blending in can prove fatal. Wearing out-of-season clothing was dangerous for a man in Britain. In July 2005, hyper-vigilant police shot dead Jean Charles de Menezes, a twenty-seven-year-old Brazilian native who was on his way to work in London wearing a winter coat. Police said they feared Menezes was a terrorist concealing explosives. Where on earth is anyone legally free to wear what he or she chooses? Ample such freedom exists in Britain, Canada, and the United States, which explains why the Menezes case was so shocking.

Suppose you live in a free society and have a choice. Why choose to conceal? Why hide personalities and identities underneath cloak and veil? Why do some women feel compelled by family, faith, or government to conceal their bodies? In the West such questions are often a prelude to a critique of "extreme" bodily concealment practiced by "other" cultures. In Europe and the United States, a woman whose hair and neck are covered by the hijab, whose face is covered by the niqab, or whose full body is covered by the burqa, is a troubling figure. She is "veiled." Some Westerners readily conceptualize and problematize clothing worn by Muslim women as repressive "veiling."[1] Many Western observers are uneasy about the covering up practiced in Islamic countries and even more uneasy when a preference for covering up accompanies immigrants abroad to westerners' home turfs, or springs up among western-born minorities, as it has in the US among black Muslims. In 2009, Sudanese officials punished women with forty lashes of the whip and hundred-dollar fines for the "crime" of wearing trousers. Lubna Hussein became a hero of the western media when she risked everything to change the Sudanese law allowing authorities to whip women for wearing pants. The western media does not valorize women who risk everything for hijab.

What must we hide? What must we not hide? In this chapter and the next, I explore the law of robing and disrobing as contexts of moral freedom and privacy for women in contemporary liberal nations. I stress that at the same time that some western women are ordered to take off modest, religiously and culturally significant clothing, other western women, who would dance naked if they could, are ordered to put something on. It is surprising that in liberal nations persons are not freer to dress and undress as they please. Who is coercively dressed, who coercively undressed, and why?

MUSLIMS IN AMERICA

The United States is home to millions of Muslims.[2] American Muslims are reported to be "largely assimilated, happy with their lives, and moderate with respect to many of the issues that have divided Muslims and Westerners around the world."[3] Islam is now among the most practiced religions in the country.[4] Like their Christian, Jewish, Buddhist, and Hindu counterparts, many Muslims are devoutly religious. Michigan has more Muslims than any other US state; in 2005 the Islamic Center of America, the largest of more than twelve hundred US mosques, opened in Dearborn, Michigan. The proliferation of mosques led to well-publicized protests in some US communities in 2010, where Islamic places of worship were defamed as so-called temples to terrorism.

The ethnic and national origins of US Muslims are diverse. Some of the millions of US families who practice Islam are recent immigrants from Africa, the Middle East, Europe, or Asia. Michigan has one of the highest concentrations of Muslims of Arab ancestry outside of the Arab world. However, about a third of US Muslims are long-time US residents and citizens.[5] Of these, some were born into families who practice Islam, while others converted to Islam as children or adults.

While most American Muslims dress in standard western secular clothing, some US women who practice Islam do not. A number wear hijab headscarves in everyday life, and keep their arms and legs covered. A few wear the niqab, a garment worn outside the home or in the presence of unrelated men that cloaks a woman's head and neck, leaving only her eyes exposed. A very few US Muslim women don a burqa, the full-body mantle worn outside the home that covers the woman's entire body and face. Among indigenous US Muslim population groups are African American adherents, many of whom adopt Islamic dress.[6] Black women wearing black or brown burqas with or without full facial coverings are a common sight in the majority African American neighborhoods of west and southwest Philadelphia. Although American women who visit Muslim counties—including Secretary of State and former First Lady Hilary Clinton and Congresswoman and Nancy Pelosi—have donned headscarves to show respect, not everyone in the United States accepts the sight of partly or fully veiled women. For many US non-Muslims and many US Muslims, too, face covering symbolizes female oppression and subservience, religious extremism and radical politics. Many women who wear headscarves report that they have experienced anti-Muslim discrimination, have been prohibited from wearing the veil in schools, and have even endured violent attacks.[7] Professor of Islamic Studies Aminah McCloud argues that African American women who wear the hijab attract more hostility than Muslim immigrants because although many non-Muslim Americans may accept that immigrants dress differently, they may find it difficult to accept native-born locals who wear headscarves.[8]

Compared to the governments of some countries, government in the United States has been tolerant of Muslim attire. Governments around the world have banned or placed restrictions on wearing the burqa, niqab, and hijab.[9] In 2004, the French government banned the hijab from public schools. In the spring of 2010, the lower house of the Belgium parliament passed legislation banning the burqa and niqab from its public streets, incurring the price of immediate criticism.[10] In the fall of 2010, the French parliament and Constitutional Council approved a similar law banning facial concealment in all public places.[11] The French law called for fines for concealing the face and for forcing anyone to conceal their face. Opponents of the measure suggested that the French ban violated the European Convention for the Protection of Human Rights and Fundamental Freedoms.[12] Concealment bans are in place in some parts of Germany (Hesse, since early 2011), and have been debated in Spain, Denmark, Ireland, and the United Kingdom.[13]

In 2005 a New Zealand judge ruled that two Muslim witnesses testifying for the prosecution in a criminal procedure could not testify while wearing a burqa.[14] On the premise that facial coverings hinder communication or visual identification, in 2010 the Canadian province of Quebec introduced a bill requiring the removal of the niqab when seeking medical and other benefits or services from government.[15] A year earlier, however, an Ontario court found that a judge could not deny a Muslim rape victim an opportunity to testify in criminal court wearing her niqab—the accused rapists were members of her own family—without first conducting a preliminary hearing to determine whether her professed religious beliefs and practices were sincere and deeply held.[16]

Debates around bodily concealment also preoccupy the public in Muslim countries. In 2010, the Cairo administrative Court upheld a ban on the niqab in university examination rooms.[17] But in 2007 the Supreme Administrative Court of Egypt found on religious freedom grounds that the American University of Cairo could not ban the niqab from campus. It was permitted, though, to require brief unveiling for verification of identity.[18] Recently, Syria prohibited the wearing of niqab (but not the hijab) in its universities.[19]

For a time, secular Turkey had banned the hijab, niqab, and burqa from its universities entirely. Leyla Sahin, a medical student who covered her hair in open defiance of the ban, was sentenced to jail.[20] The European Court of Human Rights in 2004 upheld the ban and its enforcement. Rather than unveil, some women subsequently refused to attend Turkish universities. As noted by Seyla Benhabib, in 2008 the ruling Justice and Development Party "decided to reform the law that banned the wearing of headscarves and turbans in institutions of higher learning in Turkey."[21] A constitutional amendment to permit head coverings backed by the Justice and Development Party was quickly invalidated in favor of restoring the ban, leading some university women to cover their hijab-hooded hair with wigs.[22] Although the ban remains in force, University officials no longer strictly enforce it in practice.

THE HIJAB IN FRANCE

The United States tolerates religious expression and voluntary expressions of modesty. Despite moderate anti-Muslim populism, categorical US bans on the hijab, niqab, and burqa are virtually unthinkable (an empirical claim) and ideally unconstitutional (a normative claim). Immigrant and native diversity are features of Western nations. To deal with difference, a country may seek to obliterate its symbols. But undressing Muslim women and girls from the neck up is a morally intolerant and ultimately unjust way to pursue the goal of a unified society.

On March 15, 2006, French President Jacques Chirac signed into law an amendment to his country's education statute, banning the wearing of clothing or symbols that "exhibit conspicuously a religious affiliation" in public schools.[23] Prohibited items included "a large cross, a veil, or skullcap." The ban was expressly introduced by lawmakers as an application of the principle of government neutrality, "du principe de laïcité." Yet opponents of the law viewed it primarily as an intolerant assault against the hijab, a head and neck wrap worn by many Muslim women around the world. The ban on conspicuous religious symbols applied to Jewish skullcaps and large Christian crosses as well as the hijab, but "there was never any doubt that it was primarily aimed at France's five million Muslims and what is widely perceived as creeping fundamentalism in their midst."[24]

A national law dictating that children not attend public school with their hair covered—and in the land of Liberté, Fraternité, Equalité at that—requires explanation.

It is far from obvious why the French government went after the hijab. Prior to the ban, headscarves were barely present in the schools; only a few Muslim elementary, middle, and high-schoolgirls in France wore the hijab. Only 14 percent of Muslim women in France said they wore the hijab at all, and a bare 51 percent said they actively practice their religion. Despite the limited popularity of the Muslim hijab (termed "foulard" in the French language), the hijab is a mode of dress which has become a threatening emblem of late twentieth-century and early twenty-first century anti-Western Islamic politics. Even a few yards of fabric about the head and neck—leaving the face fully exposed—is reviled as a symbol of Muslim women's oppressive femininity and, inconsistently, their radical insouciance.

Scholars in the United States have also studied veiling. Istanbul-born Seyla Benhabib has written about it in the context of Turkey.[25] Other US scholars have focused on Western discomfort surrounding the veil. Professor Nancy Hirschmann, for example, assessed the normative significance of veiling within Islam and from a liberal feminist perspective, unstymied by cultural relativism. Hirschmann set forth the various reasons given by Muslim women for their brand of covering up and explored the veil as "discursive and social symbolization."[26] Joan Scott devoted a book to the hijab in contemporary France, where it has been the subject matter of a unique political discourse. Scott argues that the study of the language through which cultures create shared realities and values is best undertaken through close readings of arguments advanced in their specific political and historical contexts. The hijab ban signaled to French immigrant minorities the felt importance of assimilation. The ban on the veil presupposed that a French identity and loyalty to the French government required the subordination of religiosity. To allow the tiny cross, the tiny star of David, the tiny Koran, but not the Orthodox garb of yarmulke and foulard was a way of raising flag above subculture and faith.

Scott insightfuly explained the attack on the hijab as resulting from (1) old-fashioned racism and colonialism towards people of North African and Muslim descent; (2) secularism—*laïcité* as a public philosophy in France; (3) individualism as a public philosophy in France; and (4) residual sex inequality as an embarrassment to French liberalism.

First, addressing racism and colonialism, Scott linked the Western obsession with the veil to sexual fantasies harbored by colonialists who encountered veiled women abroad: "the veil was a sexual provocation, and a denial of sex, a come-on and a refusal." For the confused colonial, "Islam [was] a cruel and irrational system of religious and social organization." A veiled woman might be an unruly prostitute or a slave to a husband.

Next, according to Scott, "French supporters of the law banning headscarves defined themselves as apostles of secularism." Secularism in French schools dates back to the mid-nineteenth century, when primary education was made compulsory for boys and girls and when religion was no longer taught in the classroom by Catholic priests and nuns. Yet while "militantly secular in theory," Scott argues, "French schools were more flexible," allowing, for example, recognition of the historic significance of Catholicism. Some of this flexibility was seen in the way the French approached the headscarf ban. Scarves were not banned in private schools; they were not banned for women going about their business in the streets; nor were they banned for women workers who were employed by the state. On the other hand, the law sometimes buttressed a more general expression of official disapproval of veiling. Some French people chastised women who wished to wear the veil in French naturalization ceremonies. Non-Muslims were victims of the attack on the hijab, because the ban had to be framed in neutral terms to facially comport with liberalism. Jews and Sikhs were victims of a kind of collateral damage in a war whose real enemy was Islamic difference. The education law made an issue of what had not been much of an issue in France in the past, namely the wearing of skullcaps by Orthodox Jews and turbans by Sikhs.

Scott further argued that individualism was an important dimension of the political discourse that led to the ban on the headscarf. One might suppose that individualism would point to freedom of religious choice, as it quite often has in the United States. A committee that studied Muslim girls in French schools concluded that many girls found the hijab oppressive. The foulard was not their individual preference at all. The ban on the scarf was thus presented in political discourse as a way to liberate and emancipate individual Muslim girls constrained by family and cultural pressures to cover up. Similar political discourses have emerged in other European countries, in Denmark for example.

French policy makers further imagined that the hijab might be a way Muslim parents dominated their helpless children, recruiting them willy-nilly into Islam. It is worth asking whether individualism is a public value that justifies interfering with religious choices made by parents of young children or teens. Recall that no such rescue of Old Order Amish children compelled to live a nineteenth century lifestyle in the twentieth century was endorsed by the US Supreme Court. Although dissenting Justices wondered if teenage Amish children's own desires might be unfairly subordinated to, or conflated with, their parents'.[27]

Finally, Scott explored a political discourse of sexual equality reflected in the assault on the hijab. By banning the headscarf, French legislators believed they were, in Scott's words, "removing the sign of women's inequality from the classroom" and "declaring that the equality of women and men is the first principle of the Republic." Such declarations are admirable, but the exclusion of the hijab is xenophobic. The fixation on hijab—as opposed to skirts or ponytails—as the symbol of gender inequality can only be explained by the "foreign" character of this particular feminine emblem. Mothers in the United States have sometimes fixated on the Barbie doll or the color pink as the item to purge from their daughters' lives to insure their equality with boys. But the truth of the matter is that Muslim girls without hijab, like American girls without Barbie dolls, are still subject to discriminatory treatment and unequal opportunities at home, in schools, and in the larger society.

It is tempting to think that if we are all to be the same, symbols of difference must be abolished; but another option is always to spare the symbols and change the underlying reality. For example, in the 1980s, when women began entering the legal profession in increasingly large numbers, they wore suits and not dresses. Dresses were a symbol of girly vulnerability. Female lawyers on Wall Street were encouraged to wear severe, man-tailored suits with silk scarves and neckties to work. But eventually firms and clients got used to having competent women around; women lawyers put dresses on the menu of acceptable office attire. Over time, French students and teachers might have gotten used to the hijab. The hijab might eventually have lost some of its power as a symbol of an unassimilated minority, radicalism, and gender repression.

Yet there is little evidence that the symbolic meanings of Islamic dress are abating in France, where support for Islamic clothing bans is strong. A tangible illustration of the depth of intolerance caught the eye of the international press: a week after France's constitutional court approved a ban on facial concealment in public, but before the law went into effect, a sixty-three-year-old retired schoolteacher, Jeanne Ruby, ripped off the veil of twenty-six-year-old Shaika al-Suwaidi, whom she noticed shopping in a Paris retail store. Ruby chased al-Suwaidi down, tore off her niqab, and slapped her and bit her on the hand because she had refused to comply with Ruby's demand that she unveil. Ruby, who had traveled and lived in Muslim countries, told police that "for me, wearing the veil is an act of aggression. I felt attacked as a woman."[28] A woman who claimed to feel attacked therefore felt justified in attacking another woman.

UNDRESSING WOMEN OR ADDRESSING SOCIAL PROBLEMS?

One must hope it is possible for modern liberal democracies to incorporate people of various racial, religious, cultural, and national origins in a single body politic. Yet the end need not justify the means, and legislating against symbols of difference worn by minority woman is an inapt means. Joan Scott observed that French leaders have treated French nationality as an essence rather than as a dynamic, fluid construct. "In order to come to terms with its North-African/Muslim population," Scott urged, "French politicians and intellectuals need to come up with new ways of addressing difference, ways that acknowledge its existence rather than refusing to engage."[29] Because Americans have not got it completely right, Scott's plea for engagement applies to US politicians and intellectuals as well.

Democratic nation states need adequate ideals of nation-sharing, because most are multicultural. What ideal, though, can a liberal democracy strive for? Is it integration? Is it tolerance? Could it be multiculturalism? For some, integration implies a loss of identity to assimilation; toleration sounds snobbish, in the sense that "to tolerate" is to accept that which one finds offensive. The multicultural ideal, which has had a significant life in American political discourse since the 1980s, envisions a nation of people of different sorts, each maintaining loyalty to an identity group while mysteriously composing a functioning political unit. Long after the historic 2008 election victory, Americans are still trying to figure out whether President Barak Obama prevailed politically because of or in spite of his embodiment of multiculturalism.

The United States is a better place for its acceptance of the hijab in schools, and the hijab, niqab, and burqa in most public places. But like France, the United States also struggles with how to incorporate religious and cultural minorities fully and equally into the life of the society. Americans learned the hard way that state-compelled racial segregation of African Americans places black children at risk of social alienation and feelings of inferiority. Racial segregation impairs the preparation of youth for life in a pluralistic, self-governing society, and interferes with the efficiency, productivity, and equality of the workplace. But the French surely know this by now. They have had their own hard lessons, too.

Restless disenfranchised minority youth took to rioting in US cities in the mid-1960s. The National Advisory Commission on Civil Disorders was convened by President Lyndon Johnson in 1967 to study the causes of rioting in the so-called black ghettos. The Kerner Commission, as it came to be called, issued a report that interpreted the rioting as African Americans' demand for equality and inclusion. The US rioters wanted more just police practices, jobs, housing, education, recreational facilities, political power, fair lending, and respectful racial attitudes. Something analogous to the US riots happened in France in 2005 and 2006. It began with a clash with police over the deaths of two Muslim teenagers on October 27, 2005, in Clichy-sous-Bois, a Paris suburb neighboring Saint-Denis.

> On October 27, after playing an informal soccer match with friends at a stadium, Muhittin Altun, 17, Zyed Benna, 17, and Bouna Traoré, 15, were heading home to end their Ramadan fast when they heard police sirens. Bouna told the others to run, claiming that members of the anti-criminal brigade were in pursuit. A security guard from a nearby construction site had called the police because he believed the teens were trespassing; other young men present deny ever having entered the site. Muhittin, Zyed, and Bouna jumped the fence of a nearby electrical substation to escape the police, but only Muhittin survived. Zyed and Bouna were fatally electrocuted. The police have denied

> seeing the three teens enter the substation. As word spread about Zyed and Bouna's deaths, young men from the surrounding housing projects gathered in protest. In a clash with police, they burned fifteen cars. The following evening, the conflict had expanded, pitting as many as four hundred local youth against perhaps three hundred riot police and military gendarmes called in to maintain order.[30]

The deaths of Zyed and Bouna sparked dozens of racially charged rebellions throughout the country, leading to loss of life, property destruction, injuries, and arrests. Lack of opportunity, isolation, and discrimination fueled the frustration of young people who participated in the rioting. Doubtless, ghettoized French minorities living in the *cités habitation à loyer modéré* (or HLM), the low- and moderate-income public housing projects in French cities and suburbs where many immigrants from North Africa live, want the same things ghettoized US blacks have wanted. Disaffected young men are a real, concrete problem for French democracy. The schoolgirl's hijab emerged in French political discourse as a problem too, but one the French could remedy. It was easier by far to muster political will to "liberate" Muslim schoolgirls than to adequately house, educate, and employ their brothers. It is far easier to wag a finger at a hundred or so women in burqas than to address the root causes of immigration and terrorism.

THE NIQAB IN AMERICA

A proposal for a national rule against the hijab in public schools or universities would not gain traction in the United States. Even though covering up in the conservative Muslim mode makes some Americans uncomfortable, most think it is permissible for women to cover up if they want to and if their freely held religions or cultural traditions tell them to do so. Most Americans view what they interpret as modest clothing styles dictated by religion and culture as private matters largely—though not entirely—outside the realm of legitimate state intervention. But the rule of tolerance for hijab is far from absolute. Although 65 percent of US persons polled said they would oppose a French-style niqab and burqa ban in the United States, full-face veiling has been something of a problem for Muslim women in the United States.[31] In the context of court appearances, drivers' license issuance, and air travel, US policymakers and courts have authorized laws and practices that interfere with Muslim women's freedom to wear attire that conceals their faces from view.

Muslim modesty dress has led to publicized and litigated conflicts between Muslim women and public authorities. A Florida woman clashed with the Florida motor vehicle authority.[32] Sultaana Freeman argued that state officials violated the Florida Constitution and the Florida Religious Freedom Restoration Act (FRFRA) when they revoked her driver's license because she refused to be photographed without her niqab. The FRFRA provides that "government shall not substantially burden a person's exercise of religion even if the burden results from a rule of general applicability," unless government demonstrates that application of the burden to the person—(1) is in furtherance of a compelling governmental interest; and (2) is the least restrictive means of furthering that compelling governmental interest.[33] Under FRFRA, Florida was required to show that it had a compelling interest in photographing drivers and that denying Freeman a license altogether was the "least restrictive" means of furthering its interest. Freeman's lawsuit, filed on her behalf by the ACLU of Florida, cited Colorado, Indiana, and Nebraska cases in which courts had ruled that individuals with sincerely held religious beliefs are entitled to licenses without photographs.[34] Those cases involved members of Christian sects who interpret the Bible's second commandment against graven images to prohibit them from having their pictures taken. ACLU attorney Howard Marks, who argued Freeman's case before Ninth Judicial Circuit Court, suggested that the state was using her as a scapegoat in the "war against terror," when all she wanted to do was to be able to "drive her kids to the doctor or go grocery shopping."[35] Following the litigation Florida amended the law to exempt the requirement of full face photo from FRFRA.[36]

A devout Pennsylvania woman clashed with officials at the State Correctional Institution at Graterford, Pennsylvania, who refused to allow her to visit her imprisoned son unless she agreed to remove her veil.[37] The woman brought a lawsuit in federal court to enjoin the prison to allow visitation while veiled. The judge who heard her case determined that "requiring the plaintiff to remove her veil as a condition of her right to visit her son in prison constitutes substantially burdening her exercise of religion."[38] Pennsylvania, like Florida, has a Religious Freedom Restoration Act statute.[39] The judge's constitutional analysis in the Graterford prison case conformed to a model Congress and several states courts have established for thinking about what it means to respect the fundamental right to practice one's religion. This model indicates that government may not interfere with a person's free exercise of rights other than to further its compelling—that is, urgent and important—interests. When the government's compelling interests require burdens on religious free exercise, as they will from time to time, those burdens should be minimized. In considering means to further its compelling interests, the government must select practical means that are the least restrictive of religious freedom.

Although the state has a "compelling interest in making sure that visitors to inmates are indeed the persons they profess to be," the burdens placed on the veiled woman must be the "least restrictive."[40] Rather than excluding the veiled mother from visits, the court found that the prison should inform her of the visitation times and dates when female corrections officers are on duty, so that she can briefly unveil to establish her identity prior to contact with her son.

This legal approach—the requirement of compelling state interests and use of least restrictive means—is rooted in a complex jurisprudential tradition I cannot examine here. In broad outline, however, the approach is morally satisfying. It conforms to widely embraced premises that religion is highly and uniquely important to the persons who embrace it as expressions of value and purposes (principle of exceptionalism); that government should not punish or prohibit religious practices (principle of toleration); and that government should reasonably accommodate religious practices (principle of accommodation). By application of these three principles, a just government will tolerate and reasonably accommodate an individual who wishes to reflect her religious and related cultural values through her mode of dress. If wearing specific attire is concretely dangerous or harmful (harm principle), government may have a reason to impose restrictions, notwithstanding the principles of exceptionalism, toleration, and accommodation.

Attire is rarely a practical danger, and accommodations of attire rarely require unreasonable (costly, time-consuming) measures. Californian Souhair Khatib was forced to remove her hijab headcovering while in courthouse detention facing a parole violation charge stemming from a misdemeanor welfare offense. The influential Ninth Circuit Court of Appeals held in 2010 that she was not wrongly treated and that jailers may require a woman to remove her hijab for security reasons when detained in a courthouse holding cell.[41] But surely a courthouse could find a way to accommodate a simple piece of cloth on a woman's head, while also insuring safety and security for others. The principles of exceptionalism, tolerance, and accommodation require an effort at creative problem-solving before a woman should be asked to start disrobing.

Is Muslim attire harmful in ways not directly related to concerns about concealment of drugs or weapons and terrorism? It could be argued that women who voluntarily conceal their hair or faces are actually victims of coercion. With such strong exit rights, though, it is hard to sustain such a claim in the US context, where Muslims are in the minority and the means of escaping the control of a husband, father, or religious leader are many. A related argument is that women who conceal their hair or faces are inflicting harms of self-subordination and social or economic disadvantage. This may be true, but the clothing choices of American women include crippling high heels, and dresses, skirts. and makeup whose relationship to gender equality and flourishing are rarely probed. A different analysis will be required in Iran, Pakistan, or Turkey, but in the US context, targeting Muslim women out of concern for subordination when women as a whole hold less power and earn less money is unfair to Muslims.

A woman's unwillingness to remove the niqab can have the dire consequence of denying her access to the forum of justice, as a Michigan case illustrates. Michigan District Judge Paul Paruk dismissed Ginnah Muhammad's lawsuit against a car rental company when she refused to unveil.[42] The rental company was seeking $3,000 to cover repairs on an automobile leased to Muhammad, an African American Muslim who maintained that the car had been damaged by thieves. Although she wanted access to the courts to litigate her claim, Muhammad did not wish to show her full face. She wanted to wear her niqab, as she did in daily life. Because she refused to uncover her face in his courtroom, Judge Paruk dismissed Muhammad's case. The Michigan District Judges Association sided with Judge Paruk. However, civil liberties groups sided with Muhammad. Some Muslims believe that their holy book, the Quran, requires women to cover their bodies in the presence of men outside their families. While many practicing Muslims in the United States do not wear modesty attire, for those who do, the practice is central to their faith. When a judge demands that an otherwise orderly person remove religious attire or face dismissal of her suit or refusal to hear her testimony, her religious freedom is compromised.

On June 17, 2009, by a vote of five to two, the supreme court of Michigan adopted an amendment to Michigan Rule of Evidence 611. The new rule, Michigan Rule of Evidence 611(b), provides that: "The court shall exercise reasonable control over the appearance of parties and witnesses so as to (1) ensure that the demeanor of such persons may be observed and assessed by the fact-finder, and (2) to ensure the accurate identification of such persons." This amendment would presumably allow a judge to ask a party or witness entering the courtroom wearing a ski mask or nylon stocking stretched over his head to remove it for the duration of the proceeding. But the actual events precipitating the amended rule did not involve a man wearing a ski mask or a nylon stocking. It involved instead a Muslim woman wearing the niqab. While by no means as common in the United States as the hijab, the niqab is worn by many devout urban African American Muslims, Arab Americans, and others who practice Islam. Rule 611(b) was adopted to provide positive legal authority for Michigan judges to order a woman wearing the niqab to uncover her face or leave the courtroom.

Like the hijab, the more "extreme" niqab has been reviled as a symbol of women's political oppression. But coercing a woman to remove an emblem of religious piety raises a specter of political oppression of another kind. The First Amendment of the United States Constitution protects freedom of religion: "Congress shall make no law respecting an establishment of religion, or prohibiting the free exercise thereof." As applied to the niqab of a devout Muslim, Michigan Rule of Evidence 611 (b) violates the spirit of the First Amendment. Religious attire can obscure demeanor and identity, and yet the rule includes no express exception requiring an accommodation for parties' or witnesses' religious attire. Lawyers could argue that since Rule 611 (b) permits without requiring a judge to order abandonment of Muslim modesty attire, it is not in fact unconstitutional. However the rule was adopted in the context of a dispute over the niqab precisely to authorize an interference with religious free exercise. Given the rule's affront to conceptions of moral justice as requiring tolerance and reasonable accommodation of religious preferences, let alone the rule's doubtful constitutionality, it is not surprising that the Michigan supreme court decision was not unanimous. Two judges, Chief Justice Marilyn Kelly and Justice Diane Hathaway, dissented from the decision to amend to the state's evidentiary rules.

Other US states have laws giving judges authority to control attire. Oregon has such a law, Uniform Trial Court Rule 3.010(1), authorizing exclusion of persons attired in ways that detract "from the dignity of the court." Yet an Oregon woman successfully appealed her theft conviction on the ground that the judge refused to allow a defense witness to testify when he declined to remove what the appeals court termed his "religious headgear" in the courtroom.[43] The witness in question was the woman's husband, whom an appeals court held the presiding judge improperly excluded under a misapplication of Rule 3.010(1). This obscure Oregon case brings to mind Gandhi's historic encounter with a South African judge. Upon swearing-in the nation's first "colored" bar member in a highly publicized and long-awaited ceremony, the judge asked Gandhi to remove his turban, presumably out of deference to the court. Gandhi reluctantly caved in, believing he had bigger battles to fight. But most Americans who wear religious attire in everyday life are more like the Oregon man than like Gandhi: they anticipate no bigger battles in their futures to salve their wounded dignity in the present.[44]

The Michigan Supreme Court sought to give judges the right to exercise "reasonable control."[45] It is hard to argue against a judicial power labeled "reasonable control." In the past American judges have sometimes failed to exercise "reasonable" control over states of dress and undress in their courtrooms. In an extreme instance from the past, the New York judge who tried the infamous *Rhinelander v. Rhinelander* marriage dissolution case allowed the plaintiff wife to undress in front of a jury, putatively to buttress the claim that her wealthy white husband was not a victim of fraud, tricked into miscegenation.[46] Intimate letters revealed that Mr. Kip Rhinelander had seen Mrs. Alice Rhinelander nude in sexual encounters before marriage and that he had to have known that she was "colored" when he married her. Exposing her body helped prove there had been no fraudulent pretense of whiteness.[47]

More recently, judges have demanded that an African American attorney remove an African fabric kente cloth he said was required by his role as an officer of his church,[48] that a Jewish man remove his yarmulke skull cap,[49] and that a Roman Catholic priest serving as an attorney in a criminal matter appear in court in non-clerical garb to insure a fair trial.[50] One judge erroneously ordered a new trial because a witness who was a Roman Catholic priest testified in a personal injury case wearing his clerical collar.[51] It is important to consider what kind of control over attire worn for religious purposes is truly reasonable, and specifically whether a society citing compelling state interests may justly restrict the wearing of face–coverings that are commended by religion.

Respect for religious freedom demands that there should be a very strong presumption against religious clothing bans. A Ku Klux Klan hood or a comically oversized sombero would be disruptive in court. Yet women of Muslim faith wearing the niqab are neither disruptive nor an affront. They have a religion-backed moral interest, often linked to modesty values, not to be observed, so long as they can be seen, heard and identified in other reasonably available ways.[52] But what is modesty, exactly, and what is its value and relationship to religion? Why should it be protected?

MODESTY, THE ANALYSIS

Philosophers have characterized privacy as a broad, "umbrella" concept incorporating a family of narrower concepts.[53] The narrower concepts—including seclusion, solitude, secrecy, reserve, confidentiality, and data protection—denote modes of limiting access to people and personal information. Modesty sits comfortably beneath the definitional domain of privacy. Modesty concerns limit access to people and information about them through, for example, understatement and concealment.

Viewed pragmatically, the relationship between modesty and privacy is one of mutual facilitation. In daily life, modesty facilitates enjoyment of other forms of privacy, and other forms of privacy facilitate the enjoyment of modesty. For example, individuals determined to safeguard secrets or confidences discover that modest speech is a useful habit to cultivate. Hence, the people we call "private" are often strategically modest and reserved. Likewise, especially modest and reserved people are often strategically very private. They use silence, solitude, and seclusion to achieve the modest life. They not only keep favorable information about themselves close to the vest, but they also cloak or seclude themselves.

General Modesty

Modesty in the sense that I here term "general" modesty is the tendency to avoid exaggerating or calling attention to one's virtues, material assets, and accomplishments. General modesty is a utilitarian disposition for privacy-lovers and a traditional aretaic and deontic virtue for the ethically good. The modest do not toot their own horns. I agree with a major strand in Daniel Statman's account of modesty as "a disposition to avoid arrogance and boastfulness in spite of one's (justified) high self-assessment, and to be careful not to interpret one's (true) superiority as granting one extra, more permissive moral rights."[54] Michael Ridge described the modest person in this insightful way. A person is modest just in case:

(a) She is disposed to de-emphasize her accomplishments and traits that are taken to entitle her to benefits.
(b) She is so disposed at least partially in virtue of not caring too much about whether she is esteemed and partially in virtue of not caring too much about whether she gets everything to which she is entitled.
(c) She is so disposed at least partially in virtue of caring enough that people not overestimate her accomplishments and characteristics or her responsibility for them.[55]

Modesty is akin to humility.[56] Nancy E. Snow pointed out that humility is important because it helps foster compassion, it checks boastfulness, vanity, conceit, and other vices, and because we should value self-knowledge apart from its effects.[57] Owen Flanigan argued that "the modest person may well have a perfectly accurate sense of her accomplishments and worth but she does not overestimate them."[58] Indeed, the modest person does not unduly publicize her appropriately estimated accomplishments and worth. A modest person, wrote G. F. Schueler, "cares ... about what is valuable, genuinely valuable, not about getting credit for what she has done."[59] The modest military commander will not brag about his victories; the modest Nobel prize-winning author, about her literary prowess. A modest monk will be quiet, not ostentatious, in his prayer. A modest judge will be humble in the face of the sovereign law and his or her own authority. A hundred years ago, modest, well-mannered ladies and domestic servants kept their intelligent opinions and strong passions to themselves, as expected.

General modesty is often defended as a positive character trait by secular philosophers, ancient and contemporary alike. Aristotle counted modesty as a virtue, the mean in word and deed, between shamelessness and bashfulness.[60] Immodesty out of context is undignified; it exposed one to ridicule and scorn. General modesty is a Christian virtue that is shared by other major religious traditions, including Judaism.[61] Moral critics of general modesty question whether, in the final analysis, it amounts to more than ignorance, disingenuousness, or flat-out deception. It is indeed worth considering whether it makes sense to view humbling oneself or not recognizing the truth about one's value as a virtue. Daniel Statman argued that many contemporary accounts of expressive modesty and humility make sense only if we assume the premise of the Judeo-Christian tradition that human kind is in fact lowly and unworthy of God's magnanimity.[62] I would counter that because the intent behind humble self-depiction is so often generous—for example, to let others grab the limelight or feel one's equal—it is easy to see why modesty is considered a moral good.

General modesty may have inherent value, but it has practical, utilitarian value, too. It can be socially advantageous to avoid provoking "an envy response in others."[63]

Modesty is so important to social harmony that men and women who are not modest are (or, at least, used to be) expected by the rules of etiquette to convincingly feign modesty. Pretending to be modest is of little practical value, though, when pretense fails to veil frank conceit.[64]

Bodily (and Sexual) Modesty

Modesty in the sense I term "bodily" modesty is a disposition to cloak or conceal the body, especially its eroticized zones. By contrast to general modesty, bodily modesty, a subset of which is sexual modesty, is not centrally a matter of deliberate silence, misstatement, or understatement.[65] As a personal trait, sexual modesty is the predilection to conceal the genitalia, breasts, or other parts of the body that have sexual connotations. Sexual modesty norms vary from society to society, and some population groups and individuals have idiosyncratic modesty values of their own. Societal sexual modesty norms may require persons within a group to conceal their hair, eyes, face, legs, breasts, or buttocks, no less than their genitals. Oddly, as Shasta M. Christrup observed, "current American social norms dictate that women breastfeed their infants in bathrooms because it is deemed 'inappropriate' for them to breastfeed in public where the breast might accidentally be exposed."[66] Enforcing general modesty has been left to etiquette, morality, and religion. You do not go to jail simply for being a braggart. Bodily modesty, however, has not been left to nonlegal social norms, even in the most liberal nations. Richard A. Posner and Katherine B. Silbaugh's compendium of US "sex" laws contains a whole chapter on public nudity and indecency laws in the fifty states.[67]

Sexual modesty norms, like general modesty norms, may demand restraint of speech. Only here the restraint concerns speaking of matters related to sexual attraction or sex acts. Speaking of sex is sometimes seduction, and seduction is one step removed from sex acts. American lawmakers have sometimes prohibited salty speech in the presence of women and children, as if to respect their superior entitlement to innocence and modesty. An Alabama man sitting in a cafe who told the sheriff "I will do as I God damn please" in presence of women was prosecuted in 1958.[68] A Michigan law criminalizing cursing in front of women and children was finally found unconstitutional in 2002.[69]

General and, especially, bodily modesty are mandates of organized religions. Religious groups expect diverse expressions of modesty from the faithful. In 1926, it was said that Buddhist monks must conform to a rule of "total absence of sexual intercourse."[70] Even today Roman Catholic priests and nuns submit to modest dress requirements and vows of sexual abstinence. Many religions require a certain style of dress and deportment out of a concern for sexual modesty. In diverse ways, major religions in the United States show their commitment to sexual modesty of dress and of spirit. A group of Catholic girls in the 1950s went on so-called modesty crusades in an effort to pressure retailers to offer more modest fashions and encourage young women "to use fashion choices to help them define their own religious sense of self."[71] Protestant Christian modesty and premarital chastity groups for young girls are fairly common in the United States today, especially in the South.

Eastern Pennsylvania Mennonite traditions have required that women wear a style of dress that "for modesty, includes an extra layer of fabric over the bust."[72] Black Muslims dress modestly, and girls eschew lipstick or other makeup.[73] Sikh men do not cut their hair, which may have to do with modesty.[74] For women who practice Hasidic Judaism, rules about clothing and hair are bound up with norms of modesty, referred to in Hebrew as *tzniuth*.[75] These women must cover their hair and some even shave their heads "as a symbol of modesty and marriage."[76] Modesty rules in Orthodox Judaism do not just apply to women. One authority insists that "Judaism considers modesty to be a prerequisite for true religious observance for Jews of both sexes."[77]

Traditional Mormons wore a special "temple garment" under their clothing which served as a "symbol of modesty of dress and living."[78] Quakers used to wear what was considered modest clothing when they met.[79] In many African American Protestant churches, congregations dress up "to show reverence to God"; overtly sexy attire, including jeans or trousers on women, are sometimes frowned upon.[80] As an Ardmore, Pennsylvania church I once visited instructs congregants and guests: "cover up what should be covered."

In Islam, both men and women are supposed to "lower their gaze" at one another out of a concern for modesty.[81] The most salient bodily modesty practice mandated for Muslims is the donning of concealing attire outside the home. A woman is expected to "cover her body in association with men to whom she is not related."[82] Women dress this way in public to avoid making themselves "sexually attractive to the men they might encounter there."[83] Interpretations of what parts of her body a woman should cover differ among observant followers of Islam. By scripture, women are expected "to refrain from showing off 'their ornaments,'"[84] which, under one interpretation, means their hair.[85] Many believe unrevealing, western-style clothing is acceptable; others believe women must wear a head and neck scarf or burqa, "a garment that covers [her] from head to toe, with a meshwork grill area over the eyes to permit some vision."[86] Plenty of modern Muslims themselves attack modesty requirements as repressively sectarian and unfair to women. Interestingly, though free by law to do as they please, North America Muslims nevertheless don everything from simple headscarves to the full burqas.

But modesty has not been a simple matter of choice. Bodily modesty has been a special, obligatory virtue for women. Classic philosophical accounts of female modesty explain and justify it by reference to the putative demands of civilized order and the perpetuation of the species. On Joel Schwartz's interpretation, Rousseau maintained that instilling female modesty restrains women's purported natural promiscuity and heightens men's purported physiologically restricted sexual desire.[87]

In nonwestern societies, cultural notions of bodily modesty often are more aggressively enforced than they are in North America. In fact, in some countries sexual modesty for women is strictly and brutally coerced by social norms as well as by legal and religious authorities. Women have been harassed, beaten, and punished for appearing in public uncloaked.

Disparities in the degree of modesty expected of men and women are a feature of contemporary US society. The design of public showers and toilets is one reflection of differential modesty assumptions. Acts that would be considered immodest for women may be considered modest for men.[88] An example from popular culture makes the point. In 2004, pop stars Justin Timberlake and Janet Jackson sang a live duet for millions of Super Bowl football fans of all ages watching from the stands and on television during half-time. At the dramatic end of their performance something occurred that many Americans and federal broadcast regulators considered indecent. Timberlake ripped Jackson's shirt and exposed one of her breasts, naked save for a jeweled nipple covering.[89] But it would have been considered no big deal had Jackson ripped Timberlake's shirt to reveal his chest, even if he had had a flabby set of male breasts rather than a trim physique.[90] What was an indecent and immodest exposure of Jackson would have been no worse than tasteless in the case of Timberlake. Noting the significance of women's bare breasts in art and in life, Marina Warner lamented that "the female breast, which we so quickly and reductively think of as only sexual, is as much the seat of honesty, of courage and feeling, as is the male. For both sexes it is the place of the heart, held to be the fountainhead of sincere emotion in both classical culture and our own."[91]

In recent times, teenagers' droopy trousers and flagrant display of boxers or thongs have brought out the moralizers. The Commonwealth of Virginia's House of Delegates approved a law introduced by Democrat Algie T. Howell Jr. that imposed a fifty-dollar fine on anyone who "intentionally wears and displays his below-waist undergarments, intended to cover a person's intimate parts, in a lewd or indecent manner." The silly measure was defeated in the state senate and did not become law. The proposed baggy-pants ban was aimed primarily at young men. But girls keen to show off sexy thong undergarments were targets, too. The ACLU took a stand against the proposed law: "In a free society, there are simply some things too personal for government to regulate, and one of them is the style of our clothing."[92]

Shame, modesty, and the private sphere are importantly linked. Shame is the emotion that purportedly ought to follow lapses of modesty and other virtues.[93] A woman's breasts and sex organs are inherent organs of shame in some belief systems.[94] They are instruments of shameful, if delightful, pastimes best pursued in private places to avoid censure.[95] "She ought to be ashamed of herself" was the scold heard when erotic photographs of the quickly dethroned Miss America 1983 appeared in *Penthouse* magazine. One surprising photo provided a close-up of since-successful recording artist Vanessa Williams' fully exposed genitals. Another photograph depicted a naked Williams appearing to enjoy an oral sex act with another naked beautiful woman.

The Miss America title used to demand a wholesome, chaste image. There is a close, reciprocal connection between chastity and sexual modesty. Failures of bodily modesty are a threat to premarital and marital chastity. Correlatively, to violate norms of chastity by engaging in unchaste sex acts is to violate expectations of modesty. Tocqueville speculated that nineteenth-century American women were more chaste than their European counterparts because they were trained, realistically, to see the advantages of chastity, and because they tended to seclude themselves inside their homes after marriage.[96] Michael Novak argued in 1967 that premarital intercourse is morally wrong because it fails "to fulfill the conditions of permanence implied in the symbol of intercourse," and David Carr argued in 1986 that chastity is a virtue of self-control and attachment; but Anna Stubblefield pointed out more recently that premarital and marital chastity norms have been problematic for women insofar as they have been part of a sexual double standard for men and women.[97]

Live, public nudity is restricted by law in the United States. But US cultural trends suggest a shift away from bodily modesty as a significant personal virtue. The naked body remains highly eroticized, yet public forms of nudity offline and on line are commonplace. Modesty has been unwrapped.

MODESTY RIGHTS

While unpopular within mainstream popular culture, bodily concealment is a constitutionally protected value. The US Supreme Court has not directly addressed restrictions on Muslim headscarves or facial veils. But when it does, it will have precedent to drawn on pointing toward toleration and accommodation of veiling.

In the past, admittedly, the Court has upheld laws aimed at compelling religious minorities to conform to a variety of majority practices. The Court's stance has been that "we have never held that an individual's religious beliefs excuse him from compliance with an otherwise valid law prohibiting conduct that the state is free to regulate."[98]

For example, the unrepudiated, late nineteenth-century decision *Reynolds v. United States* upheld a law applicable to the US territories, banning the practice of polygamy among the Mormons. Petitioner Reynolds was a prominent Utah Mormon who took a second wife with the approval of Mormon officials, flouting a polygamy ban enacted by Congress. Reynolds wanted to test the legitimacy of the national ban, and so he cooperated with his own prosecution, eager to appeal his conviction. Although the First Amendment clearly protects religious freedom, the Supreme Court held that the right of free exercise is a right to believe what one wishes, not a right to do what one wishes when what one wishes to do violates laws of general application. Plural marriages were "odious" to the civilized West, argued the Court.[99] And they were odious in part because of the shame they brought on women and children of such relationships, who were stained with an aura of illegitimacy. The *Reynolds* Court's interpretation of free exercise played a role in the court's decision many years later in *Employment Division of Human Resources of Oregon v. Smith*.[100] In that case members of a Native American church lost their social services jobs due to admitted use of sacramental peyote in worship. They were denied unemployment benefits on the ground that they lost their jobs "for cause"—using illegal drugs. The court held that the First Amendment did not require that the men's use of sacramental peyote be treated any differently from the use of other illegal drugs. The state interest in protecting the public from the dangers associated with drug use is a weighty one, reasoned the court.

Religious Freedom

Meyer v. Nebraska evidences a strong abhorrence to public laws whose sole purpose is to ensure assimilation. In this case, the Supreme Court struck down a state law prohibiting instruction in the German language in a parochial school. The law in question criminalized teaching German to children younger than thirteen, a crime for which Robert Meyer, a teacher at Zion Parochial School was prosecuted in 1920. The apparent purpose of the Nebraska law was assimilation—to ensure that young children became well-assimilated citizens who spoke and thought like "Americans." The court held that the Fourteenth Amendment does not permit compelling English language instruction: "[The Fourteenth Amendment] denotes not merely freedom from bodily restraint but also the right of the individual to contract, to engage in any of the common occupations of life, to acquire useful knowledge, to marry, establish a home and bring up children, to worship God according to the dictates of his own conscience, and generally to enjoy those privileges long recognized at common law as essential to the orderly pursuit of happiness by free men."[101]

In *Wisconsin v. Yoder*, in 1972, the Supreme Court struck down convictions of members of the Old Order Amish religion who refused to send their children to school for formal education beyond the eighth grade (a Wisconsin state law mandated that children attend private or public school until the age of sixteen years). The Court stressed that the application of the compulsory school attendance law could very well destroy the ability of the Amish to practice their faith as a community and perpetuate their unique way of life: "The record in this case abundantly supports the claim that the traditional way of life of the Amish is not merely a matter of personal preference, but one of deep religious conviction, shared by an organized group, and intimately related to daily living."[102] Only the Amish youth's absence from school was at issue in the *Yoder* case, not the "different" clothing they wore to school when they attended. Yet part of the Amish way of life the Court seemed reluctant to disturb included the Amish style of dress. The Old Order Amish reject what some of them call "English" dress. Instead they wear simple rural attire, not unlike their nineteenth-century ancestors.

Deference shown to the Amish way of life and educational values suggest that other groups' religiously inspired requirements of their school-aged children would be similarly protected by the Court. If government may not constitutionally ban instruction in a minority language in a parochial school or require formal secondary education for members of a minority religious group, it arguably could not ban the hijab, an article of clothing worn by a religious minority.

Although the US Supreme Court has not been asked to address the constitutionality of a hijab ban in schools or a niqab in the courts ban, it has been asked to review decisions that concern the constitutionality of dress and uniform codes for school children, public employees, and members of the armed forces. The Court's dress and uniform cases are further evidence of how it might assess the constitutionality of a hijab or niqab ban.

Individuality

In the landmark US Supreme Court case, *Cohen v. California* (1971), the Court threw out the disorderly conduct conviction of a California man who donned a jacket bearing the offensive words "F—k the Draft" in a court house corridor.[103] The decision was not unanimous, but the majority stressed that the First Amendment is not obliterated simply because a man uses a single crude expletive to express his political position on military conscription. The *Cohen* decision rested on the requirements of freedom of expression protected by the First Amendment. The First Amendment also protects the free exercise of religion. If the first Amendment protects tasteless jackets, it could be expected to protect tasteful modesty attire worn for religious purposes.

Wearing a Muslim headscarf to school could be compared to wearing a particular hairstyle and choice of clothing. May public schools demand a uniform appearance of their pupils? In the late 1960s and 1970s, many public secondary schools adopted strict hairstyle codes in response to the popularization of the long styles preferred by entertainers, college students, and "hippies." In the 1990s there was a resurgence of school uniform requirements in urban public schools. Uniforms appear to improve school discipline and promote safety.[104] On a number of occasions the federal courts have addressed the question of whether school children are constitutionally entitled to wear their hair in styles prohibited by school administrators. Analogous questions have arisen in relation to public employees' hairstyles.

In *Stull v. School Board of Western Beaver, Junior-Senior High School*, the Third Circuit Court of Appeals recognized in 1972 that "the length and style of one's hair is implicit in the liberty assurance of the due process clause of the Fourteenth Amendment." A school rule prohibited styles in which a boy's hair covered his ears or fell below his collar line. The court held the policy invalid and unenforceable, "except as applied to shop classes," where safety was an apparent issue.[105]

In *Kelly v. Johnson* (1976), the Supreme Court refused to invalidate hair length regulations promulgated by a police department. Chief Justice William Rehnquist argued for the majority that "choice of organization, dress, and equipment for law enforcement personnel is a decision entitled to the same sort of presumption of legislative validity as are state choices designed to promote other aims within the cognizance of the state's police power."[106] The requirement that police officers wear their hair in short styles was a requirement of uniform and uniformity. In a dissent joined by Justice William J. Brennan, Justice Thurgood Marshall made the case for individuality. Justice Marshall's reasoning in *Kelly* was in line with that of the Third Circuit Court of Appeals in *Stull*, which struck down a categorical hairstyle requirement for high school boys: "To say that the liberty guaranteed of the Fourteenth Amendment does not encompass matters of personal appearance would be fundamentally inconsistent with the values of privacy, self identity, autonomy, and personal integrity that I have always assumed the Constitution was designed to protect."[107]

Kelly v. Johnson is Supreme Court precedent for this principle: courts should presume the validity of uniform grooming requirements that confer public benefits, notwithstanding any individual's interest in individuality. Following this principle, one reasonably could conclude public schools may constitutionally impose uniform dress requirements that impair individuality, as indeed many public and private schools do. Some schools have uniform requirements that dictate clothing style and color. Boys are often asked to wear khaki pants and polo shirts in conservative colors. Girls are sometimes asked to wear plaid jumpers or skirts and blouses. Short of a strict uniform requirement, some schools ban logo shirts, excessively baggy pants, short shorts, tank tops, baseball caps, and ostentatious jewelry, even "chastity rings."[108] Certain clothing is prohibited because it can be used as a place to conceal contraband. Some school districts are persuaded that school uniform requirements further the goal of instilling pride and improving school discipline.[109]

It is one thing to tamp down individuality and something else to interfere with a person's religion. Schools with uniform requirements could be constitutionally required to make exceptions to accommodate bona fide religious difference among their pupils. Some schools explicitly exempt from dress code requirements the hijab and yarmulke, the Jewish head covering worn by men and boys. In Shermia Issac's Howard County, Maryland, public school, hats and other head coverings were prohibited in the classroom, but an exception was made for the yarmulke and hijab.[110] An African American eighth grader of Jamaican ancestry, Issac lost her court battle to wear an ethnically inspired headdress to school. The girl admitted that the multicolored head wrap her school forbade was not required by her religion or cultural traditions, and that she chose to wear it some days for style to conceal a "bad hair day." However, the wraps were also an expression of her ethnic pride, and were of a sort commonly worn by her mother. Shermia Issac's case suggests that head coverings not dictated by religion or cultural traditions of modesty need not receive the deference given a schoolgirl's hijab.

Some schools with dress codes, like the Maryland school cited above, have concluded that they should or must make exceptions for bona fide religious attire. As a logical matter, the constitutionality of dress codes and school uniform requirements does not entail the constitutionality of banning the hijab or other religious attire. The case must be made that the First and Fourteenth Amendments permit a substantial interference with religious liberty. Based on the precedent of *Meyer* and *Yoder*, and the evidence of the Hearn case and public reaction to it, I believe it is unlikely that a federal court would sustain a school dress code or uniform requirement that did not make an exception for pupils' bona fide religious or cultural modesty garb.

Uniformity and Public Service

The courts should—and I predict would—distinguish schools and courthouses from the military, a limited context where concerns about uniformity have been held to trump religious expression. The Supreme Court has upheld military policies limiting the right to wear the yarmulke. In *Goldman v. Weinberger*, the Court held that a Jewish rabbi and clinical psychologist, serving as an active duty member of the military, could be prohibited from wearing a yarmulke.[111] The case for permitting the military to ban religious headgear was based on the same reasoning used to make the case for permitting municipal police departments to prohibit long hairstyles—the importance of uniformity. Uniforms and uniformity communicate discipline, professionalism, and submission to a common authority.

It can be argued that categorical uniformity in the military—and in law enforcement—is a legitimate, important, or even compelling state interest. The case for categorical uniformity in school is less strong. The needs of schools on the one hand, and police departments and the military on the other, are sufficiently different to warrant constitutionally different approaches to religious or cultural exceptions. A boy in khakis, a polo shirt, and yarmulke, like a girl in a plaid jumper and hijab, inherently offends no legitimate state interest such as school discipline or safety. Categorically banning religious or cultural headgear in schools is incompatible with due respect for the religious and expressive freedom of children and their families.

A Peculiar Modesty Bias in US Law

Religious Muslims sometimes say that wearing the hijab or niqab is an expression both of religious identity and of modesty required by religion.[112] Thus another pertinent angle from which to view government imposed restrictions on the hijab would be US modesty laws. By "modesty laws," I mean the dispersed set of legal norms that dictate that adults cover up their bodies for the sake of chastity, humility, decency, or morality.

One notable manifestation of constitutional respect for women's modesty was the Supreme Court case *Union Pacific Railroad v. Botsford* in 1891. This case is a landmark of the Court by virtue of its immediate recognition of the "right to be let alone" defended by Samuel D. Warren and Louis D. Brandeis the year before.[113] The case held that a woman who filed a tort action alleging physical injuries need not submit to a medical exam at the request of the defendant. The woman's modesty was at stake. The *Botsford* decision has been effectively overruled by modern rules; rules of civil procedure now authorize courts to order the examination of personal injury plaintiffs. But what endures is the sentiment about the importance of privacy advanced in the *Botsford* case: "No right is held more sacred, or more carefully guarded, by the common law, than the right of every individual to the possession and control of his own person, free from restraint or interference of others, unless by clear and unquestionable authority of law."[114]

A fourteen-year-old US boy was suspended from school in 1983 after delivering a speech containing an extended sexual metaphor. His words were condemned by school officials as "indecent, lewd, and offensive to the modesty and decency of many of the students and faculty in attendance at the assembly."[115] The Supreme Court upheld the school's disciplinary actions, nothwithstanding the youth's free speech interests: "The pervasive sexual innuendo in Fraser's speech was plainly offensive to both teachers and students—indeed to any mature person. By glorifying male sexuality, and in its verbal content, the speech was acutely insulting to teenage girl students. The speech could well be seriously damaging to its less mature audience, many of whom were only 14 years old and on the threshold of awareness of human sexuality."[116]

Schools expect students to respect modesty and US federal judges expect schools to respect modesty. The 2009 Supreme Court's decision in *Safford Unified School District v. Redding* underscores the legal obligation of the state to recognize and respect female modesty.[117] The case held that public school administrators violated a middle school girl's Fourth Amendment rights against warrantless search and seizure when they conducted a strip search to look for contraband ibuprofen. Two adult women, a school nurse and administrative assistant, observed the embarrassing unveiling, with little regard for the girl's sense of modesty, as she removed her clothing and was compelled to shake out the cups of her bra and the crotch of her panties to dislodge the nonexistent contraband. The Ninth Circuit Appeals Court sided with the girl, who, along with her mother, sued the school district: "The overzealousness of school administrators in efforts to protect students has the tragic impact of traumatizing those they claim to serve." The court referred to the "psychological trauma intrinsic to a strip search" no matter how courteously or professionally conducted, and the "feelings of humiliation and degradation associated with forcibly exposing one's nude body to strangers for visual inspection."[118] The teenager won her case in the Supreme Court. Prior to *Redding*, the Supreme Court had held that a "special needs" exception to the Fourth Amendment warrant requirement permits public schools to conduct non law-enforcement searches of children and youth in public schools to check for illegal drug use or possession of contraband. But with the *Redding* decision, the Court recognized protection of modesty as a privacy constraint on schools' right to conduct bodily searches of youngsters.

The choice of modesty is typically a prerogative of the US women who want it. This is not to say a schoolgirl without a religious excuse can excuse herself at will from school uniform requirements that compel her to cover up less than she might prefer for reasons unrelated to her religion. This is also not to say that women have not had to fight for the right to wear Islamic dress to work. Women wearing the hijab have been denied employment opportunities, belittled, and harassed. A woman employed in security business claimed that a job reassignment prompted by her religious use of the hijab violated rules against discrimination in employment; a woman employee of Dominick's alleged that the real reason she was fired was that she wore a hijab and used break time to pray; a woman employee of rental car company claimed harassment due to wearing the hijab and praying at work.[119] Still, in the United States, the salient legal modesty battles of our time are mainly about women seeking the freedom to dress less modestly than others expect, and only occasionally about women seeking freedom to be more modest than expected.

Without success, tavern dancers and owners have gone to the Supreme Court seeking a right to totally nude performances. A battle for compelled modesty has been symbolically won in the Supreme Court in cases concerning bans on totally nude dancing (examined in detail in my next chapter).[120] Over First Amendment objections, the Supreme Court has twice upheld laws that require women to cover up, at least to some degree. The Court has bought the argument that public safety in some communities hinges on the difference between total nudity and the donning of g-strings covering the genitalia and pasties covering the nipples of performers. In a country in which states attempt to impose a symbolic vestige of modesty on its female citizens to such an absurd degree, it is unlikely that women and girls exhibiting greater than average modesty would ever be required to remove modesty garments, solely for the sake of uniformity or cultural assimilation.

The refusal to let go of the pastie and g-string reflects a cultural nudity taboo. Judge Richard Posner has argued that a "nudity taboo" is a feature of American society that requires deference under the Eighth Amendment even in the context of prison life, where providing same-sex guards is an administrative inconvenience and employment rights issue. Judge Posner made the case for respecting "Judeo-Christian" modesty values, and his argument, forgiving the attack on "radical feminists," is easily extended to Islamic modesty values embraced by many Muslim Americans:

> The nudity taboo retains great strength in the United States. It should not be confused with prudery. It is a taboo against being seen in the nude by strangers, not by one's intimates. . . . It is strongest among professing Christians, because of the historical antipathy of the Church to nudity. . . . The taboo is particularly strong when the stranger belongs to the opposite sex. There are radical feminists who regard "sex" as a social construction and the very concept of "the opposite sex," implying as it does the dichotomization of the "sexes" (the "genders," as we are being taught to say), as a sign of patriarchy. For these feminists the surveillance of naked male prisoners by female guards and naked female prisoners by male guards are way stations on the road to sexual equality. . . . I think that the interest of a prisoner in being free from unnecessary cross-sex surveillance has priority over the unisex-bathroom movement.[121]

One domain for respecting the Muslim modesty values would be the contexts at issue here—prohibiting dress and demeanor codes that would compel Muslims to remove the hijab or niqab. A woman without hijab or niqab is not naked, but her sense of modesty may be strongly implicated in what she chooses to wear. So what is the harm of letting her have her way?

A "COMPELLING STATE INTEREST"

The events of September 11, 2001 unfortunately left many Americans with a bad taste for Islam and a phobic suspicion of religious Muslims and people suspected of being from Muslim countries. Even the events of 9/11 did not result in calls for banning the veil from public places, however. Post-9/11 air travel is one of the few contexts in American life where modesty garments have come into potentially serious conflict with public purposes. Screening policies require that all men and women be asked to remove head coverings, jackets, and shoes when passing through inspection. Authorities have not sought to deny categorical passage to veiled Muslim women, though there have been outrageous casualties. One American-born Muslim woman was strip-searched after refusing to remove her hijab in a public passenger screening area of an airport.[122] Authorities have struggled to devise respectful means of screening veiled women for security purposes, but are supposed to provide screening by a female professional in a secluded area.

Some US judges are persuaded that hijab is protected free exercise of religion, consistent with reasonable security. Accordingly, in 2007 a woman in Galveston, Texas was awarded $17,250 after she alleged that a security guard refused to allow her to enter the courtroom unless she removed her headscarf "worn in observance of hijab."[123] Her case led to official measures to remind local "judges to be sensitive to the constitutional rights of people in the courtroom and specifically noting that people who wear their religious clothing or head wear are not required to remove [it] upon entering the courtroom."[124] The religious free exercise clause of the First Amendment must surely be interpreted to require toleration of the modesty garments of Muslim women. But hijab, which leaves a woman's face fully observable, is not niqab, which leaves only a woman's eyes in view. The difference may not be so relevant in assessments of risk and harm, if what one is concerned about it the ability to conceal contraband. The difference between hijab and niqab widens when concerns about the interests of government relate to the capacity identify persons and to confront witnesses and accusers. The central question that must be addressed is whether the state has a sufficiently important interest that warrants excluding niqab from the courtroom. Five main concerns—veracity, accountability, demeanor, identity, and fairness—have prompted courts to seek to exclude face-veiled women (as opposed to mere hair-veiled women) as parties and witnesses.

Government has a strong interest in a judicial system governed by rules and procedures that enable those responsible for fact-finding—judges, lawyers, prosecutors and juries—to assess the veracity of witnesses and parties. The government also has a very strong interest in holding accusers accountable for the statements they make and serious allegations of wrong-doing the levy against others. As for veracity and accountability, niqab interferes with the obligation to confront those whom one has accused. Facing a niqab-draped woman satisfies the bare desire to confront, but frustrates the ability to ascertain veracity on the evidence of overall facial expression and body language.

Demeanor is evidence of truthfulness and also of mental and emotional fitness to stand trial. Demeanor is evidence of character and of whether a person is making a serious effort to pay attention and show respect to others in court. Government has a compelling interest in a judicial system in which participants act with rationality, civility, and seriousness. The sight of niqab-drapped women invites inferences of femininity, modesty, and religiosity—but blocks inferences of immaturity, indifference, anger, boredom, or contempt. Behind her veil the Muslim party or witness might be sticking out her tongue, yawning, dozing, pursing or biting her lips, smirking, grinning, or frowning.

While it may be easier to judge the veracity and demeanor of a person who is not wearing a veil than to judge the veracity and demeanor of a person who is, judges, lawyers, and juries nevertheless have significant bases for judgment. They can rely upon assessments of the veiled woman's tone of voice, choice of words, and the consistency and plausibility of her statements. They can judge the woman wearing the style of niqab which leaves the eyes unveiled, based on the look and movement of her eyes, as well as her carriage, her gait, her posture, the manner in which she uses her hands. The assessment of demeanor does not depend upon seeing the face or entire face of the speaker. In fact, "according to the empirical evidence, ordinary people cannot make effective use of demeanor in deciding whether to believe a witness. On the contrary, there is some evidence that the observation of demeanor diminishes rather than enhances the accuracy of credibility judgments."[125]

In *Morales v. Artuz,* the Second Circuit Court of Appeals considered whether the defendant's right to confront a witness was violated when the key witness (a woman) testified wearing sunglasses so "dark... that you can't see through them."[126] The court held that the jury was still able to observe the witness's delivery, nervousness, and body language. The court explained that it was more important that the jury was able to triangulate observable aspects of demeanor with the substance of the testimony, the witness's opportunity to observe, the consistency of the testimony, and whether the witness had any hostile motive. It could be argued that the right to confront one's accusers goes to core public values and undercuts the right to veil. But that right to confront accusers cannot be interpreted as a right to force a person who is completely willing to appear in a courtroom and be questioned, to take off attire called for by her faith. The wearing of the niqab is a kind of personal religious conduct that courts must tolerate and accommodate.

As for identity, it is easy to verify the identity of a person whose full face is in plain view, but the female form behind the niqab could be almost anyone of similar weight, height, and color. There are plenty of ways a judge or other court personnel can identify a woman short of asking her to appear for the duration of a trial unveiled. The guidelines of the Maryland state Attorney General for meeting the identification needs of Maryland courts call for asking a woman wearing a modesty veil momentarily to remove it in the presence of a female security officer.[127]

In 2005 a New Zealand judge ruled that two Muslim witnesses testifying for the prosecution in a criminal procedure could not testify while wearing a burqa.[128] This case presented two difficulties. First, the burqa not only covers the face but the whole body; thus, the witnesses' body language would be difficult to assess. Second, in a criminal case the stakes are high and thus testimony is more crucial than in a civil case. Criminal cases transcend the relations between two parties and become a matter of public interest. The public has the right to a transparent and open criminal justice system and has an interest in the conviction of criminals. Arguably, the defendant's right to fair trial entitles him to cross-examine witnesses whose faces are uncovered. The judge in this case ruled that the court and litigants needed to see the faces of witnesses. Otherwise, the court stated, how could they know "that the person re-entering the witness box today is the same person who was there yesterday?" The court added that even with visual identification it is difficult to distinguish between people of similar build and facial characteristics. The court emphasized the significance of watching witnesses' faces while they are under cross-examination and the public's right to observe justice unfolding in the courts. Nevertheless, the court allowed significant accommodations for the witnesses. The court ruled that screens would be used to ensure that only the judge and counsel would see the witnesses' faces while they testified and that the court's staff would be comprised entirely of women. The court also ordered that steps be taken to ensure that the witnesses would not be seen unveiled in the entrance to the courtroom or when they departed. The court specifically mentioned that the witnesses were allowed to express their religious views by wearing a hat or scarf that covered their hair.

Finally, as to the concern for bias, the niqab in the courtroom will seem extreme and exotic to some judges, jurors, parties, witnesses, attorneys, prosecutors, and others. Ethnic prejudice and unfair bias may be amplified by the appearance of veiled women in a US courtroom. Muslim women may value their modesty and integrity more than they value marginal reductions in racial and ethnic prejudice. Clearly, bodily modesty is not something all women value or value equally. But modesty ought to be available, by right, for those consider it a core religious virtue.

In a 1991 memorandum addressed to his state's judges, New Jersey Chief Justice Robert N. Wilentz directed judges he supervised not to restrict litigants or witnesses from dressing as they choose: "I do not believe we should try to influence how litigants or witnesses dress, absent something that approaches the obscene."[129] (Muslim modesty attire is, by US standards, virtually the opposite of obscene since it conceals breasts, sex organs, and then some.) Furthermore, Justice Wilenz wrote, "I believe the fact finder, albeit the jury or the judge, should see the litigant or witness as the person wishes to appear and reach whatever conclusions flow from that 'fact.'"[130] Many jurists would find Wilenz's anything-short-of-obscenity standard too permissive. But the

United States and England share a legal heritage, and a recent U.K. study calls for an open mind and case-by-case pragmatism in responding to religious attire.

Indeed, the Equal Treatment Advisory Committee of the United Kingdom's Judicial Studies Board urged tolerance, sensitivity, and pragmatism in its 2007 guidelines for managing religious attire worn by parties, witnesses, judges, jurors, lawyers, and incidental courtroom staff: "There is room for diversity, and there should be willingness to accommodate different practices and approaches to religious and cultural observance."[131] The board found that while sensitive, well-explained requests that a woman remove her niqab will sometimes be warranted by the facts and circumstances at hand, "it is often possible," the board concluded, "to assess the evidence of a woman wearing a niqab." Judges sometime take evidence over the telephone and some judges are sight-impaired, hence the judiciary may not consistently presume that "the veil represents a true obstacle to the judicial task."[132] In sum, "In many cases, there will be no need for a woman to remove her niqab, provided that the judge is of the view that justice can be properly served."[133] A recent case in England provides an example of the way sensitivity and consideration can resolve more complicated situations. In this case, a fully veiled woman was required to testify in court. Her counsel ensured in advance that the judge presiding over the case would be a woman. The counsel was screened from the Muslim woman's view by a large umbrella and the courtroom was guarded to ensure that other men did not enter during her testimony. In this manner, the woman was able to testify without the veil.[134]

Tolerance, accommodation, and pragmatism are not inherently inconsistent with the popular US emphasis on judges having control over their courtrooms. Judges should have substantial control over their courtrooms, including the power to ban clothing or nudity that disrupts, demeans, or trivializes the forum of justice.[135] Judges can exercise control and yet be highly tolerant of personal style and religious preferences. A New Jersey judge was reversed when he held a female attorney in contempt of court for wearing slacks and a sweater in court.[136] In the American northeast, slacks and a sweater are less formal professional attire than a black suit and tie. But, unlike Mickey Mouse ears, a Batman costume, or a comically oversized sombrero, a pants and sweater outfit does not demean, trivialize, or disrupt a courtroom.

Under the principles I have identified, moral justice will not allow a blanket niqab-removal policy based either on the need to judge demeanor or veracity, to identify, to compel accountability, or to identify and avert bias. Women of Muslim faith wearing the niqab are neither disruptive nor an affront. They have a right not to be observed, so long as they can be seen, heard, and identified in other straightforward and appropriate available ways.[137] As a constitutional matter, respect for religious freedom appears to demand that there be a very strong presumption against religious clothing bans and a strict requirement of accommodation in those instances in which the state asserts a truly overriding interest in undressing its people. Courts in the United States should avoid the quick conclusion that the niqab is "a true obstacle to the judicial task."

CONCLUSION

Concealment bans have caught on in Europe. From a US perspective, the demand made by the French government that Muslim women and girls who wear hijab and niqab disrobe is counterintuitive. These women are told that in their private lives they may cover up, but in the public sphere they must undress. Never mind that they are modest or obliged to conceal their hair, face, or bodies by modesty rules of their religious traditions as they understand them. The French anti-privacy demand is paternalistic and also culturally hegemonic. It says to women of Islam: view your religious garb as coerced modesty; we order you, empower you, to be free.

In the United States, most modest clothing choices are properly situated in a domain of privacy for women, whether they are Muslim, Amish, or Orthodox Jews. The niqab in the courtroom represents a short list of exceptions—Americans mostly let women cover up, as a just, tolerant polity ought. But bodily modesty is not a matter strictly for private choice in the United States. Gripped by the Judeo-Christian "nudity taboo," US lawmakers have gone to great lengths to make sure women keep *something* on—even in the context of purposely raunchy erotic entertainment.

In the next chapter I will examine US and Canadian bodily modesty laws with the values of feminism and liberalism in mind. Canadian courts have espoused principles that seem to offer women more autonomy about states of dress and undress than American courts have offered—yet Canadian pronouncements reflect an unsatisfying blend of feminism and sexual repression that does little to enhance the lives of female sex workers or their clientele. The task of making sense of western norms of dress and undress is more difficult than one might expect, and the diverse options for liberalism, confounding.

4
NUDITY

A Canadian might just get away with topless nudity on a city street.[1] But a New Yorker could expect to wind up in jail (or a mental hospital) for strolling half naked down the street. In 1972, a New York woman was arrested for sunbathing naked at the beach, but shortly after a court cleared her of criminal charges on the ground that she had not behaved lewdly, the legislature changed the law to clarify that all public nudity is forbidden, even if the intent is not lewd.[2] Law, custom, and morality demand keeping clothing on around strangers in the United States.

Nudity is commonplace in the arts.[3] Yet with a few exceptions, the nudity and eroticism the law permits in artwork is not permitted on the streets, beaches, or parks. Laws in the United States even restrict some nudity behind closed doors. One variety of nakedness-behind-closed-doors that the law restricts is totally nude dancing, a popular form of adult entertainment.[4] Consenting adults pay other consenting adults to perform in the nude at private parties and in bars, clubs, casinos, and peep shows open to the general public. A strong belief that it is a good thing to leave sexually immodest people alone to strut and gyrate in the nude competes in the United States with a strong belief that it is a good thing to protect society from nakedness that endangers, demeans, and shames. The result is local and state laws that ban totally nude dancing.

The First Amendment of the United States Constitution protects freedom of speech and expression.[5] The Fourteenth Amendment protects liberty of action.[6] Still, state and local laws compel sexual modesty. Of course, law cannot make anyone truly modest. The sanctions the law threatens, however, can impel even the least modest men and women to behave in public as if they were paragons of that saintly virtue. Modesty practices can be and are coerced.

The US Supreme Court has upheld statutory bans on totally nude dancing.[7] Over First Amendment challenges, the Court has validated efforts by state and local officials, first, to force vestiges of traditional moral conceptions of sexual modesty onto performers through pasties and g-string clothing requirements; and, second, to address societal harms—mainly prostitution, drugs, sexually transmitted infections, and violence—that officials reflectively link to public nudity.

Striking polarities of jurisprudential thought surround the issue of commercial nude dancing. According to judicial perspectives at one end of the spectrum, it is constitutionally permissible to prohibit totally nude dancing to protect the moral traditions of society, quite apart from vital concerns about public health and crime control. Supreme Court Justice Antonin Scalia has asserted this view.[8] According to perspectives at the other end of the spectrum, it is constitutionally impermissible and ridiculous to prohibit totally nude dancing. Court of Appeals Judge Richard Posner has expressed this opinion.[9] For the most part, US opponents of nude dancing in places open to the public have lost the legal battle. Nude dancing and seminude dancing are perfectly legal in numerous parts of the country, though regulated through zoning and indecency laws. But opponents have won a kind of victory in the Supreme Court, which has held that although the state cannot categorically ban nonobscene, partially nude entertainment, it can ban totally nude nonobscene nude entertainment.

Are ideals of justice necessarily violated by laws that restrict nude dancing? What count as legitimate reasons for restricting nude performances in a just state? Can liberal law prohibit nude dancing on the ground that it is immoral, offensive, or dangerous; or because gender, race, and income disparities appear to play a role in making nude dancing an appealing amusement and profession? I consider these questions through an examination of popular nude dancing practices and nudity-related US and Canadian law.[10] In the United States legal ideals of sexual modesty exist in tension with legal ideals of free speech, expression, and conduct. The US and Canadian Supreme Courts have both handed down major nude dancing decisions in recent decades. Canada, it turns out, has a more permissive nude dancing law than its free-wheeling neighbor. Canada also boasts a more credible—though ultimately problematic—understanding of the ways in which nude dancing can and cannot be harmful. I believe that in just, free societies, persons are owed strong, consistent rationales for their laws, including relatively minor laws like nude dancing restrictions. The US public has not gotten a good set of reasons for widespread fig-leaf-cum-nipple-cover-up modesty laws restricting totally nude dancing. There are reasons to care about what goes on in strip clubs, but they turn out to have little to do with the ethics of nakedness as such.

THE BARNES CASE: LEGAL MORALISM

American laws compel modest behavior: first, by restricting nudity on the streets, on beaches, and in places of public accommodation; second, by prohibiting modes of public undress that could be characterized as obscene, lewd, or indecent; and third, by restricting the time, place, and manner of sexually oriented public theatrical performances, dancing, and touching.[11] Laws have demanded that women cover up their breasts.[12] Even infant breast-feeding in public was once treated as an indecency offense in the United States, but is gaining respect.[13] Various laws prohibit topless sunbathing by women.[14]

Barnes v. Glen Theatre, Inc. (1991) tested the constitutionality of an Indiana statute that defined "public indecency" and "indecent exposure" to include appearing "in a state of nudity."[15] In the 1980s two South Bend establishments, the Kitty Kat Lounge and the Glen Theatre, along with individual dancers who wished to offer totally nude entertainment, sued and lost, and then appealed a lower court ruling upholding the statute. Dancer Darlene Miller speculated that she would make more money dancing totally nude than partly covered. She wanted the opportunity to test her theory, but did not get it.

She almost did. The Seventh Circuit Court of Appeals held that the statute was unconstitutional under the First Amendment because it infringed the appellants' right to engage in nonobscene expressive activity with a message of eroticism and sexuality.[16]

In his anti-censorship reflection on the Kitty Kat lounge case Judge Richard Posner introduced a refreshing realism, speculating that the real reasons judges are reluctant to extend First Amendment protection to erotic dancers include the judges' typical ages, genders, and snobbery. Posner said judges feel "that the proposition, 'the First Amendment forbids the State of Indiana to require striptease dancers to cover their nipples,' is ridiculous." Further,

> it strikes judges as ridiculous in part because most of us are either middle-aged or elderly men, in part because we tend to be snooty about popular culture, in part because as public officials we have a natural tendency to think political expression more important than artistic expression, in part because we are Americans—which means that we have been raised in a culture in which puritanism, philistinism, and promiscuity are complexly and often incongruously interwoven—and in part because like all lawyers we are formalists who believe deep down that the words in statutes and the Constitutions mean what they say, and a striptease is not a speech.[17]

Scolding his colleagues on bench, Posner argued that any element of the ridiculous is not all on one side of the debate:

> Censorship of erotica is pretty ridiculous too. What kind of people make a career of checking to see whether the covering of a woman's nipples is fully opaque, as the statute requires? . . . Most of us do not admire the Islamic clergy for their meticulous insistency on modesty in female dress. Many of us do not admire busybodies who want to bring the force of law down on the heads of adults whose harmless private pleasures the busybodies find revolting. The history of censorship is a history of folly and cruelty.[18]

Posner also pointed out that striptease dancing is no longer considered obscene and that women's clothing styles have become "progressively less modest," women appearing in public "in states of undress (mini-skirts, hot pants, slit skirts, body stockings, see-through blouses, décolletage becoming outright topless evening wear) that would have been considered nakedness, or the garb of prostitutes, thirty years ago."[19] When the Kitty Kat Lounge case went to the Supreme Court, Posner's realism lost out. But it was accurate and prophetic, nonetheless.

Mainstream popular cultures of immodesty are all the rage. In the present context, moralizing about modesty will feel to many as quaint as medieval sumptuary laws. Consider the themes of conspicuous consumption and prideful sexuality in the billion-dollar hip-hop music industry. An evening cruising topless bars, watching cable television's sex shows, or making buddies on the Internet leaves little doubt that the audience for modesty lessons is limited. People of all ages have found arguably educational, entertaining, and artistic reasons to be naked around strangers.

In *Barnes* the Supreme Court ruled on appeal that state and local authorities in Indiana may require cloaking the nipples and genitalia notwithstanding the admitted First Amendment interest of dancers in free expression.[20] A plurality opinion by Justice William Rehnquist defended the Indiana law as justified legal moralism. According to Rehnquist, the Indiana law's heritage and purpose were clear: "protecting societal order and morality" through "public indecency statutes... of ancient origin" that address "gross and open indecency."[21]

Justice Scalia wrote a concurrence expressly attacking the dissenting views that offense and harm, but not morality, were constitutionally sound bases for limiting a First Amendment freedom. Justice Scalia took on the dissenting Justices's seeming assumption that the statute could not stand if its only purpose were to avoid the offense of public nudity (because the nudity in question took place behind closed doors) or to enforce morality (since morality was not a matter for public regulation):

> Perhaps the dissenters believe that "offense to others" ought to be the only reason for restricting nudity in public places generally, but there is no basis for thinking that our society has ever shared that Thoreauvian "you-may-do-what-you-like-so-long-as-it-does-not-injure-someone-else" beau ideal—much less for thinking that it was written into the Constitution. The purpose of Indiana's nudity law would be violated, I think, if 60,000 fully consenting adults crowded into the Hoosier Dome to display their genitals to one another, even if there were not an offended innocent in the crowd. Our society prohibits, and all human societies have prohibited, certain activities not because they harm others but because they are considered, in the traditional phrase, "*contra bonos mores*," *i.e.*, immoral. In American society, such prohibitions have included, for

> example, sadomasochism, cockfighting, bestiality, suicide, drug use, prostitution, and sodomy.[22]

This opinion was written more than a dozen long years before *Lawrence v. Texas* decriminalized consensual adult sodomy in 2003 and took it off the Court's list of acts permissibly criminalized because it is thought to be *contra bonos mores*.[23]

The harm principle rather than moralism was at the core of Justice David Souter's concurrence.[24] Nudity has harmful "secondary effects," he argued. His evidence of harm, though, was speculative: "live nude dancing of the sort at issue here is likely to produce the same pernicious" secondary effects as the adult films displaying "specified anatomical areas," at issue in *Renton v Playtime Theatres, Inc.*[25]

The *Renton* case announced the low standard of proof to which the Supreme Court will hold government when it comes to establishing that nudity is harmful.[26] States, towns, and cities need not spell out exactly how nudity is of a piece with vice and crime, or otherwise harmful to society.[27] They may rely on studies by other jurisdictions, or no studies at a1l.[28] Guns, prostitution, alcohol, and drugs indeed plague too many communities. It is widely believed that adult entertainment establishments, including adult theaters and clubs or peep shows featuring erotic dancers, attract serious crime and vice; the Supreme Court has concluded that this belief is reasonable.[29]

A second related "reasonable" belief is that would-be nice neighborhoods deteriorate when nude entertainers move in. Property values plummet as women take off their clothing. Requiring sexually modest cover-ups supposedly counteracts the tendency of nudity to breed dangerous geographic communities of crime and vice. Yet it is not obvious that banning totally nude dancing—while allowing virtually nude dancing in the name of constitutional freedom—addresses this concern. Through zoning laws a city can address problem of bad neighborhoods growing up around nude dancing venues.[30] Adult entertainment venues could be disaggregated and isolated, reducing the potential for the "bad neighborhood" problem.

But its opponents say public nudity also raises public health risks.[31] Uncovered bodies are more vulnerable to infectious agents in the environment. And casual sex precipitated by nudity can spread disease. The transmission of diseases like HIV/AIDS and hepatitis through exposure to others' body fluids is a risk of the unprotected casual sex that sometimes occurs in and around nude dancing venues. To avoid the public health problem, persons practicing nudity could be better educated about precautions and motivated or compelled to practice them. Persons viewing nude dancers would be prohibited from touching them or masturbating. If unhealthy sexual contact between dancers and patrons is more likely in the case of totally nude dancing, then this collateral activity, rather than the dancing itself, could be prohibited and prohibitions enforced.[32] Excessive alcohol, drug, and tobacco use are public health problems, but there is no unique association between nudity and substance abuse or addictions—although one can certainly imagine substance abuse as a way to lower dancers' and bashful customers' inhibitions.

Dissenting Justices Byron White, Thurgood Marshall, Harry Blackmun, and John Paul Stevens rejected the Indiana law on the ground that nonobscene public nude dancing is a form of constitutionally protected free expression without distinct and discernable harm. Justice White, writing for the dissenters, asserted that a legitimate purpose for laws prohibiting public nudity would be the avoidance of offense. Justice White concluded that an application of the offense principle would not justify upholding the Indiana law as applied in this case: The "offensive" conduct takes place behind closed doors in a location no person liable to offense need ever enter. Justice White continued: "The purpose of forbidding people to appear nude in parks, beaches, hot dog stands, and like public places is to protect others from offense. But that could not possibly be the purpose of preventing nude dancing in theaters and barrooms since the viewers are exclusively consenting adults who pay money to see these dances."[33]

The true purposes motivating prohibitions on totally nude dancing are paternalistic and content nonneutral; in White's view, "to protect the viewers from what the State believes is the harmful message that nude dancing communicates."[34] It is not just that the state thinks nudity is offensive and immoral; the state is also trying to protect its citizens from sexual messages they voluntarily seek out. The state treats adults, paternalistically, like children. Justice White pointed out that the state's concerns about the secondary effects of nude dancing, if genuine, could be addressed effectively by means less restrictive than a ban on totally nude dancing. If the concern were prostitution, the state could more vigorously enforce prostitution prohibitions and require that dancers and patrons keep a safe distance from one another (e.g., no lap dancing).[35]

In the wake of the splintered *Barnes* decision in the Supreme Court, some lower courts believed there was no clear precedent to follow. One court characterized attempting to follow *Barnes* as "like reading tea leaves."[36] Some courts adopted the morality rationale of Justice Rehnquist's plurality opinion, while others got behind Justice Souter's secondary effects analysis to justify prohibitions on public nudity.[37] Rather than follow *Barnes*, Pennsylvania's Supreme Court chose to adopt its own rules for governing nude dancing laws—a choice overruled by a second Supreme Court nude dancing case nine years later, this one originating in the lakeside city of Erie, Pennsylvania.[38]

When policymakers condemn acts as indecent, it is not always clear that they are expressing mere offense, strict moral disapprobation, or both. Preferring to live in a society in which they are not offended by others' conduct, some Americans seem to subscribe to what philosopher Joel Feinberg labeled "the offense principle."[39] They believe they are entitled to the protection of law from others' offensive acts. To the extent that public nudity or sex acts offend—even in the context of art or entertainment—the offense principle might allow government to prohibit them.

Finally, some people in the United States believe sexual immodesty is harmful. Immodest acts are thought to harm the soul, character, or welfare of the person acting immodestly, giving rise to the need for coercive, paternalistic laws. Some would say that paternalistic interference is warranted to the extent that nude dancing is degrading or demeaning to willing dancers or their willing audiences. Sexually immodest acts are believed to have pernicious social effects more widely. Immodest acts in places of public accommodation are believed to spawn harmful secondary effects such as prostitution, sexually transmitted diseases, the obscenity trade, illegal drugs, and violence. The pervasive line of reasoning about remedies for harm is simple to state: enforce modesty, contain crime and vice.

CITY OF ERIE: THE HARM PRINCIPLE

Erie, Pennsylvania successfully enacted an ordinance banning totally nude dancing in September of 1994. Although lawmakers debating the measure identified morality as a core purpose of the ordinance, the official preamble to the ordinance stated that its enactment was prompted by secondary effects: "For the purpose of limiting a recent increase in nude live entertainment within the City, which activity adversely impacts and threatens to impact on the public health, safety and welfare by providing an atmosphere conducive to violence, sexual harassment, public intoxication, prostitution, the spread of sexually transmitted infections and other deleterious effects."[40]

The corporate owner of Kandyland, a club featuring totally nude erotic female dancers, brought a lawsuit in the Court of Common Pleas seeking declaratory and injunctive relief against the enforcement of the nudity ban ordinance. The Court of Common Pleas struck down the ordinance in 1996, but the Commonwealth Court reversed. The Pennsylvania Supreme Court reversed on the grounds that the ordinance violated the First and Fourteenth Amendments. Nude dancing, the court reasoned, is expressive conduct meriting protection.

Victory for the corporate owner of Kandyland was short-lived. The City of Erie did not give up on its bid to get rid of nude dancing. Instead it appealed the Pennsylvania Supreme Court's decision to the Court of final authority on the First and Fourteenth Amendments, the US Supreme Court. In 2000, in *City of Erie v. Pap's A.M.*, the US Supreme Court reversed the Pennsylvania Supreme Court. Justice Sandra Day O'Connor, joined by Chief Justice Rehnquist and Justices Anthony Kennedy and

Stephen Breyer, made four substantive findings. They followed a precedent set by an earlier case, *United States v. O'Brien*, for constitutionally sound content-neutral restrictions on symbolic speech.[41] O'Connor reasoned that the statute was within the city's police powers; furthered an important government interest in combating the harmful secondary effects of crime and vice posed by public nudity; did not amount to government suppression of free speech; and did not restrict conduct more than necessary.[42]

Dissenting Justices raised important questions about the reality of the harmful secondary effects of totally nude dancing alleged by city government. What empirical evidence did Erie rely on to conclude that nude dancing breeds criminal misconduct in its midst? Doesn't the constitution require more than speculation about the existence of alleged secondary effects? City authorities were content to have partially nude dancing continue, so long as dancers were clad in at least pasties covering the nipples of their breasts and g-strings covering their genitals—but how could wearing a few inches of cloth alter the alleged tendency of sexually-oriented dancing to attract crime or vice and transmit sexually-transmitted infections?

These sensible questions go to the core of why the Court's decision cannot be taken at face value, as upholding a constitutionally protected state interest in public health and safety. Framed as a response to harm, *City of Erie* is not John Stuart Mill's harm principle at work; it is instead legal moralism. According to Mill, government possesses the moral authority to prohibit conduct that harms others, but lacks authority to moralistically or paternalistically prohibit conduct that only harms a willing actor or violates society's moral or social standards:

> The only purpose for which power can rightfully be exercised over any member of a civilized community, against his will, is to prevent harm to others. His own good, either physical or moral, is not a sufficient warrant. He cannot rightfully be compelled to do or forbear because it will be better for him to do so, because it will make him happier, because, in the opinions of others, to do so would be wise or even right.[43]

Philosophers and lawyers sometimes defend the legal paternalism and legal moralism Mill rejected. But today it is perhaps more common to stretch and bend to find an element of "harm" in conduct that one really objects to on moral or offense grounds.[44] In *City of Erie*, the Court's symbolic (and awkward) nod at the harm principle by upholding the fig leaf is barely concealed moralism, a replay of the overtly moralistic *Barnes* case.

Many lower courts have tried to apply the precedent of *Barnes* and *City of Erie*.[45] Even after *City of Erie*, the permissible rationales for restricting nude dancing was still a matter of debate and confusion. For example, in 2005, a Michigan court endorsed Rehnquist's doctrine of moralism from the *Barnes* case, stating that "the promotion of public morality through the prohibition of indecent exposure is a sufficient governmental interest."[46] Courts fret, understandably, about the lack of a limiting principle behind the "pasties and g-string" rule. For example, one court approached ridicule by observing that "We recognize that dancing with a G-string and pasties is also not nude dancing. And, government entities may constitutionally require the wearing of this attire. But at some point, nude dancing while wearing clothing cannot be described as nude dancing."[47] Judges expected to uphold total nudity bans to fight secondary effects, feel put upon in view of the flimsy claims they are expected to honor in the wake of *City of Erie*: "To wit, each additional piece of required clothing must result in a further reduction in pernicious side effects. Without demanding this connection at each step, each additional layer of restriction can be legally added simply on the basis that the previous restriction was valid, until the entire activity is banned: i.e. nude dancing is permitted so long as the dancers wear pasties and G-strings; then bathing suits; then t-shirts; then long pants and a sweater."[48]

A frustrated Massachusetts court parted ways with the Supreme Court. The court held in *Mendoza v. Licensing Board of Fall River* (2005) that the Massachusetts state constitution provides greater protection for public nudity than does the federal constitution, effectively striking down the both the *Barnes* and *City of Erie* holdings that municipalities may require dancers to appear partially covered. Writing for the court, the judge Robert J. Cordy pronounced that "we reject the city's argument that erotic dancers, clad in the oft-cited sartorial combination of 'pasties and G-strings,' may nevertheless express an equivalent 'message' without dropping 'the last stitch.'"[49] The court also quoted from the White dissent in the *Barnes* opinion, stating that "the nudity is itself an expressive component of the dance." Rather than shy away from or try to cover up the fact that their decision granted less leeway for municipalities in regulating nude dancing than did *Barnes* and *City of Erie*, the court openly acknowledged that "we recognize that our analysis departs from the Supreme Court's treatment of similar ordinances under the First Amendment." It is fair to say that the US judiciary is both confused and divided on how best to enforce public modesty norms.

CANADIAN CASES

Many western nations are more accepting of nudity than the United States. Going topless—or even nude—in public is acceptable in major European locales. The Netherlands instituted a policy in 2006 of showing prospective immigrants an official educational video on Dutch culture that includes scenes of the country's nude beaches.[50] Women may go topless on beaches in France, but even in the heart of Paris there is a place "known for near-nude sunbathing."[51] At the 2006 World Cup in Germany, a special meadow was reserved especially for nude sunbathing.[52] Nude sunbathing is common in the famous Tiergarten in Berlin. In the English Garden in Munich, it is apparently not "unusual to see business people walk into the garden at lunch, fold up their suits, and lie around naked until it's time to go back to the office."[53]

The Canadian Supreme Court has announced that categorical bans on nude dancing are unconstitutional restraints on freedom. *R. v. Tremblay* (1993) and *R. v. Mara* (1997) are leading Canadian judgments concerning nude entertainment.[54] The Canadian Supreme Court parts ways with the US Court in an important respect. The Canadian Court has unequivocally ruled that bare morality, offense, and paternalism grounds for restricting nude dancing are out of bounds. In bounds is a harm principle whose satisfaction requires nonspeculative evidence of harm.

The Canadian Court has explicitly embraced a harm principle to define constitutionally permissible limits on nude dancing. Applying its harm analysis, the Canadian Court would reject US style laws requiring that otherwise nude dancers cover their nipples and genitals. The Canadian Supreme Court has held that lawmakers can no longer require nude dancers to cover up their private parts—not to satisfy moral ideals of modesty and not to ward off merely presumed social harms. Nude dancing can be punished as indecent under local laws, but only if it violates what the Canadian Court terms the "community standard of tolerance" which "depends largely on an analysis of social harm."[55]

The Canadian high Court has adopted a remarkably permissive, third-party harm requirement in its nude dancing cases. In Canada, officials' unsubstantiated, speculative claims of nudity-related harms simply do not cut the constitutional mustard. Under the Charter of Rights and Freedoms, the Canadian Supreme Court now rejects arguments that casually link totally nude dancing per se to antisocial crime and vice. Accordingly, the Canadian Court in *Tremblay* struck down indecency convictions where the facts included that totally naked female dancers masturbated alongside their masturbating male patrons.[56] On the surface, until one understands what the court means by "harm," the Canadian requirement is strikingly reminiscent of John Stuart Mill's classic articulation of liberal freedom in his essay *On Liberty*.[57]

Cleansed of the most overt moralism of modesty, Canada's constitutional stance on nude dancing retains moral idealism. The Canadian Court has established a jurisprudence of nudity that attempts to take both tangible and intangible harms of nude conduct seriously. The Canadian Court construes harm discursively as that to which contemporary Canadians cannot tolerate fellow Canadians' exposure. Polling data does not enter into the picture; the test is satisfied by judges' hypothetical reasoning about countrymen's conventional mores. Applying this unique definition of harm, the court has determined that commercial nude dancing which includes sex acts in public is intolerable and (in that sense) harmful. Paid performers offering sex in taverns open to the public amounts to prostitution, a permissibly criminalized offense.

Yet what the court considers sex in public is sufficiently narrow as to leave rational moralists baffled by the line-drawing. As cited in *Mara*, the Canadian Court of Appeals held that seminude lap-dancing was lawfully prosecuted as harmful indecency because dancers and patrons intimately touched one another. Close human contact of the sort, said the appeals court, intolerably "degrades," "dehumanizes," "desensitizes," and "objectifies."[58] I would characterize the court's concerns as legitimate moral concerns, to be sure—concerns shared both by progressive liberal feminists and church-folk. Oddly, applying the Canadian national standard of tolerance, the court had no such concerns about naked dancers and naked patrons masturbating side by side, however repellent to local authorities. Because nudity and masturbation are undisturbed freedoms, owners and patrons of the totally nude erotic dancing industry in Canada can rejoice in the knowledge that they have little reason to fear a shut-down—or sexual frustration.

R. v. Tremblay: Community Tolerance

The Canadian Court's landmark *R. v. Tremblay* decision in 1993 denied the status of indecency to the performances of nude dancers at the Pussy Cat Club. Here is a description of the Pussy Cat Club, which like the Kitty Kat Club in the United States is a feline-denominated adult entertainment venue:

> The client would be taken to a private room that was furnished with a mattress and a chair. In that room the selected dancer would, for a fee of $40, undress and perform an erotic dance for the client on the mattress. For an additional fee of $10 the dancer would caress herself with a vibrator while she danced. During the course of the performance the dancer would assume a variety of suggestive positions while caressing herself in simulated or actual masturbation. The clients were invited to remove their clothes. The . . . majority of them masturbated while the dancer performed.[59]

In the majority view of the Canadian Court, justices Claire L'Heureux-Dube, Peter Cory, and Beverley McLachlin asserted that it is not degrading, dehumanizing, or subordinating to allow a paying stranger to select you to dance, masturbate while dancing, and himself masturbate in the nude as you perform. Performers have a constitutional right to perform totally nude, to masturbate while performing, and to invite customers into private cubicles to remove their clothing and masturbate alongside them. Such conduct is not prostitution, *Tremblay* assumes, and does not reach the level of legal indecency because it harms no one in the required legal sense of "harm."

The Canadian high court has determined that some nude dancing is in fact harmful, however. The court in *Mara* arguably betrayed its libertarianism, or stamped it with a brand of feminism, in crafting its broad definition of harm. Nude dancing will violate the community's standard of tolerance only if it is harmful, but the law is not waiting for broken bones and blood. The law will infer harm from "activities ... [that] involve degradation and objectification of women, or perhaps children or men." In form, this is a ruling feminists could laud; yet, like *Tremblay*'s dissenting justices Charles Gonthier, and Gérard La Forest, feminists might wonder why consensual totally nude simultaneous masturbation for a fee at the Pussy Cat Club is not considered degrading or objectifying to women. What is degrading or objectifying? We need a clear case paradigm. By my lights, paying for the right to rape and sling acid into women's faces would degrade and objectify women.

R. v. Mara: Look, Don't Touch

The *Mara* court thought the degradation-objectification line could be crossed without that kind of grotesque cruelty. The answer to the question "what is degrading and objectifying," gleaned from the 1997 judgment in Mara, is this: that performers and customers cross the line from nonharm to harm when they touch one another in a sexually stimulating manner. In an opinion by Justice John Sopinka in *Mara*, a unanimous Canadian Court found seminude table dancing to be an indecent performance violative of the community standard of tolerance. The case tested the constitutionality under the Canadian Charter of Rights and Freedoms of a criminal prosecution of the owner and manager of Cheaters Tavern, a midtown Toronto club. The two were charged with allowing an indecent performance in violation of a statute. Guilt under the statute depended upon *mens rea*, and the court found that there were sufficient grounds to convict the manager of the club, though not the owner, who had delegated responsibility for entertainment to the club manager.

It is a responsibility of the court, wrote Justice Sopinka, quoting precedent, to "determine as best it can what the community would tolerate others being exposed to on the basis of the degree of harm that may flow from such exposure."[60] He argued that the harm at issue in this case was centrally "the attitudinal harm on those watching the performance as perceived by the community as a whole."[61]

At Cheaters, performers and customers engaged in what the court described as public sexual contact when customers paid an additional fee for a table dance:

> The conduct of each dancer with the customer is clearly detailed in the evidence and includes: (a) being nude except for wearing an open short or blouse; (b) fondling her own breasts, buttocks, thighs and genitals while close to the

> customer; (c) sitting on a customer's lap, reaching into his crotch and apparently masturbating the customer; (e) permitting the customer to touch and fondle her breast, buttock, thighs and genitals; (f) permitting the customer to kiss, lick and suck their breasts; (g) permitting what appeared to be cunnilingus.[62]

The court endorsed the idea that the sexual contact at issue was indecent insofar as it involved "sexual touching between dancer and patron." Again, for the Canadian court, indecency is not a vague moral matter but a measure of harmfulness and a question of law. The table dancing at Cheaters was held to be "harmful to society in many ways: it degrades and dehumanizes women; it desensitizes sexuality and is incompatible with the dignity and equality of each human being; and it predisposes persons to act in an anti-social manner."[63] Interestingly, the claim of harm did not rest on the fact that the sexual activity in question could result in sexually transmitted infections. But the possibility of disease and the similarity of the activity to prostitution, the court suggested, is an aspect of what makes the conduct degrading.

With touching, sexual stimulation potentially becomes degrading and objectifying—therefore harmful and indecent, and therefore constitutionally open for criminalization. The Canadian Supreme Court broadly defines harm inclusive of dignity-reducing expression. The Canadian Court in *Mara* used the powerful terms "degrading" and "dehumanizing," but did not mean by those words only conduct such as sexualized torture or sexual slavery that would also constitute a plain human rights violation. Degradation for the court includes acts that are cruel, violent, or dehumanizing, as a human rights violation might be; but also those that merely portray women in an unequal, subordinate, or submissive manner.

The puzzle we are left with is why sexually stimulating *touching* makes the difference, if the harm is essentially one of undignified or demeaning behavior rather than risk of physical injury. One might argue that actual sexual contact to orgasm is *more* dignifying than exciting voyeurism and masturbation.

A major obstacle for making principled sense of *Mara* is that words like "objectifying," "degrading," "dehumanizing," and "undignified" do not have exact meanings. Usually terms like "demeaning" are used without carefully definitional analysis. Deborah Hellman's account of what it means for conduct to be morally demeaning is one of the most careful and may shed some light here, although it was designed for another arena of moral concern.[64] Hellman argued that the kind of discrimination a society should view as wrongful is the discrimination that is demeaning. Discriminatory conduct is demeaning when it meets two criteria. First, the conduct must show disrespect for another by debasing or degrading the person; and second, the conduct must be a material put-down, an exercise of power. Does Hellman's answer to the question she wanted to ask, which is "when is discrimination wrong?" also suggest an answer the Canadian court's question "when is sex work wrongfully objectifying and degrading?" Perhaps sex work is wrong enough for legal intervention when it is morally demeaning, and it is morally demeaning when it represents a debasement of stature and an exercise of power. Understood in this way, sex workers potentially demean their customers, and their customers and employers potentially demean them. It all depends on the context.

The ability to control one's own body is one indication of freedom from other's control. A woman is in power if she can freely decide what to do with her own body. Consensual sexual relationships are acts of freedom, not slavery; pleasure, not cruelty. Yet touching marks a critical pragmatic boundary of self-sovereignty. As long as sex does not involve touching, the man who pays for sexual stimulation lacks the critical material power, physical power over the sex worker that could make what is erotic become unacceptably demeaning. Unless the woman is touched or confined, she cannot be overpowered. She cannot be raped.

But a law that merely disallows the acts which, when performed without adult consent, qualify as rape—permutations of contact between genitalia, bodily orifices, and objects of penetration—does not make women and her customers and employers equal citizens of a free society. Moreover, anti-touching rules deny sex workers a business opportunity they do not regard as rape and their customers a pleasure they do not regard as rape. The boundary the Canadian court is looking for may be violence, including the violence of terrorizing and knowingly transmitting illnesses. Yet as a practical, bright-line rule, "touch" is more serviceable than "violence." The rule against physical contact protects women from one particularly cruel, subordinating, dehumanizing danger, physical rape, and all of its biological and emotional consequences.

MODESTY ON THE RUN

Laws in the United States restrict nudity, but US culture is full of countertrends. Little girls want to become sexy pop divas, not reserved nuns. Their sisters use phones and webcams to send naked pictures of themselves to friends, and post nude and nearly nude photographs of themselves on social networking websites. To stay in shape, their mothers sign up for erotic pole-dancing classes at the gym. Some people like to feel natural and uninhibited. Whole families practice nudism.[65] Should we care?[66]

From a conservative Judeo-Christian religious perspective, modesty is an ethical virtue, worthy of legal protection.[67] Adam and Eve taught a lesson on modesty to the American courts. Schooled in the Bible, one nineteenth-century judge adjudicating an indecency case wrote:

> The enquiry, therefore, arises for this court to answer, is the exposure, in a public place, to divers persons there assembled, by a person, of his or her private parts, a public indecency? ... [It] historically appears that the first most palpable piece of indecency in a human being was the public exposure of his or her, as now commonly called, privates; and the first exercise of mechanical ingenuity was in the manufacture of fig-leaf aprons by Adam and Eve, by which to conceal from the public gaze of each other their, now, but not then, called, privates. This example of covering their privates has been imitated by all mankind since that time, except, perhaps, by some of the lowest grades of savages. Modesty has ever existed as one of the most estimable and admirable of human virtues.[68]

The history of the matter is surely more complicated than this quaint passage suggests. Yet longstanding Judeo-Christian and related ethical beliefs do seem to help explain why contemporary US law regulates nudity in the peculiar way that it does, subscribing to the principle of the fig-leaf apron, supplemented by the fully opaque nipple cover-up. Ironically, the Constitution Americans value so much for its protection of wanted privacy, they also value for its protection of unwanted privacy—mandatory bodily modesty. Liberalism may be the dominant abstract political aspiration, but when it comes to nudity, many Americans subscribe to their own brand of legal moralism—a belief that freedom and toleration are important, but core moral standards may be enforced. Many believe public nudity and public sex are inherently wrong and should be criminalized. In defending the Erie law designed to prohibit nude dancing,[69] one self-revealing lawmaker clearly identified what was on his mind: "We're talking about what is indecent and immoral."[70] First it was James Fitzjames Stephen attacking John Stuart Mill in the nineteenth century, then Patrick Devlin squaring off against Herbert Hart over the Wolfenden Committee Report in the twentieth.[71] The same tensions continue with theorists like Robert George worrying about the "moral ecology" of American society even as permissive liberalism seems destined to win the day.[72]

The regulation of nude dancing reflects the continuing allure of a particular vision of modesty as a human virtue: the virtue displayed by the painter Botticelli's depiction of Venus on a shell, her head tilted demurely, hand laid across her comely breasts, impossibly long hair draped across her pubis. General modesty was a virtue in western philosophical thought prior to the Christian era and bodily modesty took on special importance in the Christian era. Today's curious nude dancing regulations reflect religious and moral values at play in the nation, and US lawmakers' discomfort with nudity for a host of psychological and pragmatic reasons.

Should we care about nudity and the demise of modesty? I do not believe that getting paid for entertaining in the nude is categorically and invariably wrong. However, making one's living as a nude dancer for hire in bars, clubs, casinos, peep shows, and at house parties can get a woman branded as having bad judgment and a poor character. She takes too many risks, has too much sex, has too little pride and self-respect—this is how Americans think. It is not all about modesty and decency. I surmise that lawmakers' discomfort with nudity is partly a function of fear and distrust. The United States is in many ways an emotionally immature society that seems to need a restraining sexual morality that includes sexual modesty. One doubts that fellow citizens have sufficient self-control to handle a fully libertarian regime of permissible public nudity. We are not certain we can trust our fellows not to sexually assault and harass.[73] We fear others will turn what is supposed to be nonobscene and natural into something obscene, lurid, or perverse. We fear shame, undue objectification, and victimization.

Conditions of Work

The barrier in my own thinking to wholesale embrace of nude entertainment has little to do with the nudity involved. The nude body is a morally neutral entity. It rather has to do with opposition to apparently unfair, subordinating and exploitative conditions of work. The city of Seattle's saga with strip clubs is especially instructive. In Seattle, strippers have had to pay for the privilege of dancing and then earn wages through tips from customers eager for physical contact. For example, dancers at a club called Rick's reportedly paid club owners $130 per shift and were considered to owe "back rent" if they missed a scheduled shift; they also paid club owners 10 percent of earnings from "private dances."[74] These labor conditions resulted in a kind of indentured servitude, in which strippers had to resort to prostitution to meet their debts. Women did not invent this business model. In 2005, the Seattle city council passed a law forbidding customers to touch strippers or place money in their g-strings, forcing customers and dancers to stay at least four feet apart, demanding that dancers stay behind a three-foot-tall railing, and banning dim lighting. The following year, a public referendum defeated the new rules and the old rules went back into effect. In 2008 police and federal agents raided Seattle clubs run by local strip club boss Frank Colacurcio, Sr., alleging that his business was built "on the backs of women" who "turn to prostitution to pay the exorbitant fees required to dance in his clubs."[75] It may just be true that in some communities the authorities are not mere moralizers who find nudity distasteful: "The strip club industry in this country has a pattern of public corruption, money laundering, coercive violence and prostitution."[76]

Mutual Disrespect

My second reservation about nude dancing is harder to advance. Recall the descriptions of the masturbating and table dancing venues at issue in *Mara* and *Tremblay*, the two Canadian cases. And consider the following description of a US nude dancing venue: "The live entertainment at the 'bookstore' consists of nude and seminude performances and showings of the female body through glass panels. Customers sit in a booth and insert coins into a timing mechanism that permits them to observe the live nude and seminude dancers for a period of time."[77] This obviously describes not an art school drawing class or the Broadway shows *Equus, Hair,* or *Oh! Calcutta*! This is Indiana's Kitty Kat Lounge, at issue in the *Barnes* case. Women respond on demand to coins dropped in a box by others intent on voyeurism or masturbation; performers encourage others, especially strangers, to view them solely as a means of fleeting erotic pleasure. Persons should not treat one another merely as, to borrow a phrase from Samuel DuBois Cook, "means of self-satisfaction," but as equals.[78] This could be labeled a Kantian intuition about a familiar class of nude dancing settings. (The Kantian intuition will be dismissed by some libertarians as judgmental Puritanism.) I mean to point out a two-way street. It is both the performers and the customers whose consensual conduct violates Kantian intuitions. It is commerce without reciprocal respect.

Aristotelian ethical responses are also evoked by consideration of the quality of the interpersonal exchanges at the Kitty Kat Lounge. In the words of the philosopher, "praise is extended to the modest man."[79] No categories of human excellence and exemplary character easily fit the goings-on at the Kitty Kat. Admittedly, one can be a very skillful erotic dancer: fit, creative, and amusing. And one can be a very appreciative and attractive masturbating voyeur. Club owners can be skillful, savvy businesspeople. But being good at what one does, without regard to what one is doing, is a dubious criterion of excellence. The case for excellence must rest on something inherent to the activity, lest navel-gazing or contract killing win the title of a virtue. Of the best at given tasks, one can still say, better that they occupy themselves doing something else. Spend your time, earn your way doing something else is the advice I would want to give typical nude dancing venue owners, patrons, and dancers.

It is possible that "Ashley Dupre," the twenty-three-year-old prostitute who serviced Governor Eliot Spitzer, actually respected him, and he her. It is possible she was very good at her job, very private, and that he appreciated her for it. In an interview with *People Magazine* Dupre described Spitzer blandly as "strictly business," "transactional," and "not wanting to talk"; she said that they had practiced safe sex, that she felt sorry for his wife, and that she had had no idea he was the married governor of New York until she saw him on television after the sex ring scandal broke. But it can be alarming to hear less pricey sex workers describe the low regard they have for most of their clients and customers when they call them tricks, losers, and pervs. I do believe sex work can raise concerns about respect for others and about self-respect, although I do not believe all categories of sex work undermine subjective self-respect. After all, someone like Ashley Dupre admits to prostitution with a public official and wins a book deal and a reality television show. She can feel good about herself.

CONCLUSION

It is an invalid leap of logic from the premise that typical nude dancing work is morally troubling to the conclusion that (1) totally nude dancing should be legally banned, or that (2) only partially nude dancing should be permitted. Moral wrongness is not a sufficient reason in principle to outlaw conduct in a free society. Qualitative moral concerns of the sort I have raised here are not addressed at all by the fig-leaf partial nudity compromises found in US statutes and endorsed by the US Supreme Court, or by the Canadian "look don't touch" rule.

The male streaker, mooner, or sincere philosophical nudist faces restraints of freedom, perhaps too many. As for nude dancing, North Americans need to grow beyond valorizing the fig leaf as modesty's savior. I believe that liberal democratic regimes can embrace mandatory modesty laws restricting nudity grounded in principles of harm avoidance. And the harms we ought to recognize legitimately include mutually subordinating debasements of the sort broached but not clearly delineated by the Canadian Supreme Court.

Notwithstanding legal traditions pervasively emphasizing individual freedom and tolerance, US policymakers coerce sexual modesty through laws demanding concealment of eroticized regions of male and female bodies. As might be expected of a paradigmatically free society, the coercion is restrained. But the coercion is peculiarly restrained and ambiguously motivated. State and local governments appear eager to mandate what is arguably only symbolic, outward conformity to sexual modesty norms held by some members of their communities. Whether in the name of morality, offense, public health, or safety, US lawmakers persist in coercing modest speech and behavior, even when not clearly warranted by justice or logic.

Government should try to protect women's free modesty choices. Modesty mandates ought to be reluctant and rare. However, governments around the globe routinely coerce modesty practices. Compelling modesty can conflict with a robust commitment to personal liberty. The problem is not that modesty is an inherently good or bad thing; I believe many forms of modesty deserve a place among virtues endorsed by world religions and secular philosophies. The recent demise of modesty as an ethical virtue warrants concern. The problem is rather that coerced modesty is a ready tool of subordination for illiberal, authoritarian states.

The overall direction of the North American courts, which has been to decriminalize nude and nearly nude dancing, is the right one: judges and lawmakers in free societies should rarely attempt to coerce sexual modesty. If the North American constitutional nude dancing case law is any indication, pinning down or even characterizing the harm that supposedly flows from public nakedness is fraught with practical and normative difficulties. If nudity is to be restricted on grounds of harm, the burden on government of proving causally related, harmful secondary effects to nude dancing is very great. And when one considers all of the voluntary, mainstream nudity in advertising, magazines, music videos, commercial films, health broadcasting, and on the Internet, concerns about the immorality and dangers of nude dancing seem overstated. It is a mistake to attempt censorship of immodest conduct when secondary effects claims are weak; and when protecting the Constitution would entail busy jurists and juries devoting themselves to the formalistic humiliating, silly, and unsavory business of determining whether, as required in Indiana, a particular woman's nipple is fully covered by a fully opaque covering. Some anti-nudity laws may be reasonable responses to danger, but in the twenty-first century, all such laws merit suspicion as illiberal impediments to personal choice.

PART THREE

Information Privacies: Confidentiality and Data Protection

5
CONFIDENTIALITY

The law mandates confidentiality. For men and women with a range of occupations, confidentiality is a legal obligation to remain strictly silent about some matters and limit communications about others. Lawyers, for example, are bound by law, along with their codes of professional responsibility, to maintain the confidentiality of communications with their clients.[1] The American Bar Association (ABA) promulgates codes of professional responsibility for lawyers. The federal government and forty-nine of the United States have enacted ABA standards into law, either the ABA Model Code of Professional Responsibility or the later ABA Model Rules of Professional Conduct. The official rules of evidence employed in state and federal courts recognize an attorney-client privilege, empowering clients to expect attorneys to keep quiet about the contents of their private, undisclosed communications. Lawyers routinely meet legal obligations of confidence-keeping with respect to those who seek their advice through silence, selective disclosure, and securing electronic data.

An accused thief confesses to her lawyer that she is indeed the person who stole a prized artifact from her town's history museum. The lawyer must keep the thief's admission a secret, foregoing the righteousness and rewards of solving a despicable crime. It is not easy for lawyers to remain silent when there is something interesting or important to talk about. Obligations of silence burden the conscience, and frustrate the passion for dialogue and recognition, gossip and curiosity-feeding. Viewed in this light, obligations of confidentiality are potentially unpopular privacies.

In the 1980s I briefly worked as an attorney at Cravath, Swaine & Moore, a prominent Wall Street law firm in Manhattan with a long history of representing big business. When I remarked on the unusually large number of male clerical workers employed by the firm, a senior partner described the aging men as relics of an era in which his colleagues believed men were better at keeping client confidences than women.[2] The truth of the matter is that keeping quiet when you should is a challenging discipline for most any man or woman.

Take, for example, Paul Gianamore. In 1999 Gianamore worked as a financial analyst at Credit Suisse First Boston, a major investment bank. Through e-mail, phone calls, and regular get-togethers, he told his best friend Ryan Evans about confidential tender offers and mergers discussed at the bank. Gianamore must have known what he risked. Evans could profit by secretly trading securities on the basis of information about pending deals, but Gianamore seemed not to care. Another friend said that the loquacious Gianamore told him business secrets, too. Because Gianamore gave Evans what courts have called "the gift of confidential information," and because Evans quietly used the information to make thousands of dollars trading securities, both men ended up in hot water with the Securities and Exchange Commission.[3] Evans was sentenced to fines and twenty-one months in prison for the crime of unlawful insider trading.

From a public policy perspective, laws that mandate professional silence for lawyers and financial analysts are generally good laws. I will argue that mandated confidentiality is a limit on the freedom to exchange information a liberal society justifiably imposes on many common occupations and professions. My claim is not that coerced confidentiality is all good or always good, however. The practice of confidentiality dams the flow of useful information. Confidentiality can lead to an innocent person getting killed or the wrong person being put to death. Many criticized Georgia attorney William M. Smith for silence that contributed to the conviction of Jewish factory manager Leo Frank for the murder of thirteen-year-old Mary Phagan in 1913.[4] Smith's client Jim Conley might well have committed the murder, and Smith knew it. On the basis of doubtful evidence, Frank was sent to prison for life. But before Frank could appeal, a brutal anti-Semitic mob, later organized as the Ku Klux Klan, kidnapped Frank from prison and lynched him.

Professional silence should sometimes be broken. Moreover, in some cases the right to the cloak of confidence is beneficially waived. Setting aside confidentiality can help address injustice. Setting aside confidentiality can also undercut the isolation of living with painful secrets. This is one of the reasons best selling-author and sexual abuse victim Truddi Chase gave in an 1987 memoir for waiving her right to psychotherapist-patient confidentiality and requesting that her therapist tape all their sessions.[5] Chase's session tapes became instructional videos documenting her trauma and resultant mental illness. A movie starring actress Shelley Long called "Voices Within—The Lives of Truddi Chase" aired on television in 1990. Oprah Winfrey has said that it was only after interviewing Chase that she came to realize she was not to blame for the abuse she suffered as a child.[6] The published stories of other people affected by mental illnesses have had an even wider impact.[7]

THE PRACTICE OF CONFIDENTIALITY

The most commendable confidentiality mandates imposed by law are those that clearly should admit no exceptions, and don't; or clearly should admit exceptions, including voluntary waiver, and do. I will soon come back to assessing the law. But I want to note three general features of confidentiality practices, legal or otherwise, found in the United States and similar societies. Confidentiality practices are (1) called for by a range of personal and professional relationships and occupations; (2) often relate to regulating access to personal documents, official records and restricted spaces; and (3) are frequently demanded by overlapping and conflicting sources of practical directives, everything from religious traditions and everyday morality, to professional codes and the law.

Relationships and Occupations

First, the practice of confidentiality is called for in a wide variety of common relationships and occupations. Everyday morality treats friendships and marriages as highly confidential relationships of trust in which intimate secrets may be safely shared. The procedural law applied throughout the US federal court system formally regards marriage as a confidential relationship, by incorporating, through the Federal Rules of Evidence Rule 501, the common law "spousal privilege." Spouses cannot be compelled to disclose the content of private communications or to testify against one another. The Massachusetts state statutes provide in like vein that neither spouse may testify as to private conversations with the other (even if one or the other wishes to waive the privilege) and that in criminal matters spouses cannot be compelled to testify against one another.[8] Same-sex marriage is permitted in Massachusetts, but in states where it is not, same-sex couples and cohabiting partners are not presumed to have the same protection of law for their private conversations. Recognizing that private conversations are not the sole province of married couples, some legal advocates have argued for expanding the spousal privilege to other intimate groupings, even parents and children and siblings. Yet from a feminist perspective, there are good reasons to consider contracting intimate relationship privileges. A married victim of domestic violence is severely disadvantaged in a proceeding against her abusing spouse, to the extent that the spouse is protected by the spousal privilege from having to testify.[9]

Laws mandating confidentiality may further justify the sorts of subordination, paternalism, or other injustice liberal feminism asks societies to caution against in assessing public policies and social practices. Confidentiality is a social practice that can do much good, but carries no presumption of legitimacy. Even people in illicit relationships premised on adult-child incest or extortion may expect confidentiality and successfully extract it. Criminal conspiracies are governed by strong expectations of confidentiality, backed by threats of violence. Corrupt corporate managers have relied upon corporate confidentiality norms and hierarchy to secret their wrongdoing and discourage whistle-blowing, a problem the corporate accountability law, the Sarbanes-Oxley Act, was designed to address.[10]

Important spiritual and consumer ties come with practices of confidentiality. The attorney-client, doctor-patient, and clergy-penitent relationships are ready examples. Adults can expect varying degrees of confidentiality from the lawyers, doctors, and clergy with whom they deal; and these professionals can often assert confidentiality as a privilege when called upon to give evidence in a judicial or administrative proceeding. Some professions' confidentiality obligations originate in ancient customs or religion. A duty of physician confidentiality was included in the fourth century B.C. oath of Hippocrates, updated in 1964 for modern physicians by Louis Lasagna: "I will respect the privacy of my patients, for their problems are not disclosed to me that the world may know."[11] When a Catholic priest has heard a penitent's confession of marital infidelity, he is required by the traditions of his faith to keep the sins to himself.

Individuals performing in a long list of occupations are expected to keep quiet: lawyers, doctors, and clergy are not alone in shouldering the burden of silence. Accountants, real estate agents, pharmacists, and tax professionals are also expected to keep information quiet. So are the government workers with access to the personal information contained in tax, census, and Social Security filings. State Department employees who breached confidentiality by accessing the passport files of President Barak Obama and other 2008 presidential candidates lost their jobs. Grand jurors and grand jury witnesses operate under obligations of secrecy for reasons that include the fairness of protecting the reputations of innocent people whose conduct comes under investigation. In the words of the Supreme Court: "By preserving the secrecy of the proceedings, we assure that persons who are accused but exonerated by the grand jury will not be held up to public ridicule."[12] Judges, maids, hairdressers, military personnel, police officers, school administrators—all of these serve in roles that call for confidentiality.

Documents, Records, Spaces

Confidentiality practices also regulate access to personal documents—like diaries, text messages, and e-mail; official files maintained in the context of confidential relationships, such as medical or tax records; and the restricted spaces where such personal documents and official files are likely to be stored (homes, bank vaults, office file cabinets, and computer drives). Accordingly, personal information recorded in diaries, journals, correspondence, and similar documents is commonly tagged "confidential." Medical records, academic records, and personnel files are generally described as confidential, along with banking and financial records, library circulation records, motor vehicle records, video rental records, and telephone transaction logs. In the United States, dozens of federal statutes and hundreds of state and local laws regulate access to confidential record data.[13]

Overlapping and Conflicting Directives

Revealing confidential information without consent may violate overlapping and conflicting social norms or positive rules—such as oaths, professional ethics, business policies, or the law. Confidentiality practices are demanded by complex combinations and permutations of customs and religion, ethical codes of self-regulated professions, ethical codes of government-regulated professions, company policies, and the law—substantive and procedural law, civil and criminal law, state, federal, and local law. Consider examples drawn from publicized legal disputes.

A woman wanted to keep her pregnancy a secret, but her doctor's assistant told the woman's mother about it anyway.[14] A man with AIDS expected confidentiality, but a hospital receptionist notified his coworkers.[15] The administrative assistants in both cases violated both medical ethics and the health privacy laws. Yet they may have acted from conscience.

The worried CEO of a publicly traded company quietly unburdened himself to his wife about his company's financial problems. The CEO's wife telephoned her brother to reveal the gist the corporate secrets she'd learned so that he and a friend could sell their shares of the company's stock before stock values plummeted. The CEO's wife violated the morality of marital trust and a legal regulation prohibiting the family members of a corporate insider from tipping off third parties based on information learned in confidence.[16]

A student at a private Christian school told the school's chaplain that he was gay. The chaplain then disclosed the information to school administrators, and the student was expelled.[17] An Orthodox Jewish woman spoke to two rabbis about marital difficulties that led to a divorce. The rabbis later revealed the personal matters she discussed with them in affidavits submitted in connection with a child-custody battle with her ex-husband.[18] The chaplain and the rabbis may have violated neither clergy ethics nor the law, despite the emotional distress they caused the student and mother who confided in them.

A New York lawyer sent a *Business Week* magazine reporter with whom he was chummy a copy of a sealed confidential document pertinent to a pending case—a mistake for which he was formally sanctioned by the state bar.[19] A criminal defense lawyer in a murder trial knew facts that, if revealed, might lead to the death penalty for his client but spare the life of a codefendant. Initially, he kept quiet, but many years later brought the matter to the attention of the court.[20] The criminal defense lawyer initially acted as he had good reason to believe his profession's code of ethics and the law required, but ultimately acted in accord with conscience, despite uncertainty about what professional ethics and the law truly permitted.

LAW, COERCION, AND JUSTICE

I turn now to a focus on the law. Legal confidentiality mandates sit alongside an array of nonlegal confidentiality norms and practices, as described in the preceding section. Professionals and others with access to interesting, exploitable information are required by law to keep silent about it. What, if anything, makes the silence mandates imposed on various professions and occupations just public policies? Asking a business or a person to not make use of information at their disposal is imposing a burden the justice of which is an important philosophical question. But it is not one that is amenable to easy abstract generalization. Lawmakers take fairness, efficiency, and political concerns into account when determining whether confidentiality will be legally mandated for an occupation or profession and coerced for the individuals those occupations or professions serve. Confidentiality laws are not expressions of pure principle, but rather the results of practical compromises forged in concrete contexts. An illustration helps make the point clear.

Lawmaking as Practical Compromise

The tax laws of the United States embody a policy of respecting taxpayer's personal information as confidential. Suppose private tax preparation firms retained by tax payers would like to earn revenue using taxpayers' personal data mined from electronic income tax returns. Indeed, one reason for offering free online tax preparation services could be precisely to get access to marketable personal data from filers. Suppose taxpayers are indifferent about the matter, or even supportive, because they want the cheapest tax preparation services and other financial products the market can offer. Should Congress or the Internal Revenue Service (IRS) enact a coercive rule prohibiting commercial tax preparers from making secondary uses of taxpayer data, or at least making such uses harder by requiring the written informed consent of customers? Would coercion be inconsistent with overall free-market strategies?[21] When these exact questions arose in Washington in 2006 while George W. Bush was in the White House, some privacy advocates argued against allowing the use of taxpayer data, even with consent. Although the tax preparation firms could make lucrative uses of taxpayers' data cheaply, by exploiting electronic resources, privacy advocates argued that taxpayers' informed consent was necessary and impossible. They maintained that businesses cannot obtain meaningful informed consent from most consumers, who are easily snowed by the complexity of financial concerns and lack data management literacy.

The IRS acted. New regulations governing business opportunities and secondary uses of taxpayer information went into effect January 1, 2009.[22] The new rules expressly allow firms to use taxpayer data to market products. But tax preparers may disclose taxpayer data usually only with consent and for purposes related to tax preparation. The rules address some of the privacy advocates' concerns about consent by requiring "opt-in" consent using a written instrument which includes mandatory disclosures and language. Taxpayers cannot be presumed to permit secondary uses of their data because they have not opted out; on the contrary; they must be presumed to object to secondary uses unless they have opted in, by electronically or physically signing the required consent agreement. While the IRS expressly intended to keep the taxpayer in the driver's seat by allowing him or her to consent to the use and disclosure of personal data, some confidentiality is coerced on the taxpayer. Firms cannot disclose Social Security Numbers to non-US entities, even with a taxpayer's consent. If the final outcome of this consumer confidentiality-related policy problem feels like an unprincipled patchwork of compromises, no one should be surprised: such is the reality of the law.

Sanction and Deterrence

We ethically assess the law, understanding that it is an imperfect product of practical compromise. We also understand that there is a limit to what the law can do. The law cannot prevent breaches of confidentiality; it can only hope to deter and punish them. Professionals have the power to speak and act on the basis of what they know, if they so choose. Lawyers could strike it rich writing tell-all books about their clients. (Although doing so would harm their ability to attract new clients.) Popularity and profit hold special allure. Revealing the medical secrets of the rich and famous could earn a fortune from the tabloid press, yet the physician of a famous recording artist keeps mum, forgoing profit. Why? Speech and acts that reveal patient privacies violate legal rules mandating silence, subjecting healthcare professionals to sanctions, not the least of which are civil liability. Many professionals face criminal liability and loss of license for breaching confidentiality. Confidentiality is forced; it is coerced.

THE RIGHT TO SAY WHAT YOU KNOW

In societies otherwise governed by the principle of free speech, how is it just to compel keeping mouths shut? Is such coercion warranted? The answer is surely "yes"—coercion is warranted, although there are costs to demanding it.

At first blush, it might seem obvious that individuals and institutions can be required with justice to keep silent about what they know when the truth hurts or embarrasses. The requirement of silence would seem to flow from the harm principle: coercion is justified when it prevents harm to others.

Yet obligations to refrain from communicating about sensitive matters are by no means found everywhere in the law. The US common law rule is that persons may disclose private facts unless doing so would be "highly offensive to a reasonable person"—that is, cause a reasonable person who is not hypersensitive to feel offended or aggrieved.[23] But the interpretations some courts give to common law principles bias in favor of public disclosures. Recall the case with which chapter 1 of this book began—the woman's intrusion case against the man who shared with others surreptitiously snapped photographs of an intimate bedroom scene involving his ex-wife was thrown out of court.[24] Lawsuits brought against employers or professionals privy to sensitive information concerning gay and lesbian plaintiffs have had mixed results.[25] Scott Greenwood believed he was fired from his position as an associate in the law firm Taft, Stettinius & Hollister after its management learned he was gay.[26] When he amended what he thought were confidential employee benefits forms to include his male partner as the recipient of his pension, personnel department staff within the law firm disclosed the information to others. An appeals court concluded that a reasonable person could be highly offended by being "outed" in the workplace, and denied the law firm's motion to grant a summary judgment without a trial on the facts.

The US Supreme Court has held that the media—newspapers, radio, and television—may publish highly personal information that falls innocently into their hands, even if the information came their way in violation of state confidentiality law. In two cases during the 1970s and 1980s, the Court refused to punish media: a newspaper and television station who published the names of rape victims in violation of state laws.[27] In both cases, negligent police departments handed over the identities of the victims to reporters; the victim in *Florida Star v. B.F.J.* was alive when her name was made public, and her perpetrator had not yet been apprehended. In a more recent case in 2001, the Court refused to punish media who broadcast tape-recorded phone calls, recorded in flagrant violation of federal electronic communication privacy statutes.[28] The principles of free speech and press embodied in the first amendment of the Constitution provide a rationale for not requiring confidentiality in the context of journalism. The principle of free speech trumps: speak at your own discretion, even though it will hurt.

PAID-FOR SILENCE

I have described confidentiality as a burden, but confidentiality requirements surely conform organically to how many professionals see their work anyway. Persuaded of its rewards, virtues, and business sense, professionals are often glad to shoulder the burden of professional silence. The rules of mandatory professional silence are so popular with professionals that they have been known to fight hard against compelled disclosures. Clergy have resisted compelled testimony. Physicians have opposed nonanonymous public health reporting laws. Corporate attorneys have not been eager to blow the whistle on corporate accounting fraud. Lawyers for terrorism suspects have begrudged requests to allow authorities to listen in on conversations with their clients. Many lawyers truly believe in the justice of the adversary system, and see confidentiality as an integral part of it.

Still, confidentiality can be burdensome, and the rationales for imposing it must be made clear. As a starting place, consider whether the case for the burden of confidentiality could begin with notions of contractual justice. People are paid for being silent about what they know.

Professionals are compensated for their silence with high social status, monopolies, and higher than average incomes. The argument that professionals are especially well paid for the burden of silence will only take us so far, however. If we are talking about partners or principals in top US law, investment or accounting firms, the argument makes some sense. It also makes sense with respect to the top tier at advertising, design, and publishing houses, as well as management or the most skilled senior surgeons in private practice. Yet the justification for mandated confidentiality cannot be that those required to keep secrets are highly compensated, because some of the educated professionals required to keep secrets are not in fact well paid. A public interest lawyer can earn considerably less than a suburban plumber or stone mason. Many professionals bound to keep secrets work *pro bono publico*, for free. And some low-paid professionals are threatened and condemned rather than celebrated for the work they do on behalf of illegal immigrants, minorities, or pregnant women.

Moreover, if one wants adequately to study the justice of coercing confidentiality, one cannot focus solely on the so-called learned professionals who, as a group, do indeed earn larger than average incomes, possess stature, and benefit from state-granted service monopolies. As I have been stressing, the law imposes duties of confidentiality on an exceedingly broad range of people. Confidentiality is a duty of workers rather than professionals or learned professionals alone.

Start listing the economic and social roles that require keeping silent about what one knows, and it quickly becomes clear that secrecy rather than disclosure is normative in all employment. Housekeepers and gardeners are morally bound to keep confidences, and could in theory be sued in tort for invasion of privacy for publicizing private facts about the people in whose homes they work. The confidentiality of the assistants once called "secretaries" was apparent from their very name. People who work in blue-collar capacities in business and industry are bound too keep intellectual property and trade secrets. Modestly paid and modestly educated school administrators are required by law to keep student records confidential. Editors in publishing houses have to keep quiet about the content of the books they edit or face legal liability. Police officers, prosecutors, and local elected judges and law clerks have professional secrets to keep. So do some sequestered petite jurors and all grand jurors. Government workers and military personnel of any rank have secrets of state to keep. It goes without saying that many military and government professionals must keep quiet. Employment at the Pentagon, the National Security Agency, the White House, the Federal Bureau of Investigation, and the Central Intelligence Agency characteristically demands silence.

In America, we are all supposed to keep quiet about what we learn about others' affairs through our work. This is a rule of civility implicit in social practice. Confidentiality is a civility rule that is exceedingly commonly broken, however, under cover of friendship, trust, promises, and group interest. Paul Gianamore, the financial analyst who told his friend Ryan Evans all about the deals he worked on and heard about, might have said "I'll tell you if you promise not to tell anybody I told you"—how often does one hear that? "I am not supposed to tell, but you really deserve to know" is another familiar prelude to confidentiality breaches. Many such breaches are costless to the person who breaches. Yet the importance of secrecy to achieving the core goals of some work—investment banking, legal representation, psychiatry, military intelligence—is monumental. Our society has enacted coercive, punishing legal rules to reduce the appeal of idle gossip and other unauthorized disclosures in this work.

If employment is construed as a fair bargain, a contract between employees (who understand going in the requirements of the job) and employers (who lay out all the expectations and compensation in advance), the reciprocity argument for imposing coercive duties of confidentiality is plausible. The salaries we receive are the result of a bargain; they reflect a willingness to assume voluntarily the burden of confidentiality for a price. Both the big-time lawyer the public needs for expert advice and the small-time clerical worker the public needs to administer public entitlement programs equally embrace the legal obligations of confidentiality attendant to their work in exchange for compensation. But there is more to the justice argument for confidentiality that "you get paid for it, so do it."

FLOURISHING IN A FREE SOCIETY

The story of the justice of government-imposed confidentiality is richer than the idea of payment-for-services. The case for confidentiality, where the things kept confidential are the personal lives and sensitive secrets of individuals, includes the importance of the state's role in enhancing major modes of flourishing critical to free societies by requiring comparatively minor sacrifices of liberty. Those modes of flourishing matter because of the dignity of individuals, and the importance of respecting their moral agency, autonomy, and welfare. Mandating confidentiality in the context of certain business, government, and professional relationships is consistent with the overall goals and principles of a free society. We need expert advice and a range of competently performed services in order to flourish as citizens. We need others to help us manage risk, meet responsibilities, pursue ambitions. To meet some of these needs, modern liberal societies have set up administrative bureaucracies and fostered the creation of learned professions.

To encourage people to seek out the advice of competent experts, a society can first adopt a system of regulatory monitoring to insure the quality and fitness of professionals; and second, establish rules of confidentiality that protect the flow of information between professionals and their clients. These quality and fitness measures are onerous. They require, for example, that US lawyers pass standardized examinations, complete continuing legal education courses, and be accountable to state disciplinary officials.

Silence imposed on work roles fosters the deep trust needed for the effective delivery of vital services. Legal and medical services are characteristically vital. But so are many government functions and social services and many educational and financial services. If the absence of confidentiality rules turns people away from getting help meeting tax obligations, applying for food stamps, or going to high school, the quality of lives can be substantially diminished, with adverse consequences for the common good.

Rules of occupational silence adopted in the United States often exemplify what I've been calling in this book "strong" privacy mandates. Under threat of punishing sanctions, rules of professional confidentiality in the law and medicine, for example, and evidentiary privileges, give many professionals little choice about whether they opt to keep clients' information secret. As a consequence of confidentiality rules, clients and patients know that doctors and lawyers typically cannot be compelled to reveal their secrets in court. Insider trading laws impose strong confidentiality mandates on the family members of corporate insiders. Insiders themselves are coaxed into silence by common-law confidentiality and fiduciary duties, and by US securities laws that severely punish family and friends caught knowingly and secretly trading on the basis of their "gifts of confidentiality."

An overall prima facie liberal case can be made for occupational silence mandates. Yet the case for government-coerced confidentiality will not be equally strong in every diverse context of business and industry. The unique silence mandate once imposed on a category of US government employees deserves special attention. Under a set of rules put into place during the presidency of Bill Clinton, homosexuals could serve in the US military, but only on the condition that they did not reveal their sexual orientation to others through word or deed. Requiring unwanted silence under threat of serious sanction, the effectively repealed "Don't Ask, Don't Tell" requirements are an example of strongly coercive mandatory privacy laws. They are also an example of coercively silencing public laws not readily defended. Defense officials who believed keeping gays in the closet by force argued that doing so met one of the criteria I have posited here for justly mandating silence: that it "fosters the deep trust needed for the effective delivery of vital services." Yet the claim that gay and straight individuals cannot work in trusting collaboration in the military bespoke prejudice and lacked the weight of solid empirical evidence. An historic signature by President Barak Obama in December 2010 took the muzzle off gay and lesbian service members and the intimate friends and families who knew their secrets.[29]

CONFIDENTIALITY IN CONTEXT

The positive rules governing confidentiality in one field may look significantly different from the rules adopted for another. Confidentiality may not serve the ends of liberal justice in just the same way in every domain of responsibility. The rules of confidentiality applicable to the legal profession and the rationales for the rules are in some respects peculiar to the profession. American lawyers operate in an environment tightly constrained by the constitutional demands of procedural justice. The factual information and secrets a client discloses to her attorney are protected by rules of confidentiality that give her a right against her lawyer in cases of breach. She can sue for malpractice. She can seek to have her lawyer disciplined. She can demand the right to appoint a new attorney or to be given a new trial. Confidential communications between attorneys and clients are protected by the attorney-client privilege, giving attorneys a right to refuse to produce certain requests for information in judicial proceedings.

What is the reason for such rules? In the modern US criminal law content, the rules of professional silence can function as an adjunct to the Fifth Amendment right against self-incrimination, a right defended by Thomas Hobbes on natural law grounds in the *Leviathan,* centuries before the U.S came into existence.[30] The idea of an attorney-client privilege is indeed many centuries old. John Henry Wigmore, the influential authority on the common law of evidence, explained it as having roots in Old World notions of honor and discretion. Wigmore defended the privilege on a number of prudential grounds and one with an Aristotelian flavor having to do with the cultivation of moral habits. Revealing clients secrets amounts to treachery, he urged, something that would "create an unhealthy moral state in the practitioner," the "concrete impropriety of which could not be overbalanced by the recollection of its abstract desirability."[31]

Legal ethicist David Luban has defended attorney-client confidentiality on Kantian grounds, arguing that the duty of confidentiality may be stronger in criminal than in civil representation. To respect human dignity, we treat individuals' claims as asserted in good faith until proven otherwise. We offer fair opportunities to articulate defenses with the help of trusted lawyers. Alan Donegan similarly argued that the attorney-client privilege promotes an aspect of human dignity—namely, the right to put on a credible defense with skilled assistance from an attorney.[32] Monroe H. Freedman defended confidentiality as a duty so strong that an ethical lawyer may in good conscience destroy the credibility of a truthful witness.[33] Robert J. Kulak has argued that the attorney-client privilege has a special relationship with the liberal, free-market ideal of competition: "The basic premise of virtually all our institutions is that open and relatively unrestrained competition among individuals produces the maximum collective good."[34] Liberal individualism entails that a principal (client) be able to entrust an agent (her attorney) with information not disclosed to adversaries.

HEALTHCARE

Ultimately, the strongest and best informed case for the justice of confidentiality mandates will have to be made in context. In the healthcare context, coerced confidentiality can be defended on grounds that include some peculiar to the domain. Good health is of vital importance to human well-being and flourishing. Because confidentiality contributes to good health, confidentiality is properly a major obligation in healthcare, one properly backed by the force of law. While the legal rules of health privacy continue to evolve in the United States in response to genetic testing and imaging technologies, at present entities and individuals who participate in the delivery of healthcare-related services are ascribed legal duties of confidentiality. This includes doctors, nurses, dentists, psychotherapists, and technicians directly involved in patient care, along with hospitals, data processors, insurance companies responsible for managing risk and payments, and health investigators using patient data for biomedical research.

Government may impose confidentiality to limit its own power over citizens. Confidentiality is required by fair relations with government and businesses. Because knowledge is power, special concerns have been raised about the extent to which government collects and manages personal medical information. The case for confidentiality can also be framed as a matter of contractual rights or property. Returning to the pay-for-service idea, patients pay for care and confidentiality and are entitled to it as the benefit of a legally enforceable bargain. Patients "own" information about them and should control its release. Ideals of fair business practices require that personal data collected about individuals be accurate, secure, and disclosed to third parties only with consent. Some patients believe they own personal information about themselves, especially genetic information, and should control its release. But the state interest in imposing confidentiality goes beyond the idea of enforcing contract and property rights.

First, confidentiality encourages seeking medical care. Individuals will be more inclined to seek medical attention if they believe they can do so on a confidential basis. It is reassuring to believe others will not be told without permission that one is unwell or declining, has abused illegal drugs, been unfaithful to one's partner, obtained an abortion, or enlarged one's breasts. Medical confidentiality enables abortion patients, fertility treatment patients, and indeed all patients to exercise constitutionally protected liberties of autonomous medical decision making. Many people are particular about when and whether they share health information. They view the right to make decisions about sharing information as an aspect of their freedom.

Second, confidentiality contributes to full and frank disclosures. Individuals seeking care will be more open and honest if they believe the facts and impressions reported to health providers will remain confidential. It may be easier to speak freely about embarrassing symptoms if one believes the content of what one says will not be broadcast to the world at large. People are often embarrassed and ashamed by symptoms of illness. They may be reluctant to speak, for example, of urinary incontinence. They may be reluctant to reveal disfiguring growths, depression, loss of memory, or delusional thoughts. Caregivers display concern for moral persons with rational interests and feelings when they keep information about their health and health needs private. Individuals concerned about discrimination, shame, or stigma have an interest in controlling the flow of information about their health, and arguably the moral right to do so. Mental and other behavioral healthcare consumers continue to face stigma and discrimination in a world in which getting what they need requires a virtual surrender of confidentiality to a bevy of other people including family members, doctors, social workers, teachers, hospitals, insurers, and law enforcement.

Third, health costs may be lower if people seek prompt medical attention—something they may be more likely to do if confidentiality is reliably promised. Preventive medicine, early diagnosis, and treatment save money. The cost of healthcare and insurance might be considerably higher if people avoided routine check-ups and prompt medical attention because confidentiality was not credibly promised. Individuals will be more inclined to get medical attention if they believe they can do so privately.

Confidentiality thrives as a legal duty and institutional practice, despite the emergent trend towards voluntary openness about medical information. The specifics of health and medical care have become acceptable topics of ordinary conversation outside the family circle. In the United States, public figures have taken the lead, speaking out about their AIDS, erectile dysfunction, dementia, Parkinson's disease, melanoma, prostate enlargement, and breast cancer. Disclosures that would have been considered indelicate or stigmatizing thirty years ago are made freely today, whether to pass the time, share concerns, endorse a pharmaceutical product or educate the public. Carnie Wilson, of the rock band Wilson Phillips, had gastric bypass surgery on the Internet in 2004 to educate the obese public, she said. Over 50,000 people watched her surgery.[35] Citing educational objectives, in 1999 a woman named Patti Derman permitted the Health Network to webcast live her double mastectomy.[36] At the time Derman was a nurse with a family history of breast cancer. Her breasts contained numerous calcifications, a small cancer, and a precancerous lesion. She underwent surgery to remove and reconstruct her breasts on October 20, 1999 at St. Mary Medical Center in Langhorne, Pennsylvania. Her decision to be at the center of the historic broadcast was remarkable at the time. Medical matters are among those that people generally cloak in confidentiality and privacy. Breast cancer and the removal of the breast were, until quite recently, regarded as topics which one did not speak about at all or only obliquely.

Openness about medical matters is often today voluntary. Yet, to a noteworthy degree morals and law compel openness. Medical accountability stands as a feature of modern life. In the wake of the AIDS epidemic, new levels of accountability among sexual partners gained public acceptance. Many people speak openly about health matters with strangers, because they have no choice. They must, as a condition of receiving and paying for healthcare. For example, a family needing the assistance of a county mental health agency unavoidably places reams of sensitive information in the hands of government. The same is true of a family who needs to apply for federal Medicaid to pay for aging or disabled family members' care.

Laws Mandating Health Privacy

The major federal health law in the United States coercing confidentiality is the Health Insurance Portability and Accountability Act (HIPAA), enacted in 1996. Congress delegated authority to the Department of Health and Human Services (HHS) to enact national (1) data privacy (meaning, confidentiality) and (2) data security standards. Data security standards include national standards for electronic transmission of health data and unique health identifiers for financial and administrative purposes. The department issued its Standards for Privacy of Individually Identifiable Health Information on December 28, 2000, after a contentious period of public comment on the proposed rule.

The HHS Office for Civil Rights is responsible for implementing and enforcing the privacy rule. As explained by the HHS, the HIPAA privacy rule applies to "covered entities," defined as healthcare providers who engage in certain electronic transactions, health plans, and so-called healthcare clearinghouses such as hospital billing services and insurers. "Covered entities" are prohibited from using or disclosing individually identifiable "protected health information" without consent, except as provided in the rule.

The HIPAA standards target for protection "individually identifiable" information, broadly defined. Information deemed individually identifiable might include a person's names, exact postal addresses, telephone and fax numbers, e-mail addresses, Social Security Number, medical record numbers, health plan beneficiary numbers, driver's license numbers, auto tag numbers, biometric identifiers, and photographs.

The act also limits the right of covered entities to share protected health information for purpose of marketing products and services to patients. Mental health information is subject to heightened protection under the HIPAA rule. The act does permit disclosure of health information without consent for many routine purposes. It also permits disclosures for purpose of scientific research and judicial process. The act does not address concerns of modesty or physical privacy that patients may have in healthcare settings.

How coercive is HIPAA? Is it paternalistically coercive with respect to patients? Is it coercive with respect to the covered health care entities it regulates? HIPAA is not paternalistic. The act does not require patients to protect their own privacy. While HIPAA requires that others protect the health information of patients, it does not require that patients keep their own health information private. The act does not by design encourage patients to view medical information as the sort of thing that ought to be concealed in cases where concealment is not the patient's own naked preference. HIPAA and its privacy and security rules do not educate the public about the risks of shame, discrimination, or lost opportunity that might flow from voluntary disclosures of health information. An HHS webpage aimed at the general public only asserts that: "Most of us believe that our medical and other health information is private and should be protected, and we want to know who has this information."[37] As if to discourage impractical privacy zealots, the HIPAA privacy rules are characterized as a balance: "The Privacy Rule is balanced so that it permits the disclosure of personal health information needed for patient care and other important purposes."[38] Although HIPAA and its rules are not paternalistic, the rules allow a degree of paternalism by health care providers. HIPAA's default standard is that patients must have access to their own health records and provided copies upon request. But a licensed health care professional is permitted to keep patient mental health information provided to others away from the patient herself to avert serious physical harm to the patient (or a third party).[39]

HIPAA does not confer a private right of action. That is, a patient whose provider breaches confidentiality cannot directly sue. Instead, he or she can file a complaint with HHS for an administrative remedy. The number of such complaints rose steadily from just over 3,000 in 2003 to over 8,000 in 2007. HHS's Office of Civil Rights enforces HIPAA in suits seeking civil and criminal sanctions.[40] Until 2011, HHS typically responded gently to a HIPAA complaint by requiring noncompliant covered health entities to revise their practices. In one case, a patient alleged that a hospital disclosed protected health information when a member of its staff person left a message on the patient's home phone answering machine rather than on her mobile or work phone as requested. To remediate, "the hospital provided additional specific training to staff members whose job duties included leaving messages for patients; and, revised the Department's patient privacy policy."[41] Where "an outpatient surgical facility disclosed a patient's protected health information (PHI) to a research entity for recruitment purposes without the patient's authorization or an Institutional Review Board (IRB) or privacy-board-approved waiver of authorization," the remedy was to require that the facility "revise its written policies and procedures regarding disclosures of PHI for research recruitment purposes to require valid written authorizations; retrain its entire staff on the new policies and procedures; log the disclosure of the patient's PHI for accounting purposes; and send the patient a letter apologizing for the impermissible disclosure."[42] Heralding new toughness, in February 2011, HHS announced penalties of $4.3 million against Cignet Health Center of Prince George's County, Maryland for HIPAA violations and lack of cooperation.

The confidentiality of genetic information is protected by a federal statute passed in 2008. The Genetic Information Non-Discrimination Act (GINA) aims more to prevent discriminatory uses of confidential genetic data by insurers and employers than to protect confidentiality itself. Several years before the law's passage, a company seeking to lower costs through strategic hiring and retention secretly performed genetic tests on workers to determine their susceptibility to develop repetitive stress injuries. Following the passage of GINA, this sort of use of genetic information and underhanded tactics of acquiring it are clearly unlawful.

Tort law enables individuals in the United States to sue for breaches of confidentiality outside the scope of HIPAA. Unauthorized disclosures of personal information have prompted both "public disclosure of private fact" and breach of confidentiality lawsuits.[43] In these personal injury cases, the law permits plaintiffs to seek monetary damages because they believe they have been injured by defendants' nonconsensual disclosure of confidential information. Interesting variants on medical breaches of confidentiality are cases in which a healthcare provider reveals a patient's confidences to a member of the patient's family and sometimes intends no harm by it. For example, in *Humphers v. Interstate* (1985), a physician was sued after he orchestrated the disclosure of his patient's identity to the adult daughter she had placed for adoption in infancy.[44] In *Bagent v. Blessing Care Corporation* (2007), another illustrative case, an Illinois hospital and hospital phlebotomist were sued by a patient whose sister was told of the patient's positive pregnancy test.[45] The phlebotomist falsely assumed the patient had discussed the pregnancy with her sister. In *Yath v. Fairview Clinic* (2009), disclosures to family members were intended to harm. A member of Candace Yath's husband's family worked at a clinic where she was tested and treated for sexually transmitted infections.[46] The curious relative accessed Yath's electronic medical record to find out why she was a patient and then reported to another family member, resulting in someone setting up an insulting MySpace page depicting Yath as a rotten adultress.

The fact that confidentiality is mandated by law makes for special challenges in the technological age. Healthcare providers, even those who work alone or in small groups, must adopt responsible information practices—or fail to do so at their peril. Thirty years ago, a hospital employee who happened to see an acquaintance in the lobby could not swiftly access her medical record and learn why she was there. If a disappointed family member wanted to shame one of her own, she would not have had the ready tool of Myspace or Facebook to let the world in on the health consequences of extra-marital intimacy. The ethical imperatives are clear. Office practices must be designed to protect the identity of clients and the privacy of conversations. Practitioners must be judicious in the collection of information. They should store treatment notes and records in a secure manner. They should share information only with consent or as required by law. They should protect sensitive information in its online and offline forms using locks, passwords, encryption, and other appropriate devices. Sensitive information that is no longer needed should not be retained indefinitely. Healthcare providers must work hard to comply with the legal and ethical demands of confidentiality, and must do so consistently. Healthcare providers must avoid casually discussing confidential client matters in e-mail that may not be entirely private or secure. They must avoid discussing client matters on cell phones in public places, such as in office corridors, hospital lobbies, and on trains.

Mental Health

Philosopher H. J. McCloskey argued that loving family relationships may be inconsistent with privacy.[47] Yet in practice, family members keep secrets from one another and a spouse cannot be presumed a desired confidant. In *Gracey v. Eaker* (2002), a married couple sued their marriage counselor for breach of confidentiality.[48] The couple alleged that the therapist, who had met separately with the spouses, revealed sensitive information that neither spouse had revealed to the other. While this sort of disclosure may be an effective way to address a breakdown in spousal communication, it violates the 2001 Code of Ethics of the American Association of Marriage and Family Therapists, Confidentiality Principle 2.2: "In the context of couple, family or group treatment, the therapist may not reveal any individual's confidences to others in the client unit without the prior written permission of that individual."[49] More to the point, the disclosure resulted in a lawsuit for money damages that the state of Florida deemed legitimate.

Some would argue that confidentiality is inadequately coerced in the mental and behavioral health domains. Certain practices that are not illegal raise ethical concerns. Medical and behavioral health providers must be wary of technological risk and abuse. Social workers and therapists commonly videotape sessions for training purposes or to help patients see themselves as others see them. Just because photographs and videos are easy to make and potentially useful in clinical training, does not mean one's clients should be called upon to sacrifice the privacy of their homes, communications, and expressions of emotion. One should never record a conversation with a patient without the patient's express consent, and even then, professionals must be circumspect about motives for asking. These days, a video recording could easily wind up on YouTube or viewed disrespectfully by employees of a county mental health agency. Data security breaches are so common at hospitals, health maintenance organizations, and health agencies that it is important to take special care in the creation and storage of digital recordings of patients.

The duty of confidentiality is a core consensus norm within healthcare, but it can be abused by practitioners who believe they are in full compliance. Health professionals can offend privacy values in ways that may not strictly speaking violate the law or the recognized, positive ethical standards of their professions. For example, a psychiatrist with a small two-room office suite treats both adults and children. As parents sit with young patients in the doctor's cramped waiting room, an adult patient might be overheard graphically describing and the effects of her antidepressants on her ability to have orgasms and enjoy intercourse. This psychiatrist does not have a noise machine outside her office door. Her walls are thin. Has she behaved unethically? She has certainly behaved thoughtlessly, even though she has gestured towards the technical requirements of confidentiality by not discussing her patients' problems with others and by holding sessions in a "private" office suite with a separate waiting room.

Mental health patients and their families are often bewildered by ethically contradictory institutional confidentiality practices. Imagine a ten-year-old boy hospitalized for observation following a suicide threat. After checking their son into the pediatric mental hospital designated by their medical insurers, the boy's parents ask to see the room where he will sleep. They are told that this is not possible, because there are other children in the hospital whose privacy must be respected. But when the parents return for visiting hours the next day, they and their son, along with all the other sick children and their parents, are led into a small common lounge. A physician comes into the group visitation lounge discuss a particular child's medication changes with her parents, in plain hearing of the other visitors. Confidentiality is honored when it is easy to do so (denying a parent the right to see a patient's room) but not when it is not (accommodating thirty visitors during a designated visiting hour during which busy doctors need to update numerous parents).

Waiver

In the United States, legal rules of professional silence generally allow for what is called a knowing waiver. A client, patient, penitent, or customer may authorize a trusted professional to tell what she knows. The thief may want her lawyer to disclose his nefarious secrets and broker a deal with prosecutors. Although clients may readily waive confidentiality, attorneys of their own accord may not.

But government policy makers have not permitted waiver options in every instance. Are there reasons for mandating professional silence that should lead us to refuse waiver? Government can care more about our privacy than we do. Thus, an elementary school student cannot waive the confidentiality requirements that federal law imposes on her teachers. As discussed earlier, privacy advocates have opposed allowing tax preparers to use or disclose tax return data, even with the filer's consent.

In some instances, the capacity to waive the protection of rules of coerced professional silence furthers aims that feminists have commended. There are cases in which one might applaud individuals who elect to alienate their privacy rights. Sometimes secrets need to be disclosed as an antidote to victimization. It is a good thing that the law allows waiver in these instances.

When Rabbit Howls (1987) is the curious memoir of Truddi Chase, a psychotherapy patient who maintained that she had been subjected to abuse by an uncommonly cruel stepfather.[50] Chase was raised in rural America. She reports in her book that her stepfather sexually assaulted her. The first assault, an unthinkable act of penile-vaginal penetration, occurred at the age of two. Later assaults included forcible sex with dogs and farm animals. Severe physical and emotional abuse continued until the young woman left home at sixteen. She was ultimately diagnosed with disassociative identity ("multiple personality") disorder (DID).

As a result of her trauma, Chase developed a bizarre mental illness that impaired her adult relationships and undermined her career as a realtor. She reported repeatedly blacking out, making odd remarks, losing track of time, and feeling dizzy. She sought the help of numerous mental health professionals and was eventually diagnosed with disassociative identity disorder; her therapist believed she had developed as many as ninety distinct personalities to deal with her past.

Professional psychotherapists, like physicians, inhabit a world of legally mandated privacy: professional silence. What their patients tell them in the course of care is supposed to be kept confidential. Psychotherapists who breach confidentiality by disclosing patient information to third parties expose themselves to liability for malpractice and invite other legal problems under state and federal law. Because DID is a rare disorder, imagine the difficulty of keeping silent when you are a therapist who believes on good evidence that one of your patients is afflicted. You are only human.

You want to share your excitement with family, friends, and colleagues. Conversation about a case like could entertain a dull dinner party, enliven a date. You could write a fascinating book! But there is a legal barrier: confidentiality, in this case, is coerced. It may be easy to abide by the rule of silence when you are caring for a predictable stream of depressed and anxious patients, but if you get an unusual case, you will want to talk about it. Now the privacy mandate suddenly feels like a burden. It is real coercion.

Chase's therapist did not have to face the problem of embracing unwanted privacy restrictions, as his patient freely and aggressively waived her right to confidentiality. Chase walked across the threshold of care demanding that her therapy not be private. She wanted to share her secrets. She wanted to become a crusader for the truth of domestic violence and abusive incest. Accordingly, she requested that all of her therapy sessions be tape-recorded, and they were. Chase, who died in 2010, believed the recordings helped her therapist substantiate her highly unusual diagnosis. The book she wrote about her experience of abuse and treatment relies on the recordings. Using the recordings, she shared her experience with her therapist's students and colleagues, and with victims and perpetrators of sexual abuse. Viewed as a credible DID survivor, she appeared on the famous *Oprah Winfrey Show*.

Traditionally, the sessions of a psychotherapist and patient are sealed in bonds of confidence. However, it is important that the law permits beneficiaries of professional silence to waive the requirement. Voluntary waiver can put an end to dysfunctional secrecies. To be able to tell the public what one is expected to hide or share with mental health professionals can have important therapeutic and educative advantages. But as beneficial as shedding secrecy can be, compelled professional silence remains an important category of mandatory privacy. The laws that require confidentiality and secrecy of lawyers, physicians, therapists, and clergy are sound public policy—coercion without unwarranted paternalism, subordination, or inequality.

Voluntarily disclosing mental health secrets can be an antidote to sexual victimization—but refusing to disclose such secrets under cover of law can be a way of avoiding accountability for alleged sexual abuse. A priest used both the psychiatrist-patient privilege and the clergy-penitent privilege to seek to withhold mental health records in a personal injury case brought by a former parishioner who alleged sexual harassment. Fortunately for the alleged victim, the court required that the priest's records be turned over to her. The court held that the priest had constructively waived his right of confidentiality by sharing his records with another priest, who acted in an unprivileged administrative capacity on behalf of the church.

Unauthorized disclosure of secrets revealed in counseling and therapy can function as a way of dominating women. The New York Court of Appeals held that Orthodox rabbis, who believed it was their religious duty to disclose a female congregant's secrets to her husband, may not be sued for breach of confidence. The court held that the First

Amendment prevented it from punishing a practicing cleric for breaching confidentiality when required by a religious duty.[51] The court thus prevented Chani Lightman from winning a suit against disloyal rabbis who sided with her husband in a bitterly fought divorce and child custody dispute.[52] Lightman's husband, a successful physician, wanted full custody of the pair's children. The rabbis claimed that Ms. Lightman admitted to faults her spouse needed to know about, including discontinuing Orthodox bathing requirements to avoid sex with her husband and initiating a social relationship with a male friend. Yet it was far from clear that Lightman's rabbis deserved to hide behind their faith. Several rabbinical experts told the *Jewish News* that the Jewish law of *lashon hara* instructs people to refrain from gossip or other harmful language, and breach of confidentiality is an ethical failing people doing therapeutic work, whether as rabbis or counselors, need to understand.[53] This extraordinary case gives rise to questions of general import. If patients can waive confidentiality at will in the public interest, why can't their therapists breach it at will in the interest of the public or some segment of it?

Exception

Healthcare providers are normally bound to keep quiet. There are, of course, exceptions to the general rule. A pharmacist repeatedly asked to fill prescriptions written by a particular physician for a particular patient for suspicious quantities of controlled substances can choose to notify authorities. In certain instances disclosure, rather than nondisclosure, is the mandate. Professionals and the general public embrace exceptions to the rules of professional silence in the medical context.

There are two major recognized exceptions to the obligations of professional confidentiality in medicine, and both exceptions imply that physical health and safety are more important than the confidentiality of medical records and relationships. First, all healthcare providers are obligated to report child neglect and abuse uncovered while treating patients. Parents who bring a child to the emergency room covered with cigarette burns or suffering from multiple unexplained fractures or severe malnutrition are supposed to be reported to child welfare authorities.

Second, mental health providers have ethical and legal duties to warn potential victims of a mentally disturbed person's violent intentions. Again, psychotherapists are expected to keep their patients' secrets. The American Psychological Association's (APA) ethical code requires that "Psychologists respect... the rights of individuals to privacy, confidentiality, and self determination."[54] Psychotherapists are not permitted to reveal infidelity, closeted sexual orientation, or ruined finances. Yet psychotherapists are required by state law to breach confidentiality as necessary to warn potential victims of patients' violent intentions. The landmark decision *Tarasoff v. Regents of the*

University of California in 1976 imposed on California mental health providers a legal duty to warn potential victims.[55] In that case, a therapist failed to warn a woman that a psychotherapy patient had made a credible threat against the woman's life. Although the therapist notified the police, she did not notify the endangered woman, whom her patient then killed. The family of murder victim Tatiana Tarasoff sued the therapist and her university employer, seeking damages for breach of a duty to warn, and won. Others states followed California in adopting the duty to warn. Psychotherapists must also disclose mental illness to third parties to secure the hospitalization of a person under their care whose mental illness makes them a suicide threat or violent threat to others.

There is another exception to the rule of professional silence. Therapists can speak to their own professional therapists. Because all professional therapists are bound by the rule of silence, a therapist who seeks the professional services of another therapist may disclose client confidences in confidence.

CONCLUSION

The laws that demand confidence-keeping by professionals are generally popular—that is, they are generally applauded by the public and embraced by practitioners in the field, along with experts who study the field. This popularity stems in part from the fact that the laws take sensibly into account notions of what should and should not be exceptions to duties of silence.

The laws that require confidentiality of healthcare professionals are open to criticism, but are also generally popular. The medical confidentiality laws are known to include a number of exceptions. The laws do not require the keeping of the confidences of child predators who are molesting children under their care (the child abuse/neglect exception), or mentally ill psychiatric patients who announce plans to murder innocent acquaintances (the *Tarasoff* rule exception). Indeed, the law imposes a duty to report child abuse in the first instance and a duty to warn potential victims in the second.

The people who manage businesses have a number of obligations of confidentiality. First, they are duty-bound to remain silent about trade secrets. The laws that require confidence-keeping by corporate executives with access to valuable trade secrets (such as the formula for a soft drink) do not have major exceptions, and their popularity depends on their being rather absolute. Indeed it is difficult to imagine a situation in which we would regard it as warranted for an employee of Coca-Cola to disclose the formula for Coke Zero.

The laws that require confidentiality of lawyers are also open to criticism, and may be somewhat less popular. The reason is that many people are ambivalent about the adversary system that enables lawyers to profit handsomely from keeping the confidences of despicable people. In a notorious case, Syracuse attorney Frank Armani represented Robert Garrow, a man being prosecuted for murder. Armani knew that his client was guilty and also knew the secret location of the corpses of two other people Garrow told him he had murdered.[56] But the ethical law of attorney confidentiality and privilege are helped by a number of exceptions that make the rule of silence more palatable. The laws that require legal confidentiality do not compel an attorney to remain silent about a client's plot to blow up a public building (the future crimes exception), nor do they require an attorney to secret away a murder weapon or written kidnap plan given to her by a client or a client's friend (the smoking gun exception).[57]

Discretion and reserve are high-toned virtues, reflecting the need for externalized restraint. Information sharing is acceptable; go too far, however, and you risk being branded a gossip, chatterbox, snitch, or tattler. Keeping appropriate silences has been recognized as a challenging goal of personal virtue since the days of Aristotle. Ethics often demands we do things that feel difficult, until they become a habit.

When persons obtain knowledge of others in the course of their work, they incur an ethical responsibility to comply with a complex set of civility rules, including rules of confidentiality. When social importance is attached to silence, rules of silence may be spelled out in ethical codes or enacted into law. Plenty of financial incentives exist for voluntarily assuming especially difficult legal burdens of silence. Yet payment for secrecy is not the whole story of why confidentiality is justly coerced. The larger story is the dignitarian one of respecting the moral agency, autonomy, and welfare of citizens of a liberal democracy and requiring practices of occupational confidentiality that further such respect.

6

RACIAL PRIVACY

Much of policy making surrounding personal information is premised on the notion that government has a key role in the protection of sensitive data. Data can be called sensitive because it falls into a category of data presumed worthy of concealment, such as health or genetic information. Data can also be considered sensitive when it concerns groups of people, such as children and the elderly, whose vulnerabilities merit special protection. Finally, data can be called sensitive if it falls at the intersection of norms regarding the importance of protecting certain data from disclosure and certain people from harm: the genetic data of children merits special protection, for example, because genetic data is subject to concealment and because children are vulnerable. There is a politics of sensitive data that seldom gets the attention it deserves. From a political perspective we might want some data to be considered sensitive in order to limit access to it, keeping it out of the hands of people whom we fear will use it in support of policies with which we do not agree. Or, we might want certain data not to be deemed sensitive, so that it will be available for use to further policies with which we do agree. The debates over racial privacy in the United States is the perfect context for exploring the politics of sensitive data.

WHAT IS SENSITIVE DATA?

"Sensitive data" is not a Platonic essence. It is a pragmatic concept. We consider information sensitive in a given place and time because of the harm to welfare or dignity we believe its collection, use, or disclosure entails. Moreover, as citizens and consumers in a certain time and place, we label data held by government and businesses as sensitive to reflect concerns about whether it is accurate, whether it is secure, and how long it will be retained. In the early twentieth century, the fact that a person was born to an unmarried mother might have been considered a sensitive piece of information, one that could result in a diminished social status; contemporary Americans no longer look down on children born outside of marriage, and do not regard legitimacy status as sensitive information.

If you ask the typical American today to list the broad categories of sensitive information, they might start with information of the sort contained in health, financial, and education records they know to be protected by law. They might add that sexual orientation is sensitive information in some contexts and that criminal histories are sensitive, too. If you asked about the categories of people whose personal information is sensitive enough to merit special legal protection, they would likely mention children, the elderly, people with HIV/AIDS, and the seriously mentally ill.

Understanding sensitive data as a pragmatic category reserved for information we believe merits special protection, should race be considered an important category of sensitive information? Should people belonging to racial minority groups be seen as vulnerable to privacy and data-protection harms, along with people who are young, ill, and elderly? Do we already think of race and racial minorities this way?

In the United States we routinely speak of sexual, medical, and financial privacy. We also refer to family, electronic communications, and online privacy. All of these privacies receive explicit protection in the law. None is treated as an absolute, unqualified right against public or private entities; in fact, national security, law enforcement, public health, free speech, and even routine business and administrative conveniences are cited by our courts and legislatures as legitimate limits on privacy.

Several years ago, there was a novel discussion in the United States of yet another category of privacy potentially meriting legal protection: racial privacy.[1] The United States has no national racial privacy statute as such, and no prominent racial privacy provisions within its major information policies. It is worth considering why. A broader, more philosophical question worth addressing is whether racial privacy is a vital category of legal protection in the kind of just, free society the United States aspires to be. In 2003, California voters rejected Proposition 54, a proposed Racial Privacy Initiative that would have outlawed state collection of race and ethnicity data. The U.S. public is ambivalent about racial privacy, is not clamoring for racial privacy, and a majority may oppose the idea of racial privacy laws.

But in other western-style democracies, popular, existing laws limit the collection and dissemination of race, ethnicity, and other population-group data, even for some benign purposes.[2] Is an ethically imperative body of law missing in the United States? Is it missing because American culture is a "racially saturated field" in which blacks, for example, are not allowed autonomous modes of anonymity but must retain identities as "impure, savage, immoral, stupid, dull in imagination, ugly, the white man's burden, evil, simian, childlike, and naturally fit to serve whites"?[3] Or is it missing because it makes no practical sense and would impair the quest for racial equality? After all, the United States is governed by a wealth of antidiscrimination laws and is a signatory to the legally binding United Nations International Convention on the Elimination of All Forms of Racial Discrimination, which opposes "any distinction, exclusion, restriction or preference based on race, colour, descent, or national or ethnic origin which has the purpose or effect of nullifying or impairing the recognition, enjoyment or exercise... of human rights and fundamental freedoms."[4]

A MISSING JURISPRUDENCE

Informational privacy receives protection in contemporary U.S. law through a large volume of constitutional, statutory, and common law. However, racial information receives little legal protection. This has always been true. Infamous Supreme Court decisions like *Dred Scott v. Sandford* (1857), *Plessy v Ferguson* (1896), and *Korematsu v. United States* (1944) might have prompted mid-twentieth century lawmakers to prohibit government classification by race as an antidote to slavery and discrimination.[5] But they did not. In these cases peoples of African, mixed, and Japanese ancestry were denied equal procedural and substantive rights solely on the basis of race. Dred Scott was returned to slavery, Homer Plessy was relegated to segregated train cars, and Fred Korematsu was dispatched to a concentration camp. As a consequence of the *Korematsu* decision, which upheld restrictions on Japanese Americans after announcing that all restrictions based on race were immediately suspicious, race has come to be treated as a "suspect classification" in U.S. equal protection law.[6] The Supreme Court held in 2005 that an unwritten policy of the California Department of Corrections under which prisoners were segregated based on their races was subject to strict judicial scrutiny, because race was a suspect class and especially so when used in a coercive environment.[7] But protecting fundamental liberties and righting the wrongs of the past have not included definitive constitutional interpretation or federal law banning official notice of a person's race.

Far from banning racial identification, U.S. legislation requires classification by race. Concealing race is not an option because racial identification and self-identification are mandated by law. As recently as 1982, the state of Louisiana refused to allow Susie Guillory Phipps to change her official race designation from black to white, even though she and her family have always lived as whites and look completely Caucasian; Louisiana records said that Ms. Phipps had "three thirty-seconds" part "Negro blood."[8] Race designations no longer appear on every birth certificate and marriage license, but they do appear in school, employment, and health records. Aided by efficient electronic technologies, business and government routinely compile and share racial, ethnic, and other population-group statistics today.

The concept of racial privacy makes rare appearances in U.S. law—but it slips a quiet, problematic foot into the courthouse from time to time, as I will later describe. Racial privacy requirements remains absent from the massive, main body of information privacy law. Moreover, under existing U.S. law, compiling race data or disclosing another's race is not per se an established ground for civil liability, criminal punishment, or constitutional objection.

First, a number of state constitutions now explicitly protect the right to privacy, but without special reference to racial privacy. The Florida Constitution's right to privacy provision provides that: "Every natural person has the right to be let alone and free from governmental intrusion into the person's private life except as otherwise provided herein. This section shall not be construed to limit the public's right of access to public records and meetings as provided by law."[9] California's provides that "All people are by nature free and independent and have inalienable rights. Among these are enjoying and defending life and liberty, acquiring, possessing, and protecting property, and pursuing and obtaining safety, happiness, and privacy."[10] Neither mentions race. When state constitutes do mention domains of privacy, they tend to mention homes or correspondence. For example, the Constitution of the State of Washington provides that: "No person shall be disturbed in his private affairs, or his home invaded, without authority of law."[11]

The federal constitution does not expressly protect race data, and federal courts have upheld the constitutionality of race and ethnic data collection.[12] In 1976, the United States won a suit against the state of New Hampshire, which had refused to adhere to federal race and ethnic data collection requirements under Title VII of the Civil Rights Act of 1964 and regulations of the Equal Employment Opportunity Commission. The Court rejected New Hampshire's argument that requiring race and ethnicity disclosures violates the federal constitution. Asking states to provide racial and ethnic data to the federal government is both constitutional and consistent with the goal of equal of employment opportunity, the Court determined.[13]

Neither the expectations of privacy protected under the Fourth Amendment nor the privacy protected under the substantive due process holdings of *Griswold v. Connecticut* (1965) and *Roe v. Wade* (1973) extend to racial data. Our homes and many of our intimate decisions are private, but not, under these cases, are our races. One federal judge made this point outright in a 1978 decision. Teachers, school board officials, and a parent-teacher association in New York sought to prevent city, state, and federal government from collecting racial and ethnic data on public school teachers and supervisors. The government wanted the information to help with their efforts to remedy discrimination against minority children in teacher assignments. The court held that requiring the collection and reporting of race and ethnic data was lawful. Data collection did not involve a search and seizure within the meaning of the Fourth Amendment or violate the substantive due process privacy principles laid down in *Griswold* or *Roe*. "The Constitution itself does not condemn the collection of this data," the court wrote.[14] The Supreme Court's 1977 decision in *Whalen v. Roe* recognized a Fourteenth Amendment interest in informational privacy, but with no hint that race information would merit the privacy protection medical information plainly did.[15]

Second, although an expanding number of state and federal statutes protect privacy, lawmakers have enacted none specifically to protect racial privacy. The focus of federal statutory lawmaking has been privacy protections for federal records containing personally identifying information, health data, credit, tax, and financial data, along with school records, video rental records, Internet transactions, and electronic communications.[16]

Third, although state common law recognizes privacy rights, race has not been generally treated as a private matter protected by the intrusion and public disclosure torts. Nor is it an aspect of identity whose distortion or appropriation is wrongful under the false light, misappropriation, or publicity torts.[17] In *Cheesman v. Ameritite* (2010), a federal district court in the state of Washington dismissed the invasion of privacy tort claim of a woman of Filipino ancestry for reasons that capture a pervasive attitude about race information in the United States. Ameritite, a company that provides title and escrow services, hired Ms. Cheesman but soon fired her. She claimed discrimination under federal civil rights statutes and invasion of privacy under state law, but the court found neither. The court held termination of Cheesman for well-documented incompetence was legitimate and nondiscriminatory; asking about her race, her children's race, and her national origin was "not highly offensive to a reasonable person because people regularly ask new acquaintances similar questions."[18] Derogatory racial slurs are poor manners, but not generally torts. It appears that revealing someone's race without consent would not count as "highly offensive to a reasonable person" either.[19] Collecting and disclosing race data is more typically lawful than unlawful in the United States.

Notwithstanding the historic election of a president with African ancestry in 2008, race problems in the United States remain. Combating racial discrimination has been a major public policy priority since slavery was officially abolished in the 1860s. Post-Civil War amendments to the constitution, principally the Thirteenth, Fourteenth, and Fifteenth amendments, sought to end slavery and governmental discrimination against African Americans. The Civil Rights Act of 1964 prohibited state and federal government, larger employers, and places of public accommodations from discriminating on the basis of race and related traits, color, creed, and national origin.

Government prohibitions on collecting and reporting race have not emerged as favored paths to addressing the problem of racial discrimination. Policy makers in the United States have generally viewed racial disclosures as key to righting racial wrongs and ending pernicious social and economic disparities. Maintaining racial statistics premised on racialized population-group classifications has been mandatory for public schools, larger employers, and lenders. Controversial affirmative action, racial quotas, and set-aside policies require public and private employers to collect race and similar population-group information about individuals. Within federal discrimination law,

Congress and the courts do not define race data collection as racial discrimination. Federal entities freely collect racial, ethnic, and national origin data about individuals and use the data that they collect for a variety of public purposes.

The constitutionally mandated national decennial census collects population-group data, requiring Americans to classify themselves (or tolerate being classified) in one or more ever-changing official racial and ethnic categories. Race data collection continues in the face of mixed-race families protesting racial pigeonholing, and scientists reporting the limited biological basis for the racialization of phenotypical and cultural population-group differences among human beings. The fifteen official categories of the 2010 census included white, African American/black/Negro, Native American, and Asian/Pacific Islander. A question apart from the race question asked whether respondents were Hispanic, Latino, or Spanish. The option first offered in 2000 of selecting more than one race was offered again in 2010. About 2 percent of Americans identified themselves as having more than one race in the 2000 census, although the number of children and young adults claiming more than one race was higher. In 2010, a person whose ancestors were once classified as octoroon, mulatto, or Negro could classify herself as "African American/black/Negro," and also had the option of selecting an additional race from among the categories provided or naming "some other race." She could also designate herself as Hispanic, Latino, or Spanish.

Privacy challenges to race data collection for purposes of the census have failed. In the illustrative *Morales v. Daley* case from 2000, the plaintiffs argued in a federal district court in Texas that requiring answers to race, ethnicity, legitimacy, alienage, and sexual preference questions on U.S. Census forms violated both privacy and equal protection guarantees.[20] Plaintiffs also objected to an additional question for "Hispanic" persons. The court held in 2000 that the offending census questions intruded on an individual's privacy only to a limited degree, given the methods used to collect the data and the statutory assurance that the answers and attribution would be kept confidential. The court also found that the state interest in gathering the information was significant and that Congress had never insisted on a mere headcount alone.

The government's use of racial categories is not exhausted by census-taking and civil rights law enforcement and monitoring. For example, polices of the National Institutes of Health require inclusion of racial minorities in medical research. Policies further require that research investigators describe the racial and ethnic composition of any proposed study population and address racial and ethnic issues when developing a research design and sample size. To take another example, the federal government acknowledges and embraces racial classification in pursuit of its public education mission. The Federal Trade Commission makes public education materials available to the public in English and Spanish at no cost. But in some instances the public is invited to select race-specific versions of official agency materials. The assumption seems to be that community outreach is more effective if it involves a kind of racial matching: individuals may be more receptive to a public announcement about the availability of the National Do Not Call Registry, for example, if it bears photographs of people who look like them. Hence, it is possible to request materials by referring to the race (and also age and family status) of the persons depicted.[21] The public can select Hispanic, Caucasian, and African American versions of the announcement.

If racial classification by government is immoral and unjust, the evidence suggests that few U.S. Americans see it that way. Historically, many countries have engaged in race-conscious census-taking and maintained race registries; the United States is not exceptional.[22] Americans commonly embrace racial, ethnic, and national origin classifications as their own, even those that are of recent vintage such as "Hispanic." Race and ethnicity are matters of self-identification and pride. Many African Americans and Native Americans see official group classification schemes as essential to reparations claims or resolving disputes over entitlement to tribal assets. Racial classification is popular with proponents of affirmative action in education and employment. Public health experts believe racialized population-group identification is useful for targeting appropriate health interventions and resources. African Americans joke about the seeming illegality of "Driving While Black," given that they are more likely than whites to be stopped by police. All Americans understand the risks of appearing to be Middle Eastern, Mexican, or Chinese, but few voice wholesale objections to group classification by employers and government.

At the same time that some experts are discounting race as a social construct erected atop observed variations in human phenotype and documented or remembered ancestry, others are glorifying racial self-understanding through science. Entrepreneurs have marshaled emergent genetic technologies to create genetic testing that promises to reveal perhaps undetected racial ancestry. A Sarasota, Florida firm purported to use DNA testing to tell people their hidden race or race mixtures, primarily for entertainment value.[23] Yet racial identification is more often about pride in group membership than entertainment.

A cynic bent on access to affirmative action benefits reserved for racial minorities—for example, for establishing membership in a well-off Native American tribe—could turn to genetic testing. A Texas company called Family Tree DNA—Genealogy by Genetics, Ltd. claimed the ability to determine whether a person has Native American ancestry. For about $300, the company inspects mitochondrial DNA and Y-chromosomes to search for markers shared by the vast majority of known Native Americans. The service perhaps could, according to one analyst, "help [Black Seminole] Freedmen identify their American Indian ancestry and thus resolve their membership problems."[24]

Ferreting out hidden race using genetic analysis is also proposed as a way to improve the nation's health. Research to uncover race-group linked genetic markers is ongoing. Medications (e.g., heart drug BiDil for African Americans) and medical protocols are already aimed at specific groups. Individuals might want to know their hidden racial ancestries as part of measures to address health risks.

The motivations for questing after knowledge of race are varied. People want to establish entitlements, but also to know who they really are, corroborate family stories, and reconnect with kin. Harvard professor Henry Louis Gates hosted an illustrative documentary television series in 2006. Gates, an African American, asked a number of other prominent African Americans to submit to genetic testing to uncover their racial ancestry.[25] Remarkably, a famous neurosurgeon, an astronaut, a writer, a professor, and several entertainers agreed. If race data is private, these highly successful and educated Americans showed little reluctance to go public.

With the support of his extremely light-skinned elderly father and aunt, Gates also submitted to testing. As revealed in the documentary, Gates's tests suggest that he is substantially of European ancestry, notwithstanding his brown skin. Tests performed on behalf of Gates's celebrity guests revealed Asian ancestry in the case of a brown-skinned astronaut with almond-shaped eyes, and the lack of long-presumed Native American ancestry in the case of a black actress. Tests performed on one celebrity purportedly revealed evidence not only of race, but of actual tribal ancestry on the African continent. Gates made a journey to Africa to introduce the young African performer to a tribe whose genetic markers said he could claim as distant kin.

An Unpopular Referendum

A proposed change in the California state constitution would have gone against the grain of U.S. jurisprudence by mandating racial privacy. Affirmative action foe Ward Connerly spearheaded an effort to enact California Proposition 54, a so-called Racial Privacy Initiative, in 2003.[26] The referendum would have amended the state constitution to prohibit state officials from collecting data about a person's race, ethnicity, color, or national origin.[27] Californians voted down the initiative in an October special election in which they also voted to replace former governor Gray Davis with actor Arnold Schwarzenegger. Proposition 54 was an effort to undermine race-conscious public policies across the board by mandating a form of privacy that few people really wanted, and few people really cared about.[28]

Had the initiative passed, the state university system would no longer have been able to collect racial data from its current or prospective students, unless required by federal law. Information needed to monitor public elementary and secondary education would not have been available. The Racial Privacy Initiative's passage would have meant educators could not "determine accurately whether California's diverse student population is being adequately served in [its] schools, whether certain groups are facing higher dropout rates, whether students are in need of particular services, whether they have access to advanced courses or are being warehoused in special education classes, and whether they are merely enrolling in the state's colleges or are graduating from them."[29]

The implications of prohibiting racial data collection would have reached far beyond education, however, into the realms of public employment, health, and law enforcement. The initiative would have impaired collecting statistical data on conditions which impact different racial groups differently, including sickle cell anemia, breast cancer, HIV/AIDS, and Tay-Sachs disease; reporting and gathering data on racial profiling by police, hate crimes, and organized hate groups;[30] and, finally, keeping track of discrimination in housing, public accommodations and employment.[31]

Supporters of Proposition 54 argued that a racial privacy law would further the civil rights goal of nondiscrimination.[32] A number of nationally prominent opponents of affirmative action and so-called reverse discrimination supported the measure, including Shelby Steele, George Will, and Thomas Sowell. At the same time, the Racial Privacy Initiative attracted nationally prominent opposition. The National Association for the Advancement of Colored People (NAACP) voted to oppose the initiative. The initiative's limit on state race data collection would have meant that authorities could not "understand the positive or negative impacts of their policies or programs on ethnic communities including in the area of education, delivery of public services and public assistance," the NAACP concluded.[33] African American Julian Bond blasted the initiative as a "deceptively titled effort to eviscerate civil rights enforcement." As long as race counts, we have to count race, Bond said.

The Racial Privacy Initiative had little to do with traditional privacy concerns, but the rhetoric of privacy may have won it credibility in some quarters. As explained by Stanford University professor Richard Banks, the initiative's rhetoric was "postured to appeal to the popular notion of preserving privacy in much the same fashion as one preserves medical history, credit information, or religious affiliation from prying eyes," and "the race/privacy nexus reinforces the traditional image of the state as the oppressive force against which individuals struggle to maintain their identity."[34]

The racial privacy measure in California failed, but it placed an important set of questions on the public agenda. Assuming we can speak meaningfully of race at all, should race be protected by privacy rights? Is racial privacy a requirement of liberal justice? If justice requires racial privacy, ought it to be mandated through law? And as a practical matter, what type of laws can prevent and deter use of information that exists not only in paper and electronic files, but also in a person's face, name, pattern of association, and historical memory?

Recognition in the Courtroom

Widespread support for a racial privacy law could not be garnered in California, one of the most populous and racially diverse states. But the noisy defeat of Proposition 54 should not drown out the quiet life the concept of racial privacy has begun to play in isolated U.S. courtrooms. Express and implicit racial privacy claims have been asserted both in state and federal court. Isolated racial privacy claims have forced a few judges to grapple with the question of whether, when, and why racial information should be immune from collection or disclosure.

Typically these judges embrace both the concept of racial privacy and racial privacy as a legitimate legal interest, but reject the racial privacy claims before them. Courts do not reject racial privacy claims as a matter of principle. They do not argue, for example, that racial privacy is an incoherent or pernicious concept, or that individuals lack cognizable interests in the privacy of racial information. Rather, racial privacy claims are losing out in balancing tests that compare the heft of legitimate interests in race privacy against the heft of legitimate interests in race disclosure. Most judges are concluding on the facts in individual cases that the public interest in race data disclosure outweighs both public and the private interests in race concealment. Courts have rejected racial privacy claims that would block efficient attempts to fight racial profiling or employment and housing discrimination.

Profiling in New Hampshire

In the spring of 2000, the New Hampshire Civil Liberties Union (NHCLU) discovered that the city of Manchester Police Department had a policy of photographing drivers stopped in their cars but not arrested.[35] The photographs were taken with the consent of the detainees in question. The NHCLU decided to request information about the police photographing practice and to seek access to the actual photographs. The NHCLU believed an analysis of the photographs could reveal race or gender-bias in the pattern of officers' decisions concerning whom to stop.

New Hampshire has a statute analogous to the federal Freedom of Information Act (FOIA) called the Right to Know Law. To make government more accountable to the general public, the both the federal and the analogous state laws grant members of the public broad access to records held or compiled by officials. The FOIA contains an express exception—5 U.S.C. (b)(6)—limiting access to "medical, personnel, and similar files" that contain private information about named individuals. The New Hampshire Right to Know Law includes an express exemption, whereby officials need not disclose records whose disclosure could constitute an invasion of privacy.[36]

When the NHCLU filed a request for photographs under the Right to Know Law, the request was turned down. The law grants neither journalists nor civil liberties groups special access to records deemed private. The municipality of Manchester maintained that "the release of the photographs would be an unwarranted invasion of the privacy of the individuals in the pictures," and also that disclosure "would interfere with and reveal investigative techniques."[37] The NHCLU sued for access to the information and photos, and won. The city took an unsuccessful appeal to the Supreme Court of New Hampshire.

Writing for the state high court, Chief Justice David A. Brock argued that the case called for balancing the public interest in disclosure to unmask racial and sexual profiling (asserted by the civil liberties group) against the government's interest in nondisclosure to protect investigative techniques and the individual privacy interest in nondisclosure (both asserted by the City of Manchester).

The court's analysis of the privacy interests individuals were presumed to have in their photographs was brief. The New Hampshire statute did not specify the type of state-held information that should be deemed private, and Justice Brock declined a general characterization of his own. Lacking specific legislative guidance, he simply assumed the premise that individuals have a privacy interest in photographs that disclose their faces, races, and sexes. Emphasizing the minimal character of a privacy interest in the face in isolation from other identifying information, Justice Brock then quickly concluded that: "Any privacy interest in the photographs at issue does not outweigh the public's interest in disclosure."[38] Brock stressed that no inference about the person's involvement with a crime can logically be drawn, no personal identifying information such as name, address or date of birth would be provided; and the photographs did not "reveal intimate details of individuals' lives."[39]

The court noted that the police photographs were not stigmatizing or taken without the subjects' consent: "Although the defendant correctly asserts that individuals have a strong interest in not being associated unwarrantedly with alleged criminal activity... that assertion is not relevant here because the pictures at issue were taken with the consent of the subjects, and the trial court explicitly exempted from disclosure photographs that are or were part of police investigations, including pictures of victims, witnesses and suspects."[40]

Faces can reveal races, and under New Hampshire law, people have a privacy interest in photographs of their faces. Yet because faces are typically evidence of race, and race information is vital to municipal accountability for police misconduct, facial photographs taken with consent may be shared with a private civil liberties entity for purposes of proving or disproving racial profiling, and without seeking the further consent of the photographs' subjects.

Lessons from Georgia

More than a century ago, another U.S. state high court looked harder at the privacy interest in the human face, limiting nonconsensual use by a private party of a white man's photograph. The reasons offered lend deeper, more philosophical insight into why a mere face in a photo might deserve legal privacy recognition.

An artist named Paolo Pavesich awoke one day in 1904 to discover that a photograph of him taken by a professional photographer named J. Q. Adams was included in an advertisement for insurance.[41] The advertisement appeared in Atlanta's main newspaper, the *Constitution*. Accompanying the photograph was the following statement, supposedly a quote from Pavesich: "In my healthy and productive period of life I bought insurance in the New England Mutual Life Insurance Co., of Boston, Mass., and to-day my family is protected and I am drawing an annual dividend on my paid-up policies."[42] In reality, Pavesich had never purchased insurance from New England Mutual Life; nor had he given Adams or the insurance company permission to use his photograph.

Seeking $25,000 in damages, Pavesich sued the photographer, the insurance company, and the general agent of the insurance company (whose name appeared in the ad). Pavesich alleged "a trespass upon plaintiff's right of privacy," as well as "breach of confidence and trust."[43] The original trial court threw out the claims, but on appeal to the Georgia Supreme Court, Pavesich won a reversal.

That Pavesich prevailed on his privacy claim was remarkable, as privacy jurisprudence was barely in existence at the time. Samuel Warren and Louis Brandeis argued in the 1890 *Harvard Law Review* for a right to privacy broad enough to encompass the right to prevent third parties from placing our photographs on public display.[44] They agreed with a New York City magistrate that Marion Manola had an interest in inviolate personality to block her employer from plastering the streets of Manhattan with images of her dressed in a theatrical costume.[45]

However, in 1904, the New York Court of Appeals had refused to recognize a similar right to privacy asserted by a young woman whose photograph was used without her consent on packaging for baking flour.[46] The court declared in good positivistic fashion that "there is no precedent for such an action to be found in the decisions of this court."[47] A dissenting judge would have recognized a right to privacy, since "new conditions affecting the relations of persons demand the broader extension of those legal principles which underlie the immunity of one's person from attack."[48]

Unrestrained by positivism, the Georgia high court bravely announced that a right to privacy protecting the human face must be recognized as a matter of fair inference from common law principles.[49] Moreover, the right to privacy has roots in "the instincts of nature," the court argued; "each individual as instinctively resents any encroachment by the public upon his rights which are of a private nature as he does the withdrawal of those of his rights which are of a public nature."[50] A person's face is a private matter; the ability to choose to display or conceal it is an aspect of liberty. A photographic representation of a person's face circulated to the general public without consent violates the person's general liberty to choose the manner in which he or she lives:

> One may desire to live a life of seclusion; another may desire to live a life of publicity; still another may wish to live a life of privacy as to certain matters and of publicity as to others. One may wish to live a life of toil where his work is of a nature that keeps him constantly before the public gaze; while another may wish to live a life of research and contemplation, only moving before the public at such times and under such circumstances as may be necessary to his actual existence. Each is entitled to a liberty of choice as to his manner of life, and neither an individual nor the public has a right to arbitrarily take away from him his liberty.[51]

Who would voluntarily surrender the natural liberty to choose between seclusion and publicity—to a sovereign who was not bound to protect them? No rational man, the court reasoned in classic contractarian fashion:

> The individual surrenders to society many rights and privileges which he would be free to exercise in a state of nature, in exchange for the benefits which he receives as a member of society. But he is not presumed to surrender all those rights, and the public has no more right, without his consent, to invade the domain of those rights which it is necessarily to be presumed he has reserved than he has to violate the valid regulations of the organized government under which he lives.[52]

Neither a photograph nor "the body of a person can . . . be put on exhibition at any time or at any place without his consent," the court opined in the previously mentioned 1890 case of a woman who successfully enjoined the publication of photographs in which she wore a revealing theatrical costume.[53] In the Pavesich case, the court determined that "the right of one to exhibit himself to the public at all proper times, in all proper places, and in a proper manner is embraced within the right of personal liberty," and that "the right to withdraw from the public gaze at such times as a person may see fit, when his presence in public is not demanded by any rule of law is also embraced within the right of personal liberty."[54]

The *Pavesich* decision is significant in the history of U.S. law for two reasons. First, it represents the first time that an American court explicitly based its decision on the premise of a freestanding right to privacy, a denomination of legal entitlement that would require nearly sixty years more to find recognition in an explicit form in constitutional law,[55] and seventy to become a routine part of legislative law-making in the United States.[56]

Second, and more immediately, the case essentially created the right to privacy tort. Born as a right to be free from unwanted commercial use of one's face, within just a few decades the right broadened into a cluster of rights most states recognize: to be free (1) from appropriation of name, likeness or identity; (2) from intrusion upon seclusion; (3) from publicity placing one in a false light; and (4) from unwanted publication of private facts.[57] Today, tort law includes protection for privacy, and so too does statutory and constitutional law. A New York statute originally enacted in the months after the *Roberson* case extends privacy protections to a person's name and likeness.[58] Federal and state statues create special privacy rights in genetic information because lawmakers believe genes, like faces, bespeak our identities.

Although contemporary American tort law recognizes a right to control commercial uses of a person's face, there are limits placed on the right. News media may profit handsomely from photographic images taken without the subject's consent, where the subject is caught up in a news story.[59] Because news publications enjoy First Amendment rights and common law "newsworthiness" privileges, a person caught up in a news event may find her photo in the newspaper and have no valid legal claim against anyone. The level of personal outrage, embarrassment, or humiliation in photographic publicity is irrelevant where news reporting is concerned.

Outside of the news, legal limits on nonconsensual publication of our photographs are recognized. Yet faces are hardly private. No legal right bars others from gazing at our faces in public places. People can stare. They can photograph us with their cell phone cameras from a distance. Business and government can made video recordings of us as we enter and exit subways, enter and exit retail establishments, or bank at an automatic teller machine (ATM).

Law enforcement authorities shocked the nation when they used FaceTrac facial recognition technology to scan the crowd at the Tampa football stadium that hosted Superbowl XXXV in 2001. By comparing the faces in the crowd to a data bank of the faces of individuals being sought in connection with crimes, authorities identified nineteen known criminals.[60] Some people cried foul, but other cried fair, arguing that people who attend televised public events with tens of thousands of others should have no expectation of privacy.

Yet the pervasive use of video cameras and the emergent use of technology far more accurate than FaceTrac rewrites the rules of social exchange, adding to the costs and risks of appearing in public. People with jobs and families must leave their homes and therefore cannot escape surveillance. Recreation is risky. A man sought by police for parole violations was detected when a "kiss cam" surveillance device identified him in the stands of a baseball game.[61] Gone is the anonymity of the crowded sports stadium or the flaneur's city street. Google Street View places random people on view globally. Widespread use of facial recognition technologies and ordinary video surveillance cameras evokes an Orwellian or *Minority Report* nightmare of overmonitored existence that can make us feel less free.[62] A federal statute addresses one aspect of the problem of video voyeurism—capturing images of people's private parts. The statute criminalizes, with a fine and up to a year in prison, intentionally capturing a photographic image of a person's "naked or undergarment clad genitals, public area, buttocks of female breast," under "circumstances in which the person has a reasonable expectation of privacy."[63] One commentator proposed a new tort action to deter sharing and electronic transmission of some digital photographs.[64]

We could distinguish *Pavesich* from the New Hampshire profiling case by stressing that the unwanted disclosure in *Pavesich* was a private, commercial appropriation of a photographic likeness, rather than a public, noncommercial disclosure. And it is one thing to have your photo appear in the morning newspaper of a major city, and something else to have it tucked away in an ACLU filing cabinet or included among stacks of court papers in a lawsuit alleging racial profiling. Yet if losing control over a photograph profoundly impacts a person's very freedom to decide how he or she lives, as the Georgia court contended in *Pavesich*, the differences between the two cases just may not be all that important. In both cases the freedom of the photographic subject has taken a trampling.

Politics and Race in Illinois

Richard M. Daley was a candidate for the mayor of Chicago, Illinois, in 1989. He was also Illinois State's Attorney General. Media giant CBS wanted to investigate candidate Daley's record on minority employment and decided to look into how many of his assistant state's attorneys had been members of racial minority groups.

The network filed a request under the Illinois Freedom of Information Act to obtain the racial data.[65] Patterned on the federal Freedom of Information Act (FOIA),[66] the Illinois act seeks to make the machinations of government transparent and hold officials accountable by granting the press and general public ready access to government records. Like its federal counterpart, the Illinois statute does not permit the government responding to a FOIA request to disclose personal information about individuals, such as medical and personnel information.

Illinois officials maintained records containing just the detailed data CBS requested. The data had been collected and compiled for purposes of federal Equal Employment Opportunity Commission (EEOC) compliance. However, the state officials refused to give CBS precisely what it wanted, which was a list of the names, races, and positions held by each individual assistant state's attorney.[67] The government was only willing to provide CBS with what it gave the EEOC: the aggregate number of minorities in each of five federally specified categories of white, African American, Asian, Hispanic, and Native American. Asserting a right to independently verify statistics reported to the EEOC, CBS sued in Cook County Circuit Court for an injunction mandating disclosure of the names and races of individuals. The court dismissed the suit and CBS appealed. An Illinois appeals court held that the lower court had not abused its discretion in finding that the Illinois FOIA exempts from disclosure personnel information that is private, including information about a person's race.[68]

The state appeals court relied heavily on a major U.S. Supreme Court case, *United States Department of Justice v. Reporters Committee for Freedom of the Press* (1989). In this case, the court denied the media plaintiffs request from the Justice Department copies of its criminal histories or "rap sheets" on four members of the Medico crime family.[69] All of the information contained in the Medico criminal histories was a matter of public record, a rap sheet being little more than a compilation of arrests, charges, convictions, and incarcerations, along with the date of birth and physical characteristics of the record subject. The secreting of government rap sheets potentially furthered effective criminal investigations, but in the *Reporters Committee* case the government emphasized that concealment protected record subjects' privacy interests in "practical obscurity."[70]

The *Reporters Committee* Court appears to have had something like this in mind. When publicly available information about a person is aggregated and the aggregation publicized, that person's life becomes less private, as a practical matter. New, differently colored attention is paid to the person. Certain forms of repackaging and republication of publicly available information are offensive to privacy, even though the individual facts revealed are a matter of public record. Extending the reasoning of *Reporters Committee* to the facts at hand, the Illinois court concluded that even if the fact of a person's race is a matter of public observation or record, it would not follow that a government record documenting his or her race should be revealed to the public through the media; this would call attention to individuals' races and thereby diminish their racial privacy. The government's release of name and race data would have implications for the level of privacy people enjoy. Government should not act so as to call attention to facts on record about a person, which will result in the person's being an object of perhaps unwanted, perhaps negative scrutiny.

Should the media giants of the world lose in the face of the foregoing line of argument? Do strangers who use our race data or photographs without our permission, as the *Pavesich* court pronounced, run our lives? My answer to these questions is "no." I agree that we should run our own lives in a free society. And we do—even if as past or present state employees the press is given our names, races, job descriptions, and photographs. Fighting racial discrimination by holding public officials accountable for their employment practices rather than barring public race data collection is the better way—maybe the only practical way—to make sure equality and liberty are protected in the long run.

Racial Privacy Outweighed

The *CBS* case went the other way, but courts have permitted racial disclosures sought by private litigants on the ground that doing so furthered the goals of equality and public accountability. In 2002, in *Department of Fair Employment & Housing v. Superior Court,* a court permitted racial disclosures to help establish housing discrimination claims.[71] The department served a subpoena on Nancy Keller, the manager of rental property, seeking the disclosure of the identities of past rental applicants and tenants, after a prospective tenant filed a complaint alleging discrimination based on race and marital status. The applicant was a African American woman whose roommate was to have been a Caucasian woman. Keller refused to provide information arguing that disclosure would have violated the right of privacy of third parties—former and current tenants and rental applicants. The court held that disclosure of the identities of tenants and housing applicants was required because gathering personal information sufficient to ascertain race and gender was relevant to housing discrimination investigations. The compelling state interest in protecting against race and marital status outweighed the intrusion on the privacy of third parties. Fighting discrimination was described as a compelling interest, one stronger than privacy.

In a similar vein, in 1999, a court in *Hicks v. Roberson County* ordered an employer to produce race data about individuals in its work force over the privacy objections of the employer, who faced suit by a white man for employment discrimination.[72] The white man sought documents relating to the race of all defendant's employees. The county argued that it would be a violation of the privacy of third parties to release the data. The court disagreed, and ordered the defendants to produce all documents regarding the race of the defendant's employees, despite the confidentiality concern. In another case, a major department store was accused of prosecuting black shoplifters more frequently than whites committing comparable offenses. The court ordered the retailer to make its confidential store logs available to plaintiffs seeking to prove racial bias against blacks detained and accused of theft.[73]

Other cases repeat this pattern. In 2003 in *Waters v. U.S. Capitol Police Board,* a federal court plaintiff in the District of Columbia successfully sued to obtain a "racial snapshot" of the defendant employer's workforce. The plaintiff was a former police recruit, suing the police for race discrimination. The court readily held that an employer must disclose race and other identifying information, reasoning that such information was necessary to make out a prima facie case of racial discrimination.[74] The court held that the defendant was required to disclose the races of persons terminated, polygraph results, and previous complaints of race discrimination.

In *Lissner v. United States Customs Service* in 2001, two customs officers were arrested after their involvement in an alleged crime.[75] Lissner, an interested party, sought information about the incident, including a complete description of two officers. The customs service refused racial information, providing only information about height, weight, and eye color. Lissner sued. The court held in 2001 that information about race would not reveal intimate, private details about the officers of the sort that required protection. The public interest in disclosing the information outweighed the privacy interests of the officers.

The *CBS* court treated racial status as inherently private and subject to individual control. Indeed most courts seem to assume that race is a private matter, even where racial privacy claims lose out in the courts' own balancing tests. The *Lissner* court, by contrast, did not readily assume that racial disclosures invade privacy at all. The court asserted that knowing a person's race does not amount to knowing anything about the intimate details of his or her personal life. Two errors in reasoning are evident here. First, revealing intimacies of personal life is only one criteria of privacy; not everything that merits privacy protection has to do with intimacy. The poor performance evaluation an employee received from an employer may merit privacy protection, for example. Second, racial identity is commonly a matter of secrecy and social reserve in American life, precisely because knowing a person's race means knowing something about the intimacies of sexual, family, and marital life—who has sexual and social intercourse with whom. If racial privacy is going to be recognized as a legitimate legal interest, it should not be merely because control over personal information is a brand of freedom—but also because what we call "race" can be deeply tied the intimacies of a personal life and ought to be afforded some measure of respect where possible. Yet race has undeniably public dimensions.

AMBIVALENCE AND PARADOX

Race is public and private, publicized and secreted, imminent and intimate. If by "private" one means hidden or unknown, the races with which most Americans identify—and the racial categories at play in the society by which others identify us—are rarely private. Indeed, what we call race in the United States is a set of human traits and associations generally in plain view. At one time, African Americans were labeled "colored," referring to their typically darker skin tones. "Red and yellow, black and white, they are precious in His sight," went the words of a song I learned as a Christian preschooler in the 1950s. American society has largely moved beyond the practice of using crayon colors—white, black, yellow, red, and brown—as shorthand for complex sets of observable and ancestral traits, but "people of color" remains a term used for population groups not primarily of Anglo-European ancestry.

Race, as U.S. Americans define it, is chiefly visible in the face. Moreover, observable traits that include names, voices, language, dress, gait, and affiliations are reliable clues to race not visible in the face. Racial categories in widest use in the United States today map onto observable characteristics, but we also know race by history and memory. President Barak Obama's mother was unquestionably "white," but he, by appearance and convention, because his father was a very dark-skinned Kenyan, is "black."

SECRETS AND SENSITIVITIES

Faces do not always reveal race and ethnic heritage. Few can tell by quick visual inspection of facial features that someone's origins are Slovenian, Cuban, Libyan, or Hmong. Many people take special pride in ethnic, national, or cultural roots that happen to be difficult to discern by superficial observation. Like ethnicity and national origin, what we think of as race can be invisible.

Some self-identified African Americans and Native Americans, for example, are not obviously African American or Native American; they have to announce their racial identities if others are to know for sure. Pioneering conceptual artist and philosopher Adrian Piper is such a person. She began incorporating her personal story of racial ambiguity into compelling art work in the 1970s. Piper, who was born with light skin, wavy hair and European features, has a strong African American identity. She is the daughter of fair-skinned Caribbean, African, European, and East Indian ancestry parents who raised her in Harlem, New York.[76] Piper once created a set of mock business cards on which she disclosed her racial self-identity. She passed them out to strangers who assumed she was white and made offensive remarks about minorities.

Race for some is experienced as a delicate, personal matter, tied to feelings of shame, anger, or sorrow. A biracial man with honey-brown skin might wish to conceal his white ancestry to cap anger and sorrow over abandonment by his white mother. A biracial woman may want to conceal black racial ancestry to fit in better with white peers. Because of social taboos against interracial sex and marriage, whole families may conspire to keep their racial backgrounds and other-race kin in the closet.[77]

Some people are not aware that their family trees include members of racial groups with which they do not identify. A prominent lawyer, former law school dean, and university president, Gregory Williams looks white. His father was a fair-skinned black man who looked a little Italian, and his mother was white. In his book *On the Color Line*, Williams described living first as a white child in a white community in which his father passed as white, and then as a black child in his father's hometown of Muncie, Indiana.[78]

However, the social salience of racial categories has a lot to do with the fact that what we call race is generally not capable of concealment. Not only is race often visible by the face; a person's race also often a matter of common knowledge in their communities of origin and documented in a diverse assortment of official and unofficial sources. Neighbors in Harlem knew that Adrian Piper's family were "Negroes," some of whom passed for white. Greg Williams's neighbors in his father's hometown knew that the Williams kids were black, even though for the longest time Greg and his brothers did not. Race is a social practice, a set of social networks. As Williams discovered, although racial ancestry can be buried, the race or races we care most about are generally the ones that are on the surface of our skins, and at the forefront of our vital inner lives and interpersonal relationships.

In the United States race is a matter of ancestry and attachments rather than appearance alone. Yet officials often use appearance to gauge race.[79] The "look and see" test of race works pretty well in most instances. The Equal Employment Opportunity Commission (EEOC) guidelines for racial data reporting cited in the *CBS* case presuppose that race is usually visible and that most people will identify themselves by race and ethnicity if asked, but that a minority of people will not want to disclose their race to their employers. Out of respect for that preference, employers are not authorized to compel disclosure of race; however, if an employee declines to provide the information, the federal guidelines require that the employer ascertain the person's race by visual inspection. This policy against compelling racial self-disclosure costs the government little since the fact of race will be apparent to the eye (and ear) in the vast majority of cases. Again, race is in the face. Race is so much in the face that, while racial data collectors are not supposed to second-guess racial classification asserted by an individual, an exception applied in the 1987 EEOC *Compliance Manual* if a person asserts a racial identity that is "patently" inaccurate.[80]

Racial privacy preferences vary with context. A person might favor race data collection for benign remedial or welfare enhancing purposes by government in her life as citizen voter. Many people go online for the purpose of finding same-race partners. They want their races to be known and valued. A woman may gladly disclose her race on employment applications, but enjoy racially anonymous Internet surfing in her private life. Many people travel the Internet and intentionally conceal or fake their races in their online communications. The rewards of racial anonymity have been touted and the pitfalls acknowledged.[81]

Still, some people build whole lives around the concealment of race or ethnicity. Some blacks live their whole lives posing—"passing"—as white. I have known mixed-raced blacks who did not speak about their white parents, and have heard of whites concealing remote African or Jewish ancestry. Racial information should be treated as private, the argument goes, because some people regard their racial ancestry as sensitive and should be at liberty to conceal it.

Living in the racial closet is not necessary in the United States today, and for most Americans, the closet is not an option. Race is not generally a secret, and is not generally secreted. Race is, however, something we can deliberately de-emphasize and ignore at times. In some social settings, gratuitous attention to another's race would be considered impolite and impolitic. Race is sensitive that way—like disability, religion, sexual orientation, gender, and weight. But where there is no suspicion of serious bias or denigration, Americans freely disclose and discuss one another's races all the time.

We are accustomed to thinking of race overwhelmingly as a matter of public knowledge and public record. Race data has gone from being perniciously a matter of public record in the 1950s, to being beneficently a matter of public record today. This set of facts makes the ascription of a legal interest in racial privacy a more puzzling and troubling proposition than the U.S. courts have been forced to acknowledge thus far.

One could argue for racial privacy laws on the grounds that many sensitive people prefer the privacy of their race, and if people prefer the privacy of race, liberal democratic government should respect that preference by refusing to document race and disclose. In my experience, few people care if others know their race. However, an argument for racial privacy could be premised on the assumption that although racial privacy is not a popular majority preference, it is a vitally important minority preference worth protecting.

The largely public character of race severely limits the ability of a state to protect racial privacy through law. There is nothing wrong with trying to respect people's sensitivities, and uninvited race disclosure happens to offend people's sensitivities the way unauthorized financial disclosures often do. But it may not be practical; there may be few meaningful ways to do it.

The obvious impracticality of racial privacy laws that meaningfully conceal what Americans call "race" may explain why there has been no great demand for laws protecting racial privacy in the United States. Racial privacy was not among the rallying cries of the civil rights movement. The California anti-affirmative action referendum aside, racial privacy has barely been a part of debates over the justice of color-conscious remedies for discrimination. Still, a society which acknowledges sensitive, intimate dimensions of racial information and its own history of race prejudice could be understandably tempted to consider racial privacy laws limiting discriminatory use of race data by government.

PERSECUTION

What could racial privacy amount to in the present day for residents of the United States? How can what is so thoroughly known and knowable be rendered legally private? Yet people may seek to control the collection and use of racial data because they value the capacity to hide intimate secrets. They may disapprove the purposes to which racial data would be put. They might not wish to facilitate race-specific medical, scientific, or social science research. They may oppose race-conscious public programs, such as affirmative action or minority set-asides. They may prefer a color-blind society. They might not wish, as the *CBS* court pointed out on behalf of Mr. Daley's assistant state's attorneys, to have their races become a matter of public debate. It is worth looking more closely into whether there are good normative arguments for public policies that treat persons' races as private information.

For those who can manage it, concealing race is a way to avoid getting hurt. One of the points of racial categorization in the United States has been to sort human beings on the basis of phenotypical traits and ancestry, and then to allocate social, political, and economic entitlements. African Americans, Native Americans, Asian Americans, and Hispanic Americans have histories of extreme government and government sanctioned discrimination on account of their races and ethnicities. Chinese, Japanese, Jewish, Arab, Irish, and Italian Americans have histories of bias and discrimination on American soil. Racial discrimination and racially motivated violence have been longstanding problems. Formerly a nation of slaveholders, segregationists, and white privilege, the United States remains burdened by racial and national origin discrimination. In easily imagined instances, concealing race to thwart unfair treatment would be warranted.

The risk of group persecution exists even in the most "civilized" societies. Legal precautions must be taken against apartheid, slaughter, and genocide. For many contemporary western Europeans, the concept of racial privacy is embraced with enthusiasm for that very reason. Europeans accept racial privacy as a way of protecting individuals from extremes of government persecution. So-called Aryan racial statutes and Jewish identity were officially assigned in Germany in the first half of the twentieth century, with catastrophic consequences.[82] The movement to define who was Jewish spread to other countries as well. In the Netherlands, for example, "a Jew was anyone with three Jewish grandparents, or, if he or she were observant, two Jewish grandparents."[83] In the Netherlands in 1940, all gainfully employed persons were required to fill out forms listing racial background. Physical identification of one's Jewish heritage was also mandated in Holland, where by 1942, the Nazis ordered Jews to wear the yellow star. In Belgium in 1940, Jews (also defined as anyone with at least three Jewish grandparents) were required to carry identity papers stamped "Jood-Juif," and were required to register their home addresses and property with the state. In 1942 in Belgium, a military administration ordered Jews to wear a badge. In France, laws were enacted "declaring anyone with two [Jewish] grandparents to be a Jew," and in 1942 the Nazis ordered Jews in the Occupied Zone aged six years and older to wear the yellow star. The most extreme of the classifications was in Slovakia, where any person with one Jewish parent was considered Jewish. In Warsaw in 1936, the Ministry of Commerce ordered that all shops throughout Poland to include, as part of the shop sign, the name of the owner as it appeared on his birth certificate. There would be no hiding. Other countries had policies as well, including Croatia, Greece, and Bulgaria.

An historic European Union Directive on Race went into full effect in November 2003, requiring member states to adopt laws applicable to public and private entities prohibiting direct and indirect forms of discrimination based on race or ethnicity in employment, housing, education, social security, healthcare and services.[84] (Nationality-based discrimination is not prohibited.) Since World War II, European national lawmakers and the European Union have enacted regulations limiting the collection and dissemination of personal data pertaining to race, ethnicity, and similar traits or group memberships.[85] In 1995 the European Union adopted a directive for "the protection of individuals with regard to the processing of personal data and on the free movement of such data."[86] Under Article 8 of the directive, "Member States shall prohibit the processing of personal data revealing racial or ethnic origin, political opinions, religious or philosophical beliefs, trade-union membership, and the processing of data concerning health or sex life."[87] The restriction has exceptions for health, safety, and employment, but creates a strong presumption. Racial privacy is not a matter of complete choice. Legislated restrictions on data transfer cannot necessarily be waived by individuals who wish to consent to racial disclosure. Privacy can be coerced if "the laws of the Member State provide that the prohibition . . . may not be lifted by the data subject's giving his consent."[88]

The risks of government racial classification are clear when considering recent experiences in Rwanda, Bosnia, and Iraq. In those countries, slaughter and genocide were facilitated by quick reference to group membership recorded on an identification card. In Bosnia, Serbs threw away their identify cards, hoping to survive by blending in with the Muslims they feared.[89] In Rwanda, a Hutu identity card or passport, or at least "looking" Hutu rather than Tutsi, meant the difference between life and death.[90] In Iraq, possessing identity papers that read Sunni rather than Shia or vice-versa kept families together and saved lives.[91]

POLITICAL LIBERALISM: THE QUESTION OF IMPARTIALITY

Should the United States enact the racial information privacy laws that it does not have and that a majority of its citizens may not want? Such laws would aim at preventing embarrassment, discrimination, or persecution, presumably by placing limits on the ability to collect, disseminate, and publicize information. Lawmakers would need to settle on what categories of information to restrict. Would race and ethnicity data be enough? Should national original be included? And what about nationality? Lawmakers would also have to decide who would be banned from race data collection. Perhaps the laws would aim solely at government, or they might also apply to employers and schools. An extensive law might ban race information collection throughout the private sector—prohibiting, for example, an Internet dating service from collecting race and similar population group information from its clients.

Waiting until extremes of race hatred have erupted to introduce bans on race data collection could be pointless and imprudent. Yet enacting bans in the face of a cultural openness about race and the absence of extremes of race hatred could subject lawmakers to ridicule. Many of the people newly governed by a regime of racial silence would surely find it odd. And even if they did not, the observable, public character of race would limit the usefulness of information laws purporting to take race out of the picture. What are clearly needed are laws prohibiting racial discrimination. Whether an adequate package of antidiscrimination laws necessarily includes race data limitations is an interesting, open question.

It is sobering to note, however, that social and political evil do not require formally maintained sources of racial data. Government classifications, compulsory identification cards, and yellow stars aid human rights violations. But serious harm against a targeted group can be accomplished without them. There is so much racial and ethnic segregation in the United States that everyday patterns of life reveal race. If extremists declared genocide against African Americans, they would not need official records held by employers, schools, and government to round up targets for extermination. It's no secret what most African Americans look like, and in what neighborhoods and schools the vast majority can be found. Anti-Semites know how to find Jewish targets. They know the communities, places of worship, and child care centers to strike.

The question to consider, then, is what practical point racial privacy laws might have as an adjunct to race discrimination bans, given the social imminence of race. In considering the point of such laws, the national and historical context at hand is very relevant. Racial privacy rules that might make sense in Rwanda or Germany might not make sense in the United States or Canada. Yet valuable lessons from abroad and a nation's own history should not be overlooked.

The point of racial privacy laws in the United States would be partly symbolic. They would be a way of saying that, officially speaking, race does not matter: we are a society committed to impartiality. However, as some proponents of race-conscious public policies believe, official recognition of race is consistent with an overall commitment to the impartiality demanded by liberal justice.[92]

Justice for individuals in free societies requires wide liberty of action, plus impartiality in the allocation of public benefits and burdens. Race does not matter when it comes to allocating voice and respect, but it may matter in the context of specific programs and policies needed to secure equal voice and respect for all. Drawing on John Rawls's 2001 reformulation of "justice-as-fairness," consider how a Rawlsian liberal might approach the argument.

John Rawls presented his two main principles of justice as principles that would be adopted by persons in "the original position," placed behind the "veil of ignorance."[93] in traditional social contract theory, we are not asked to imagine that parties to the social contract are ignorant about their own characteristics. However, persons in the Rawlsian analogue—the original position—are ignorant about race and other social identities: "In the original position, the parties are not allowed to know the social positions or the particular comprehensive doctrines of the persons they represent . . . [or] persons' race and ethnic group, sex or various native endowments such as strength and intelligence."[94]

Parties to the original position are "veiled" against information and points of view that could result in bias in the design of political justice. Rawls assumed that the end product of the original position would reflect some sort of bias if the parties possessed racial (or ethnic) information. Thus, he stipulated ignorance about the parties' own racial identities. Rawls did not maintain that thoroughgoing colorblindness is a requirement of substantive justice; the race-ignorance stipulation of the original position does not flow from a general principle mandating colorblindness in all government affairs. It is an open question whether a just, well-ordered society based on Rawlsian principles would permit government to collect race data vital for, for example, securing the health, educational achievement, or economic well-being of all its citizens.

The first principle of justice emerging from the original position was this: "Each person has the same indefeasible claim to a fully adequate scheme of equal basic liberties, which scheme is compatible with the same scheme of liberties for all."[95] A person's race will be irrelevant to the strength of his or her claim on basic liberties. Racial data collection aimed at treating some people unequally with others would be prima facie unjust, much as the use of gender data collection criteria would be unjust. However, racial data collection with other purposes, objectives, and consequences is not obviously ruled out.

Is racial privacy a basic liberty, though? If it were, we would have to worry about racial data collection both because of its potential for facilitating unequal treatment, and for its implications for liberty itself. Among those basic constitutional liberties could be the liberty imagined by the *Pavesich* court—equal basic liberty to choose the manner of one's life, whether to live in relative seclusion or in the public eye. But to argue that basic liberties include rights of informational privacy, as they surely do, does not lead in any straightforward manner to claims for the protection of racial information privacy. At a minimum, race has to be understood as something that is amenable to meaningful concealment. In addition, it is partly an empirical question whether state data collection is more benign than harmful. Racial labeling could be a feature of a society in which "the political and social conditions essential for the adequate development and full exercise of the two moral powers of free and equal persons" is satisfied.[96] Freedom not to be labeled by any racial or ethnic category by the state would not appear to be a basic liberty in the abstract.

A society could find that race and ethnic information is pertinent to legislative efforts to secure equal basic constitutional liberties. It could also find that affirmative action programs and minority business set-asides are called for by the first principle of justice and pass muster with the second.[97]

Rawls's second principle was this: "Social and economic inequalities are to satisfy two conditions. First, they are to be attached to offices and positions open to all under conditions of fair equality of opportunity; and second, they are to be to the greatest benefit of the least-advantaged members of society (the difference principle)."[98] Government collection of racial data may serve benign purposes tied to public health and the delivery of social services. Knowing the racial and ethnic background of newborns and fully grown adults can be pertinent to their care, as some medical abnormalities are more common among some groups than others. A public hospital might want to collect such information. In addition, taking into account ethnic customs, religions, diets, and lifestyles might be relevant to fair, efficient, and sensitive delivery of social services. Making free flu shots available to a community on its day of religious worship is probably a bad idea. Government needs to take notice of facts that bear on social identities.

Racial minorities are not inherently among Rawls's least advantaged. Opponents of affirmative action and proponents of the racial privacy initiative seem to think that race is a poor proxy for need and disadvantage today. Rawls looks "conservative" to the extent that he operated in the world of ideal theory in which neither race nor gender are among the contingencies that (predictably and negatively) affect life prospects: "Justice as fairness focuses on inequalities in citizens' life prospects—their prospects over a complete life... as these prospects are affected by three kinds of contingencies:... (a)... social class...; (b) native endowments...; (c)... good or ill fortune."[99]

Rawls was aware that his American readers might wonder at the exclusion of gender and race from the list of major contingencies affecting life prospects. Thus, several pages later he writes:

> It is natural to ask: Why are distinctions of race and gender not explicitly included among the three contingencies noted earlier? How can one ignore such historical facts as slavery—(in the antebellum South) and the inequalities between men and women resulting from the absence of provisions to make

> good women's extra burden in the bearing, raising, and educating of children so as to secure their fair equality of opportunity?[100]

Rawls came to his own defense, justifying the exclusion on the ground that his primary concern is "ideal" theory and the well-ordered society, not "partial compliance theory." The least advantaged are defined, he further explained, by deficits of wealth and income, not properties of race or gender, for the least advantaged "share with other citizens the basic equal liberties and fair opportunities but have the least income and wealth."[101]

Although Rawls underemphasized the roles played by race and gender traits in our society, he acknowledged potential structural impacts:

> Suppose, for example, that certain fixed natural characteristics are used as grounds for assigning unequal basic rights, or allowing some persons only lesser opportunities; then such inequalities will single out relevant positions. Those characteristics cannot be changed, and so the positions they specify are points of view from which the basic structure must be judged. Distinctions based on gender and race are of this kind. Thus if men, say, have greater basic rights or greater opportunities than women, these inequalities can be justified only if they are to the advantage of women and acceptable from their point of view. Similarly for unequal basic rights and opportunities founded on race. It appears that historically these inequalities have arisen from inequalities in political power and control of economic resources. They are not now, and it would seem never have been, to the advantage of women or less favored races.[102]

It is pretty clear from reading Rawls that he did not want race to matter in just societies. Just societies are supposed to be impartial. But I see nothing in a Rawlsian perspective to rule out race-conscious programs that stand to benefit the less advantaged in society. Rawls offered "hope that in a well-ordered society under favorable conditions, with the equal basic liberties and fair equality of opportunity secured, gender and race would not specify relevant points of view."[103] And yet in a society that is not perfectly well-ordered, in which equal basic liberties and fair equality of opportunity have not been secured, race and gender may specify relevant points of view. Far from furthering justice, a law like California's proposed Proposition 54 could limit the kinds of remedial measures a society can take to extend equality of opportunity. Racial minority group members have often lacked an important primary good, "the social bases of self respect" and a "lively sense of their worth as persons . . . able to advance their ends with self-confidence."[104] And while many privacy rights are surely among primary goods, racial privacy—with its impracticalities, lack of appeal, and inconsistency with robust egalitarianism—is not a condition of the social contract.

Racial privacy laws could have purposes beyond symbolizing impartiality. Such laws would validate the sensitivities of the minority of persons for whom racial designations are inherently offensive. Racial privacy laws would disable harmful acts or bigoted policies dependent upon racial statistics. Finally, the laws would reduce the probability of individual acts of racial bias against particular people. Americans of Middle Eastern ancestry and Mexican-Americans, for example, have a tale to tell about loss of freedom and livelihood, especially in this post-9/11 era. We know that racial and ethnic disclosures in the United States can harm the interests of individual minority group members in being let alone. Group-classification schemes effected by government or the business sector play a role in making race detection and injury more likely. Race classification and data collection can be used to injure interests in intimacy, dignity, safety, or nondiscrimination.

Racial privacy laws, which seem both impractical and counter-productive at present, could, in theory, have a point. In specific, well-defined contexts racial information, like medical and financial information, may demand protection.[105] Philosophers maybe more tempted than I have argued the hard facts presently warrant to ascribe individuals a moral claim to positive laws guaranteeing freedom from official racial classification, and a degree of control over the collection and uses of racially identifying information. Should the day arrive when racial privacy were necessary to protect through law in the US, it would be an open question whether ascribing individual "control" would be the best way to protect such privacy.[106] Indeed, if there were rights of racial privacy, perhaps they should be understood as rights that cannot be waived by persons indifferent or opposed to the benefits they confer. And there are other options for race-related data privacy, too.

PRIVATE ASSOCIATION AND CIVIL RIGHTS

The problem of persecution on account of race or population group is real, and government can have an important role in supporting measures to obscure racial affiliation, if not race itself. Although typical African Americans cannot conceal their race, they can conceal race-related affiliations and memberships, publicity about which would expose them to added discrimination and danger. Since the 1950s, the First Amendment principle of freedom of association has functioned as something of a proxy in the United States for one of the few sorts of racial privacy that makes good sense.

In *NAACP v. Alabama* (1958) the Supreme Court held unanimously that the constitutional rights of speech and assembly include a right of private group association. Finding that the National Association for the Advancement of Colored People (NAACP) had standing to defend the privacy interests of its members,[107] the court held that the civil rights group had a right to keep its rank and file members' identities secret.

The NAACP was dangerously visible in the 1950s.[108] It had made enemies by boldly pushing for black civil rights for decades.[109] In 1956, Alabama took definitive steps to expel the group from its borders. The NAACP's mission to rid American life of race discrimination was at variance with the state's aim of maintaining race segregation premised on white superiority. Setting aside traditions was painfully difficult. In 1954, the Supreme Court handed down its decision in *Brown v. Board of Education* officially ending state-imposed public school segregation.[110] Yet most white Alabamans refused to permit their children to attend schools with black children. Getting rid of the NAACP was a part of public resistance to desegregation.

An Alabama statute similar to those in other states required out-of-state ("foreign") corporations to register or "qualify" prior to transacting business.[111] To qualify to conduct operations in Alabama, a foreign corporation was supposed to file its charter with the secretary of state, designate a place of business, and name an agent to receive service of process. The penalty for transacting business without having first qualified included fines for the organization and criminal prosecution of its corporate officers. Alabama maintained that the NAACP was a foreign corporation operating in Alabama. The state alleged that the NAACP had flagrantly violated state law by operating extensively in the state without taking the steps to qualify. The state pointed out that the NAACP had opened a regional office, organized chapters, and recruited members throughout Alabama; solicited contributions in Alabama; and provided both financial support and legal aid to black students attempting to gain admission to the white-only University of Alabama. The state also alleged that the unregistered civil rights group had instigated the famous Montgomery bus boycott that followed Rosa Park's arrest for refusing to give her bus seat to a white passenger.

The Montgomery Bus boycott had not been the work of the NAACP and the NAACP had provided only legal support to African Americans seeking to attend the University of Alabama. Yet it was true that the NAACP had failed to comply with the state's corporate qualification law prior to setting up shop in Alabama in 1914. Based on this act of noncompliance, state officials successfully obtained a court order enjoining the NAACP from continuing to operate in the state. Alabama persuaded a court that the NAACP was causing irreparable injury to the property and civil rights of the residents and citizens of the State of Alabama for which criminal prosecution and civil actions afforded no adequate remedy. In addition to ordering that the NAACP cease operations, the court also granted a harsh request that the NAACP not be permitted to comply with the state corporate qualification law even if it wanted to.

The NAACP attempted to fight ouster by tendering the missing corporate qualification documents to officials. The state fought back by refusing to accept the documents and with a motion in state court seeking the names and addresses of the organization's agents and members. The state court granted the motion. The NAACP partly complied by handing over the identities only of its officers and directors. At a time when civil rights advocates faced death, injury, and loss of property, the NAACP refused to reveal the identities of its general membership. For this refusal, the NAACP was held to be in contempt of court and fined $100,000.

The NAACP appealed the decision of the state court to the U.S. Supreme Court. Attorney Robert Carter argued on behalf of the NAACP that the names and addresses of members could be kept private even granting the argument that the organization ought to have formally complied with the foreign corporation qualification law when it first arrived in Alabama in 1914. The Supreme Court rendered an opinion siding with the NAACP. (A series of four Supreme Court cases were necessary, however, before Alabama abandoned its bid to eject the NAACP.[112])

The Court ruled that the due process clause of the Fourteenth Amendment confers to each individual the rights of free speech and free association. These are rights protected from federal violation by the First Amendment and from state violation by the First and Fourteenth Amendments. The idea that Americans are free to join private groups was already established by 1958.[113] However, the court's decision to allow private groups to keep membership information confidential from the state was a major constitutional milestone. Revealing the group's membership, argued Justice John Marshall Harlan, "is likely to affect adversely the ability of [the NAACP] and its members to pursue their collective effort to foster beliefs which they admittedly have the right to advocate, in that it may induce members to withdraw from the Association and dissuade others from joining it because of fear of exposure of their beliefs shown through their associations and of the consequences of this exposure."[114] The state can legitimately demand to know the officers and agents of an organization, its purposes, and general activities, but not the identities of its members. Yet, when Americans voluntarily join a private peaceful political, religious, or social association—even an unpopular or controversial one—they are entitled to as much confidentiality as to their names and addresses as the association chooses to confer.

In the age of surveillance—a common descriptor in the United States for the years after the terrorist attacks of September 11, 2001—there has been pressure to permit racial profiling and deep probes into minority groups' membership.[115] But in *NAACP v. Alabama*, the court reassuringly characterized official demands for membership lists as substantial restraints on freedom of association.[116]As such, courts must strike down such demands unless the state can show a "controlling justification" in disclosure.[117] Demonstration of a compelling state interest in disclosure may be called for.[118]

NAACP v. Alabama has left an indelible mark on constitutional law. Major decisions of the Supreme Court have followed the authority of the *NAACP* case. *Bates v. City of Little Rock* (1960) upheld the NAACP's refusal to provide the names of its members to city tax revenue officials.[119] Lower courts have also followed the *NAACP* decision. In *Wallace v. Brewer* (1970), Alabama lost its bid to obtain the membership list of a group of black Muslims who purchased land with the intent to settle in the state.[120] A curious Alabama state law required the registration of "communists, Nazis, and Muslims." The law required all Muslims who remain in Alabama for more than one day to register with the department of public safety and any Muslim organization to list all of its members. The federal district court declared the law unconstitutional. The court cited *NAACP v. Alabama* and the "vital relationship between freedom to associate and privacy in one's association."[121]

Anil Kalhan, citing the *NAACP* case in defense of informational privacy rights in the immigration law enforcement context in 2008, argued that "as a result of being compelled to disclose immigration and citizenship status, both unauthorized and lawfully present noncitizens may become more vulnerable to discrimination or harassment based on that revealed status itself."[122] In this respect, maintained Kalhan, "the individual interest in maintaining some measure of privacy in one's status is analogous to the associational privacy and anonymous speech interests that the Supreme Court has recognized and protected under the First Amendment, where the Court has also been concerned with the vulnerability that members of disfavored groups may face if forced to disclose their group membership or identities as speakers."[123] Kalhan stressed a Pennsylvania court's decision in *Lozano v. City of Hazleton* (2007) "to permit plaintiffs with 'uncertain immigration status' to proceed anonymously with litigation.... because of 'potential for harassment and intimidation of the plaintiffs on the basis of their race, immigration status, and involvement with the 'highly publicized and controversial lawsuit.'"[124] The *Lozano* litigation—initiated by public interest organizations challenging the city of Hazleton, Pennsylvania's ordinance penalizing residents who rent to or employ undocumented immigrants—loudly echoes *NAACP*.

Beyond race-specific applications, *NAACP* is increasingly the centerpiece of a constitutional jurisprudence of information privacy and anonymity. Read broadly, the *NAACP* decision established a strong constitutional interest in the protection of sensitive data. *NAACP* gets cited whenever questions arise about the right of government to demand access to information obtained in confidence and deemed sensitive. For example, it was cited in *Whalen v. Roe* in 1977.[125] The New York legislature passed the New York State Controlled Substances Act, requiring that pharmacists report the names of people who filled prescriptions for certain dangerous medications. Five years after its enactment, *Whalen* brought the 1972 law before the Supreme Court. Although the Court did not find the law to be an unconstitutional violation of the right to privacy on its face, it noted that there is a constitutionally significant interest in the protection of data regarded as sensitive, such as medical data. Like *NAACP* itself, *Whalen* stands for the ideal of constitutional protection for sensitive data.

The *NAACP* decision has not always protected individuals seeking to remain anonymous. The courts have sometimes found that the state's interest in the accountability of potential wrongdoers outweighs the privacy interest in confidential group association, individual expression or anonymity. In *Uphaus v. Wyman* in 1959, the court upheld the right of the state of New Hampshire to order a group with ties to known communists to turn over a list of individuals who had been guests at one of its camps.[126] In *Church of the American Knights of the Ku Klux Klan v. Kerik* (2004), the Second Circuit Court of Appeals held that hooded masks worn by KKK members did not constitute expressive conduct entitled to First Amendment protection, and that New York's anti-mask statute was not facially unconstitutional. The information that one is a member of the Klan can be sensitive, but appears less protected: "The Supreme Court has never held that freedom of association or the right to engage in anonymous speech entails a right to conceal one's appearance in a public demonstration." In 2010 the District of Columbia District Court acknowledged *NAACP's* potential relevance to cases in which anonymous internet users seek to block ISPs from complying with subpoenas demanding the identities of their customers.[127] But that court rejected rights of anonymity claimed by an Autoadmit.com forum participant who posted insulting and defamatory statements about a Yale Law student.

Nicole A. Ozer cited the *NAACP* case in 2008 in support of the case she sought to build against expanding the use of insecure radio frequency identification (RFID) technology.[128] The technology impacts the fundamental rights to privacy and chills the ability to exercise rights to free expression by preventing people from remaining anonymous. Ozer argued that "forcing people to carry a government ID with insecure RFID technology is tantamount to requiring people to potentially identify themselves whenever they walk, speak, or meet in public... since it would be practically impossible to be in a public place without wondering whether the government was monitoring and recording who you were, where you were, and what you were doing."[129] Recent information technologies capable of capturing sensitive data about our identities suggests that the principles of private association, confidentiality, and anonymity embodied in the NAACP case will remain in view.

Thanks to *NAACP v. Alabama*, government may not force even a controversial group to identify its members, absent establishing a compelling state interest in disclosure. The right of private free association belongs to all who respect the rights of others. It belongs to Muslims, Jews, Christians, Hindus, and Buddhists. It belongs to communist, socialist, or liberal ideologues. And it belongs to the native-born as well as the immigrant American. Technology has made it easier to collect, store, and share data revealing individuals' population groups or group memberships. But, here, as elsewhere, "can easily do" does not entail "should do" or "must do".

CONCLUSION

In the United States race is in the face—seen, heard, and known. It is a talked-about source of pride and identity. (Consider this the social imminence of race.) U.S. laws aimed at a policy of shoving race into a closet would be at odds with its social imminence. Official bans on race data-collection and sharing would be impractical, futile and unpopular.

I have suggested that a useful racial privacy right of a kind is already embodied in U.S. law—namely, the informational privacy right established in *NAACP v. Alabama.* The Equal Employment Opportunity Commission's interpretation of Title VII reflects the ideal that official use of race information should be restricted—discriminating against someone of the basis of the race, ethnicity, color, or culture of a person or the person's associates is considered unlawful.[130] Yet the concept of racial privacy is not well-integrated into U.S. moral, political, and legal discourse. As an instance of the politics of sensitive data, I have tried to explain why, and to lay out the case against expanded usage. Racial privacy laws, were they adopted widely, would have a point. They would express disapproval of pernicious uses of information about a person's race. Acknowledging that they would have an expressive point falls short of making the case for their enactment.[131] As feminist philosophers have long argued, some privacy is not good for promoting the things we care about, including safety at home and equality. Racial privacy of the sort Californians considered but rejected would not have been good for public health or the struggle for equal opportunity. Race-conscious public policies that promote social welfare, equality, and inclusion have little in common with the discrimination and persecution they aim to repair.

7

THE ELECTRONIC DATA GIVE-AWAY

It is difficult scientifically to measure such a thing, but the taste for privacy seems to be dwindling. Or maybe, before electronic technology entered our lives, informational privacy was just a happenstance fact of life rather than a passion. Whatever the state of taste, I believe that mature adults, young adults, teens, and children, have privacy and data protection needs of which they may fail to be fully mindful or feel helpless to address on their own. With this in mind, consider the vast sweep of existing privacy and data protection statutes adopted by Congress, nearly all of which permits adults to waive or alienate their privacy rights. We have a great deal of privacy law aimed at regulating the flow of information, but only a small portion of it functions to protect the privacy people do not care or take care to protect. We are allowed to give privacy away.

Congress has enacted dozens of privacy protection statutes, resulting in a rich sector-by-sector patchwork quilt of special-purpose rules. (Congress has not followed the approach of the European Union, which has enacted several comprehensive multi-sector data-directives. In chapter 5, I described the Health Insurance Portability and Accountability Act (HIPAA), the federal health privacy statute. In chapter 8, I will assess the Children's Online Privacy Protection Act (COPPA), a paternalistic statute designed to protect the informational privacy of young children and their households; and by way of comparison to COPPA, I will highlight features of other statutes—the Privacy Act of 1974, the Family Education and Right to Privacy Act of 1974, and the Video Privacy Act of 1988. Along with chapter 8, the present chapter explains why and how privacy laws matter, exploring the social and ethical significance of real and imagined technologies propelling the on-going phenomenon I call "the great privacy give-away."

THE FEDERAL PRIVACY STATUTES

A complete list of major privacy protection laws enacted by Congress would include, chronologically: the Fair Credit Reporting Act (1970), regulating confidential credit reports; the Privacy Act (1974), regulating access to federal records; the Freedom of Information Act (FOIA, 1974), including privacy exemptions to a federal open records law; the Family Educational Rights and Privacy Act (FERPA, 1974), regulating access to school records; the Right to Financial Privacy Act (1978), regulating access to banking records; the Privacy Protection Act, regulating the search and seizure of work products protected by the First Amendment (1980); the Computer Fraud and Abuse Act (1986), creating criminal sanctions for intentionally accessing a protected computer without authorization; the Video Privacy Protection Act (1988), regulating access to video rental records; the Employee Polygraph Protection Act (1988), prohibiting employee lie-detection testing; the Telephone Consumer Protection Act (1991), regulating access to consumer data and amended to create the National Do Not Call Registry; the Driver's Privacy Protection Act, regulating access to motor vehicle records (1994); the Health Insurance Portability and Accountability Act (HIPAA,1996), regulating the privacy and security of medical information; the Telecommunications Act (1996), limiting disclosure of telecommunications consumers' personal information; the Children's Online Privacy Protection Act (COPPA, 1998), limiting website operators' access to children's personal information; the Identity Theft and Assumption Deterrence Act (1998), making it a federal crime to intentionally steal another's identity; Title V of the Gramm-Leach-Bliley Financial Services Modernization Act (GLB, 1999), regulating disclosures of financial information, data security and pretexting; the Controlling the Assault of Non-Solicited Pornography and Marketing Act (CAN-SPAM, 2003), prohibiting certain forms of unsolicited e-mail; and the Genetic Information Non-Discrimination Act (2008), limiting the use of confidential genetic data by employers and insurers.

This impressive list of statutes creating information privacy rights is only a part of the US privacy protection regime. To it must be added the crucial federal statutes that—along with the Fourth and Fifth Amendments to the Constitution limiting search and seizure and compulsory self-incrimination—protect the privacy of telephone and e-mail communications from unrestrained private and government surveillance. The Foreign Intelligence Surveillance Act (FISA, 1978), sets the ground rules for top-secret intelligence gathering. The Electronic Communications Privacy Act (1986) amended Title III of the Omnibus Crime Control and Safe Streets Act of 1968, broadly regulating access to wire, oral, and electronic communications; stored communications, such as e-mail and voice mail; and "dialed" phone numbers, call records, and GPS and cell tower location data. The Communications Assistance for Law Enforcement Act (CALEA, 1994) facilitates official surveillance of electronic communications. The controversial Uniting and Strengthening America by Providing Appropriate Tools Required to Intercept and Obstruct Terrorism Act (USA PATRIOT Act, 2001), extensively amended and supplemented federal laws to facilitate investigations of terrorism after the events of September 11, 2001.

MANY STATUTES, INADEQUATE PROTECTION?

It is reassuring that Americans have a bevy of federally protected information privacy rights. But it is no small matter, if you agree with me that privacy rights should do more than simply offer the opportunity of privacy, that individuals are free to repudiate the protections of nearly all of them at will. What about the actual experience of privacy? Are there any "inalienable" statutory privacy rights that insure that?

European Union (EU) law contemplates possible privacy protections data subjects cannot give up at will. In October 1998 the EU Data Protection Directive enacted in 1995 went into effect. The purpose of the directive was to mandate uniform, minimum privacy standards to safeguard the informational privacy of persons residing in EU member states. The original directive, which has been amended in an effort to address recent developments in electronic communications and data storage, regulates the types of personal information that can be sought, collected, and shared without the consent of the individual. It applies to all sectors of industry and to nearly all personal data. Personal data is defined broadly by the EU to include "sensitive information" such as "racial or ethnic origin, political opinions, religious or philosophical beliefs, trade union membership" and data concerning "health or sex life."[1] To reiterate a point made about this directive in the last chapter, legislated restrictions on data transfer cannot necessarily be waived by individuals who wish to consent to disclosure. Privacy can be coerced under Article 8.2a if "the laws of the Member State provide that the prohibition . . . may not be lifted by the data subject's giving his consent."[2]

The directive does not apply to public sector data transfers having to do with criminal law enforcement and national security; or to the communications of natural persons concerning "purely personal" or "household" matters. The EU directive prohibits the transfer of personal data to countries outside of the European Union that do not meet the directive's high standards of privacy protection. (But EU officials do not believe their directives are a holy grail. Paul M. Schwartz agrees. He explains EU data law as a product of path dependence and other practical and historical factors.[3] The EU is acutely aware of the limitations of its current data protection regime, large parts of which were designed nearly twenty years ago when communications and networking practices were vastly different. On November 4, 2010 the European Commission adopted a strategic communication on a comprehensive strategy on data protection in the EU.[4] EU standards are likely to change.) Under existing EU standards, lacking an omnibus privacy protection law or equivalent combination of laws, the United States does not make the grade. To enable US multinational organizations to transfer data about Europeans across the Atlantic, and to thereby preserve a several hundred billion dollar international trade relationship, the United States and the European Union successfully negotiated a Safe Harbor agreement in 2000. The European Parliament adopted the safe harbor plan and it has been implemented. The accord was designed to protect the privacy of EU citizens, while avoiding the need for the US government to mandate EU-style privacy rules. Under the agreement, US firms may transfer data from Europe if they participate in a voluntary program of certification. The required certification is a self-certification process. Companies in the United States wishing to participate must join a self-regulatory privacy program (such as Trust-E) and develop a policy that conforms to Safe Harbor principles. After the September 11, 2001 terrorist attacks, the European Union and the United States negotiated a separate privacy agreement to handle trans-border flows of airline passenger data. The original "agreement between the European Union and the United States of America on the processing and transfer of passenger name record (PNR) data by air carriers to the United States Department of Homeland Security" carried a sunset date of July 31, 2007, but was subject to extension "by mutual written agreement."[5]

Privacy advocates and consumer groups criticized the Safe Harbor agreement. They said that it let the United States off the hook for its failure to adopt stronger privacy protection laws for its own residents. Insisting that the United States should have stronger privacy laws, critics point out that privacy is recognized in the international context as a human right. Article 12 of the United Nations Universal Declaration of Human Rights explicitly affirms the right to privacy, as does Article 8 of the European Convention for the Protection of Human Rights and Fundamental Freedoms. The Organization for Economic Cooperation and Development (OECD) adopted privacy guidelines in 1980.

How might the United States make its privacy laws stronger? Arguably stronger privacy laws would require firms seeking to disclose personal data to provide notice and consent about the use of the data on an informed opt-in basis, and forbid certain disclosures altogether. This would entail letting data subjects know in advance what a firm would like to do with their data and seek affirmative permission.

Some US privacy advocates were stunned in 1999 when a federal appeals court declared that requiring a company to obtain customers' opt-in consent before using customer's personal data could violate the constitution. The former US West, Inc. was a major regional telecommunications carrier formed as a result of the breakup of AT&T. From its formation in 1983 it served Pacific and mountain states of the western United States. The company was acquired in a merger with Qwest Communications in 2000. Qwest is a provider of voice, video, and data services in the United States and abroad. A Federal Communications Commission (FCC) regulation required that telecommunications carriers provide their customers an opportunity to opt in to disclosure of "customer proprietary network information" (CPNI) rather than opt out. US West sued, claiming that the First Amendment entitled the company to opt-out consent policies and make use of lawfully obtained information for business purposes. *US West v. Federal Communications Commission* (1999) struck down the FCC regulation. The 10th Circuit Court of Appeals held that defendant FCC failed to show that the restraint of speech represented by limiting plaintiff's disclosure of CPNI (through a requirement of obtaining each customers' opt-in consent to disclosure) was narrowly tailored to further a substantial state interest in privacy.

Congress imposed the constitutionally safer opt-out rather than an opt-in consent approach to protecting data when it enacted Title V of the Financial Modernization Act of 1999, also known as the Gramm-Leach-Bliley Act or GLB. But critics of the opt-out law say the GLB privacy rules are therefore too weak to be effective.[6] GLB establishes three privacy-related rule sets: the Financial Privacy Rule, the Safeguards Rule, and Anti-Pretexting Rule. GLB applies primarily to financial institutions—companies that are significantly engaged in the business of offering financial products or services to individuals, including loans, financial or investment advice, or insurance. GLB authorizes eight federal agencies and the states to administer and enforce the Financial Privacy Rule and the Safeguards Rule, including the FTC and the SEC.

The GLB Anti-Pretexting Rule prohibits use of false pretenses, including fraudulent statements and impersonation, to obtain consumers' personal financial information, such as bank balances. The Safeguards Rule requires all financial institutions to design, implement and maintain safeguards to protect customer information. The Safeguards Rule applies to financial institutions that collect information from their own customers and those "such as credit reporting agencies" that receive customer information from financial institutions.

The Financial Privacy Rule governs the collection and disclosure of customers' personal financial information by financial institutions and other companies who receive such information. The most conspicuous obligation for financial institutions under GLB is the fair information practice obligation to provide consumer and customer notices. The notices are supposed to disclose how "nonpublic personal information" the company gathers and discloses about consumers and customers is treated. The privacy notice must be a clear, conspicuous, and accurate statement of the company's privacy practices. It must state what information the company collects about consumers and customers, with whom it shares the information, and how it protects or safeguards the information. The privacy notice must be given to individual customers or consumers by mail or in-person delivery. An online lender may post its notice on its website and require online consumers to acknowledge receipt as a necessary part of a loan application. A company's precise obligations under the GLB Act depend on whether the company has "consumers" or "customers" who obtain its services. A "consumer" is an individual who obtains or has obtained a financial product or service from a financial institution for personal, family or household reasons. Consumers are entitled to receive a privacy notice from a financial institution only if the company shares the consumers' information with companies not affiliated with it, with some exceptions. A "customer" is a consumer with a continuing relationship with a financial institution. A customer is entitled to receive a financial institution's privacy notice automatically every year for as long as the customer relationship lasts.

Consumers and customers have the right to opt out of—refuse consent to—having their information shared with certain third parties and company affiliates. An affiliate is an entity that controls another company, is controlled by the company, or is under common control with the company. The privacy notice must explain how, and offer a reasonable way that consumers and customers can opt out. For example, providing a toll-free telephone number or a detachable form with a pre-printed address is a reasonable way for individuals to opt out; requiring individuals to write a letter as the only way to opt out is burdensome and thus unreasonable.

An ability by individuals to opt out of certain data disclosures is denied. An individual who opts out cannot opt out of financial institution's sharing nonpublic personal information with outside companies which (a) provide essential services like data processing or servicing accounts, or (b) market the company's products or services. But by the same token, a service provider or marketer may only use the information for limited purposes and may not sell it. Individuals may not opt out of a disclosure that is legally required. If an individual elects not to opt out, he or she effectively permits financial institutions to use the information for its own purposes or re-disclose it to a third party, consistent with the financial institution's privacy notice. Even if individuals have not opted out of sharing the information for marketing purposes, however, GLB prohibits financial institutions from disclosing their customers' account numbers to nonaffiliated companies in the context of the company's telemarketing, direct mail marketing, or other marketing through e-mail.

The notice requirement was a well-intended fair information practice. But people rarely read their notices. And people rarely out opt of disclosures. The security safeguards of GLB are potentially more useful. Under the GLB Act, a financial institution must comply with security safeguards. They must develop, "implement, and maintain a comprehensive written information security program"; "identify reasonably foreseeable internal and external risks to the security, confidentiality, and integrity of customer information"; and "design and implement information safeguards to control the risks."[7] The Federal Trade Commission has brought highly publicized enforcement actions against firms like Choicepoint and TJX that have failed to comply with the requirements of GLB and experienced serious data breaches because of it. ChoicePoint, a publicly traded company based in suburban Atlanta, obtains and sells to more than 50,000 businesses the personal information of consumers, including their names, Social Security Numbers, birth dates, employment information, and credit histories. The FTC prosecuted ChoicePoint for carelessly selling consumer data to a bogus company. The 2006 settlement required ChoicePoint to implement new procedures to ensure that it provides consumer reports only to legitimate businesses for lawful purposes, to establish and maintain a comprehensive information security program, and to obtain audits by an independent third-party security professional every other year until 2026. The order requires ChoicePoint to establish, implement, and maintain a comprehensive information security program designed to protect the security, confidentiality, and integrity of the personal information it collects from or about consumers.

As pretexting has become a massive problem for the financial services industries, the GLB pretexting rules have taken on added significance. As explained by the FTC, "pretexting is the practice of getting your personal information under false pretenses."[8] This is dangerous because pretexting can lead to identity theft, whereby "someone hijacks your personal identifying information to open new charge accounts, order merchandise, or borrow money."[9]

PRACTICAL OBSCURITY: A SWAN SONG AFTER THE WEB

In a well-known open-government case, *US Department of Justice v. Reporters Committee for Freedom of Press* (1989), the Supreme Court held that Freedom of Information Act (FOIA) Exemption 7(c) prohibits federal disclosure of FBI rap sheets to the media. To qualify under Exemption 7(c), information should be of a sort that could "reasonably be expected to constitute an unwarranted invasion of personal privacy."[10]

Philosophically speaking, the fact that information is not wholly private does not mean that an individual has no interest in limiting its disclosure or dissemination.[11] The purpose of FOIA is not fostered by disclosure of information about private citizens that is accumulated in various governmental files but that reveals little or nothing about an agency's own conduct. The privacy interest in maintaining the practical obscurity of rap sheet information will always be high.

The *Reporters Committee* case is significant for its willingness to extend privacy rights under a federal statute even to criminal offenders concerning their public criminal records. But the case is also significant today as a kind of swan song, maybe a dirge. Thanks to electronic records, the Internet and search engines web, the vaunted "practical obscurity" of data is soon to be a memory. Data once resigned to the dustbin of history is now at anyone's fingertips. The media can easily construct its own rap sheets. Bad behavior today, or unwise or inadvertent disclosures, are not forgotten; they will never become practically obscure. A society that coerces privacy seeks to help us avoid falling prey to uses of information otherwise given away or taken away.

GIVE AWAY, TAKE AWAY

My focus on legitimately coerced and imposed privacy could be resisted as a distraction from the many ways in which government is taking privacy away and putting it at risk. This is not the intent, and problematic regimes like the REAL ID Act of 2005 merit criticism. We give away privacy the government confers, but government takes away privacy that some of us want.

In a country that has not had a national identification card, the REAL ID law was bound to kick up controversy. The act was signed into law as part of the Emergency Supplemental Appropriations Act for Defense, the Global War on Terror, and Tsunami Relief Act.[12] Congress gave the Department of Homeland Security authority to promulgate rules under the act. Real ID rules were originally scheduled to go fully into effect in May 2008, but the period of compliance was extended. By May 11, 2011, states were expected to have methods in place to verify that the identity documents provided by driver's license applicants, such as birth certificates, are valid. They will also be expected to start issuing Real ID-compliant licenses. By December 1, 2014, all Americans under the age of 50 will be expected to present Real ID-compliant licenses when boarding airplanes and entering federal buildings. All Americans, regardless of age, will have to meet those requirements by 2017.[13] One objective of the REAL ID Act is to implement the recommendation of the 9/11 Commission to enhance the security and integrity of driver's licenses. (The 9/11 terrorists used authentic driver's licenses that they obtained on the basis of unverified identification.) The new rules would prescribe verification standards and security features for state-issued ID cards. The rules would also make presentation of an identification card that complies with federal standards a condition of boarding most commercial aircraft, and entering federal buildings or nuclear power plants.

Although federal funds would pay for a part of the states' obligations to implement REAL ID, many states have expressed opposition to a policy of national identification standards. Privacy advocates objected to an original, abandoned proposal to place radio frequency identification technology (RFID) in new driver identification cards. The government has no plan to encrypt the data on the new identification cards, opening the possibility that data from these machine-readable cards will be easily appropriated. Appropriated or not, the cards will award authorities superior, unprecedented knowledge of the comings and goings of all citizens and residents. So we must worry about government taking away our privacy even as we worry about our own penchant for giving it away. The double-edged problem of privacy give-aways and take-aways is nicely illustrated by the only partly futuristic concept of "lifelogging."

LIFELOGS: REMEMBERING EVERYTHING

Children give away their privacy, but adults do too. The temptation and opportunity to give privacies away will only expand and intensity. The technologists' concept of a lifelog represents the ultimate privacy give-away. The term "lifelog" refers to a comprehensive multimedia archive of an individual's quotidian existence, aided by pervasive computing technologies. Comprehensive full-life lifelogging technology is moving outside the laboratory and into everyday life. Products in the spirit of lifelogging are already in use.[14] Every iPhone has lifeloging functions. Systematic, intentional lifelogging could someday signifcantly complement existing memory preservation practices. It could do the work of a diary, journal, or day book; a photo album, scrapbook or home video; a filing cabinet or cardboard box; a laptop, cell phone, or personal digital assistant (PDA). The lifelog of the future could store data pertaining to biological states derived from continuous self-monitoring of, for example, heart rate, respiration, blood sugar, blood pressure, and arousal.

While still in its infancy, consumer-driven comprehensive electronic personal archiving is ripe for philosophical speculation. How will this technology make it more attractive for adults to give away personal data, and create personal data that can be given away or taken by government? What would it mean for society if typical individuals retained a detailed record of their entire lives? What would it mean for interpersonal relationships to know that shared experiences are probably being recorded? How will intimacy, confidentiality, and privacy be affected? Who would have the right to forbid, restrict, initiate, or require lifelogging? Who would have the right to access the content of a person's lifelog? What, especially, would be the lifelogging-related entitlements of parents, employers, and the government? And what of access by spouses, researchers, business partners, accountants, lawyers, and private physicians presumed to have confidential relationships with the individual?

MyLifeBits is the name of a Microsoft Research company-sponsored full-life lifelogging project conceived in 1998 to explore the potential of digitally chronicling a person's life.[15] MyLifeBits focuses on recording the life of veteran researcher Gordon Bell. MyLifeBits is high-concept, high-tech, labor intensive, and Warhol-like: continuous storage of a life in durable electronics rather than paper cartons. Andy Warhol's low-tech lifelogging project—he called it time-capsuling—began in 1974: Warhol filled, sealed, and sent to storage 610 cardboard containers of "photographs, newspapers and magazines, fan letters, business and personal correspondence, art work, source images for artwork, books, exhibition catalogues, and telephone messages, along with objects and countless examples of ephemera, such as announcements for poetry readings and dinner invitations,...placed on an almost daily basis into a box kept conveniently next to his desk."[16] Bell's lifelogging is distinctly high-tech. Using a geeky infrared Sensecam camera worn around his neck, along with scanners and computing devices, Bell records nearly all of his conversations and experiences. He stores them electronically, along with documents, photographs, and memorabilia chronicling his past. In addition, Bell electronically preserves all of his e-mail, typed documents, and web page visits.

Technologists predict that full-life, lifelogging devices will one day be integrated into everyday existence, becoming as ordinary as telephones. Researchers maintain that technologies to amass experiences from the individual perspective through the use of personal sensors and recording devices will potentially change social structure itself.

They anticipate mostly positive changes and net benefits relating to education, law enforcement, the military, healthcare, and sense and memory enhancement for the disabled. The US military has already begun to experiment with lifelogging. The Pentagon canceled a lifelog project which was to have been an effort to build a database tracking a person's entire existence; the program was canceled after the Defense Advanced Research Projects Agency's request in 2003 for proposals to develop lifelog technology spawned controversy and concerns about privacy. However, a smaller-scale lifelogging project, Advanced Soldier Sensor Information System and Technology, was premiered in 2007 at the Aberdeen Proving Grounds.[17]

Lifelogging preserves individually produced "capta"—defined as "units of data that have been selected and harvested from the sum of potential data."[18] Because lifelog data is conceived as self-produced, researchers Martin Dodge and Rob Kitchin have characterized lifelogs—"socio-spatial archives that document every action, every event, every conversation, and every material expression of an individual's life"—as personal "sousveillance," a term borrowed from the Canadian technologist Steve Mann.[19] Lifelogging has sousveillance and surveillance dimensions. It is sousveillance to the extent that it captures data about oneself or from the perspective of oneself. But it is surveillance to the extent that it is designed to capture data about others, including others who may also be engaged in acts of sousveillance or surveillance. Human individuals live social rather than solitary lives. One person's comprehensive, full-life lifelog would inevitably capture biography and expressions of the lives of other persons. How, if at all, should the capture and surveillance implicit in personal sousveillance be regulated? How can security against harmful falsification, deletion, data breaches, or identity theft be assured? Would lifelogs turn individuals into surveillance partners of government? How much access should the government have to an individual's lifelog for national security, law enforcement, public health, tax compliance, and routine administrative purposes?

Privacy concerns arise because lifelogs are not destined solely for storage until the subject's death like Warhol's cardboard boxes, or sealed for five thousand years like a World's Fair time capsule.[20] By design, lifelog capta will be accessible and useable. Two of the most obvious and important categories of privacy problems raised by comprehensive, full-life lifelogging are (1) pernicious "memory" (that is, recordation, recall, replay, and remembrance, and (2) pernicious surveillance (that is, watching, observing, tracking, spying). Both involve threats to privacy. Memory can be a very good thing, but it can also encourage harmfully dredging up or revisiting past conduct. Surveillance can also be a very good thing, but it turns into a social evil when it trains watchful, spying eyes needlessly and hurtfully.

The capacities to recall, to be reminded, and to review records of the past can be valuable. Suppose that you could invisibly record and store conversations in electronic memory for convenient retrieval on demand. You could be spared professional disapproval and social embarrassment. Despite practical utility, electronic memory enhancement is not an unqualified good. Electronic memory enhancement enables destructive reminding and remembrance. Lifelogging—like social networking—would extend the longevity of personal experience. Yet people typically have a legitimate moral interest in distancing themselves from commonplace misfortunes and errors.[21]

Say I get drunk, lose my temper, and slap a dear friend at a party. My lifelog records the incident. After making amends and being forgiven, I decide to delete the episode from my log. But a dozen other party guests have captured the slapping incident on their lifelogs, too. I may be unable to prevent acquaintances from someday throwing my fault in my face. Once a dustbin, in the lifelog context, history becomes a freezer.

Dredging up the past can hurt feelings, stir negative emotions, and ruin lives. We can see clearly the potential cruelty and harmful consequences of resurrecting the past in the patterns of a familiar line of privacy tort cases. In these cases, someone suffered humiliation and loss of standing in the community because someone else chose to bring up—the victims might say, dredge up—the truths of their pasts. In 1931, *Melvin v. Reid* pitted a homemaker, who had once been a prostitute acquitted of murder, against filmmakers who used her actual maiden name in *The Red Kimono*, a movie based on her life.[22] William James Sidis brought a lawsuit against the *New Yorker* magazine in 1940, after a reporter weaseled into his apartment for an interview and then published a story that belittled Sidis's eccentricities and shabby circumstances.[23] Mr. Sidis had been a celebrated child prodigy, the youngest person ever to attend Harvard, and a college graduate by age sixteen. In 1971 a case of the same ilk, *Briscoe v. Reader's Digest Association*, was brought by a convicted armed hijacker turned solid citizen and parent who sued a newspaper for publishing a reference to his crime.[24]

Three short decades ago, reliance on expectations of substantial privacy about the past were highly reasonable. One could build a new life on a premise of de facto concealment. One could earn trust and honor. One could walk with dignity before others. Respecting expectations of privacy about the past in a world of mere human memory and mostly paper archives was a moral obligation. There was a kind of moral right to forget and to be forgotten.

In an era of electronic archives, traditional predictions and expectations of privacy about the past have begun to look less reasonable. Information about the past is readily at hand. Much of the focus of information science is on how to eliminate what the Supreme Court has termed "practical obscurity" through electronic archive and retrieval. Electronic accessibility renders past and current events equally knowable.[25] The very ideas of "past" and "present" in relation to personal information are in danger of evaporating. The past is on the surface, like skim. There is much less dredging required to get to the past; one can simply point and click for almost instant replay.

Today's "Melvins" and "Briscoes" must expect their crimes to have a rich afterlife—not only in newspapers and government records but via, for example, cell phones, blogs, discussion forums, YouTube videos, Bing, Twitter, Facebook, and MySpace, as well. As privacy and concealment become more difficult to obtain, they may come to matter less or differently. In a universe of cheap, massive lifelog data retention, individuals would perhaps come to understand digital capture and unwanted data disclosure as mundane risks, like swallowing bugs at a picnic. More radically, they may come to understand themselves not as longitudinal well-integrated personalities, but as ever-present navigable data streams no one fully controls.

Security measures will help to keep lifelog data private. But the law may not permit privacy. Just as laptop hard drives are subject to search at the US border, so too would be any other portable data storage device. Government need not honor keep-out signs: it can demand that we provide passwords or decryption keys, notwithstanding concerns about self-incrimination. Courts can require disclosure of information previously posted on Facebook, whatever the account holder's privacy settings. Moreover, social norms may fail to ascribe individuals the right to keep their own lifelogs sufficiently private from family and friends to securely protect their emotional lives and careers. And in any case, individuals will be featured in other people's lifelogs, probably without a legal right to fully control how the data about them is used, shared, or construed.

Improvements in mental health diagnosis could flow from the accessibility of lifelog data. Therapists could actually see and hear the behavior of clients not sick enough for monitoring in a hospital—the equivalent of the Holter Monitor ambulatory electrocardiograph machine that cardiologists employ to detect subtle heart disease. Yet the vivid recall lifelogs will permit might turn out to be a psychological hazard. The lifelogging concept is insensitive to the therapeutic value of forgetting the details of experience.[26] Trauma often needs to recede into near oblivion; rumination about the past may need to be discouraged to make room for fresh experiences and perspectives.

Indeed, the ability to move on from wrongdoing is something even wrongdoers not affected by mental illness may find it hard to do in a world of lifeloggers. The expectation that lifeloggers delete memories of offensive conduct for which others have forgiven them might emerge. My deleting data about my forgiven offenses from my lifelog may have less value, though, if the others around me do not delete their records of what I have done. But incomplete networking and communication means that information of about wrongs will not be consistently followed up with and up-dated by information about moral repair. Another difficulty: interest asymmetry. The forgiven offender may be best served by data deletion, while the forgiving victim may be best served by data preservation.

I now turn from pernicious memory to pernicious surveillance. Lifelogs could someday become exceedingly comprehensive and sensitive windows into a person's life. A great deal of data is already collected and retained about individuals by themselves and by others. In the future the need for personal lifelogging could be tempered by the fact that business and government will routinely and systematically collect detailed data about individuals for purposes of marketing, security, and social control. Because sousveillance is also surveillance, lifeloggers join the state and industry as fellow people-watchers.

The potential exists for using lifelog pervasive computing technology for purposes of spying on others. Spying is sometimes prompted by genuine obligations of caretaking, such as monitoring an aging adult parent or teenager; it may also be a way to prove a humiliating adultery, gather evidence against a corporate crime, or expose injustice. Where spying is ethically permitted or required, there are ethical limits on the methods of spying.[27] The virtuous spy will violate privacy and transparency norms, but he or she will, to the extent possible, continue to act with respect for the moral autonomy and for the moral and legal interests of the investigative target. This value attached to spying thus provides no justification or defense for recreational spying, whether using lifelog technology or more traditional means. Widespread lifelogging could increase the amount of illicit, unethical recreational surveillance to intolerable levels. Dodging recreational spies and social network-addicted blabbermouths could become a major self-protective preoccupation of any privacy-sensitive members of the next generation.

People will presumably own their lifelogs, but there is no reason to think lifelogs will be immune from appropriation by government. On the contrary, there is every reason to think lifelogging will be a boon to the legal system and government surveillance. The sousveillant will be the true sibling of Big Brother. I reach this conclusion by taking notice of the spirit and letter of current federal surveillance policy. There is already fairly systematic surveillance of Americans.[28] Current laws—Fourth Amendment law, the Electronic Communications Privacy Act, the Communications Assistance for Law Enforcement Act, and the Patriot Act—give the government access to virtually all means of communications and data storage.[29] The law also demands that new communications technologies preserve powers of government access. A government that has traditionally enjoyed access to communications and correspondence will want access to lifelogs, too.

Martin Dodge and Rob Kitchin examined the ethics of lifelogging and came up with an ironic solution to the problems of psychologically risky mechanical sousveillance and sousveillance-aided government surveillance: infuse lifelogging systems with "imperfection, loss and error." Dodge and Kitchin propose designing lifelogs to function imperfectly, not unlike biological memory. In particular, they propose that the devices have the capacity to "block" recording of some details, "forget" details over time, and "tweak" memory of the past by mis-recording precisely when, where and how certain events took place. Fallibility of the lifelog will benefit the individuals who own it, too. Dodge and Kitchin argue that, free from an "unforgiving" and "merciless" memory machine, persons can "evolve their social identities, live with their conscience, deal with their demons, move on from their past to build new lives, reconcile their own paradoxes and contradictions, and be part of society."

There is still time for privacy-by-design. There is still time optimally to design full-life lifelogging products. Consumers are not yet clamoring for "perfect" memory, full-life lifeloggers—but given the choice between a deliberately imperfect Dodge-Kitchin lifelogger and a veridical lifelogger, I suspect most consumers would go for the latter, despite the attendant problems of privacy. If Jim and Jill are sentimental lovers who first met at Starbucks on a Tuesday morning, they will not want their lifelogs to have created both inaccurate and inconsistent accounts of their fateful encounter. The "unforgiving" and "merciless" veridical lifelog technology will have gargantuan appeal to consumers, the government, and the health, research, and commercial sectors. One's physician cannot be helped with data about blood pressure and heart rate if the accuracy of that data is in question. The precise color of the item you purchased at Target and the date are the sort of detailed, accurate data the commercial sector wants to collect.

Designers of the Total Recall veridical lifelog technology at the University of Southern California in Los Angeles recognized the privacy issues raised by its continuous environmental recording aspect.[30] They even considered the possibility that lifelogging recording technology might violate wiretapping laws, other privacy statutes, or fair information practice consent standards. But they seemed to find solace in their controversial observation that people in public places lack "reasonable expectations of privacy."[31] This observation is a virtual ideology. But privacy law itself—let alone ethical theory—suggests a more subtle reading of privacy in public places, and asserts that there can be a right to it. Pervasive surveillance, whether in public or private places, opens the door to the misery of perpetual judgment.

In the 1967 the Supreme Court held in *Katz v. United States* that the expectation of privacy is not limited solely to the home, and may extend to at least some publicly visible and accessible areas like phone booths on city streets.[32] The 1974 federal Privacy Act prohibits the federal government from making a record of the exercise of First Amendment rights of free speech. There are signs that more American courts and policymakers also accept the notion of privacy in public.[33] A recent federal law prohibits some forms of potentially embarrassing picture-taking, which have become more of a problem with the creation of increasingly advanced mobile telephone cameras.

The stated aim of the Total Recall project was to create a personal information management system which will securely collect, store, and disseminate data from a variety of personal sensors. The projected systems would also allow customizable searching, analysis, and querying of the data, in a secure manner. Applications of the systems could play an important role in improving people's quality of life.

The Total Recall team predicted and embraced the fact that lifelogging recordings will fall into the hands of the state. Indeed, part of their social design concept for lifelogs was after that they are available to the judicial system. They noted with seemingly uncritical acceptance that "the political climate supports access to information by law enforcement even without judicial intervention."[34] They speculated that lifelogs would be admissible as veridical under the rules of evidence because of the "legitimate needs for data" and that they probably would not be subject to Fifth Amendment exclusion because they would not be testimonial. Rather than degrade the utility of the lifelog out of concerns about privacy and government access, in the manner of Dodge and Kitchin, the Total Recall team labored to imagine design features that acknowledge privacy interests in turning lifeloggers on and off, while insuring the capacity to preserve verifiably authentic, unmodified recordings. It is that very capacity, preserved at all, that constitutes the threat.

There is an appeal to the notion of making a multimedia record of one's entire life. We feel that our experiences and achievements, however ordinary, comprise our uniqueness; preserving a record of them preserves a record of us. Lifelogging feeds the inner King Tut, the side of us that fights transience through entombment. But lifelogging is also journaling, art, entertainment, and communication. Innovators expect lifelogging products to emerge as serious tools for improving the quality of life. In its favor, lifelogging might encourage introspection and self-knowledge. The capacity to share lifelogs could increase intimacy, understanding, and accountability in personal relationships. Inheriting the lifelog of a deceased parent, spouse, or child could help preserve family history and ease the pain of loss. Replay and remembrance machines could make us better at caretaking, work, and professional responsibility, too. Finally, lifelogs might enhance personal security. A potential mugger or rapist would have to think twice in a society of lifeloggers.

To the extent that it preserves personal experience for voluntary private consumption, electronic lifelogging looks innocent enough—as innocent as Blackberries, home movies, and snapshots in silver picture frames. But lifelogging could fuel excessive self-absorption, since users would be engaged in making multimedia presentations about themselves all the time. The availability of lifelogging technology might lead individuals to overvalue the otherwise transient details of their lives. The content of many a YouTube video and Twitter message reflects a narcissitic over-engagement with forgettable fun. Furthermore, the potential would be great for incivility, emotional blackmail, exploitation, prosecution, and social control surrounding lifelog creation, content, and accessibility.

Although comprehensive full-life lifelogging technology does not yet exist outside of the laboratory, legal and ethical limitations and parameters suggest themselves.[35] No one should be required to keep a lifelog. No one should be suspected for not keeping a lifelog. Lifelogs should be deemed the property of the person or persons who create them. No one should record or photograph others for their lifelogs without consent. The owner of a lifelog should be able to delete or add content at will. No one, for example a commercial provider of cloud computing storage, should copy a lifelog or transfer a lifelog to a third party without the consent of its owner. We must hope that the changes in the quality of life affected by the proliferation of lifelogs will not result in a further deterioration in the taste for privacy or fewer legal privacy protections. Existing privacy laws pertaining to intrusion, publication, communication, search and seizure, surveillance, data protection, and identity should be presumed to apply to lifelogs. Existing intellectual property laws should be presumed to apply to lifelog content. The rules of evidence, privilege, and professional ethics should be presumed to govern the use and disclosure of lifelog data, but these do not always keep private dairies, letters, and business papers private.[36] These presumptions may prove unworkable or merely unpopular.

CONCLUSION: CARING ABOUT NOT CARING ABOUT PRIVACY

Privacy is not always popular. It is not as popular as it should be. The tendency and the willingness to throw privacy away is troubling. It is troubling when children toss the pearls of privacy back into the ocean; and it is troubling when young adults and mature adults thoughtlessly do the same. Why? It is troubling because the value of privacy is not just the opportunity for optional privacy states, but the experience of privacy and the habits of respect for privacy it constitutes. The argument has been made that privacy is already gone and in any case unnecessary. I agree with neither proposition, but fear we are inching towards the former state of affairs.[37]

Since the 1970s, when scholars first began to analyze privacy in earnest, philosophers have linked the experience of privacy with dignity, autonomy, civility, and intimacy. They linked it also to repose, self-expression, creativity, and reflection. They tied it to the preservation of unique preferences and distinct traditions. Privacy is a foundational good. The argument that privacy is a *right* whose normative basis is respect for persons opens the door to the further argument that privacy is also potentially a *duty*. "To respect someone as a person is to concede that one ought to take account of the way in which his enterprise might be affected by one's decision," S. I. Benn wrote.[38] And to respect oneself may require taking into account the way in which one's personality and life enterprises could be affected by decisions to dispense with foundational goods that are lost when one decides to flaunt, expose, and share rather than to reserve, conceal, and keep.

The idea that the experience of privacy is ethically mandatory is logically consistent with leading normative accounts. It is consistent with Robert Post's (citing Erving Goffman and Jeffrey Reiman) "characterization of respecting privacy as respecting civility norms" of deference and demeanor.[39] It is likewise consistent with Helen Nissenbaum's analysis of privacy. She defines privacy and its value in relation to norms of the appropriateness of specific behaviors and the distribution of certain information in social and cultural context.[40] If people are completely morally and legally free to pick and choose the privacy they will experience, such as deferential civility, appropriateness and limited data flow, they are potentially deprived of highly valued states that promote their vital interests, and those of fellow human beings with whom they associate. We need to restrain choice—if not by law, then somehow. Respect for privacy rights and the ascription of privacy duties must both be a part of a society's formative project for shaping citizens.

Lior Jacob Strahilevitz has argued that privacy violations can be understood as rechanneling information flow, so that information unknown or obscure in a network becomes known: "Where a defendant's [in a suit alleging informational privacy invasion] disclosure materially alters the flow of otherwise obscure information through a social network, such that what would have otherwise remained obscure becomes widely known, the defendant should be liable for public disclosure of private facts."[41] Viewed in this way, it may not seem to matter that privacy is invaded unless the person whose information flows out against his will cares. We have to go back to dignitarian ideals about privacy to see why we, as liberals, should care about optional dismissals of privacy.

Jeffrey Reiman defined privacy as the "social rituals" that serve to teach us that we are distinct moral persons and autonomous moral agents.[42] Liberals agree that there is something wrong with being watched and investigated all the time. As legal theorist Daniel Solove argues, surveillance can make "a person feel extremely uncomfortable" and can lead to "self-censorship and inhibition."[43] Surveillance is a form of social control. As such, it impacts freedom. I have been urging that dispensing with one's privacy is yielding to social control, and that that impacts freedom, too. Realizing this, the notion that some privacy should not be optional, waivable, or alienable should have instant credibility.

Pushing the idea that privacy is appropriately coerced in some contexts is not to align with the "theory of social rights" rejected by John Stuart Mill in *On Liberty*. A theory of "social rights," he said, maintains the "monstrous" proposition "that it is the absolute social right of every individual, that every other individual shall act in every respect exactly as he ought; that whosoever fails thereof in the smallest particular, violates my social right, and entitles me to demand from the legislature the removal of the grievance.[44] But the liberal ideal becomes an ironic joke in a society in which people freely choose to be always in others' lines of sight, much as it is a joke in a society in which they freely choose utter domination.[45]

8
POPULAR PATERNALISM

When my friend Vincent took a new job, he was dismayed that the company's desire to stringently protect the privacy of employees' e-mail meant he could not use his favorite old password at work: "123OceanAve", the street address of a childhood home. His employer instructed him to select a password that did not contain any word found in the English language dictionary, plus at least four numerals, a mix of four upper- and lowercase letters of the alphabet, and an exclamation point. "Zj34uc!91B" met the criteria, but my friend would have preferred to take on the slight risk of someone hacking into his e-mail than to have to memorize a random stream of characters.

Vincent is one of the many people who consider data privacy measures a bother. Their attitudes of annoyance raise questions about the extent to which paternalistic impositions of privacy by particular people or entities in particular contexts are warranted. In Vince's case the motives for imposing a strong data protection regime on workers were not purely paternalistic. The firm was seeking both self-interestedly to protect the integrity of company data, and paternalistically to protect the privacy of employees' personal e-mail sent from the office or company webmail. Mandating a secure password is weak paternalism, coercion barely worthy of objection; but mandated data protection can have significant implications for choice, speech and other freedoms.

PATERNALISTIC MANDATES

Paternalism by government is not rare, but requires special warrant. In a society with liberal aspirations, we expect regimes of choice concerning personal information to be preferred over regimes of coercion whenever possible. Indeed, policy makers with free market stripes work especially hard at times to avoid and minimize state coercion. But coercion can be, in a way liberals commend, advantageous to the individuals coerced. Freedom has to be forced on the loyal slave or subservient wife who cannot imagine a better life without a master.

As an example of privacy-related policy making in which the specter of state paternalism raised its head and had to be confronted, in chapter 1 I described how U.S. Federal Trade Commission regulators created an optional Do Not Call registry to give Americans a choice about whether to stop receiving the nightly tsunami of telemarketing calls that interrupted otherwise private time at home. Faced with the problem of telemarketing call abuses, federal policymakers had several plausible choices: (1) doing nothing, beyond better enforcing then-existent laws aimed at deterring and punishing telemarketing abuses; (2) enacting new coercive rules, banning most commercial telemarketers from placing calls to phone customers; or (3) enacting new rules of choice, empowering individual phone customers to voluntarily place their numbers on a national Do Not Call registry, which would deny most telemarketers the right to call their homes; and even (4) requiring telemarketers to pay a fee for calls to phone customers. The FTC regulators chose option (3). Had they chosen option (2) and thereby forced phone customers to give up privacy-invading unsolicited telemarketing calls, I believe customers might have come to delight in the coerced bit of additional uninterrupted solitude and intimacy at home. But regulators preferred the less paternalistic, weaker privacy mandate over the more paternalistic, stronger privacy mandate. Option (3) allowed regulators to enhance consumer choice and freedom, while preserving socially useful political and charitable telemarketing. The tradeoff was not perfect. Socially useful, noncommercial telemarketing calls can get pretty intrusive. During the 2008 presidential primary campaign season, Americans received an unremitting stream of calls from supporters of Hillary Clinton and Barak Obama, both of whom sought the Democratic Party nomination that eventually went to Mr. Obama. The calls, many just taped-recorded messages from local mayors, ex-presidents, and governors, continued through primary voting day. My friend Vincent had an intense encounter with overzealous young Obama supporter who called his house after he had already voted, asking whether he had gone to the polls. When he told her he regarded her call and question as invasions of privacy, she was taken aback: "Well, sir, you are a registered voter, and your home phone number is a public record. I make calls like this all day, sir, its just the way politics are done, for your information."

The task of making sound liberty, equality, and efficiency-enhancing public choices regarding privacy and personal data protection can be exceedingly complex. Policymakers must take full measure of practical limits, norm tradeoffs, and competing plausible policy alternatives. One plan to impose privacy may be arguably sound (e.g., banning all commercial telemarketing calls, requiring medical confidentiality of hospitals, forcing spouses of corporate insiders to retain company secrets), while another arguably not sound (e.g., not allowing gays in the military to reveal their sexual orientation, never allowing letter recipients to sell intimate letters from celebrities, banning all government race data collection). As discussed in chapter 6, proponents of the failed racial privacy initiative referendum in California doubtless believed that, forced to give up the practice of disclosing race, members of racial minority groups would delight in unimagined benefits of a reduction in officials' race-based decision making. However, as my extended examination of the concept of racial privacy was designed to illustrate, the proposed racial privacy mandate in question was conceptually problematic, impractical, and an impediment to distributive and reparative justice.

A JOB FOR THE NANNY STATE

While state paternalism prima facie impairs the freedom that liberalism—especially the libertarian interpretation of liberalism—ascribes to normal adults, the story is different with children and youth. Young children are properly subjected to paternalistic interventions of all sorts. Protecting children from both harm by others and self-imposed harm is a responsibility of family and government caretakers. The "nanny state" is exactly what children need.

Overall paternalistic concern for children and youth has led to public sector programs and policies that reflect frank disregard for children's legitimate privacy interests. A striking example is the webcam scandal that rocked the Philadelphia suburb of Lower Merion in 2009. On November 11, 2009, Lindy Matsko, an assistant principal at Harriton High School (HHS), approached fifteen-year-old Blake Robbins, then a sophomore at HHS, and informed him that school administrators believed that he was "engaged in improper behavior in his home."[1] Matsko cited as evidence an image taken by means of the webcam of Robbins's school-issued MacIntosh laptop computer.[2] Matsko may have suspected that captured laptop-derived images or conversations implicated Robbins in drug usage and/or dealing.[3] School administrators claim that the image was a screen shot of Robbins's computer showing a troubling on-line chat between Robbins and another student.[4] Robbins, however, has claimed in at least one television interview that the image was not a screen shot, but rather an external webcam shot of him consuming Mike and Ike candy, which school administrators mistook for drugs.[5]

No disciplinary action was taken against Robbins as a result of any images captured from the laptop.[6] However, shortly after the incident, Robbins's father, Michael Robbins, contacted Assistant Principal Matsko to discuss the situation and confirm that HHS administrators in fact had the ability to remotely activate the webcam in a student's school-issued laptop "at any time it chose and to view and capture whatever images were in front of the webcam."[7]

Neither Michael Robbins nor any other parent or student in the Lower Merion School District (LMSD), which includes two state-of-the-art academic high schools,[8] had been officially notified in advance of the district's ability to capture screenshots and webcam images from pupils school-issued laptops. Yet the district could capture webcam shots "of anyone or anything appearing in front of the camera at the time of activation"[9] taken from "any location in which the [school-issued] computer was kept," such as the student's home.[10] In a statement to a newspaper after Robbins filed a lawsuit claiming privacy intrusions prohibited by state and federal law, school district official Virginia DiMedio confirmed that the District did not disclose the TheftTrack remote activation feature to teachers or students "for obvious reasons" since "it involved computer security, and that is all it was being used for."[11] On October 11, 2010, the Lower Merion School Board voted to settle Robbins's and another invasion of privacy lawsuit that resulted from webcam surveillance for a total of $610,000, agreeing never to again use tracking software on student-issued laptops without the consent of students and their parents.[12]

Perhaps it was not surprising that within a decade of widespread Internet use, the U.S. Congress enacted legislation designed to protect the privacy of children who use the web. (Congress never imagined that one of the risks of using the web would be spying by public schools utilizing school-issued computers.) Limiting the right of website operators to collect personal data from children under the age of thirteen, the Children's Online Privacy Protection Act (COPPA), federal legislation that became effective in the year 2000, imposed electronic information privacy on children that children themselves often did not want or value. Like children, many adults display a remarkable lack of concern for their own electronic information privacy. They can be tricked and exploited by website operators, by fellow social networkers, identity thieves, and spammers. Congress has been slow and less paternalistic about stepping in to address the data protection needs of adult users of communications technologies, leaving some privacy advocates asking, in light of the magnitude of the problem, why.

The Internet (by which I shall mean the Internet and the World Wide Web) is a resource for communication, commerce, education, entertainment, art, friendship, charity, and politics. The Internet comes with problems and costs, some of which can be effectively addressed through positive legal regulation. The perils of Internet use include the dignitarian and reputational harm that befalls individuals when online information enables the government or other third-parties to gain access to personal data and communications. The Internet exposes users to financial peril. Failure to use secure websites, websites with meaningful privacy policies, and privacy-enhancing technologies (such as encryption, digital signatures, and pseudonyms) can lead to inadvertent disclosures of sensitive financial data or personal identifiers. Disclosures of personal data can mean financial losses, consumer inconvenience, and identity theft.

Now an indispensable tool for daily life, the Internet can be an exhilarating domain for social experimentation and personal growth. But at the same time, it exposes users to sexual predators, stalkers, and emotional injury. Why, if at all, should government decline to regulate information practices through coercive, even paternalistic, legislation?

THE CHILDREN'S INTERNET PRIVACY LAW

Children love pop music and social networking. That is why they visited at least 196 of the more than 1,000 websites operated by Sony BMG Music Entertainment. To register to use these cites, children gave their birth dates and other personal information to Sony Music, without seeking parental approval. On some of the Sony Music sites children could create their own personal fan pages, review music, upload photographs or videos, post comments, join discussion forums and send private messages.

Children love cookies and candy, too. Hershey Foods Corporation manufactures some of America's most popular chocolate candies, including Hershey's Kisses and the Hershey chocolate bar. The company operated more than thirty websites featuring candy-related information and entertainment aimed at children. To use these sites, children were supposed to ask their parents to complete Hershey's official permission form. Hershey Foods accepted the online forms once completed, but without any proof that actual mothers, fathers, or other adult guardians had filled them in. The Mrs. Fields company, which produces the popular cookie, operated "birthday club" websites for children twelve and under. After enrolling in a birthday club, an eligible child could expect to receive a personal birthday greeting and coupons for free merchandise. To enroll, children were asked to provide their full names, home addresses, e-mail addresses, and birth dates. More than 84,000 children signed up. Ms. Fields allowed children to join the birthday club on their own, without seeking parental approval.

Pop music and sweets are more important to children than electronic information privacy and data protection. This ordering of priorities gets things wrong, and the United States Congress decided to do something about it. To protect families from the immature preferences of children under the age of thirteen, Congress enacted the Children's Online Privacy Protection Act.[13] The statute went into effect in 2000, limiting the right of website operators to collect personal data from children. The act was preceded by private and public sector studies citing informational privacy losses and exploitation by advertisers, along with accessibility to child sexual predators and exposure to adult content, as major risks of children's use of the Internet.[14] The intent of the legislation was to make it more difficult for websites to collect personal information directly from young children without a parent's knowledge and consent. Specifically, COPPA requires commercial website operators to obtain the verifiable consent of a parent or guardian before collecting personal information from children under thirteen. The act also limits operators' right to condition prizes and contests on the disclosure of personal information. Charged with enforcing COPPA, the US Federal Trade Commission (FTC) files complaints against website operators accused of inadequate privacy protection practices or violating specific rules governing how personally identifiable information may be obtained from families with young children. Complaints filed with the FTC against Sony Music, Mrs. Field's Cookies, and Hershey Foods have resulted in more than $1.2 million dollars in civil penalty assessments.

FAIR INFORMATION PRACTICES

Fair information practice standards first promulgated in the 1970s are embodied in COPPA's requirements of notice, access, and security.[15] Fair information practice principles are standards for collecting, maintaining, and disclosing personal information about individuals that have often guided the hands of government and the private sector.[16] Common to fair information practice codes are five core principles of privacy protection: Principle (1) Notice/Awareness; Principle (2) Choice/Consent; Principle (3) Access/Participation; Principle (4) Integrity/Security; and Principle (5) Enforcement/Redress.[17] COPPA requires certain fair information practices of covered websites. For example, operators must provide clear notice on the website of what information the operator collects and how the operator will use or disclose information collected from children. The act applies to operators of commercial websites and certain other online services that are directed at children under thirteen.[18] A website operator is defined as primarily those operating websites for profit; COPPA's definition does not distinguish between domestic and foreign-based websites. As long as websites are directed at, or knowingly collect information from, children in the United States, COPPA applies. Foreign-based website operators who advertise in offline media in the United States or on popular US websites place themselves within the FTC's jurisdiction and are also supposed to comply with COPPA's regulations.

Specifically, COPPA requires that operators provide parents or guardians with: (1) "a description of the specific types of personal information collected from the child by [the] operator"; (2) "the opportunity at any time to refuse to permit the operator's further use or maintenance... of personal information from that child"; and (3) "a means that is reasonable... for the parent to obtain any personal information collected from that child."[19]

The second requirement, that parents be permitted to prohibit further use of information at any time, is a particularly strong consumer right vis-à-vis the commercial sector. This requirement merits special emphasis. The right of parents is not simply an ordinary right to "opt out" of unwanted third-party disclosures, or even a right to limit secondary uses of information. These ordinary rights appear in many formulations of fair information practices. Under COPPA, parents are ascribed a powerful right to veto primary collection, primary use, secondary use, and even maintenance of data. This strong right goes beyond typical formulations of fair information practices.

The strong veto right is needed to further the objectives of the statute, and the parental veto rule is clearly needed to effect meaningful adult control. Through

COPPA, parents are granted the power to function as gatekeepers of children and households' personal information; and because small children sometimes slip personal information past unsuspecting parents, the power to recapture information previously disclosed is critical. An adult lacks the power to recapture personal data concerning household income and habits that he, she, a spouse, or older teen has rashly disclosed—but under COPPA that same adult is able to recapture data imprudently disclosed by a young child.[20] COPPA has no exceptions for "mature minors," analogous to the required exceptions to laws requiring parental notification or consent for abortion services.[21] In the realm of data privacy, unlike the realm of reproductive privacy, for children under thirteen, parents rule officially and absolutely.

But COPPA binds and limits parents, too, as targets of regulation. Parents cannot waive the protection entailed by certain COPPA requirements and prohibitions. For example, COPPA requires operators to establish procedures to protect the "confidentiality, security, and integrity of personal information collected from children."[22] This obligation cannot be avoided through parental waivers. Nor can COPPA's prohibition against operators conditioning a child's participation in online activities (e.g., games and prizes) on the provision that they provide more personal information than is reasonably necessary.[23] This last prohibition disables the use of incentives that would turn simple children's games into data bonanzas for online businesses. Policy makers did not want e-commerce to have this ability, even if parents do not care.

A so-called safe harbor is provided for operators who follow COPPA-approved self-regulatory guidelines issued by representatives of the marketing or online industries or other designated persons.[24] Several groups and companies applied for safe harbor status right away, as soon as the law went into effect. To encourage compliance and limit the need for formal enforcement actions, the FTC has sought to educate the public, and operates multiple websites designed to provide education about online privacy.[25]

A LAW IN ACTION

Website operators' willingness to comply with COPPA is a mixed story. Many major, popular sites comply; some do not. Early indications of rampant noncompliance with the statute suggested that COPPA might not achieve its ends. In July 2000, just a few months after its effective date, the FTC undertook to determine whether website operators were complying with the act; of the children-oriented sites investigated, only about half were compliant. The FTC issued warning letters to several sites. A report by Professor Joseph Turow, an independent academic researcher, indicated at the time that most commercial websites geared for children ignored children's privacy and the requirements of COPPA. A striking illustration of the problem occurred more than a year after COPPA went into effect. Operators of popular, adolescent (at the time) singer Britney Spears's official website voluntarily closed down in order to revamp for COPPA compliance.[26] Of course, the easiest way to revamp for COPPA compliance is simply to stop asking anyone for personally identifiable information.

As noted, Congress authorized the FTC to enforce COPPA's provisions. The FTC can bring enforcement suits under COPPA and seek to impose civil penalties. But even before the compliance rules went into effect, the FTC displayed an interest in the privacy of young families. The FTC's first Internet privacy complaint was a deceptive practices suit brought and settled in 1998 against GeoCities. The commission alleged that "GeoCities misled its customers, both children and adults, by not telling the truth about how it was using their personal information."[27] The settlement required GeoCities to ensure parental control by obtaining parental consent prior to collecting personal information from children twelve and under. According to the FTC, industry self-regulatory guidelines already in effect in 1998 but ignored by GeoCities urged sites to obtain parental consent for at least some transactions with children.

In another pre-COPPA case, in May of 1999 the FTC announced that the Young Investor website operated by Liberty Financial Services, a large Massachusetts asset management company, had settled an action alleging false promises of anonymity. As reported by the FTC, the website operators used contests, prizes, and promises of anonymity to induce children to provide detailed financial data about their allowances, stocks, bonds, mutual funds, spending habits, college plans, and family finances.[28]

The FTC began sending warning letters to noncompliant websites in July 2000, just a few months after COPPA went into effect. That same month, a COPPA complaint was added to the FTC's unfair and deceptive trade practice lawsuit against Toysmart.com. The FTC initiated its first enforcement action under COPPA in a case alleging a violation of the provision against the conditioning of participation in a contest on disclosure of personal information. On July 21, 2000, the commission filed an enforcement action under COPPA against Toysmart.com, concurrent with its settlement of charges that Toysmart had violated its own privacy policy when it sought to sell its customer database to discharge obligations in bankruptcy.[29] The firm's policy had been reviewed and approved by TRUSTe, an industry self-regulation group.[30] The COPPA violation alleged against Toysmart was that a trivia contest, which first appeared on the Toysmart website in May 2000, collected personal information from children under thirteen without obtaining the consent of the children's parents. The contest conditioned participation on the disclosure of the requested personal information.[31]

On April 19, 2001, the FTC announced the settlements of its first line of civil penalty cases brought under the act. Monarch Services, Inc. and Girls Life, Inc., operators of www.girlslife.com; Bigmailbox.com, Inc., and Nolan Quan, operators of www.bigmailbox.com; and Looksmart Ltd., operator of www.insidetheweb.com, were all charged with violations of COPPA for illegally collecting personal information from children without parental consent and requiring children to disclose more personal information than was needed for participation in the activities involved. To settle the charges, the operators agreed to pay $100,000 in civil penalties. Furthermore, the settlements barred any future COPPA violations and required the companies to delete all personally identifying information collected from children online at any time since COPPA became effective. In addition, the operators were required to post a privacy policy on their website that complied with the law, as well as a link to www.ftc.gov/kidzprivacy, the FTC-operated site that provides information about COPPA.[32]

In recent years numerous successful enforcement actions have been brought by the FTC. The American Pop Corn Company, maker of Jollytime Popcorn, paid a $10,000 fine in 2002 for collection of personal data without parental consent.[33] The same year the firm that makes the classic Etch-A-Sketch toy, the Ohio Art Company, agreed to pay $35,000 to settle FTC allegations that it unlawfully collected personal information from more than 2, 500 children on its website without first obtaining parental consent. The government alleged that the company collected information including children's first and last name, street address, e-mail address, age and date of birth; while the website asked children to get their parent or guardian's permission first, there was no official method of notifying or obtaining verifiable consent from any parent or guardian before collecting the personal information in question.[34]

In 2003, enforcement actions against Hershey Foods and Ms. Fields led to substantial fines. The FTC filed a complaint against Mrs. Fields Cookies for failing to obtain parental consent for the disclosure of personal information, and the baked goods manufacturer agreed to pay $100,000 in civil penalties. After the FTC filed a complaint against Hershey Foods, the candy maker agreed to pay $85,000 in civil penalties for failing to obtain verifiable parental consent before allowing children to use its sites. Flexing its muscle, the FTC filed a complaint against the giant Sony Music, alleging that Sony failed to obtain verifiable parental consent and notify parents of its data management practices. To settle the suit, Sony agreed in December of 2008 to pay a $1 million civil penalty.[35] As social networking options for children on the web multiply, the FTC may have gone after Sony to make the point about the seriousness of creating portals for gullible and exploitable users.

WHY AGE THIRTEEN?

Why is age thirteen the dividing line between freedom and coercion? According to COPPA, the term "child" means an "individual under the age of 13."[36] Although the statute applies only to children under thirteen, it is no secret that older children imprudently disclose financial information about themselves and their households as well.

In fact, one study suggested that teenagers may be a bigger problem for online disclosures of private information about their households than children under thirteen.[37] Why then are children over thirteen excluded?

While COPPA disempowers the parents of older teenagers, other key federal privacy laws do not. Under the federal Privacy Act, originally passed by Congress in 1974, parents may access government records about their teenage children, over the teens' objections. Parents also may seek to limit unwanted disclosures about their teens.[38] Also known as the Buckley Amendment, the Family Educational Rights and Privacy Act of 1976 (FERPA)[39] withholds federal funds from institutions that disclose students' academic and disciplinary information to third parties without parental consent. Under FERPA, parents are permitted access to their under-eighteen teenagers' school records even over the teens' objections; parents can also veto disclosures of school records sought by their teenage children.[40]

The FTC has stated that the age of thirteen is the standard for distinguishing adolescents from young children who may need special protections. Yet it fails to explain the assumption that only young children may not understand the safety and privacy issues and are particularly vulnerable. Children over the age of thirteen recklessly disclose personal information, just like their younger siblings. There is no generic difference between the categories of personal information that teens disclose and that younger children disclose. The privacy interests of teens and their families can be harmed by teens' disclosures of personal information. Perhaps we can assume parents, schools, libraries, government, or industry could simply educate older teens to take the appropriate precautions that children under the age of thirteen must be coerced to take.

The framers of COPPA may have excluded older teens from the act's reach , not from belief in their superior educability, but knowing they can more readily use deception to circumvent parental involvement. As applied to a savvy fifteen-year-old, the consent requirements seem futile. Still, there are grounds to doubt that youth over thirteen are sufficiently sophisticated about advertising and marketing to release them as free game for e-commerce. Offline, state, local, and federal governments impose many restrictions on the commercial sector's ability to advertise and sell to older teenagers. Examples of these restrictions are tobacco advertising, glue sales, and body piercings.

Consider the other ways COPPA seeks to protect only young children. The determination of whether a website is directed to children under thirteen is based not only on the intent of the website operator, but on the language, images, and overall design of the site as well. COPPA also applies to websites and online services that are not specifically directed to children, but whose operators have "actual knowledge" that they are collecting information from a child. The act only applies to websites that collect personal information, but defines it broadly to include a person's name, address, e-mail address, phone number, Social Security Number, and any other identifier deemed to enable physical or online contact.

Under COPPA, "verifiable parental consent" is mandated for data collection. The FTC has specified an array of methods of obtaining verifiable parental consent. The operator of a website may obtain parental consent online and verify that consent via e-mail or telephone if the personal information is used only internally. Prior to disclosing information to the general public (via chat rooms or message boards) or to third parties, an operator of a website must get parental consent in a more rigorous fashion, such as by a signed fax, credit card number, parent-initiated phone call, or secure e-mail.

Exceptions apply to the requirement of parental consent for data collection. Obviously, operators must be permitted to capture e-mail information in order to provide parental notice and seek parental consent. Website operators are also permitted to collect personal information to protect the safety of children, the security of the site, and to satisfy the demands of law enforcement. In addition, website operators may collect an e-mail address (but not other kinds of information) on a one-time basis to process a request from a child if the operator then deletes the information. Parental permission must be obtained if children are to receive newsletters sent to their e-mail addresses on an ongoing basis.

IS THE PATERNALISM JUSTIFIED?

What does this regime of rights and rules mean for children? Is it just that children's access to Internet-based goods and services has been made to depend on the privacy preferences of their guardians and the federal government? What of children's own wants and desires? Is COPPA's cyber-paternalism well-designed and well-justified? These are philosophical questions about the limits of government and parental paternalism.

Some civil libertarians have taken the side of children (and the industries that want to sell them things and shape their market preferences), decrying the impact of cyber-paternalism on freedom of speech, "the right to know," and free market competition.[41] But in this context, libertarians are in a minority. For while too little access to computers was a genuine equity concern in the 1990s, the digital divides between young and old and rich and poor have begun to narrow, with mobile phones, free WiFi in public places, and Internet access in more private homes, schools, or in libraries. Too much unchaperoned text messaging, social networking and web browsing by minors has emerged as a larger concern than equity of access. The ubiquitous Internet is perceived as a threat to youth. Some children's advocates would like to see minors shielded and segregated in supervised, filtered,

G-rated, advertisement-free corners of the World Wide Web. The unlimited, unfiltered, and unfettered access to the Internet and social media enjoyed by many minors stands as a special policy concern in the United States.

Responding to the call to protect children from threats to their safety and moral development, COPPA purports to protect children's informational privacy, mainly by investing parents with the right to bar certain disclosures of information to third parties.[42] COPPA is not entirely unlike FERPA in that regard. Consumer privacy advocates have generally accepted the paternalism implicit in FERPA as reasonable. From a libertarian perspective, COPPA has been more controversial than FERPA, and the reason is clear. FERPA keeps transcripts under wrap. By contrast, COPPA places parents and the government between children and the most powerful source of knowledge and vehicle of communication of all time—the Internet, the World Wide Web.

Privacy advocates are not so sure about COPPA, despite the characterization of its passage as a consumer privacy victory. On June 9, 2000, in testimony before the Commission on Child Online Protection (a body created by Congress in the COPPA), the former general counsel of the Electronic Privacy Information Center (EPIC), David L. Sobel, urged the rejection of age verification requirements as a condition of access to the Internet. Instead of blocking access, efforts should be made to help young people learn to safely and responsibly navigate the Internet. Sobel argued that a new regime for the collection of personal data in the name of "child online protection" would impose additional burdens on Internet users.[61] The American Civil Liberties Union (ACLU) also took a strong position against government attempts to restrict Internet content, calling self-rating "the greatest danger to free speech online."[62] Information privacy protections that barely protect privacy, that seem morally arbitrary, that aggravate parents, frustrate children, create false promises, and block access to information and communication may come at too high a cost.

Without a doubt, Internet use can be something of a threat. First, Internet use, like television viewing or comic book reading, competes with activities many of us believe are better for children. These include homework, physical exercise, music lessons, and conversing face-to-face. Second, inappropriate exposure to sex, violence, hate, and advertising content on the Internet can undermine parental values and authority. Neither filtering practices nor rating systems have become pervasive or effective enough to reduce the threat of inappropriate exposure to children. Third, the Internet can facilitate bullying voyeurism and sexual exploitation of minors by adult predators. Children who make friends over the Internet and agree to face-to-face meetings may discover that their new friend is actually an adult harboring criminal intent. Law enforcement is using the Internet to deter potential sex offenders and crimes against children. In 2000, Patrick Naughton, an ex-Disney executive, flew from Seattle to Santa Monica to meet and seduce a person he met online; he thought she was a thirteen-year-old girl, but the person turned out to be an undercover FBI officer.

The fourth reason Internet use is a threat to families is that it can compromise child welfare by facilitating knowing and unknowing criminality by children. Juvenile hackers, identity thieves, and viral agents are familiar banes. White-collar crime among teens online was made a little more interesting by Jonathan Lebed, an early offender. This New Jersey youth capitalized on the anonymity of the Internet and the gullibility of greedy adults to earn $800,000 by trading stocks. Lebed's parents—and the Securities and Exchange Commission—eventually "grounded" the high-flying high schooler. Lebed reluctantly agreed to give up some of the money he had earned. Bewildered by the SEC's rare enforcement effort, Greg Lebed, Jonathan's father, blamed access to the Internet for his family's woes: "Ever since that computer came into the house, this family was ruined."[43]

Finally, Internet use is viewed as a threat to families is because informational privacy is threatened by children's participation in e-commerce. Children are often indifferent to the forms of informational privacy and data protection of concern to adults. This is a major finding of Joseph Turow's and Lilach Nir's Annenberg Report.[44] At present, e-businesses generally must collect personal data to process purchases; they may, and often do, collect personal data simply to create customer profiles for lucrative marketing purposes or to compile commercially valuable customer mailing lists. Children and adults can be lured by clever online games into disclosing personally identifiable information and family finances to businesses.

While COPPA was enacted to curb informational privacy loss, it was not designed to bring a halt to data collection, advertising, and sales practices that target young people and their families.[45] Rather, the act was designed to protect the informational privacy of children and their families from excessive and unwanted disclosures of personal information. It was designed to impose certain fair information practices on e-commerce, and to educate the public.

Some have argued that parental control software, rather than strict compliance by industry with COPPA, is the real key to protecting children from making harmful disclosures because, without close supervision, "it is clear that many of today's tech-savvy children will be able to get around parental notification and consent."[46] There is little evidence that parents are substantially more involved in supervising their children online in response to COPPA.[47] The statute "forces" parents who would otherwise be content to give their children free reign over their computers, and other web-enabled devices, to monitor their use of Internet sites that collect personal information. Not all parents welcome the veto power COPPA confers.[48]

Parents may want their children to have free access to the World Wide Web because they believe the risks are minimal, or because they do not have the time or interest to deal with their children's online activities. It is worth observing, however, that some parents may want their children to have free access to the Internet for moral or political reasons. They may believe that children should have unfettered access to the web and the public library equally, as a matter of free speech, free expression, and the right to know. They may want their children to develop judgment and taste by exposure to the best and worst of civilization in the relatively safe and private terrain of books and the Internet. COPPA's requirements are not specifically designed to deny children access to content, but, as civil libertarians observe, that is one of their effects. Civil libertarians may rejoice today in the fact that the average child's access to the Internet and ability to independently navigate the web have increased significantly since COPPA's passage. The current FTC emphasis on education and enforcement seems warranted. But the climate of the Internet is changing, and children's online privacy protection is a moving target. The FTC is being forced to rethink COPPA in light of easy methods available to children to lie about their ages to gain access to adult sites; and children's use their own legitimate bank-issued debit cards as "proof" of parental consent.[49] Furthermore, COPPA looks like a weak measure to protect children's online privacy considering the popularity among young children and teens of posting intimate personal information and photographs on social networking sites like Facebook and Myspace.[50]

While Congress has passed statutes governing the privacy and security of health and financial information, no comprehensive Internet privacy law has been enacted.[51] COPPA was the nation's first specific online privacy protection law. COPPA was cyber law, but it was also family law. COPPA does what family law does: it confers legal power over children to parents or other adult guardians, enabling paternalistic and authoritarian intervention. It is a paternalistic, authoritarian measure designed to limit the ability of children under the age of thirteen to disclose personally identifying information without the knowledge and consent of their parents.

The wants and needs of the young generate billions of dollars in revenue for the U.S. economy. Given the economic significance of youth and their families, normative reflections about their ideal roles in the Internet economy ought to be major concerns. To what extent should the commercial sector have access to children, and on what terms? Are efforts to shield children from the commercial sector denying them access to information and transactions to which they are entitled as a matter of political morality?

With COPPA, Congress attempted to strike a balance between the social good of youth access to the Internet and the free market, on the one hand, and the social good of parental supervision of Internet use and market transactions by youth on the other. But what, really, are the normative implications of making parents the guardians of children's and household privacy? Is doing so good family law? Good privacy law?

COPPA is family law when viewed as a governmental effort to compel parental child protection in the best interests of children, and to privilege parental over nonparental influences on young children. COPPA seeks to buttress the family by regulating the flow of information about children and their families to the public.

In May of 2000, researchers at the University of Pennsylvania's Annenberg Public Policy Center released a study showing that children are more likely than their parents to reveal personal family information online.[52] Although most parents surveyed had concerns about their children's Internet use, 89 percent said they believe the Internet is beneficial to schoolwork, and 85 percent said that children find fascinating and useful information on the Internet. Parents believe Internet use benefits their children, but also that children may be more likely than adults to make poor judgments about yielding personal information in the context of electronic commerce. A 1996 report by the Center for Media Education noted that the "interactive nature of the Internet gives marketers unprecedented power to gather detailed personal information from children."[53] Prior to COPPA, marketers could freely elicit data from children overtly, using games and prizes as incentives, and covertly, using software that tracks online behavior. Some parents may want help in limiting their children's access to the Internet and potentially deceptive trade practices.[54] They may value COPPA for that reason; others may not.

From a family law perspective, COPPA has several normative weaknesses. First, it draws a line of dubious justification between teenagers and "tweenagers." A number of younger children will be as able as many teenagers when it comes to circumventing the requirements of the statute. Some children under thirteen are no more or less in need of parental control than teenagers. Thus the statute seems morally arbitrary.

Second, the policy objective of protecting children from the harmful consequences of Internet use is barely served by COPPA. The act limits access to commerce, but not to adult content. Nor does it prevent children from posting personal information on social networking sites. Now, as before COPPA's enactment, direct and constant parental supervision is needed to keep children from adult content and dangerous levels of voluntary self-disclosure. It bears emphasis that most websites that do not collect personal information, and many with explicit adult content can be visited in part or in full by children of any age.

Third, COPPA's paternalism and authoritarianism places parents between beneficial information and online activities. The act is paternalistic in the sense that it presumes that young children lack the judgment needed to know when the disclosure of personal information is safe and warranted. It is authoritarian in the sense that it presumes that government may authorize parents to, for reasons of their own, prohibit children from exchanging personal data for access to Internet-based commerce, however desirable or useful to the children. Like other legal measures that place parents between a child and a mainstream social good, COPPA is morally problematic.

From the point of view of family law, placing parents between children and the Internet is arguably suitable. As a general rule, children need protection. The societal mandate is that public authorities protect children by looking after their best interests. In the first instance, parents (meaning, in most instances, mothers or other female caretakers) are those with whom primary responsibility for executing this mandate rests. Parents should be a part of the decisions made by the minor children for whose safety and well-being they are ultimately responsible. We have heard this principle asserted with varying efficacy in connection with everything from teen abortion rights to the V-chip. So it should come as no surprise to hear it in connection with the Internet.

Parents fear unfettered access. James M. Knight is an apt illustration. A parent in Exeter, New Hampshire, Knight brought a lawsuit to compel public school authorities to give him access to the "computer files that would reveal the Internet sites visited by all computer users in the schools of two local districts."[55] The Supreme Court has often sided with parents who wish to restrict children's access to information and services provided by public schools. The Court has famously held that Amish parents may keep children older than thirteen out of school, in order to inculcate Amish values.[56] COPPA can be read in that same tradition: as the Congress of the United States saying that all parents may keep children under thirteen away from e-commerce in order to inculcate parental values.

When viewed in the vein of the Video Privacy Act of 1988 or Title V of the Financial Services Modernization Act, COPPA is commercial sector information privacy law. They are all measures to regulate the flow of personal information entrusted to others with expectations of confidentiality and security in an economically sensible way.[57] Again, children may be more likely than adults to make poor judgments about yielding personal information in the context of electronic commerce. To make it more difficult for industry to prey upon children's indifference to disclosing personal information about themselves and others of the sort e-businesses most want, COPPA compels parents to get involved in the monitoring of data collection.

As privacy law, COPPA falls into a small class of privacy laws that challenge purely voluntary notions of privacy. An implicit message of COPPA is that privacy is too important to be left to the judgment of minors. The same message is implicit in the Privacy Act of 1974, which authorizes "the parent of any minor" to "act on behalf of the individual."[58] Looking at the entire body of American privacy law as a whole, it is remarkable that children are not permitted to waive their informational privacy rights online.

Children are accorded rights under major privacy laws.[59] They are permitted to waive their privacy rights in a number of contexts. Indeed, most informational privacy rights recognized in American law can be waived by most people. Fourth and Fifth Amendment rights protecting expectations of privacy can be waived. A schoolchild can decide she wants to show her teacher what is in her backpack, for example, whether or not the teacher's search would meet an exception to the warrant requirement.[60] We adults are free to invite the police into our homes, give them our blood, our thoughts, and our diaries, even though the consequences may mean criminal prosecution and loss of liberty. Children are similarly free.

The Video Privacy Act does not prohibit anyone from authorizing release of one's prior video rentals to third parties. The Health Insurance Portability and Accountability Act does not prohibit anyone from telling someone else his or her medical history. Although those seeking to release their records must give informed consent, they may disclose personal medical information freely. The Privacy Act does not prohibit one from revealing the criminal history contained on his or her own rap sheet. The national Do Not Call Registry, aimed at protecting the privacy of the home from intruders, does not require that anyone place their phone number on the list, even if they have children in their homes. An impulsive teenager can disclose sufficient financial information to a used-car dealer to purchase a lemon on credit.

What COPPA does, however, is block voluntary disclosures of personal data. Prohibiting voluntary disclosures by children lacking parental consent in situations in which they and their parents may be indifferent to privacy losses and resentful of government intervention, COPPA is among the most paternalistic and authoritarian of the federal privacy statutes thus far. The Family Educational Rights and Privacy Act is more paternalistic in one sense: it extends the parental right to veto third-party disclosures of their children's educational records up through the child's eighteenth year, while the COPPA veto expires at the thirteenth year. But FERPA admits more in the way of voluntary waivers by parents and youth.

In sum, the Children's Online Privacy Protection act is U.S. federal information privacy law, governing the commercial sector and the market for information. The statute is also family law, governing families in the combined interests of child welfare and parental autonomy. The COPPA statute is coercive, both as it relates to parents and as it relates to children. Congress believed the coercion was justified by the danger to children and their families posed by the Internet, dangers to which both children and their parents may be unduly inattentive. Using the Internet without close adult supervision can be dangerous for minors.[63] Children may recklessly or unknowingly give personal information to strangers set on illegal sexual or other exploitation, and minors may be less cautious than their parents about giving out embarrassing or intimate personally identifying information about other members of their families. Parents may worry about Internet use for reasons unrelated to informational privacy. Children's obsession with Internet-based games, music, research, and communication can impair the ability of families to spend quality time together. They make families vulnerable to predators and identity theft. Moreover, a few notorious youth have used their computers for mischief—hacking into government networks, spreading viruses, or influencing the stock market.[64] COPPA is not a solution to all of these problems. However, COPPA has incentivized website operators to adopt practices that reduce the likelihood that personally identifiable information will be sought from young children. While the law is paternalistic, coercive and draws arbitrary lines, it's moral and political legitimacy are by now scarcely in doubt.

DO YOUNG ADULTS NEED PATERNALISTIC LAWS, TOO?

The Children's Online Privacy Protection Act could be viewed as part of a nation's formative educational project: the young are to be taught the value of privacy by imposing privacy protection rules limiting their choices until they are old enough to choose responsibly. But it will be difficult for children to get the message that privacy is a duty of self-care if they closely observe the actual behavior of teens and young adults. Everyone under the age of forty seems to be freely sharing personal facts, ideas, fantasies, and revealing images of themselves all the time. Everyone seems to be on Facebook, Youtube, Twitter or the latest equivalents. People seem to be trusting other people not to misuse information and to keep secrets. Children see teens and young adults giving unseen Internet website operators and their real names, addresses, phone numbers, photographs, credit card numbers, salaries, Social Security Numbers, auto registration numbers, and work identification numbers in order to get things done that must be done. How can they be taught what is safe and what is unsafe? How could they come to regard any personal identifiers as sensitive enough to hide?

Young adults are voracious users of text messaging, e-mail, online shopping, blogs, discussion forums, and social network sites. There is no shortage of intentional and inadvertent self-disclosure on Facebook, where users create online profiles and then share them with their friends and other site visitors.[65] People post just about everything, from photographs to political perspectives. On Myspace and Facebook, users can also choose to affiliate with interest groups. These groups include alumni of particular schools, biological families, professional colleagues, political parties, and social causes. Although some individuals have professional reasons for social networking and groups have ideological aims (for example, a vegan group called "Live and Let Live"), others seem to be just about fun.

In the youthful domain of social networking, privacy and modesty seem passé. Bragging and self-disclosure are *au courant*. Myspace once supported groups with names like "Truly Beautiful Women" (with over 3,500 members in June 2006); "Myspace Hottyz" (over 1,000 members in June 2006); "hotties & cuttiez" (730 members in June 2006); and "CCC: Cute, Confident, Conceited" (492 members in June 2006). On Facebook there are groups whose sole purpose seems to be bragging about how great the people in it are, how the students at one school are better than the students at another, or even how one ethnicity is better than another.[66]

Revealing oneself on a social networking site can have far-reaching consequences. In a lawsuit against Myspace, a mother sought $30 million after her 14 year old daughter was allegedly sexually assaulted by a man she met on the site.[67] In another case, a predator trolling Facebook pretended to be friends with girls and then extorted nude pictures from them.[68] There are also more mundane—but nevertheless potentially devastating—consequences of exposing oneself on these websites. Employers have begun to check applicants' profiles and base hiring decisions on what they find. One candidate lost a job opportunity because he mentioned using an illegal drug.[69]

Feminists have been among the most astute observers and critics of North American and European cultures of self-disclosure spawned by the Internet.[70] The potential for online community, self-expression, and self-definition must be weighed against the potential for victimization in the hands of anonymous, unaccountable, unscrupulous people and enterprises. The image of Amy Boyer, murdered by a stalker who learned where to find her by purchasing her personal data online, is one such nightmarish reminder.[71] The image of "Jenni," on the other hand, is empowering to some women.

Jennifer Ringley is a true legend of cyberspace. From 1996 to 2003, Ringley, known to her fans as "Jenni," operated the popular web site "JenniCAM," open to all comers for a small fee.[72] Ringley had several cameras trained on the rooms of her dormitory and home to allow visitors to observe her in real time. Her life was on view most of each day, so that her fans could watch her perform the mundane activities ordinarily performed in the privacy of one's home: hygiene, socializing, rest, avocations. Ringley made decisions that represented a sharp break with past expectations of female modesty. To earn money, expand the creative potential of the web, and gain notoriety, Ringley decided to overturn traditional privacy norms generally thought to work to a person's and the political community's advantage. Ringley's web site serviced artsy and prurient interests. Visitors paid to see something that social traditions say they were not supposed to see: namely, the body of a strange woman.

Ringley is not the only person who has lived in front of a webcam. Other women were involved in early websites seriously catering to savvy voyeurs. Ana Voog, an artist and musician, broadcast herself having sex with a boyfriend, and was still online at www.anacam.com in 2009. Carla Cole cofounded The Sync with her boyfriend in 1997, one of the first Internet video program companies. The Sync sponsored the Jenni Show, Snack Boy, and a sexy Internet talk show Cole herself hosted called CyberLove. Voyeur Dorm Dolls' House websites placed college-aged women in front of cameras for sometimes sexy and popular viewing.

Ordinary people are increasingly—and purposefully—going onto the Internet to relinquish their privacy and gain a new sense of freedom by removing their masks as well as their clothes. It seems that since 2003, when Ringley was forced to go off of the air because of Paypal's reputational concerns about nudity, prohibitive modesty and informational privacy norms have become irrelevant.[73] By 2006, some men and women, like beautician Debbie Daniels, were using webcams to attract potential suitors, stripping on webcams before going out on dates.[74] Interviewed for a news article in the United Kingdom, one woman confessed to getting "so turned on by the idea of someone else 'in the bedroom' that I really show off!" Another woman interviewed for the same article said she suffered from low self-esteem and "just wanted someone to want me." Once she got in front of the webcam she couldn't keep away: "I'm on camera most nights. I love the power I have over the men who watch me. I like dressing up and performing."[75]

Internet nudity is a way of exerting power, because it does more than feed anonymous fantasy lives. People fall in love. Sean Patrick Williams, whose 24/7 webcam www.seanpatricklive.com is no longer active, reported viewers developing romantic attachments to him in the 1990s. Williams was baffled and disturbed by the effect his immodesty had on others: "The purpose is not for them to create a personal relationship with me. The purpose is for them to see me and go out and create a personal relationship with someone else."[76] To be disturbed by the emotional response of people whom he has targeted for "intimate" exposure reflects one of the ways in which modesty still matters. At one time, many individuals would aspire only to expose their bodies to people with whom they hoped to form a mutual emotionally intimate bond. Some Internet users today are oddly still capable of inferring an intimate relationship simply from having seen a nice person naked online. A troubling dimension of webcam exposure is that many people have been caught on webcams without their knowledge, thus involuntarily relinquishing their modesty and physical privacy.[77] One notorious webcam broadcasted live scenes from a bar. A man in another country viewing the broadcast telephoned the bar offering to buy "the girl in the pink outfit" a drink. Without her knowledge, "he'd been watching her for two hours."[78] Webcams can be secretly stashed anywhere, including the bathrooms of bars and the dressing stalls of swimming pools. Landlords have been known to sneak cameras into tenants' bedrooms. A high school remotely activated webcams on school-issued laptops, recall chapter 7.

Online self-exposure can be altruistic. The Internet's educative potential was apparent from its the early days. In the mid-1990s, Elizabeth, a middle-aged married mother of three, gave birth on the Health Network, an Internet site affiliated with the FOX Entertainment Group. Childbirth was once a deeply private act shrouded by conventions of privacy. This part of our past is well-illustrated by the famous 1881 case *DeMay v. Roberts*,[79] in which a married couple successfully sued the physician who came to their tiny house on a dark, stormy night to deliver their child. The doctor's mistake was to bring along an "unprofessional young unmarried man" who observed the delivery.[80] Childbirth is understood by many to be an intimate family experience from which strangers should be excluded. Women are no longer burdened with the nineteenth century's expectations of modesty in childbirth, though some twentieth-century women still demanded it.[81] Childbirth has developed into a joyous family experience that is commonly observed by and shared with spouses, children, and parents. Inviting others into the birth chamber is a kind of sharing that sometimes includes the general public. Many television shows follow pregnant women through the process of birth and delivery, with special attention to women having difficult pregnancies or multiple births.

Elizabeth said she allowed the web broadcast because she wanted to educate others. Sometimes, immodesty has educational aims. Journalists condemned Elizabeth for making her newborn child into a public curiosity. Writer Ellen Goodman characterized the Internet birth as a blow to privacy, albeit a voluntary blow: "As private space shrinks, the public's hunger for authenticity grows. As the hunger grows, the deeper we invade private life to find something real, and the shallower it gets."[82] Goodman's concern is that the appetite for other peoples' private lives may lead to the end of private life as more and more people publicize otherwise private acts to a community of strangers. Indeed, Elizabeth may have been self-deceived about the educational impact of her Internet delivery; how babies are born is not something about which the general public is especially ignorant.

In chapter 5 I mentioned Patti Derman, the woman whose mastectomy was webcast with her consent for educational purposes. Derman's decision, and others' support and encouragement, suggest a new attitude toward women's bodies. Here we had a woman who did not regard the fact of her surgery as a matter for strict confidence; who was not ashamed to reveal to strangers that she had breast cancer and that her breasts had been removed hoping to cure it; and who was unafraid to disclose her breasts in public despite the taboo. Derman is plainly not a woman confined by domestic roles and conventions of modesty and concealment. Her abrogation of modesty and shame for the sake of educating the public about an important public health problem is something many progressives would applaud.

Derman rejected forms of privacy and modesty that hurt and isolate women. Under the old privacy regime,[83] women could rarely feel comfortable sharing and obtaining detailed knowledge of their bodies. Under the new regime, health privacy is optional. A woman can choose when to elect privacy, when to choose publicity. To elect tasteful publicity for so noble a cause as women's public health education may be something we should all praise. Her conduct does not point directly to the need for paternalistic laws that prohibit sharing.

The artist Matuschka's photographic self-portrait appeared on the cover of the *New York Times Magazine* in 1993.[84] Matuschka bared her chest to the camera to reveal the disfiguring scar of a mastectomy that she believed was probably unnecessary to cure her cancer. The photograph was nominated for a Pulitzer. Graphic breast reconstruction, reduction, and augmentation surgery on television is now routine, along with images of breast and chest disfiguration. Any discussion of online disclosures must consider the opportunities that exist for offline disclosure; moreover, the worlds merge. *The New York Times* is accessible offline in hard copy, and online as well.

The Internet's culture of self-disclosure is merely in tune with the rest of the world. The revealing personal memoir is a thriving genre in the book publishing business. Television programs feature crime victims and trauma survivors telling their stories. Television programs also feature elective cosmetic surgery patients seeking to perfect breasts, bellies and vaginas. Indeed an episode of "Dr. 90210" about "vaginoplasty" (plastic surgery to alter the vagina) was "the highest-rated show in [the E! network's]" history."[85] There are whole shows devoted to people who live with unusual genetic disorders or acquired diseases. How is "privacy" preserved in this and similar contexts? The g-string-and-pasties principle assessed in chapter 4 has made its way to primetime health "infotainment" television. The common convention is freely and graphically to display cosmetic imperfections, morbid obesity, injuries, pathological disfigurement, and congenital abnormalities, while blurring or boxing out patients' genitals and female nipples. Yet some late-evening cable television shows reveal fully nude persons and even couples having sexual intercourse.

For mature adults, Facebook and the web in general are places to work and do business. Many people do virtually all of their banking and bill paying online, hopeful that data security and privacy policies and laws will protect their financial privacy. Travel arrangements, shopping for consumer goods (books, clothing, flowers)—all of this happens online. Internet sites like Second Life have actually blurred the line between lives on and offline. A complex fantasy game, Second Life allows players (called Residents) to navigate a realistic-looking three-dimensional world, through avatars who perform social and commercial activities.[86]

Sharing personal data is the way of the contemporary world. There is no chance the United States government will intervene in a strict censorship mode to curb radical forms of self-disclosure online. Government will protect Americans from inadvertent access to adult-themed spam (with CAN-SPAM Act), and punish data breaches, identify theft, and computer hacking.[87] But government will not—and constitutionally perhaps cannot—do much to protect adults from voluntary conduct that erodes the taste for privacy and modest self-restraint. That important task is largely left to moral and ethical sectors, which, one must hope, will not neglect it.

AFTERWORD

Why hide anything?

An answer to the question is suggested by the entry in John Adams' diary dated Monday, August 20, 1770. In Adams' view, privacies of concealment, secrecy, and reserve are both moral virtues and duties. Worldly wisdom dictates that we protect ourselves from "damage, danger and confusion" by generally keeping "our sentiments, actions, desires, and resolutions" to ourselves. Revelations to enemies and indiscreet friends alike risk "loss, disgrace or mortification." On occasion, however, virtue and duty run in the other direction, Adams wrote: "the cause of religion, of government, of liberty, the interest of the present age and of posterity, render it a necessary duty for a man to make known his sentiments and intentions boldly and publicly."

Adams' take is modern. Privacy aligns not with raw preference, but with prudent self-interest. The good of privacy is contingent. Sometimes we ought to go public when we might prefer to hide; sometimes we ought to hide when we might prefer to go public. The important thing is that privacy, like information sharing, has a place in free society. Our moral interests include freedom from judgment, freedom to don masks, freedom to build and maintain reputations, and freedom to and from intimacy.[1]

What must we hide?

Adams' diary points to a general answer: hide the things whose disclosure would lead to danger, disgrace, and dishonor. But a distinctly different answer is suggested by the book of Matthew in the New Testament of the Bible. We should hide the things whose disclosure leads to approval and admiration. The righteousness of pious acts such as giving to the poor, praying, and fasting is undermined by intentionally seeking public notice. Through modesty and reserve we are taking God alone into confidence. Thus:

> Concerning Almsgiving
>
> So whenever you give alms, do not sound a trumpet before you, as the hypocrites do in the synagogues and in the streets, so that they may be praised by others. Truly I tell you, they have received their reward. But when you give alms, do not let your left hand know what your right hand is doing, so that your alms may be done in secret; and your Father who sees in secret will reward you.

Concerning Prayer

And whenever you pray, do not be like the hypocrites; for they love to stand and pray in the synagogues and at the street corners, so that they may be seen by others. Truly I tell you, they have received their reward. But whenever you pray, go into your room and shut the door and pray to your Father who is in secret; and your Father who sees in secret will reward you.

Concerning Fasting

And whenever you fast, do not look dismal, like the hypocrites, for they disfigure their faces so as to show others that they are fasting. Truly I tell you, they have received their reward. But when you fast, put oil on your head and wash your face, so that your fasting may be seen not by others but by your Father who is in secret; and your Father who sees in secret will reward you.[2]

There is a ready secular rendering of the message in this religious passage. Keeping your goodness to yourself makes you really good. Virtue is its own reward. Don't be a show-off.

Ancient and early American texts suggest a way of thinking about privacy that the buzz of continuous networking threatens to drown out. Status updates on Facebook and Twitter risk offending the ethics of Adams and the ethics of Matthew. "I am giving a lecture in Paris" sounds like bragging—as well as an "all clear" message to house thieves and rivals in romance. Does anyone care about all the monitoring, data give-aways, and data collection that have come to characterize daily life? Are modesty and confidentiality dying virtues? Is there anything to be done about it?

I have tried in this book to engage readers in a sustained reflection about moral and political values that inform privacy law and policy. I urged in part II that there can be virtue in voluntary seclusion and concealment, but injury in forced isolation, closeting, and selective legal moralism. I further urged, in part III, that there can be pragmatism in confidentiality, plus prudence and dignity in limiting access to personal information and electronic communications.

My claim here has been that we should live some of our lives in private, some in public; and that there is often a role for government in requiring us to live this way. Privacy is too important to be left entirely to chance and taste. We need laws that require government to leave us alone. We need laws that require government to help us make sure that others leave us alone. And we may even need laws that help create and preserve forms of privacy to which we may be unwisely indifferent that are nonetheless important to lives of opportunity promised by a free and democratic society.

We may be unwisely indifferent to our own privacy because we are young, or because we are busy, or because we are unfamiliar with the risks of data collection, sharing, and storage that come with the mysterious technology we enjoy. The recoil at the specter of paternalism can be nearly instinctive for political liberals. But the modest paternalism defended here is consistent with—and indeed required by—a robust liberalism, appreciative of the respects in which unchecked loses of privacy can leave one, in the words of an historic judicial opinion, slave to merciless masters.[3]

The law justly identifies some of us as beneficiaries and targets of legal duties to hide, duties to embrace even unpopular privacy. What must we hide then? We must hide what is necessary to preserve our common dignity and separate virtues. We must hide what is necessary to keep ourselves safe from harm. We must hide what our roles and responsibilities and professions dictate that we hide as matters of efficacy, beneficence, or contract. And we must hide, notwithstanding all of technology's attractions, what good relationships and reputations—now and in our distant and uncertain futures—render it prudent to hide.

NOTES

Preface

1. I introduced my conception of "coerced privacy" in a symposium essay that launched this book project: "Coercing Privacy," *William and Mary Law Review* 40: 723–57 (1999).
2. Gerald Gaus and Shane D. Courtland, "Liberalism," in Edward N. Zalta (ed.), *Stanford Encyclopedia of Philosophy* (September 10, 2007). Available at http://plato.stanford.edu/archives/win2003/entries/liberalism/.
3. See Andrew T. Kenyon and Megan Richardson (eds.), *New Dimensions in Privacy Law* (Cambridge: Cambridge University Press, 2006).
4. I am referring to the "Directive 95/46/EC on the protection of individuals with regard to the processing of personal data and on the free movement of such data."
5. For example, "Dredging-Up the Past: Lifelogging, Memory and Surveillance," *University of Chicago Law Review* 75: 47–74 (2008); "Undressing Difference: The *Hijab* and the West," *Berkeley Journal of Gender, Law and Justice* 23: 208–24 (2008); "Disrobed: The Constitution of Modesty," *Villanova Law Review* 51: 841–57 (2006); "Race, Face, and Rawls," *Fordham Law Review* 72: 1677 -1695 (2004); "Minor Distractions: Children, Privacy and E-Commerce," *Houston Law Review* 38: 751–76 (2001); and "Privacy-as-Data-Control: Conceptual, Practical, and Moral Limits of the Paradigm," *Connecticut Law Review* 32: 861–875 (2000).
6. Carl S. Kaplan, "Kafkaesque? Big Brother? Finding the Right Literary Metaphor for Net Privacy," *The New York Times*, February, 2, 2001 (describing an essay by Daniel J. Solove); Oscar Gandy, *The Panopticon Sort: A Political Economy of Personal Information* (Boulder: Colo.: Westview Press, 1993); Charlotte Twight, "Watching You: Systematic Federal Surveillance of Ordinary Americans," *The Independent Review* 4 (2): Fall 1999, pp. 165–200.
7. Uniting and Strengthening America by Providing Appropriate Tools Required to Intercept and Obstruct Terrorism (USA PATRIOT) Act, Pub. L. No. 107–56, tit. II, § 209(1) (A), 115 Stat. 272, 283 (2001).
8. See Frederick S. Lane, *American Privacy: The 400 Year History of Our Most Contested Right*, pp. 31–32 (Boston: Beacon Press, 2009).
9. Alan F. Westin, respected author of the seminal *Privacy and Freedom* (New York: Atheneum Press, 1967), has conducted privacy polls in conjunction with Harris Polls. The Harris surveys suggest that most people are "privacy pragmatists" (willing to trade privacy for other goods), as opposed to "privacy fundamentalists" (never willing to give up privacy) or "privacy unconcerned" (caring little or nothing about privacy). See http://www.harrisinteractive.com/harris_poll/index.asp?PID=365.

   Numerous opinion polls were conducted in 2007 and 2008 concerning health privacy, Internet privacy, freedom from government surveillance, financial privacy, and free expression. The polls included the Health Confidence Survey (May 2008); the Pew Internet &

American Life Project Poll (April 2008); the Public Agenda Confidence in U.S. Foreign Policy Index Poll (March 2008); the CBS News/New York Times Poll (December 2007); a FOX News/Opinion Dynamics Poll (July 2007); the ABC News/Washington Post Poll (July 2007); and a State of the First Amendment Survey (August 2007). Consumer Reports conducted a poll on September 25, 2008, interpreted as showing that "Americans [are] extremely concerned about Internet privacy."

For links to privacy opinion data, see generally the Privacy and Public Opinion webpage maintained by the Electronic Privacy Information Center at http://epic.org/privacy/survey/.

10. See the Federal Trade Commission, http://www.ftc.gov/reports/privacy3/fairinfo.shtm: "Over the past quarter century, government agencies in the United States, Canada, and Europe have studied the manner in which entities collect and use personal information—their 'information practices'—and the safeguards required to assure those practices are fair and provide adequate privacy protection. The result has been a series of reports, guidelines, and model codes that represent widely accepted principles concerning fair information practices. Common to all of these documents [hereinafter referred to as 'fair information practice codes'] are five core principles of privacy protection: (1) Notice/Awareness; (2) Choice/Consent; (3) Access/Participation; (4) Integrity/Security; and (5) Enforcement/Redress."

    The American Institute of Certified Public Accountants (AICPA) and the Canadian Institute of Chartered Accountants (CICA) formed a AICPA/CICA Privacy Task Force, which developed the Generally Accepted Privacy Principles (GAPP), which are similar to fair information practices. See http://www.aicpa.org/InterestAreas/InformationTechnology/Resources/Privacy/GenerallyAcceptedPrivacyPrinciples/.
11. See http://www.law.berkeley.edu/4620.htm.
12. In 2009 and 2010, the Federal Trade Commission hosted a series of roundtable workshops on the norms that ought to govern privacy regulation. See http://www.ftc.gov/bcp/workshops/privacyroundtables/.
13. Truddi Chase, *When Rabbit Howls* (New York: Berkeley Books, 1987).
14. George Yancy, *Black Bodies, White Gazes: The Continuing Significance of Race* (Lanham, Md.: Rowman and Littlefield, 2008), p. xvi.
15. Children's Online Privacy Protection Act of 1998 (COPPA), 15 U.S.C. § 6501 et seq.
16. Richard Thaler and Cass R Sunstein, *Nudge: Improving Decisions About Health, Wealth and Happiness* (New York: Penquin, 2009).

Chapter 1

1. These are the facts of a Mississippi case, *Plaxico v. Michael,* 735 So. 2d 1036 (Miss., 1999).
2. These are the facts of an Oregon case, *Humphers v. First Interstate Bank,* 696 P.2d 527 (1985) (Or. 1985).
3. See *Boring v. Google,* 598 F. Supp.2d 695 (W.D. Penn. 2009), 362 Fed Appx. 273, 2010 WL 318281 (C.A. 3 (Pa.); *Yath v. Fairview Cedar Ridge Clinic,* 767 NW 2d 34 (Minn. App. 2009).
4. But see Daniel J. Solove, "A Taxonomy of Privacy," 154 *University of Pennsylvania Law Review* 477–564 (2006), emphasizing conceptual disarray. See generally, Daniel J. Solove, *Understanding Privacy* (Cambridge, Mass.: Harvard University Press, 2008). Cf. Daniel J. Solove, *The Future of Reputation: Gossip, Rumor and Privacy on the Internet* (New Haven, Conn.: Yale University Press, 2007).

5. See, e.g., *Washington v. Glucksberg*, 521 U.S. 702 (1997), holding that assisted suicide may be prohibited, and *Lewis v. Harris*, 188 N.J. 415, 908 A.2d 196 (2006), holding that gay marriage equivalents must be permitted in New Jersey.
6. These are the peculiar facts of a New York case, *Finger v. Omni Publications International*, 77 N.Y. 2d 138 (N.Y. 1990).
7. See *Boy Scouts of America v. Dale*, 30 U.S. 640 (2000), holding that the Boy Scouts may revoke the membership of a gay man on the basis of his sexual orientation; *Hurley v. Irish-American Gay, Lesbian & Bisexual Group of Boston*, 15 U.S. 557 (1995), holding that organizers of an Irish American parade may exclude homosexuals and bisexuals seeking to march under "gay pride" banners.
8. Cf. Neil Richards, "Intellectual Privacy," *Texas Law Review* 87: 387–445 (2008).
9. *Freedman v. America Online*, 303 F.Supp.2d 121 (D.Conn. 2004); *Theofel v. Farey-Jones*, 359 F 3d 1066 (9th Cir. 2003).
10. Anita L. Allen, *Privacy Law and Society* (Minneapolis: West/Thomson Reuters, 2011), a comprehensive textbook on privacy law.
11. *NAACP v. Alabama*, 357 U.S. 449 (1958), holding that the First Amendment protects associational and informational privacy; *Katz v. United States*, 389 U.S. 347(1967), holding that the Fourth Amendment protects reasonable expectations of privacy.
12. See *Roe v. Wade*, 410 U.S. 113 (1973) and *Lawrence v. Texas*, 539 U.S. 558 (2003), holding that the Fourteenth Amendment protects the right to choose abortion and sex partners.
13. See *Engblom v. Carey*, 677 F.2d 957 (2d. Cir. 1982), holding that the Third Amendment protects interests in private possession of homes; *Schmerber v. California*, 384 U.S. 757 (1966), holding that the Fifth Amendment protects privacy interests countermanding forced self-incrimination); *Griswold v. Connecticut*, 381 U.S. 479 (1965), holding that the Ninth Amendment protects unenumerated privacy rights. Cf. *Johnson v. Phelan*, 69 F.3d 144 (7th Cir. 1995), with Posner, dissenting and concurring on the ground that the eighth amendment prohibits privacy intrusions that are cruel and unusual.
14. See, e.g., *In re T.W.*, 551 So. 2d 1186 (Fla. 1989) and *Commonwealth v. Sell*, 504 Pa. 46; 470 A.2d 457 (Pa. 1983), holding, respectively, that the Florida and Pennsylvania state constitutions afford more privacy protection than the federal constitution.
15. For a sample framework for thinking about public sector privacy regulation, see Fred H. Cate, *Privacy in the Information Age* (Washington: Brookings Institution Press, 1997).
16. See Title III of the Omnibus Crime Control and Safe Streets Act of 1968, as amended by the Electronic Communications Privacy Act of 1986, 18 U.S.C. §§ 2510 et seq. ("Title III"); Health Insurance Portability and Accountability Act of 1996, Pub. L. No. 104–91, 110 Stat. 1936 (1996), codified primarily in Titles 18, 26 and 42 of the United States Code (HIPAA); Family Educational Rights and Privacy Act of 1974 (FERPA), 88 Stat. 571, 20 *U.S.C.* § 1232*g*. (FERPA); Children's Online Privacy Protection Act of 1998 (COPPA), 15 U.S.C. § 6501 et seq. (COPPA); and Title V, Subtitle A of the Gramm-Leach-Bliley Financial Services Modernization Act, Pub. L. No. 106–102, 113 Stat. 1338 (1999), codified as amended at 15 *U.S.C.A.* § 6801 et seq. (GLB).
17. H.L.A. Hart, *The Concept of Law* (Oxford: Oxford University Press, 1961), 89–91. Cf. Robert Cooter, "Expressive Law and Economics," *Journal of Legal Studies* 27: 585–608, 607 (1990); cf. Lisa Nelson, "Normative Dimensions of Paternalism and Security," *I/S: A Journal of Law and Policy for the Information Society* 2: 27–50 (2005/2006).

18. See *Boring v. Google*, 598 F. Supp.2d 695 (W.D. Pennsylvania). See also *Boring v. Google, Inc.* 362 Fed Appx. 273, 2010 WL 318281 (C.A. 3 (Pa.).
19. See *Bagent v. Blessing Care Corporation*, 862 N.E.2d 985 (Ill. 2007). Here, a target of a privacy law mistakenly assumed friendship erased her privacy duties.
20. The text of my Quinlan Lecture at Oklahoma City University Law School was published as Anita L. Allen, *Unpopular Privacy: The Case for Government Mandates*, 32 Okla. City U. L. Rev. 87–102 (2007).
21. An actual U.S. federal statute of this sort, the Children's Online Privacy Protection Act of 1998 (COPPA), 15 U.S.C. § 6501 et seq., is treated in detail in chapter 8 of this book.
22. Sigal R. Ben-Porath, *Tough Choices: Structured Paternalism and the Landscape of Choice* (Princeton, N.J.: Princeton University Press, 2010), 38–39.
23. Peter Applebome, "Love Letters in the Wind: A Private Affair of the Famously Private Salinger," The *New York Times*, Wednesday, May 12, 1999, p. E1.
24. Joyce Maynard, *At Home in the World* (New York: Picador Press, 1999). On a webpage devoted to her book, Maynard writes: "For more than four decades I had lived with a deep and abiding need to please others. Since the age of eighteen, I had been haunted by the fear of J. D. Salinger's disapproval and wrath. And I wasn't wrong that my decision to break a long-held silence concerning a literary icon's role in my life would bring terrible wrath and disapproval upon me."
25. Dinita Smith, Salinger Letters Sold and May Return to Author, *New York Times*, June 23, 1999. See http://query.nytimes.com/gst/fullpage.html?res=9404E3DA1F3BF930A15755C0A96F958260.
26. Julian Sanchez, "Defining 'Paternalism' Online," *The Technology Liberation Front*, available at http://techliberation.com/2010/02/12/defining paternalism-online/, last accessed May 20, 2011.
27. Amitai Etzioni, *The Limits of Privacy* (New York: Basic Books, 2000).
28. See Jean L. Cohen Regulating *Intimacy: A New Legal Paradigm*, 77 (Princeton: Princeton University Press, 2002); Jean L. Cohen, "Is There a Duty of Privacy?" *Texas Journal of Women and the Law* 6: 47, 59–64 (1996).
29. Ian Ayres and Matthew Funk, "Marketing Privacy: A Solution for the Blight of Telemarketing and Spam and Junk Mail)." See http://papers.ssrn.com/sol3/papers.cfm?abstract_id=303303. See also Ian Ayres and Barry Nalebuff, "If Telemarketers Paid for Your Time," Forbes.com, March 28, 2002; see http://www.forbes.com/2002/03/28/0328whynot.html.
30. Ian Ayres, "Disclosure Versus Anonymity in Campaign Finance." *Nomos XLII: Designing Democratic Institutions*, in ed. Ian Shapiro and Stephen Macedo (New York: New York University Press, 2000), pp. 19–54.
31. See, e.g., Margaret Urban Walker, *Moral Understandings: A Feminist Study in Ethics* (New York: Routledge, 1998). See generally, Robin May Schott, Discovering *Feminist Philosophy: Knowledge, Ethics, Politics* (Lanham. Md.: Rowman and Littlefield, 2003), pp. 87–133.
32. Legal Feminists have engaged assiduously in this work, too. See e.g., Kathryn Abrams, "From Autonomy to Agency: Feminist Perspectives on Self-Direction," *William and Mary Law Review* 40: 805–46 (1999).
33. See, for example, two earlier books, Anita L. Allen, *Uneasy Access Privacy for Women in a Free Society* (Totowa, N.J.: Rowman and Littlefield, 1988) and Anita L. Allen, *Why Privacy Isn't Everything: Feminist Reflections on Personal Accountability* (Lanham, Md.: Rowman and

Littlefield, 2003). See also Linda McClain, "Reconstructive Tasks for a Liberal Feminist Conception of Privacy," *William and Mary Law Review* 40: 759–94 (1999).

34. Judith A. Baer, *Our Lives Before the Law: Constructing a feminist Jurisprudence* (Princeton University Press 1999), pp. 124ff.
35. Gerald N. Rosenberg, "The Real World of Democratic Community," in *Nomos XXXV: Democratic Community*, ed. John W. Chapman and Ian Shapiro (New York: New York University Press, 1993), pp. 228–55, 241.
36. Michel Foucault, *The History of Sexuality; An Introduction*, translated Robert Hurley, (New York: Vintage Books, 1990), pp. 10, 35.
37. See generally Anita L. Allen, "Privacy," in Iris Marion Young and Alison M. Jaggar, eds., *A Companion to Feminist Philosophy*, (Oxford: Blackwell, 1998), 456–65. See also Beate Rössler, ed., *Privacies: Philosophical Evaluations* (Stanford, Calif.: Stanford University Press, 2004).
38. Charlotte Perkins Gilman, *Women and Economics: A Study of the Economic Relation Between Men and Women as a Factor in Social Evolution* (Boston: Small, Maynard & Co., 1898).
39. Catharine A. MacKinnon, *Feminism Unmodified: Discourses on Life and Law* (Cambridge, Mass.: Harvard University Press 1987) 93, 101–102.
40. Jane Bailey, "Life in the Fishbowl: Feminist Interrogations of Webcamming," in *On the Identity Trail: Anonymity, Privacy and Identity in a Networked Society*, Ian Kerr, Carole Lucock and Valerie Steeves, eds. (New York: Oxford University Press: 2009) 283–301; Jane Bailey and Adrienne Telford, "What's So 'Cyber' about It? Reflections on Cyberfeminism's Contribution to Legal Studies," 19 *Canadian Journal of Women and the Law*, 243–71 (2007); Anita L. Allen, "Cyberspace and Privacy: A New Legal Paradigm? Gender and Privacy in Cyberspace," 52 *Stanford Law Review* 1175–1200 (2000); Ann Bartow, "Our Data, Ourselves: Privacy, Propertization, and Gender," *University of San Francisco Law Review* 34 (Summer 2000), 633–704.
41. *Doe I and Doe II v. Individuals, Whose True Names are Unknowm*, 561 F. Supp.2d 249 (D. Ct. 2008).
42. Amy R. Baehr, *Varieties of Feminist Liberalism* (Lanham: Md.: Rowman and Littlefield, 2004).
43. Baehr, p. 15, citing Martha Nussbaum, *Sex and Social Justice* (New York: Oxford University Press, 1999), 67. (Italics in original.) The same might be said, by the way, of freedom- and equality-conscious republicanism of the sort defended by Philip Pettit, consistently followed through. See Philip Pettit, *Republicanism: A Theory of Freedom and Governmen*t (Oxford: Oxford University Press 1997), p. 140, arguing that feminist concerns for nondomination, equality, and inclusion are especially well-addressed by the ideals of republican political theory.
44. Julian Sanchez, "Defining 'Paternalism' Online."
45. Richard H. Thaler and Cass Sunstein, *Nudge* (New Haven: Yale University Press 2008), 6.
46. Thaler and Sunstein, p. 7.
47. Thaler and Sunstein, pp. 22–29.
48. David Harsanyi, How *Food Fascists, Teetotaling Do-Gooders, Priggish Moralists, and Other Boneheaded Bureaucrats Are Turning America into a Nation of Children* (New York: Broadway Books, 2007).
49. John Rawls, *Political Liberalism* (New York: Columbia 1993), p. 181.
50. See generally, Kok-Chor Tan, *Toleration, Diversity, and Global Justice* (University Park: Penn State Universty Press (2000); Will Kymlicka, *Contemporary Political Philosophy: An*

Introduction (2nd ed.) (Oxford: Oxford University Press 2002). For an interesting analysis of a debate between Martha Nussbaum and Susan Mollin Okin about whether women's autonomy and respect for religious traditions are equally consistent with political and comprehensive liberalism, see Penny Enslin, "Liberal Feminism, Diversity and Education," *Theory and Research in Education* 11:73–87 (2003).

51. Robert A. Dahl, "Why Democratic Countries Have Mixed Economies," in John W. Chapman and Ian Shapiro, eds. *Democratic Community* (New York: New York University Press, 1993), pp. 259–82.
52. See Bruce Ackerman, *Social Justice and the Liberal State* (New Haven, Conn.:, Yale University Press 1980), p. 372. See generally Joshua Cohen, "Democracy and Liberty," in Jon Elster, *Deliberative Democracy* (Cambridge: Cambridge University Press, 1998), pp. 185–231.
53. Stanley I. Benn, *A Theory of Freedom* (Cambridge: Cambridge University Press, 1988), p 268.
54. Benn, p. 268.
55. Benn, p. 168.
56. Benn, p. 271.
57. Jeffrey Rosen, *The Unwanted Gaze: The Destruction of Privacy in America* (New York: Random House, 2000). Cf. Goffman, E., *The Presentation of Self in Everyday Life* (Garden City: Doubleday, 1959); Goffman, E., *Behavior in Public Places* (New York: The Free Press, 1963); see also Gandy, O. H., *The Panoptic Sort: A Political Economy of Personal Information* (Boulder, Colo.: Westview Press, 1993).
58. Benn, p. 271.
59. Eric A. Posner, *Law and Social Norms* (Cambridge, Mass.: Harvard University Press, 2000).
60. Cf. Feinberg, Joel, "Autonomy, Sovereignty, and Privacy: Moral Ideals and the Constitution?," *Notre Dame Law Review*, 58: 445–92 (1983).
61. Philip Pettit, *Republicanism: A Theory of Freedom and Government* (Oxford: Oxford University Press, 1997), p. 267.
62. Robert C. Post, "The Social Foundations of Privacy: Community and Self in the Common Law Tort," *California Law Review* vol. 77: 957–1010 (October 1989).
63. Pettit 1997, p. 269.
64. Robert C. Post, "The Social Foundations of Privacy: Community and Self in the Common Law Tort," *California Law Review*, vol. 77: 957–1010 (October 1989).
65. *U.S. v. Katz*, 389 U.S. 347 (1967).
66. See Bruce Ackerman, *Social Justice and the Liberal State* (New Haven, Conn.:, Yale University Press 1980), pp. 173, 195–96.
67. Diana Tietjens Meyers, "Agency," in Alison M. Jaggar and Iris Marion, eds., *A Companion to Feminist Philosophy* (Oxford: Blackwell) pp. 372–82, 372.
68. See *Stanley v. Georgia* 394 U.S. 557 (1969); *Ravin v. State*, 537 P.2d 494 (Alaska 1975).
69. Jed Rubenfeld, "The Right to Privacy," *Harvard Law Review* 102: 737–807 (1989).
70. David A. J. Richards, *Toleration and the Constitution* (1989).
71. *Pavesich v. New England Life Insurance Co.* et al., 122 Ga. 190; 50 S.E. 68 (GA 1905).
72. Lisa Sternlieb, "*Jane Eyre*: Hazarding Confidences," *Nineteenth Century Literature* 53/no. 4: 452–79, 453 (March 1999). Jane depicts herself as a silent confidant all the while sharing the confidences of Rochester with the readers and not sharing the book with Rochester. "Jane's addiction to privacy is crucial to any understanding of the novel, for this marriage plot could only have been written without the husband's knowledge."

73. See Jean L. Cohen Regulating *Intimacy: A New Legal Paradigm,* 77 (Princeton, N.J.: Princeton University Press, 2002); Jean L. Cohen, "Is There a Duty of Privacy?" 6 *Texas Journal of Women and the Law* 47, 59–64, 125 (1996).
74. The "Don't Ask, Don't Tell" policy of the U.S. military is codified as 10 U.S.C.S. 654 (b): "Policy. A member of the armed forces shall be separated from the armed forces under regulations prescribed by the Secretary of Defense if one or more of the following findings is made and approved in accordance with procedures set forth in such regulations:***

    (1) That the member has engaged in, attempted to engage in, or solicited another to engage in a homosexual act or acts* * *
    (2) That the member has stated that he or she is a homosexual or bisexual, or words to that effect, unless there is a further finding, made and approved in accordance with procedures set forth in the regulations, that the member has demonstrated that he or she is not a person who engages in, attempts to engage in, has a propensity to engage in, or intends to engage in homosexual acts.
    (3) That the member has married or attempted to marry a person known to be of the same biological sex."

75. Julie E. Cohen, "Examined Lives: Informational Privacy and the Subject as Object," *Stanford Law Review* 52: 1373–438 (2000).
76. See, discussing employee drug testing, Adam Moore, *Privacy Rights: Moral and Legal Foundations* (State College: Pennsylvania State University Press, 2009).
77. Cf. Feinberg, Joel, "Autonomy, Sovereignty, and Privacy: Moral Ideals and the Constitution?" *Notre Dame Law Review* 58: 445–91 (1983).
78. Moore, Adam D., ed., *Information Ethics: Privacy, Property, and Power* (Seattle: University of Washington Press, 2005); DeCew, Judith Wagner, *In Pursuit of Privacy: Law, Ethics and the Rise of Technology* (1997); Benn, S. I., *A Theory of Freedom.* (Cambridge: Cambridge University Press, 1988); Schoeman, F. D., ed., *Philosophical Dimensions of Privacy: An Anthology* (Cambridge: Cambridge University Press, 1984); Boone, C. Keith, "Privacy and Community," *Social Theory and Practice,* 9:1 (Spring 1983); Reiman, Jeffrey H., "Privacy, Intimacy and Personhood," *Philosophy and Public Affairs,* 6:26–44 (1976); Rachels, James, "Why Privacy is Important," *Philosophy and Public Affairs,* 4:323–33 (1975); Pennock, J. R. and Chapman, J. W., eds., *Privacy: Nomos XIII* (Atherton Press: 1971).
79. Benn, pp. 299–302.
80. Cf. Patrick O. Goodridge, "Public Privacy (Self-Government)," *University of Miami Law Review* 53: 395–422 (1999).
81. Grundgesetz für die Bundesrepublik Deutschland, Artikel 1 (1): "Die Würde des Menschen ist unantastbar. Sie zu achten und zu schützen ist Verpflichtung aller staatlichen Gewalt."
82. Allison Lynn, "German Regulators After Big Bro," *Wired News,* March 7, 2000.
83. For a defense of expressive laws that seek to achieve a new moral equilibrium, see Robert Cooter, "Expressive Law and Economics," *Journal of Legal Studies* 37: 585–608 (June 1998).
84. Barry Schwartz, "Self-Determination: The Tyranny of Freedom," *The American Psychologist* 55:/1: 79–89 (2000).
85. Cf. Martin E. Halstuk, "Shielding Private Lives from Prying Eyes:

    The Escalating Conflict Between Constitutional Privacy and the Accountability Principle of Democracy," *CommLaw Conspectus* 11: 71–94 (2003).

86. *American Civil Liberties Union v. Department of Defense*, 543 F.3d 59 (2nd Cir. 2008).
87. The Freedom of Information Act, 5 U.S.C. § 552, (FOIA) is an open government statute. Using FOIA, the media, public interest groups, and the general public attempt to keep track of what the federal government is up to. The Privacy Act and nine FOIA exemptions limit disclosures under the act. Federal agencies are separately responsible for meeting their own FOIA responsibilities. Requests for records must be addressed to the appropriate agency for processing. Persons who believe they have been improperly denied a FOIA request and have exhausted their administrative remedies may sue in federal district court.
88. ACLU Press Release, "Photos Depict Abuse At Facilities In Afghanistan And Iraq," September 22, 2008. See www.**aclu**.org/ . . . /appeals-court-orders-defense-department-**release**-detainee-abuse-photos-**aclu**-lawsuit, last accessed February 12, 2011.
89. *Center for National Security Studies v. U.S. Department of Justice*, 331 F.3d 918 (D.C. Cir. 2003), holding that the government could withhold names and other identifying information sought by civil liberties groups.
90. *Associated Press v. Department of Defense*, 554 F. 3d 274 (2d Cir. 2009), holding that the government could withhold names and other identifying information about detainees sought by the media.
91. Charlie Savage, Closing Guantánamo Fades as a Priority, New York Times, June 25, 2010. See http://www.nytimes.com/2010/06/26/us/politics/26gitmo.html, last accessed February 12, 2011.
92. See Joyce Maynard's webpage at http://www.joycemaynard.com/Joyce_Maynard/WELCOME.html, last accessed February 12, 2011.

Chapter 2

1. Hanna Arendt, "Some Questions of Moral Philosophy," in Jerome Kohn, ed., *Responsibility and Judgment* (New York: Schocken Books, 2003), p. 98.
2. Arendt, p. 98.
3. Arendt, p. 99.
4. Arendt, p. 99.
5. Richard E. Byrd, *Alone* (Los Angeles: Jeremey P. Tarcher, Inc., 1938), p. 4.
6. Gaston Bachelard, *The Politics of Space* (New York: Orion Press, 1964), p. 6.
7. See generally Ann Cline, *A Hut of One's Own: Life Outside the Circle of Architecture* (Cambridge, Mass.: MIT Press, 1997).
8. May Sarton, *Journal of Solitude* (New York: W.W. Norton, 1973).
9. Keith Tester, *The Flâneur* (New York: Routledge, 1994), pp. 1–4.
10. Janet H. Freeman, "Speech and Silence in *Jane Eyre*," *Studies in English Literature,* 1500–1900, *Century* 24 (4): 1984), pp. 683–700; Carla Kaplan, "Girl Talk: Jane Eyre and the Romance of Women's Narration," *Novel: A Forum on Fiction* 30(1): Autumn 1996, pp. 5–31.
11. Mary Lyndon Shanley, *Feminism, Marriage and the Law in Victorian England,* 1850–1895 (Princeton, N.J.: Princeton University Press, 1989), pp 8–9.
12. Bette London, "The Pleasures of Submission: Jane Eyre and the Production of the Text," *English Literary History*, 58 (1): 1991, pp. 195–213.
13. Anita L. Allen, "The Jurisprudence of *Jane Eyre*," *Harvard Women's Law Journal* 15 (1992), pp. 173–238.

14. Samuel Warren and Louis Brandeis, "The Right to Privacy," *Harvard Law Review* 4 (1890), pp. 193–220.
15. E.L. Godkin, "The Rights of the Citizen. IV-To His Own Reputation," *Scribner's* 8 (1), (1890) pp. 58–67, stressing the value of separate rooms. See also E.L. Godkin, "The Right to Privacy," *The Nation*, 22: 496–97 (December 25, 1890), expressing doubt that a privacy right of the sort proposed by Warren and Brandeis would catch on.
16. *Kyllo v. United States*, 533 U.S. 27, 37 (2001).
17. Cf. Elisabeth Gill Johnson, *Privacy, Interaction, and Residential Satisfaction in a Low Income Housing Development* (Dissertation Abstracts International, Boston University, 1984), analyzing original survey of women residents of a housing project about their satisfaction with their homes.
18. *Carey v. Brown*, 447 U.S. 455, 471 (1980).
19. *Gregory v. Chicago*, 394 U.S. 111, 125 (1969).
20. See *Frisby v. Schultz*, 487 U.S. 474 (1988); *National Funeral Services, Inc. v. Rockefeller*, 870 F2d 136 (4th Cir. 1989).
21. See *Carey v. Brown*, 447 U.S. 455, 471 (1980).
22. See the Telephone Privacy Division page of he Indiana State Attorney General, last visited February 13, 2009 at http://www.in.gov/attorneygeneral/consumer/telephone/faqs.html#2.
23. See http://www.donotcall.gov/, the official website for the Do Not Call Registry, last visited February 12, 2009.
24. See *Mainstream Marketing Services v. FTC*, 358 F.3d 1228 (10th Cir. 2004).
25. *Carey v. Brown*, 447 U.S. 455 (1980).
26. Ian Ayres and Matthew Funk, "Marketing Privacy: A Solution for the Blight of Telemarketing and Spam and Junk Mail)," see http://papers.ssrn.com/sol3/papers.cfm?abstract_id=303303. See also Ian Ayres and Barry Nalebuff, "If Telemarketers Paid for Your Time," *Forbes.com*, March 28, 2002, see http://www.forbes.com/2002/03/28/0328whynot.html.
27. *Illinois v. Telemarketing*, 538 U.S. 600 (2003).
28. See http://www.washingtonpost.com/wp-dyn/content/story/2008/02/28/ST2008022803016.html.
29. Barbara Belbot, "Where Can a Prisoner Find a Liberty Interest These Days? The Pains of Imprisonment Escalate," *New York Law School Law Review* 42 (1998), pp. 1–69, 40–47.
30. Carol Steiker, "Forward: Punishment and Procedure: Punishment Theory and the Criminal-Civil Procedural Divide," *Georgetown Law Journal* 85 (1997), pp. 775–819.
31. See Markus Dirk Dubber, "On the Enlightened Punishment: The Right to Be Punished: Autonomy and Its Demise in Modern Penal Thought," *Law and History Review* 16 (Spring 1998), pp. 113–46.
32. In *Laaman v. Helgemoe*, 437 F. Supp 269 (NH 1977), the court condemned confinement at a New Hampshire state prison as unconstitutionally cruel and unusual, citing "the cold storage of human beings," "enforced idleness," and "numbing violence against the spirit."
33. Claire Schaeffer-Duffy, "Solitary Confinement: an American Invention," *National Catholic Reporter* 6 (37) (2001), p. 5. See also Christine Rebman, "The 8th Amendment and Solitary Confinement: The Gap in Consequences from Psychological Consequences," *DePaul Law Review* 49 (1999), pp. 567–619.

34. See http://www.easternstate.org/history/sixpage.php.
35. Spencer Harrington, "Teaching the Crazy: SuperMax Confinement Under Attack," *The Humanist* 57 (1): January 11, 1997, p. 14–19.
36. Matthew W. Meskell, "An American Resolution: The History of Prisons in the United States from 1776–1877," *Stanford Law Review* 51 (1999), pp. 839–65, 841.
37. Meskell, p. 855.
38. Bryan B. Walton, "The Eighth Amendment and Psychological Implications of Solitary Confinement," *Law and Psychology Review* 21 (1997), pp. 271–88, 283.
39. Walton, 283.
40. Amy Imse, "State Locks Kids in 'Hole'; Youth Prison's Use of Solitary Confinement Stirs Outrage," *Rocky Mountain News*, March 8, 1998, pg. 5A.
41. See *Wilkinson v. Austin*, 545 U.S. 209 (2005): "'Supermax' prisons are maximum-security facilities with highly restrictive conditions, designed to segregate the most dangerous prisoners from the general prison population. Their use has increased in recent years, in part as a response to the rise in prison gangs and prison violence." See also Leena Kurki and Norval Morris, "The Purposes, Practices and Problems of Supermax Prisons," *Crime and Justice* 28 (2001), pp. 385–421, 386.
42. *Wilkinson v. Austin*, 545 U.S. 209 (2005), Kennedy, J.
43. *Wilkinson v. Austin*, 545 U.S. 209 (2005), Kennedy, J.
44. Kurki and Morris, p. 389.
45. *Wilkinson v. Austin*, 545 U.S. 209 (2005).
46. Art Caplan, "Ethical Issues Surrounding Forced, Mandated, or Coerced Treatment," *Journal of Substance Abuse Treatment* 31 (2006), pp. 117–20.
47. Alex Beam, *Gracefully Insane: Life and Death Inside America's Premier Mental Hospital* (New York: Public Affairs, 2001).
48. Deborah Jones Merritt, "Communicable Disease and Constitutional Law: Controlling AIDS," *New York University Law Review* 61 (1986), pp. 739–99, 776.
49. Michael Davis, Justice and the Shadow of Death: Rethinking Capital and Lesser Punishments (Lanham, Md.: Rowman and Littlefield), p. 128.
50. See Leah Hammett, "Protecting Children with Needs Against Arbitrary Exclusion from School," *California Law Review* 74 (July 1986), pp. 1373–407.
51. Martin I. Meltzer, Inger Damon et al., "Modeling Potential Responses to Smallpox as a Bioterrorist Weapon," *National Center for Infectious Diseases Emerging Infectious Diseases* 7 (1): 2001, pp. 959–69.
52. Nancy Shute, "Germs and Guns: 'Would Quarantine Work to Control and Epidemic?'" *U.S. News and World Report*, November 19, 2001, p. 50.
53. Melissa Healy, "Are Quarantines Back: The practice has been used around the world for centuries. SARS is putting it back in the public consciousness and raising questions about the effectiveness," *Los Angeles Times*, April 14, 2003, part six, page 1.
54. Lawrence O Gostin, Scott Burris, and Zita Lazzarini, "The Law and the Public's Health: a Study of Infectious Disease Law in the United States," *Columbia Law Review* 99 (1999), pp. 59–128.
55. See Deirdre Davidson, "Inadmissible: Quarantine Proposal Sparks Debate,"*Legal Times*, November 5, 2001, p. 3.
56. Leonard J. Nelson III, "Current Development: International Travel Restrictions and the AIDS Epidemic," *American Journal of International Law* 81 (1987), pp. 230–36.

57. Keith Bradsher, "Hong Kong Resists Wide Quarantine for Mystery Illness," *New York Times*, April 11, 2003, section 8, p. 10.
58. Bradsher, p. 10.
59. Davis, p. 131.
60. See Jack El-Hai, *The Lobotomist, A Maverick Medical Genius and His Tragic Quest to Aid the World of Mental Illness* (New York: Wiley, 2007), pp. 153ff. Dr. Freeman traveled coast to coast performing psychosurgery and training others in his controversial transorbital lobotomy technique.
61. Judith Walzer Leavitt, *Typhoid Mary* (Boston: Beacon Press, 1997).
62. Paula Span, "Quarantine Island: SARS Isolation Recalls New York's Long Ago Health Efforts," *The Washington Post*, May 21, 2003, p. C 01.
63. Howard Markel, "A Gate to the City: the Baltimore Quarantine Station, 1918–28," *U.S. Department Health and Human Services Public Health Reports* 110 (2): March 1995, p. 218.
64. Sherwin Nuland, "Hate In the Time of Cholera," *The New Republic*, May 26, 1997, p. 32.
65. Warren and Brandeis, p. 195. For an earlier use of the phrase "right to be let alone" see the treatise by Thomas M. Cooley, *Cooley on Torts* 29 (2d ed. 1888).
66. A "Coalition Against Institutionalized Children Abuse" has been established as a resource for families and the general public. The stories of the deaths of dozens of children and youth appear on its website at http://www.caica.org/RESTRAINTS%20Death%20List.htm, last accessed February 22, 2009.

Chapter 3

1. Joan Wallach Scott, *Politics of the Veil* (Princeton, N.J.: Princeton University Press 2007) p. 1.

   My summary here of Scott's views is adapted from my review of her book in "Undressing Difference: The Hijab and the West," *Berkeley Journal of Gender Law and Justice* 23 (2008), pp. 208–24.
2. "Muslim Americans: Middle Class and Mostly Mainstream," from the Pew Research Center. Available at http://pewresearch.org/assets/pdf/muslim-americans.pdf (last accessed June 2, 2010). Pew describes its report as the "first ever nationwide survey to attempt to measure rigorously the demographics, attitudes and experiences of Muslim Americans" (p. 3). The Pew Research Center Report estimates the number of U.S. Muslims to be 2.35 million.
3. Pew Research Center Report, p. 3.
4. Pew Research Center Report, p. 3.
5. The Pew Research Center Report states that "roughly two-thirds (65%) of adult Muslims in the U.S. were born elsewhere," and "among native-born Muslims, roughly half are African American (20% of U.S. Muslims overall), many of whom are converts to Islam." Other estimates of the proportion of African Americans that comprise the Muslim population range from 40% to 85%. African Americans are considered the largest group of nonimmigrant Muslims in the United States. See Karan Fraser Wyche, "African American Muslim Women: an Invisible Group," *Sex Roles* 51 (September 2004), pp. 319–28.
6. Converts to Islam in the United States are "among the most enthusiastic about wearing traditional women's attire." Donna Gehrke-White, *The Face Behind the Veil: the Extraordinary Lives of Muslims Women in America* (New York: Kensington, 2006), pp. 2–5. See also Yvonne

Yazbeck Hadda, Jane I. Smith, Kathleen M. Moore, *Muslim Women in America* (New York: Oxford, 2006), p. 45 ("Most Muslim women who are black choose to adopt Islamic dress and Islamic names"). As an aside, it has also been documented that African American women are known for their creativity in designing stylish garments that also attend to the modesty requirement. Yazbeck Haddda et al., p. 13.

7. Yazbeck Hadda et al., *Muslim Women in America* at 103–107.
8. Yazbeck Hadda et al., p. 59–60 (taken from Aminah McCloud, *African American Islam* (New York: Routledge, 1995).
9. I also address this question in Anita L. Allen, "Undressing Difference: The Hijab in the West," *Berkeley Journal of Gender, Law and Justice* 23 (2008), pp. 208–24. See also Anita L. Allen, "Hijabs and Headwraps: The Case for Tolerance," in Deirdre Golash (ed.), *Freedom of Expression in a Diverse World* (New York: Springer, 2010) pp. 115–27.
10. Yassin Musharbash, "It Makes No Sense to Ban the Burqa," in *Spiegel Online*. Available from http://www.spiegel.de/international/europe/0,1518,687105,00.html (last accessed June 2, 2010); Reuters, "Muslim Woman in Italy Is Fined for Wearing Veil," *New York Times*, May 5, 2010, p. A12 (reporting that "a 26-year-old Tunisian woman has been fined for wearing a face veil while walking to a mosque in northern Italy").
11. Steven Erlanger, "France: Full-Face Veil Ban Approved," *New York Times*, October 10, 2010, p. A8.
12. Recent veiling legislation in Spain almost followed the French example. In 2010, the Senate approved a ban against wearing the burqa in all public places. This bill was later rejected by a slim majority in the Parliament. However, the government announced it will introduce a different version of the bill later. Raphael Minder, "Spain's Senate Votes to Ban Burqa," *New York Times*, June 23, 2010. Available at http://www.nytimes.com/2010/06/24/world/europe/24iht-spain.html?ref=muslim_veiling (last accessed July 18, 2010). See also Alan Clendenning and Harold Heckle, "Spain Rejects Burqa Ban—For Now," in *The Huffington Post*. Available at http://www.huffingtonpost.com/2010/07/20/spain-rejects-burqa-ban_n_653254.html (last accessed July 20, 2010).
13. See http://www.islamophobia-watch.com/islamophobia-watch/2011/2/2/german-state-imposes-veil-ban-on-civil-servants.html (last accessed February 19, 2011.
14. *Police v. Razamjoo* (2005), DCR 408 (District Court, Auckland).
15. Bill 94: An Act to establish guidelines governing accommodation requests within the Administration and certain institutions. Available at http://www.assnat.qc.ca/en/travaux-parlementaires/projets-loi/projet-loi-94-39-1.html (last visited June 2, 2010). See also Ian Austen, "Canada: Bill in Quebec Would Ban Veils in Dealings with Officials," *New York Times*, March 25, 2010, p. A15.
16. *R. v. S. (N.)* (2009), 2009 *CarswellOnt* 2268, 95 *O.R.* (3*d)* 735 (Ont. S.C.J.).
17. Jaclyn Belczyk, "Egypt Court Upholds Niqab Ban for University Examinations" in *Jurist*. Available from: http://jurist.law.pitt.edu/paperchase/2010/01/egypt-court-uphold-niqab-ban-for.php (last visited June 3, 2010).
18. Belczyk, "Egypt Court Upholds Niqab Ban for University Examinations."
19. "Syria: Islamic Scarf That Leaves Only Eyes Exposed Is Banned," *New York Times*, July 19, 2010, A9.
20. *Leyla Sahin v. Turkey*, Eur. Ct. H. R. (Application No. 44774/98, November 10, 2005). The European Court of Human Rights heard the case of a Turkish university student who had objected to a ban on the hijab in schools, a policy the Turkish Parliament

reconsidered in 2008 because it was effectively excluding nonsecular women from getting a university education at all. Today headscarves that cover the neck, the chador, and the burqa are banned on campus, but traditional scarves tied under the chin are allowed. The European Court of Human Rights heard another case regarding the veil in *Dahlab v. Switzerland* (2001) V Eur Court HR 449. Here, a schoolteacher was banned from teaching in a primary school because she wore an "Islamic headscarf," but the case was dismissed as inadmissible. For a critique of these two court cases, see Carolyn Evans, "The 'Islamic Scarf' in the European Court of Human Rights," *Melbourne Journal of International Law* 7 (2006): pp. 52–74 (Evans criticizes the court's reliance on stereotypes about Muslim women). See Reuters, "Muslim Leader Says France Has Right to Prohibit Head Scarves," *New York Times*, December 31, 2003, p. A5.

21. Benhabib, p. 25.
22. Matt Porter, "Headscarves in Turkey Wave a Red Flag," in *Global Post*. Available at http://www.globalpost.com/dispatch/study-abroad/100209/headscarves-turkey (last accessed June 3, 2010).
23. Law No. 2004-228 of March 15, 2004, Journal Officiel de la République Française [J.O.] [Official Gazette of France], March 17, 2004, 5190 ("*en application de principe de laïcité, le port de signes ou de tenues manifestant une appartenance religieuse*").
24. Elaine Sciolino, "The Reach of War: Religious Symbols; Ban on Head Scarves Takes Effect in a United France," *New York Times*, September 3, 2004, p. p.
25. Selya Benhabib, "Turkey's Constitutional Zigzags," *Dissent* 56(1) (Winter 2009), pp. 25–28.
26. Nancy J. Hirschmann, *The Subject of Liberty: Toward a Feminist Theory of Freedom* (APrinceton, N.J.: Princeton University Press, 2003).
27. *Wisconsin v. Yoder*, 406 U.S. 205 (1972).
28. Henry Samuel, "Pensioner 'Ripped Veil From the Face of Muslim Woman,'" *Daily Telegraph* (UK) October 15, 2010.
29. Scott, *Politics of the Veil*, p. x.
30. See, e.g., Paul Silverstein and Chantal Tetreault, "Algeria-Watch, Urban Violence in France," November 2005. Available at http://www.algeria-watch.org/en/policy/urban_violence.htm (last accessed March 9, 2008).
31. Pew Research Center, "Widespread Support for Banning Full Islamic Veil in Western Europe, Most Americans Disapprove," available at http://pewresearch.org/pubs/1658/widespread-support-for-banning-full-islamic-veil-western-europe-not-in-america (last accessed February 18, 2011).
32. *Freeman v. State*, 2003 WL 21338619 (Fla.Cir.Ct. June 06, 2003) (NO. 2002-CA-2828). Affirmed by *Freeman v. Department of Highway Safety and Motor Vehicles*, 924 So.2d 48, 31 Fla. L. Weekly D537 (Fla.App. 5 Dist. February 13, 2006) (NO. 5D03-2296), rehearing denied (March 29, 2006).
33. A federal Religious Freedom Restoration Act of 1993, 42 U.S.C. § 2000bb, was found unconstitutional as applied to the states in *City of Boerne v. Flores* (1997). The passage of federal RFRA was a response by Congress to Supreme Court Free exercise decisions including *Employment Division v. Smith*, 494 U.S. 872 (1990). Prior to RFRA, the court had held that minority religions are not relieved from the force of laws of general application, such as the nation's polygamy and controlled substance laws. The *Employment Division* case upheld the denial of unemployment benefits to two Native American men who lost

their state jobs because they had consumed sacramental peyote as part of a Native American church ritual. Florida has adopted its own version RFRA that mirrors the federal statute, as follows:

Fla. Stat. Ann. §§761.01-761.05 (1998)

761.01 Short title.; This act may be cited as the "Religious Freedom Restoration Act of 1998."

761.02 Definitions.;—As used in this act:

(1) "Government" or "state" includes any branch, department, agency, instrumentality, or official or other person acting under color of law of the state, a county, special district, municipality, or any other subdivision of the state.
(2) "Demonstrates" means to meet the burden of going forward with the evidence and of persuasion.
(3) "Exercise of religion" means an act or refusal to act that is substantially motivated by a religious belief, whether or not the religious exercise is compulsory or central to a larger system of religious belief.

761.03 Free exercise of religion protected.;

(1) The government shall not substantially burden a person's exercise of religion, even if the burden results from a rule of general applicability, except that government may substantially burden a person's exercise of religion only if it demonstrates that application of the burden to the person:
    (a) Is in furtherance of a compelling governmental interest; and
    (b) Is the least restrictive means of furthering that compelling governmental interest.
(2) A person whose religious exercise has been burdened in violation of this section may assert that violation as a claim or defense in a judicial proceeding and obtain appropriate relief. . . .

34. *Quaring v. Peterson*, 728 F.2d 1121 (8th Cir.1984); *Bureau of Motor Vehicles v. Pentecostal House of Prayer, Inc.*, 269 Ind. 361, 380 N.E.2d 1225 (Ind.1978); *Dennis v. Charnes*, 805 F.2d 339 (10th Cir.1984).
35. John-Thor Dahlburg, "Court Battle Over Veil Pits Religion Against Security," *Los Angeles Times*, May 30, 2003. Available at http://articles.latimes.com/2003/may/30/nation/na-veil30 (last accessed June 10, 2010).
36. Section 332.051 reads as follow: "Notwithstanding chapter 761 or s. 761.05, the requirement for a fullface photograph or digital image of the identification card holder may not be waived."
37. *Bint-Ishmawiyl v. Vaughn*, 1995 WL 461949 (E.D. Pa. 1995).
38. Ibid.
39. 71 Pa. Stat. §2401–2407 (2002).
40. Ibid.
41. *Khatib v. County of Orange*, 603 F 3d 713 (9th Cir. 2010).
42. *Muhammed v. Paruk*, 533 F. Supp. 2d 893 (E.D. Mich.2008).
43. *State v. Allen*, 113 Ore. App. 306, 308 (Or. Ct. App. 1992).
44. Mohandas K. Gandhi, *Gandhi An Autobiography: The Story of My Experiments With Truth*, trans. Mahadev Desai (Boston: Beacon Press, 1993), pp. 94ff.

45. Amendment of Rule 611 of the Michigan Rules of Evidence, available at http://courts.michigan.gov/supremecourt/Resources/Administrative/2007-13-08-25-09-Order.pdf (last accessed June 3 2010).
46. *Rhinelander v. Rhinelander,* 219 N.Y.S. 548 (N.Y. App. Div. 1927), *aff'd* 157 N.E. 838 (N.Y. 1927).
47. Earl Lewis and Heidi Ardizonne, *Love on Trial: An American Scandal in Black and White* (New York: W.W. Norton, 2001).
48. Anita Womack, "Judge Tells Lawyer not to Wear Kente Cloth in Court," *Times Daily,* 23 May 1992, available at http://news.google.com/newspapers?nid=1842&dat=19920523&id=iUweAAAAIBAJ&sjid=MscEAAAAIBAJ&pg=1385,3508784 (last accessed June 3 2010).
49. *Close-It Enters., Inc. v. Mayer Weinberger,* 64 A.D.2d 686, 407 N.Y.S.2d 587 (2d Dept.1978).
50. *La Rocca v. Lane,* 77 Misc.2d 123, 353 N.Y.S.2d 867 (N.Y.Sup. Mar 11, 1974), reversed on other grounds in *La Rocca v. Lane,* 47 A.D.2d 243, 366 N.Y.S.2d 456 (N.Y.A.D. 2 Dept. Apr 07, 1975).
51. *Ryslik v. Krass,* 652 A.2d 767 (N.J. Super. Ct. App. Div. 1995).
52. Aaron J. Williams, *The Veiled Truth: Can the Credibility of Testimony Given by a* Niqab-*Wearing Witness be Judged Without the Assistance of Facial Expressions?, U. Det. Mercy L. Rev.* 85 (2008), p. 273.
53. See, e.g., Anita L. Allen, *Uneasy Access: Privacy for Women in a Free Society* (Totowa, N.J.: Rowman & Littlefield Publishers, 1988), p. 3; Daniel J. Solove, "A Taxonomy of Privacy," *University of Pennsylvania Law Review* 154 (January 2006), pp. 486–564.
54. Daniel Statman, "Modesty, Pride and Realistic Self-Assessment," *The Philosophical Quarterly* 42 (169) (October 1992), p. 434.
55. Michael Ridge, "Modesty as a Virtue," *American Philosophical Quarterly* 37 (3) (July 2000): p. 28.
56. General modesty is akin to, but not identical to, humility. See Daniel Statman, "Modesty," p. 420, claiming that his argument about modesty "applies to the virtue of humility too."
57. Nancy E. Snow, "Humility," *The Journal of Value Inquiry* 29 (1995), pp. 211–15. Cf. Sebastian Carlson, "The Virtue of Humility," *The Thomist* 7 (2) (April. 1944), p. 136, describing humility as Christian virtue "by which every man, considering the depth of his nothingness and sin, and God's excellence as his Creator and Redeemer, is restrained from attempting anything beyond the measure of his nature and of the grace given him, yet at the same time from acting beneath that measure"); and, Anthony Skillen, "Can a Good Man Know Himself?," *Philosophical Investigations* 18 (2) (April 1995), pp. 151–55, assessing the consistency of true humility and accurate self-assessment.
58. Owen Flanagan, "Virtue and Ignorance," *The Journal of Philosophy* 87 (8) (August 1990), pp. 420–28, 424.
59. G. F. Schueler, "Why Is Modesty a Virtue?" *Ethics* 109 (July 1999), pp. 835–41.
60. See Aristotle, "Magna Moralia," in *The Complete Works of Aristotle,* ed. Jonathan Barnes, (Princeton, N.J.: Princeton University Press, 1984), pp. 1875, 1887. See Aristotle, "Nicomachean Ethics," in *The Complete Works of Aristotle,* ed. Jonathan Barnes (Princeton, N.J.: Princeton University Press, 1984), 4:1779–80. See also Michael Ridge, p. 277, discussing modern ethical perspectives on modesty influenced by Aristotle.
61. Cf. Daniel H. Frank, "Humility as a Virtue: A Maimonidean Critique of Aristotle's Ethics" in *Moses Maimonides and His Time,* ed. Eric L. Ormsby (Washington, D.C.: Catholic University of America Press, 1989), pp. 89–99; at 89 ("The right way . . . is not to be merely humble . . . but to be humble-minded . . . and lowly of spirit to the utmost").

62. Cf. Daniel Statman, "Modesty," pp. 420–38, debating whether modesty ought to be considered virtue. See also p. 430, asserting that "the endorsement of humility is connected with the `pessimistic' view of human nature which is to be found in religious thought." Cf. A.T. Nuyen, "Just Modesty," *American Philosophical Quarterly* 35 (1) (January 1998), pp. 101–109, 102.
63. See Julia Driver, "Modesty and Ignorance," *Ethics* 109 (July 1999), pp. 827–34.
64. Schueler points out a paradox about modesty through a quip he attributes to Alan Bennett: "All modesty is false modesty, otherwise it wouldn't be modesty." Schueler at 467.
65. See G. F. Schueler, p. 467, n.1 (distinguishing sexual modesty from general modesty using different terminology); cf. Roger Scruton, *Sexual Desire: A Moral Philosophy of the Erotic* (New York: The Free Press, 1986), pp. 140–48, distinguishing social modesty/shame (what I term general modesty) from sexual modesty/shame (what I term sexual or bodily modesty).
66. Cf. Shasta M. Christrup, "Breastfeeding in the American Workplace," *American University Journal of Gender, Social Policy & the Law* 9 (2001): pp. 472–502.
67. Richard A. Posner and Katherine B. Silbaugh, *A Guide to America's Sex Laws* (Chicago: University of Chicago Press, 1996), pp. 83–97.
68. *See Lowery v. State,* 39 *Ala. App.* 659, 107 *So.2d* 366 (1958).
69. See *People v. Boomer,* 250 Mich.App. 534, 655 N.W.2d 255 (2002). See also Bob Greene, "Up the Creek with a paddle—and Cussing Up a Storm," *Chicago Tribune*, August 30, 1999, p. 1, Zone C.

    Under Alabama law, Ala.Code 1975 § 15-8-150, "disturbing women at public assemblies, etc. by profanity, etc." was once an indictable offense. Until 1974, California's penal code, West's Ann.Cal.Penal Code § 415.5, governing disturbances of the peace read: "Every person who maliciously and willfully disturbs the peace or quiet of any community college, state college, or state university by loud or unusual noise, or by tumultuous or offensive conduct, or threatening, traducing, quarreling, challenging to fight, or fighting, or by using any vulgar, profane, or indecent language *within the presence or hearing of women or children,* in a loud and boisterous manner, is guilty of a misdemeanor" (emphasis added). Idaho law, ID ST § 18-6409 Disturbing the Peace, similarly once provided that: "Every person who maliciously and willfully disturbs the peace or quiet of any neighborhood, family or person, by loud or unusual noise, or by tumultuous or offensive conduct, or by threatening, traducing, quarreling, challenging to fight or fighting, or fires any gun or pistol, or uses any vulgar, profane or indecent language *within the presence or hearing of children,* in a loud and boisterous manner, is guilty of a misdemeanor" (emphasis added.) Under Georgia law, Ga. Code Ann., § 16-11-39: "(a) A person commits the offense of disorderly conduct when such person commits any of the following . . . : (4) Without provocation, uses obscene and vulgar or profane language in the presence of or by telephone to *a person under the age of 14 years* which threatens an immediate breach of the peace" (emphasis added). Georgia's penal code of 1895, section 396, prohibited obscene and vulgar language, including any "which would reasonably offend the sense of *modesty and decency of the woman*" (emphasis added). See *Holcombe v. State,* 5 Ga.App. 47, 62 S.E. 647 (Ga.App. 1908). In Puerto Rico, PR ST T. 33 § 4521- Breach of the Peace: "Any person who willfully performs any of the following acts, shall be punished by imprisonment for a term that shall not exceed six (6) months, a fine that shall not exceed five hundred dollars ($500), or both penalties, at the discretion of the court: . . . (c) Uses vulgar, profane or indecent language in the presence or within the hearing of women or children in a loud or noisy manner" (emphasis added).

A Texas child welfare rule, 40 TAC § 746.2805 (2006)- Department of Family & Protective Services' Prohibition on Certain Types of Discipline, provided that: "There must be no harsh, cruel, or unusual treatment of any child. The following types of discipline and guidance are prohibited.... (7) Subjecting a child to harsh, abusive, or profane language." Virginia has a similar child welfare rule, 22 VA ADC 40-110-830. (2006), prohibiting care-givers from discipline by "abusive or profane language." Louisiana restricted telephone communication content. LSA-R.S. 14:285-Telephone communications; improper language; harassment; penalty, provides that: A. No person shall: "... (4) Engage in a telephone call, conference, or recorded communication by using obscene language, when by making a graphic description of a sexual act, and the offender knows or reasonably should know that such obscene or graphic language is directed to, or will be heard by, a minor. Lack of knowledge of age shall not constitute a defense."

70. S. Tachibana, *The Ethics of Buddhism* (London: Oxford University Press, 1926), pp. 142–43.
71. Kathryn Jay, "'In Vogue With Mary': How Catholic Girls Created An Urban Market For Modesty," in *Faith in the Market: Religion and the Rise of Urban Commercial Culture*, ed. John M. Giggie and Diane Winston 177–98 (New Brunswick, N.J.: Rutgers University Press, 2002), pp. 178–79.
72. Beth E. Graybill, "'To Remind Us Who We Are': Multiple Meanings of Conservative Women's Dress," in *Strangers at Home: Amish and Mennonite Women in History*, ed. Kimberly D. Schmidt, Diane Zimmerman Umble, and Steven D. Reschly 53–77 (Baltimore, Md.: Johns Hopkins University Press, 2002), 59.
73. Clifton E. Marsh, *From Black Muslims to Muslims: The Resurrection, Transformation, and Change of the Lost-Found Nation of Islam in America, 1930–1995*, 2nd ed. (Lanham, Md.: Scarecrow Press, 1996), p. 44.
74. See W. H. McLeod, *Who Is a Sikh?: The Problem of Sikh Identity* (Oxford: Clarendon Press, 1989), p. 32; Margaret A. Gibson, *Accommodation Without Assimilation: Sikh Immigrants in an American High School* (Ithaca, N.Y.: Cornell University Press, 1988), pp. 14–15.
75. Barbara Goldman Carrel, "Hasidic Women's Head Coverings: A Feminized System of Hasidic Distinction," in *Religion, Dress and the Body*, ed. Linda B. Arthur (Oxford: Berg, 1999), pp. 163–79; at 165 (stating that "Hasidic women's dress and appearance are therefore specifically regulated, by *halakhoth*, or laws of the Torah, in order to ensure that *ervah* parts ore covered. The many *halakhoth* that define appropriate clothing and presentation for an observant Jewish woman are inseparably bound to tzniuth, or modesty. Tzniuth is the guiding principle for all Hasidic women, young and old").
76. Ibid., pp. 166 and 167 (footnote omitted).
77. Lisa Aiken, *To Be a Jewish Woman* (Northvale, N.J.: Jason Aronson, 1992), p. 130.
78. Bill McKeever and Eric Johnson, *Mormonism* 101*: Examining the Religion of the Latter Day Saints* (Grand Rapids, Mich.: Baker Books, 2000), p. 211 (quoting E. Asay). See also Jean A. Hamilton and Jena Hawley, "Sacred Dress, Public Worlds," in *Religion, Dress and the Body*, ed. Linda B. Arthur (Oxford: Berg, 1999), pp. 31–51; at p. 44 ("wearing the garment ensures that the wearers are modest in street dress as well").
79. The Representatives of the Religious Society of Friends for Pennsylvania, New Jersey, and Delaware, *Principles of Quakerism: A Collection of Essays* (304 Arch Street, Philadelphia, 1909), stating that "when Friends were drawn together as a distinct body of professors, they came clothed in modest, though not evidently antiquated, apparel,", p. 1982.
80. Gwendolyn S. O'Neal, "The African American Church, Its Sacred Cosmos and Dress," in *Religion, Dress and the Body*, ed. Linda B. Arthur 117–34 (Oxford: Berg, 1999), 128.

81. S. Tanya Gulevich, *Understanding Islam and Muslim Traditions: An Introduction to the Religious Practices, Celebrations, Festivals, Observances, Beliefs, Folklore, Customs and Calendar Systems of the World's Muslim Communities, Including An Overview of Islamic History and Geography* (Detroit: Omnigraphics, Inc., 2004), p. 193.
82. Murtaza Mutahhari, *The Islamic Modest Dress*, 2nd ed., trans. Laleh Bakhtiar (Albuquerque: Abjad, 1989), p. 8.
83. Gulevich, p. 193.
84. Quran 24:30–31, 35:59, Ali trans.
85. Gulevich, p. 193.
86. Gulevich, p. 193.
87. See, e.g., Joel Schwartz, *The Sexual Politics of Jean-Jacques Rousseau* (Chicago: University of Chicago Press, 1984), pp. 33–40.
88. Double standards pervade western societies. See Keith Thomas, "The Double Standard," *Journal of the History of Ideas* 20 (2) (April 1959), pp. 195–216, detailing double standards of chastity and fidelity.
89. See Kalefa Sanneh, "Pop Review; During Halftime Show, a Display Tailored for Video Review," *New York Times*, February 2, 2004.
90. But see Glazer, pp. 116–17, arguing no inherent reason why exposure to female breast is any more offensive than exposure to male breast.
91. Marina Warner, "The Slipped Chiton," in *Feminism and the Body*, ed. Londa Schiebinger, (Oxford: Oxford University Press, 2000), pp. 265–92, at 273.
92. American Civil Liberties Union of Virginia, "News Release Legislation Dictating Clothing Style Goes Too Far," February 8, 2005. Available at http://www.acluva.org/newsreleases2005/Feb8.html (discussing proposed Virginia bill).
93. *See* Carl D. Schneider, "'The Reddened Cheek'—Nietzsche on Shame," *Philosophy Today* 21 (Spring 1977): pp. 21–31, 33: "If the sense of shame protects the vulnerability of things of value to violation, it also easily serves as a cloak to hide fearful inhibitions." See generally *Gabrielle Taylor, Pride. Shame and Guilt: Emotions of Self-Assessment* (Oxford: Oxford University Press, 1985).
94. Cf. Nathan Rotenstreich, "On Shame," *Review of Metaphysics* 19 (1965), pp. 55–86, 63.
95. See generally Thomas W. Laquer, "Amor Veneris, vel Dulcendo Appeletur," in *Feminism and the Body*, ed. Londa Schiebinger (Oxford: Oxford University Press, 2000), pp. 58–86.
96. *See* Sanford Kessler, "Toqueville on Sexual Morality," Interpretation 16 (3) (Spring 1989), pp. 465–80.
97. See Michael Novak, *A Time to Build* (New York: MacMillan, 1967), pp. 373–81; David Carr, "Chastity and Adultery," *American Philosophical Quarterly* 23 (4) (October 1986), pp. 363–70; Anna Stubblefield, "Contraceptive Risk-Taking and Norms of Chastity," *Journal of Social Philosophy* 27 (3) (Winter 1996), pp. 81–100, at 81.
98. *Employment Division v. Smith*, 494 U.S. 872, 878 (1990).
99. *Reynolds v. United States*, 98 U.S. 145, 164, 166 (1878) ("Laws are made for the government of actions, and while they cannot interfere with mere religious beliefs and opinions, they may with practices").
100. *Employment Division, Department of Human Resources of Oregon v. Smith*, 494 U.S. 872, 878–79 (1990) ("We have never held that an individual's religious beliefs excuse him from compliance with an otherwise valid law prohibiting conduct that the state is free to regulate").

101. *Meyer v. Nebraska,* 262 U.S. 390, 403 (1923).
102. *Wisconsin v. Yoder,* 406 U.S. 205, 206 (1972).
103. *Cohen v. California,* 403 U.S. 15 (1971).
104. Lisa Rich, "Students Dress Up for School: Trenton Shows Off Potential Uniforms for September," *The Times*, February 22, 2008, p. A1. ("According to the federal government's 'Manual on School Uniforms,' a unified wardrobe is one way to reduce discipline problems and increase school safety."). *Kelly v. Johnson,* 425 U.S. 238 (1976).
105. *Stull v. Sch. Bd. of W. Beaver Junior-Senior High Sch.,* 459 F.2d 339, 347 (3d Cir. 1972).
106. *Kelly v. Johnson,* 425 U.S. 238 (1976).
107. *Kelly v. Johnson,* 425 U.S. 238, 50–51 (1976), Marshall, J., dissenting.
108. Luke Salkeld, "Girl's Chastity Ring Banned by School," *BSX-Daily Mail,* December 5, 2008, p. 29; Cf. "Students of Virginity," *New York Times* March 30, 2008, p. 38.
109. Cf. Lisa Rich, "Outfitting Students for Unity, Security: Presentation of Uniforms Set for Tomorrow in City," *The Times,* February 19, 2008, p. A3.
110. *Isaacs ex rel. Isaacs v. Bd. of Educ. of Howard County, Md.,* 40 F. Supp. 2d 335 (D. Md. 1999).
111. *Goldman v. Weinberger,* 475 U.S. 503 (1986).
112. See, e.g., Hirschmann, pp. 175–85.
113. Warren and Brandeis, pp. 193–220 (1890). The idea caught on, and by 1905 the first state supreme court had embraced the right. See *Pavesich v. New England Life Ins. Co.* 50 S.E. 68 (Ga. 1905).
114. *Union Pacific Railroad v. Botsford,* 141 U.S. 250, 251 (1891).
115. Modest speech is coerced by public school districts, for example. See *Bethel School District v. Fraser,* 478 U.S. 675, 678–79 (1986).
116. See *Bethel School District v. Fraser,* 478 U.S. 675, 678–79 (1986).
117. *Safford Unified School District v.Redding,* 557 U.S. ___, 129 S. Ct. 2633 (2009).
118. *Safford Unified School District v. Redding,* 531 F. 3d 1071 (2008), 557 U.S. __ (2009).
119. See *Campbell v. Avis Rent A Car System, Inc.,* No. 05-74472, 2006 WL 2865169 (E.D. Mich. October 5, 2006); *Wiley v. Pless Sec., Inc.,* No. 1:105-CV-332-TWT, 2006 WL 1982886, (N.D. Ga. July 12, 2006); *Alsaras v. Dominick's Finer Foods, Inc.,* No.00-1990, 2000 WL 1763350 (7th Cir. November 22, 2000).
120. *City of Erie v. Pap's A.M.,* 529 U.S. 277 (2000) (upholding constitutionality of city ordinance prohibiting public nudity); *Barnes v. Glen Theatre, Inc.* 501 U.S. 560 (1991) (upholding constitutionality of state statute prohibiting public nudity).
121. *Johnson v. Phelan,* 69 F.3d 144, 152 (7th Cir. 1995), with Posner, J., concurring and dissenting.
122. *Kaukab v. Harris,* No. 02 C 0371, 2003 WL 21823752 (N.D. Ill. August 6, 2003), not reported in F. Supp.2d.
123. *Boyd v.Texas,* 301 Fed. App'x 363, 364–65 (5th Cir. 2008).
124. Ibid.
125. Olin Guy Wellborn III, "Demeanor," *Cornell Law Review* 76 (1991): 1075.
126. *Morales v. Artuz,* 281 F.3d 55 (2d Cir. 2002).
127. Office of the Attorney General, State of Maryland, May 27, 2009, "Constitutional Law—Free Exercise Clause—Whether Deputy Sheriff May Require An Individual Entering A Courthouse To Remove A Religious Face Covering For Security Purposes." 94 Md. Op. Atty. Gen. 81, 2009 WL 1648560 (Md.A.G.). Available at http://www.oag.state.md.us/Opinions/2009/94oag81.pdf (last accessed 10 June 2010).

128. *Police v. Razamjoo* (2005), DCR 408 (District Court, Auckland).
129. *Ryslik v. Krass,* 652 A.2d at 770.
130. *Ryslik v. Krass,* 652 A.2d at 770.
131. Equal Treatment Advisory Committee (ETAC) of the Judicial Studies Board (JSB), available at http://www.jsboard.co.uk/downloads/etbb/2009_etbb_3_religon.pdf (last accessed June 10 2010). Chapter 3.3 Religious Dress, 3-18/1.
132. JSB, at 3-18/4.
133. JSB, 3-18/6.
134. Caroline Bridge, "Case Reports: Practice: Evidence," *Family Law* 37 (2007): 986.
135. *State v. Allen,* 113 Ore. App. 306, 308 (Or. Ct. App. 1992).
136. *In re De Carlo,* 357 A.2d 273, 275 (N.J. Super. Ct. App. Div. 1976).
137. Aaron J. Williams, "The Veiled Truth: Can the Credibility of Testimony Given by a Niqab-Wearing Witness be Judged Without the Assistance of Facial Expressions?" *University of Detroit Mercy Law Review* 85 (2008): 273.

Chapter 4

1. *R. v. Jacob,* 112 C.C.C. (3d) 1 (Ont. Ct. App. 1996).
2. *People v. Gilbert,* 338 NYS2d 457 (1972).
3. Carol Kino, "Happenings: Slicing Art Out of Life," *New York Times,* September 3, 2006, Arts p. 23. Artist Lucas Samaras' recent artwork incorporates images of people watching images of him nude and in various states of undress.
4. Nude dancing cuts into the market for elaborately costumed Las Vegas shows. See Erika Kinetz, "The Twilight of the Ostrich-Plumed, Rhinestone-Brassiered Las Vegas Showgirl," *The New York Times,* August 13, 2006, Section 2 (Arts and Leisure), p. l. A dancer performing in Donn Arden's retro "Jubilee!" at the Bally Las Vegas Casino remarked that she is "modest" and would feel uncomfortable on stage topless or in a g-string. Ibid, p. 20.
5. "Congress shall make no law respecting an establishment of religion, or prohibiting the free exercise thereof; or abridging the freedom of speech, or of the press, or the right of the people peaceably to assemble, and to petition the government for a redress of grievances." U.S. Constitution, Amendment I.
6. The Fourteenth Amendment reads in part: "No State shall make or enforce any law which shall abridge the privileges or immunities of citizens of the United States; nor shall any State deprive any person of life, liberty, or property, without due process of law; nor deny to any person within its jurisdiction the equal protection of the laws." U.S. Constitution Amend. XIV, § 1.
7. *City of Erie v. Pap's A.M.,* 529 U.S. 277 (2000); *Barnes v. Glen Theatre, Inc.,* 501 U.S. 560 (1991). But see *Pap's A.M. v. City of Erie,* 571 Pa. 375, 812 A.2d 591 (PA 2002) (state constitution compels rejection of U.S. Supreme Court decision permitting ban on totally nude dancing.)
8. See *Barnes,* 501 U.S. at 572–80.
9. See *Miller v. Civil City of South Bend,* 904 F.2d 1081, 1089–104 (7th Cir. 1990).
10. I sheepishly "speak of sex in terms of repression" following a pattern Foucault insightfully studied. Michel Foucault, *The History of Sexuality, Vol. 1.: An Introduction* (New York: Vintage Press 1990), p. 7.
11. Cf. Carol A. Crocca, Annotation, *Validity of Ordinances Restricting Location of "Adult Entertainment" or Sex-Oriented Businesses,* American Law Reports 10 (5), pp. 538, 553–55 (1993).

12. See generally Reena N. Glazer, "Women's Body Image and the Law," *Duke Law Journal* 43 (October 1993), pp. 113–47. Glazer explores Indiana and New York laws that prohibit women from exposing their breasts in public.
13. President William Jefferson Clinton signed a Right to Breastfeed Act into law in 1999. Cf. Laura T. Kessler, "The Politics of Care," *Wisconsin Journal of Law, Gender and Society*, 23 (2008), pp. 169–99.
14. See, e.g., *Belmar v. Buckley*, 453 A.2d 910, 911 (N.J. Sup. Ct. 1982), quoting Belmar Ordinance 5-1.2, which, in its then-form, read as follows: "*Indecent* Exposure: It shall be unlawful for any person to appear or travel on any street, avenue, highway, road, boardwalk, beach, beach front or waterway located in the Borough of Belmar, or to appear in any public place, store, or business in said borough in a state of nudity or in an indecent or lewd dress or garment, or to make any indecent or unnecessary exposure of his or her person"; *State v. Turner*, 382 N.W.2d 252, 253 (Minn. Ct. App. 1986), quoting PB2-21, which states: "*Proper Attire Required.* No person ten (10) years of age or older shall intentionally expose his or her own genitals, pubic area, buttocks or female breast below the top of the areola, with less than a fully opaque covering in or upon any park or parkway, as defined in PB1-1. This provision does not apply to theatrical, musical, or other artistic performances upon any park or parkway where no alcoholic beverages are sold"; *McGuire v. State*, 489 So. 2d 729, 730 (Fla. 1986), quoting rule 16D-2.04(1)(e) of the Florida Administrative Code, which provides in pertinent part: "In every bathing area all persons shall be clothed as to prevent any indecent exposure of the person. All bathing costumes shall conform to commonly accepted standards at all times".

    See W. Hampton Sides, "Eastern Exposure; Lifestyle: Along the New Jersey Shoreline is the First and Only Federal Beach Where Clothing Is Optional. Nudists Hope It's Not the Last," *Los Angeles Times*, July 8, 1993, describing a federal beach in Sandy Hook, New Jersey, where nude sunbathing is permitted, though reluctantly. Apparently, according to Sides, "the past decade has seen a spate of disappointments for the naturist movement, including the loss of traditional nudist sunning spots like Florida's MacArthur Beach and Assateague Island National Seashore in Virginia."

    See Survey, "Should going topless on public beaches be legal?" *Cosmopolitan*, June 1998, p. 54, stating that "in the United States, some beaches in Florida and New York also allow women to bare their breasts in public."
15. See *Barnes v. Glen Theatre, Inc.*, 501 U.S. 560, 569 n.2 (1991), citing Indiana Code § 35-45-4-1 (1988). The Indiana Code at issue in *Barnes* provides:

    Public indecency; indecent exposure

    Sec. 1. (a) A person who knowingly or intentionally, in a public place:

    (1) engages in sexual intercourse;
    (2) engages in deviate sexual conduct;
    (3) appears in a state of nudity; or
    (4) fondles the genitals of himself or another person;

    commits public indecency, a Class A misdemeanor.

    (d) "Nudity" . . . means the showing of the human male or female genitals, pubic area, or buttocks with less than a fully opaque covering, the showing of the female breast with less than a fully opaque covering of any part of the nipple, or the showing of covered male genitals in a discernibly turgid state.
16. *See Miller v. Civil City of South Bend*, 904 F.2d 1081, 1087–89 (7th Cir. 1990), Posner, J., *rev'd sub nom. Barnes v. Glen Theatre, Inc.*, 501 U.S. 560 (1991).

17. See *Miller v. Civil City of South Bend*, 904 F.2d 1081, 1100, 1099–100 (7th Cir. 1990) (Posner, J., concurring); rev'd sub nom. *Barnes v. Glen Theatre*, Inc., 501 U.S. 560 (1991).
18. *Miller*, at 1099–100.
19. *Miller*, at 1100.
20. *Barnes*, 501 U.S. at 571.
21. *Barnes*, at 568.
22. *Barnes* at 574–75 (Scalia, J., concurring).
23. 539 U.S. 558 (2003).
24. See *Barnes*, 501 U.S. at 584 (Souter, J., concurring).
25. Ibid. at 584.
26. 475 U.S. 41 (1986). In *Renton*, the court held that: "The First Amendment does not require a city, before enacting such an ordinance, to conduct new studies or produce evidence independent of that already generated by other cities, so long as whatever evidence the city relies upon is reasonably believed to be relevant to the problem that the city addresses." Ibid. at 51–52; *accord City of L.A. v. Alameda Books, Inc.*, 535 U.S. 425, 438 (2002). There, the court opined: "In Renton we specifically refused to set such a high bar for municipalities that want to address merely the secondary effects of protected speech. We held that *a municipality may rely on any evidence that is 'reasonably believed to be relevant' for demonstrating a connection between speech and a substantial independent government* interest." Ibid. (quoting *Renton*, 475 U.S. at 51–52) (emphasis added).
27. See *Bethel Sch. Dist. v. Fraser*, 478 U.S. 675, 678–79 (1986).
28. The Supreme Court permits zoning regulations that restrict the location of adult entertainment establishments. See *Alameda Books*, 535 U.S. at 425; *Renton*, 475 U.S. at 54. The court also upheld laws requiring exotic dancers to wear pasties and g-strings. See *City of Erie v. Pap's A.M.*, 529 U.S. 277 (2000); *Barnes*, 501 U.S. at 572. Licensing schemes that operate as prior restraints on free speech, however, have been struck down. See *FW/PBS, Inc. v. Dallas*, 493 U.S. 215 (1990). Judge Posner of the Seventh Circuit is skeptical. See *Miller v. Civil City of South Bend*, 904 F.2d 1081, 1100 (7th Cir. 1990) (Posner, J., concurring); rev'd sub nom. *Barnes v. Glen Theatre, Inc.*, 501 U.S. 560 (1991). In any event, there is no contention that the stripteases of the Kitty Kat dancers are obscene. It would be difficult to make such a contention with a straight face at a time when a career respectable in the eyes of many people can be founded on posing in the nude for men's magazines. *Barnes v. Glen Theatre, Inc.* at 1091. Ibid. at 1099–100 (internal citation omitted).
29. *See Renton*, 475 U.S. at 51–54.
30. See *Alameda Books*, 535 U.S. at 429–30 (upholding zoning ordinance prohibiting two adult entertainment businesses to operate within 1000 feet of one another or in same building). The court further concluded that based on a 1977 report it is:

    Reasonable for Los Angeles to suppose that a concentration of adult establishments is correlated with high crime rates because a concentration of operations in one locale draws, for example, a greater concentration of adult consumers to the neighborhood, and a high density of such consumers either attracts or generates criminal activity.

    Alameda Books at 436.
31. *See Hart Book Stores, Inc. v. Edmisten*, 612 F.2d 821, 829 n.9 (4th Cir. 1979), finding unhealthy, unsanitary conditions in adult entertainment establishment warrant state regulations restricting their location.

32. Public health laws have been used in New York City to address the collateral effects and activities of nude dancing. See David Rohde, "Public Health Is Invoked to Shut Strip Bar," *New York Times*, August 7, 1998.
33. *Barnes*, 501 U.S. at 590–91 (White, J., dissenting).
34. *Barnes* at 591.
35. *Barnes* at 594.
36. *Nakatomi Inc. v. City of Schenectady*, 949 F. Supp. 988, 993 (N.D.N.Y. 1997). Another complained that "serious constitutional issues would exist on the reasoning of eight of nine Barnes justices", (*Tunick v. Safir*, 209 F.3d 67, 83 (2d Cir. 2000).
37. See, e.g., *People v. Huffman*, 702 N.W.2d 621, 627 (Mich. Ct. App. 2005); *Knudtson v. City of Coates*, 519 N.W.2d 166, 169 (Minn. 1994). See *Lounge Mgmt. v. Town of Trenton*, 580 N.W.2d 156, 161 (Wis. 1998).
38. Pennsylvania would fall into line after *In Purple Orchid v. Pa. State Police, Bureau of Liquor Control Enforcement*, 721 A.2d 84 (Pa. Commw. Ct. 1998). The court explained that in Pennsylvania, "our Supreme Court decided that *Barnes* has no precedential effect on whether total nudity violated the First Amendment to the United States Constitution and that it would have to do its own analysis of whether the Ordinance suppressed free expression." 721 A.2d 84, 89 (Pa. Commw. Ct. 1998). Instead, *Purple Orchid* stated that the Pennsylvania Supreme Court had adopted "Justice White's [dissenting] view that strict scrutiny should apply" to the ordinance at issue. Although the case that *Purple Orchid* discusses as the example of the Pennsylvania Supreme Court's reasoning, *Pap's A.M. v. City of Erie*, 674 A.2d 338 (Pa. Commw. Ct. 1996), was later reversed by the United States Supreme Court in *City of Erie v. Pap's A.M.*, 529 U.S. 277 (2000), it is nevertheless still relevant because it shows that some courts did, initially at least, decline to follow the *Barnes* decision.
39. Joel Feinberg, *Offense to Others: The Moral Limits of the Criminal Law* (Oxford: Oxford University Press, 1988), pp. 22-25.
40. *Pap's A.M. v. City of Erie*, 719 A.2d 273, 279 (Pa. Commw. Ct.1998); rev'd, 529 U.S. 277 (2000).
41. 391 U.S. 367 (1968).
42. See *City of Erie*, 529 U.S. at 296–98.
43. John Stuart Mill, *On Liberty*, ed. David Bromwich and George Kateb (New Haven, Conn.: Yale University Press, 2003), p. 80.
44. Vincent J. Samar, "Gay Rights as a Particular Instantiation of Human Rights," *Albany Law Review* 64 (2001), pp. 923–1030; at 986, arguing that "this is separate from the situation where the exercise of the normative right itself may create a clear, present, and imminent risk of harm to life or property. In that case, we might want to say that the right to march is overridden by another right (such as the right not to be harmed) because it is considered a more important right. Here too, one has to be careful that the valuation of importance is not based on some altogether independent moral standard. Rather, it should be based on finding a common denominator that justifies both rights to see exactly why the latter trumps the former."
45. Despite the lack of clear precedent, courts followed the *Barnes* and *City of Erie* decisions in granting from Barnes that "nude dancing... is presumably constitutionally protected speech" (see *D.H.L. Assocs. v. O'Gorman*, 199 F.3d 50, 56 (1st Cir. 1999). See also Robert Mann Enter. v. Pasco County 15 Fla. L. Weekly D 113 at *4–5 (M.D. Ha. 2001), stating in

reference to both *Erie* and *Barnes* that "like it or not, erotic nude dancing is expressive conduct within the outer ambit of the First Amendment's protection." Courts also adopted Barnes's "pasties and g-string" allowance to municipalities (see, e.g., *Cafe 207 v. St. Johns County,* 856 F.Supp. 641, 646 (M.D. Fla. 1994)). Other courts seemed to criticize the *Barnes* case by commiserating with the towns that wanted to ban nude dancing but nevertheless needed to give it at least some protection under the *Barnes* rationale: "While the Court is sympathetic to the City of Elizabeth's efforts to prevent what it perceives to be degradation of the community's moral, environmental, and social values, the Court cannot ignore the fact that nude erotic dancing is considered by the Supreme Court to be expressive conduct that is constitutionally protected" (*Internationally Hott II v. City of Elizabeth,* Civ No. 96–1447 (WGB), 1997 U.S. Dist. LEXIS 22870, at *26 (D.N.J. 1997); *see also Internationally Hott II v. City of Elizabeth* , 134 Fed.Appx. 496, 2005 WL 1170738 (C.A. 3 (NJ)). Questions about the *Barnes* decision also arose in dissents and concurrences in lower court opinions. In Justice Anderson's concurrence in *City of Elko v. Abed,* 677 N.W.2d 455 (Minn. Ct. App. 2004), discussing *Erie* and *Barnes,* he stated that it is "unfortunate" that the Supreme Court considers nude dancing protected expression, and that he thinks "the better approach is to recognize that erotic dancing is solely conduct and not entitled to First Amendment protection" at all (677 N.W.2d 455, 470, 471 (Minn. Ct. App. 2004)). Dissenting in part in *Pel Asso v. Joseph,* 427 S.E.2d 264, 269 (Ga. 1993), Justice Fletcher wrote that the "principle of stare decisis compel[led]" him to "concur that nude dancing is protected expression," implying that if it were up to him, it would not be protected at all.

46. *People v. Huffman,* 702 N.W.2d 621, 629 (Mich. Ct. App. 2005).
47. *Town of Lyndon v. Bever,* 627 N.W.2d 548, 2001 WI App. 101, 14–15 (Wis. Ct. App. 2001).
48. *Nakatomi Inv. v. City of Schenectady,* 949 F. Supp. 988, 997 (N.D.N.Y. 1997). so *Mendoza v. Licensing Bd. of Fall River,* 827 N.E.2d 180, 189 (Mass. 2005).
49. *Mendoza v. Licensing Bd. Of Fall River,* 827 N.E.2d 180, 189 (Mass. 2005).
50. Gregory Crouch, "Nijmegen Journal: A Candid Dutch Film May Be Too Scary for Immigrants," *New York Times,* March 16, 2006.
51. Ann Goodman, "Making a Splash in Paris," *New York Times,* August 19, 1990. See also Kerry Shaw, "Travel Advisory; Palm Trees (but No Swimming) Along the Seine," *New York Times,* July 28, 2002, describing a fake beach set up in the heart of Paris, at which "yes, women are allowed to go topless."
52. *See* Jamie Trecker, "The World Cup Made Easy: Munich," *New York Times,* May 28, 2006, stating that if you are a "naturist at heart," then "the Schonfeldwiese, a meadow in the center of the sprawling Englischer Garden, is the place for you. It is reserved for nude sunbathing, and will be packed with all manner of humanity."
53. J. S. Marcus, "The Bohemian Side of Munich," *New York Times,* September 24, 1995.
54. The two leading cases are *R. v. Mara,* 2 S.C.R. 630 (1997), http://csc.lexum.umontreal.ca/en/1997/1997scr2-630/1997scr2-630.html and

    R. v. Tremblay, 2 S.C.R. 932 (1993), http://csc.lexum.umontreal.ca/en/1993/1993scr2-932-/1993scr2-932.html. The Supreme Court of Canada makes its judgments available online through an official, authoritative collaboration. See http://csc.lexum.umontreal.ca/en/. In these endnotes, I will cite the pagination of the official online PDF versions of *R. v. Mara and R. v. Tremblay.*
55. *Mara* at page 17 (paragraph 31), citing, 2 S.C.R. 932, 958 (1993).

56. *R. v. Tremblay*, 2 S.C.R. 932 (1993), http://csc.lexum.umontreal.ca/en/1993/1993scr2-932-/1993scr2-932.html.
57. A Pennsylvania court quoted *On Liberty* at length in defenses of a decision striking down convictions under a statute that criminalized deviate sexual intercourse, excepting husbands and wives. The sex in question was between performers and members of the audience in a "pornographic theater" open to adults. *Commonwealth of Pennsylvania v. Bonadio*, 490 Pa 415 A2d.d 47 (1980).
58. *Mara* at page 9, para.12.
59. *R. v. Tremblay*, 2 S.C.R. 932 (1993), http://csc.lexum.umontreal.ca/en/1993/1993scr2-932-/1993scr2-932.html.
60. *Mara* p. 17, paragraph 31., citing *Butler*.
61. *Mara* at p. 18, paragraph, 34 ("relevant social harm to be considered... is the attitudinal harm on those watching... as perceived by the community").
62. *Mara* at page 23, paragraph_44.
63. *Mara* at page 9, para.12.
64. Deborah Hellman, *When is Discrimination Wrong?* (Cambridge, Mass.: Harvard University Press, 2008).
65. See, e.g., "Bare Buns Family Nudist Club," available at http://www.takeoffwithus.com/decentexposure.html (accessed August 2, 2006), describing the Bare Buns Family Nudist Club as a gathering place for individuals and families who enjoy wholesome, social, non-sexualized nudity.
66. See generally Amy Adler, "Girls! Girls! Girls!: The Supreme Court Confronts the G-string," *New York University Law Review* 80 (October 2005), pp. 1108–55, providing psychoanalytic account of Supreme Court's nude dancing cases.
67. See Aaron Ben-Ze'ev, "The Virtue of Modesty," *American Philosophical Ouarterly* 30 (3) (July 1993), pp. 235–46, "Modesty is generally considered to be an important virtue." See also p. 235; G. F. Schueler, "Why Modesty Is a Virtue," Ethics 107 (3) (April 1997), pp. 467–85; see also Michael Ridge, "Modesty as a Virtue," *American Philosophical Ouarterly* 37 (3) (July 2000), pp. 269–83; G. F. Schueler, "Why Is Modesty a Virtue?" *Ethics* 109 (July 1999), pp. 835–41.
68. *Ardery v. State*, 56 Ind. 328, 329–30 (1877).
69. In relevant part, Ordinance 75–1994, codified as Article 711 of the Codified Ordinances of the City of Erie, provides that:
    1. A person who knowingly or intentionally, in a public place:
        a. engages in sexual intercourse
        b. engages in deviate sexual intercourse as defined by the Pennsylvania Crimes Code
        c. appears in a state of nudity, or
        d. fondles the genitals of himself, herself or another person commits Public Indecency, a Summary Offense.
    2. "Nudity" means the showing of the human male or female genital [sic], pubic hair or buttocks with less than a fully opaque covering; the showing of the female breast with less than a fully opaque covering of any part of the nipple; the exposure of any device, costume, or covering which gives the appearance of or simulates the genitals, pubic hair, natal cleft, perineum anal region or pubic hair region; or the exposure of any device worn as a cover over the nipples and/or areola of the female breast, which device simulates and gives the realistic appearance of nipples and/or areola.

3. "Public Place" includes all outdoor places owned by or open to the general public, and all buildings and enclosed places owned by or open to the general public, including such places of entertainment, taverns, restaurants, clubs, theaters, dance halls, banquet halls, party rooms or halls limited to specific members, restricted to adults or to patrons invited to attend, whether or not an admission charge is levied.

4. The prohibition set forth in subsection 1(c) shall not apply to:

a. Any child under ten (10) years of age; or

b. Any individual exposing a breast in the process of breastfeeding an infant under two (2) years of age.

Erie, 529 U.S. at 283.

70. *Erie*, at 329 (Stevens, J., dissenting).
71. See generally Peter Cane, "Taking Law Seriously: Starting Points of the Hart/Devil Debates," *The Journal Ethics* 10 (1–2): January 9, 2006, pp. 21–51.
72. Robert P. George, "The Clash of Orthodoxies: Law Religion and Morality in Crisis" (Intercollegiate Studies Institute, 2001).
73. See *City of L.A. v. Alameda Books, Inc.*, 535 U.S. 425, 451 (2002) (Kennedy, J., concurring), stating that "[the Supreme Court has] consistently held that a city must have latitude to experiment, at least at the outset, and that very little evidence is required."
74. Paul Shukovsky, Kathy Mulady, and Scott Gutierrez, "Ops and Feds Raid Seattle Strip Clubs," *The Seattle Post-Intelligencer*, June 3, 2008.
75. Shukovsky et al., quoting Seattle Police Chief Gil Kerlikowske.
76. Shukovsky et al., quoting city councilman Tim Burgess.
77. *Barnes v. Glen Theatre Inc.*, 501 U.S. 560, 563 (1991).
78. *See* Samuel DuBois Cook, "Foundation and Meaning: Human Encounters," in J. Roland Pennock and John Chapman, *Coercion* (Picataway, New Jersey: Transaction Publishers 1972), 107–125, p. 109; John MacMurrary, "The Virtue of Chastity," in *The Case Against Pornography*, ed. David Holbrook (La Salle, Ill.: Open Publishing Company, 1973), pp. 68–82.
79. Aristotle, "Nicomachean Ethics," in *The Complete Works of Aristotle*, at bk. II 1750.

Chapter 5

1. But see *State v. Olwell*, 64 Wn.2d 828, 831, 394 P.2d 681 (1964), holding that lawyers must come forward when they possess certain evidence of a crime, such as a knife used to commit a murder. The American Bar Association has urged preservation of a strong attorney-client privilege, though since 2001 measures to address corporate corruption and terrorism have arguably weakened it. See http://www.abanet.org/buslaw/attorneyclient/publichearing20050421/testimony/saltzburg.pdf, last accessed February 7, 2009.
2. Cf. Jennifer L. Pierce, *Gender Trials: Emotional Lives in Contemporary Law Firms* (Berkeley: University of California Press, 1995), pp. 38–48. Pierce devotes nearly a chapter to the history of the Cravath firm, including its transition from a mainly male staff of administrative assistants and attorneys to a staff consisting mainly of female administrative assistants and male attorneys.
3. See *U.S. v. Evans*, 486 F.3d 315 (7th Cir 2007). See also http://www.sec.gov/litigation/litreleases/lr18378.htm.

4. "Should A Lawyer Betray Client to Save Innocent Man: Distinguished Men of the bar Discuss an Interesting Question Raised by the Action of Attorney Smith in the Famous Frank Murder Case," *New York Times,* October 11, 1914.
5. Truddi Chase, *When Rabbit Howls* (New York: Jove Books, 1987). I express no opinion as to the veracity of Chase's memoir.
6. See http://www.achievement.org/autodoc/page/winoint-2, visited February 7, 2009.
7. See, e.g., Kay Jamison, *The Unquiet Mind: A Memoir of Moods and Madness* (New York: Vintage Press 1997).
8. Massachusetts General Law c. 20 Section 233.
9. R. Michael Cassidy, "Reconsidering Spousal Privileges After Crawford," *American Journal of Criminal Law* 339, 374, (2006), arguing that "state legislatures should reconsider their spousal privilege rules—many of which are poorly conceived, confusing, and outdated—and should reform these statutes... to add an express exception for criminal cases alleging domestic violence."
10. The Public Company Accounting Reform and Investor Protection Act of 2002 ("Sarbanes-Oxley Act") (Pub.L. 107–204, 116 Stat. 745, enacted July 30, 2002). The statute provides criminal penalties for retaliating against whistleblowers who breach confidentiality expectations in order to alert law enforcers of wrongdoing.
11. Hippocratic Oath. See http://www.pbs.org/wgbh/nova/doctors/oath_modern.html, last visited, Feb. 20, 2011.
12. See *Butterworth v. Smith,* 494 U.S. 624, 629 (1990). See also *U.S. v. Doe,* 481 U.S. 102 (1987). See generally Mark Kadish, "Behind the Locked Door of an American Grand Jury: Its History, Its Secrecy, and Its Process," *Florida State Law Review* 24 (1996), pp. 1–77, 19.
13. See generally Anita L. Allen, *Privacy Law and Society* (Minneapolis: West/Thomson Reuters, 2011).
14. *Delaware Ins. Guar. Ass'n v. Birch,* Not Reported in A.2d, 2004 WL 1731139 (Del.Super., 2004).
15. *Doe v. Medlantic Health Care Group, Inc.* 814 A.2d 939 (2003).
16. *S.E.C. v. Rocklage,* 470 F.3d 1 (1st Cir. 2006), construing 17 C.F.R. § 240.10b5-2(b)(3), duties of trust or confidence for spouses of corporate insiders for purposes of insider trading laws prohibiting undisclosed, deceptive trading on basis of material, nonpublic information.
17. *Woodard v. Juniper Christian School, Inc.,* 913 So.2d 1188 (2005).
18. *Lightman v. Flaum,* 97 N.Y.2d 128, 761 N.E.2d 1027 (N.Y., 2001).
19. *In Re Holley,* 729 NYS2d 128 (App. Div. 2001).
20. See Adam Lipak, "Lawyer Reveals Secret, Toppling Death Sentence," *New York Times,* January 19, 2008, p. A1. The underlying case was *Atkins v. Virginia,* 536 U.S. 304, 122 S.Ct. 2242, U.S.,2002, in which the Supreme Court held that Daryl R. Atkins could not be sentenced the death for a fatal shooting if he were determined to be mentally retarded. A later court determined that Atkins was not mentally retarded and could therefore be sentenced to death. After attorney Leslie P. Smith broke "professional silence," Atkin's sentence was reduced to life in prison. Smith revealed that prosecutors had covered up possible evidence from her client William Jones that he, rather than Atkins, had been the trigger man in the robbery and killing.
21. "Twilight of Tax Privacy," March 30, 2006, *The New York Times,* p. A24.

22. The rules that went into affect January 1, 2009 amend Internal Revenue Code Sec 7216, “Disclosure or Use of Tax Information by Preparers of Returns” for the first time since the advent of widespread electronic data-sharing. The precise rules for obtaining consents appear in Treas. Reg. §301.7216-3(b) and Revenue Procedure 2008–35.
23. The American Law Institute, *Restatement (Second) of Torts*, § 652 (1977). § 652B Intrusion Upon Seclusion provides that “One who intentionally intrudes, physically or otherwise, upon the solitude or seclusion of another or his private affairs or concerns, is subject to liability to the other for invasion of his privacy, if the intrusion would be highly offensive to a reasonable person.”
24. *Plaxico v. Michael*, 735 So.2d 1036 (Miss. 1999).
25. See generally Anita L. Allen, “Privacy Torts: Unreliable Remedies for LGBT Plaintiffs,” *California Law Review*, 98: 1711-64 (2011).
26. *Greenwood v. Taft, Stettinius & Hollister*, 663 N.E.2d 1030, 1034 (Ohio Ct. App. 1995).
27. See *Florida Star v. BJF*, 491 U.S. 524 (1989) and *Cox Broadcasting Corporation v. Cohn*, 420 U.S. 469 (1975).
28. *Bartnicki* v. *Vopper*, 532 U.S. 514 (2001).
29. Sheryl Gay Stolberg (December 22, 2010). “With Obama’s Signature, ‘Don’t Ask’ Is Repealed,” *The New York Times*. Available at http://www.nytimes.com/2010/12/23/us/politics/23military.html.
30. The text of the Fifth Amendment to the United States Constitution reads: “No person shall be held to answer for a capital, or otherwise infamous crime, unless on presentment or indictment of a Grand Jury, except in cases arising in the land or naval forces, or in the Militia, when in actual service in time of War or public danger; nor shall any person be subject for the same offense to be twice put in jeopardy of life or limb; nor shall be compelled in any criminal case to be a witness against himself, nor be deprived of life, liberty, or property, without due process of law; nor shall private property be taken for public use, without just compensation.” Thomas Hobbes outlines the powers of the sovereign and the liberties of individuals in *Leviathan* (New York: Oxford University Press 2009), chapters 21, 24, 28–30. The *Leviathan* was originally published in England in 1651.
31. 8 John Henry Wigmore, *Evidence in Trials at Common Law*, Sections 2290–91 (John T. McNaughton, ed., rev. volume 1961), pp. 553.
32. David Luban, *Lawyers and Justice: An Ethical Study* (Princeton, N.J.: Princeton University Press, 1988), p. 92. See generally David Luban, *Legal Ethics and Human Dignity* (Cambridge: Cambridge University Press, 2007).
33. Monroe K. Freedman, *Lawyer’s Ethics in an Adversary System* (New York: Bobbs-Merrill, 1975), pp. 46–48.
34. Robert J. Kutak, “The Adversary System and the Practice of Law,” in David Luban, ed., *The Good Lawyer: Lawyers’ Roles and Lawyers’ Ethics* (Totowa, N.J.: Rowman and Littlefield. 1984), p. 173.
35. On the television show *Deborah Norville Tonight*, Ms. Wilson explained: “I’m very passionate about people that don’t know what to do. They’re morbidly obese. This is an option. I am public about my struggle because I know I’m helping people.” Carnie Wilson, interview by Deborah Norville, *Deborah Norville Tonight*, MSNBC, June 29, 2004. See Rick Hepp, “His Finest Hours as a Plastic Surgeon,” *Chicago Tribune*, September 29, 1999, online edition, available at http://articles.chicagotribune.com/1999-09-29/news/9910060377_1_surgery-facelift-plastic-surgeon.

36. Craig Tomashoff, "When the Reality is Inside the Body," *The New York Times Television Reviews* (Chicago: Fitzroy Dearborn Publishers, 2000), p. 268–270, 269.
37. See the consumer information page at the Department of Health and Human Services website, http://www.hhs.gov/ocr/privacy/hipaa/understanding/consumers/index.html. Last accessed February 24, 2011.
38. Department of Health and Human Services consumer information page.
39. See 45 *Code of Federal Regulations* (CFR) 164.524—Access of individuals to protected health information, (a)(3)(i): "A covered entity may deny an individual access, provided that the individual is given a right to have such denials reviewed,... in the following circumstances: (i) A licensed health care professional has determined, in the exercise of professional judgment, that the access requested is reasonably likely to endanger the life or physical safety of the individual or another person;". Read more at http://cfr.vlex.com/vid/164-524-access-individuals-protected-19931896#ixzz1Ez87uhRK and http://cfr.vlex.com/vid/164-524-access-individuals-protected-19931896#ixzz1Ez7neRhR.
40. See Department of Health and Human Services data reported at http://www.hhs.gov/ocr/privacy/hipaa/enforcement/data/complaintsyear.html. Last accessed February 24, 2011.
41. The Department of Health and Human Services publishes illustrative enforcement actions on its website. For this one, see http://www.hhs.gov/ocr/privacy/hipaa/enforcement/examples/allcases.html#case28.
42. See http://www.hhs.gov/ocr/privacy/hipaa/enforcement/examples/allcases.html#case8. Last accessed February 24, 2011.
43. American Law Institute, *Restatement (Second) of Torts* (Philadelphia: American Law Institute 1966). Section 652D Publicity Given to Private Life provides that: "One who gives publicity to a matter concerning the private life of another is subject to liability to the other for invasion of his privacy, if the matter publicized is of a kind that (a) would be highly offensive to a reasonable person, and (b) is not of legitimate concern to the public."
44. *Humphers v. Interstate*, 298 Or. 706 (Or. 1985).
45. *Bagent v. Blessing Care Corporation*, 862 N.E. 2d 985 (Ill.2007).
46. *Yath v. Fairview Clinics*, N.P., 2009 WL 1751767 (Minnesota App.)
47. H. J. McCloskey, "The Political Ideal of Privacy," *Philosophical Quarterly* 21 (1971), pp. 303, 308–309.
48. *Gracey v. Eaker*, 837 So. 2d 348 (Fla. 2002).
49. See American Association of Marriage and Family Therapists Code of Ethics, available at http://www.aamft.org/imis15/content/legal_ethics/code_of_ethics.aspx (last accessed February 20, 2011).
50. Truddi Chase, *When Rabbit Howls*.
51. *Lightman* v. *Flaum*, 97 N.Y.2d 128, 761 N.E.2d 1027 (N.Y., 2001). New York's highest court affirmed a decision handed down by the Appellate Division, holding that CPLR 4505 does not subject members of the clergy to civil liability for sharing confidential communications.
52. Sherry F. Colb, "Suing Clergy For Divulging Confidence, Why the New York Court of Appeals Was Wrong to Hold That a Woman Could Not Sue For Violation of the Clergy-Penitent Privilege." December 5, 2001, Available at http://writ.news.findlaw.com/colb/20011205.html, last accessed February 20, 2011.
53. See http://www.jewishaz.com/jewishnews/981211/ruling.shtml, visited February 4, 2009.

54. American Psychological Association, "Ethical Principles of Psychologists and Code of Conduct" (2010), Standard 4, "Privacy and Confidentiality," available at http://www.apa.org/ethics/code/index.aspx, last accessed February 20, 2011.
55. *Tarasoff v. Regents of the University of California*, 131 Cal. Rptr. 14, 551 P.2d 334 (Cal. 1976).
56. Tom Alibrandi with Frank H. Armani, *Privileged Information* (New York: HarperCollins Publishers 1984), p. 104.
57. Cf. "Model Code of Professional Responsibility Conduct," Canon 4, DR 4–101 C (3), providing that a lawyer may reveal "The intention of his client to commit a crime and the information necessary to prevent the crime." Cf. *State v. Olwell*, 64 Wn.2d 828, 831, 394 P.2d 681 (1964), holding that lawyers must come forward when they possess certain evidence of a crime, such as a knife used to commit a murder.

Chapter 6

1. A preliminary discussion of this topic was published as Anita L. Allen, "Race, Face, and Rawls," *Fordham Law Review* 72 (2004), pp. 1677–96.
2. See generally, Patrick Simon, *"Ethnic" Statistics and Data Protection in Council of Europe Countries: Study Report* (Strasbourg: Council of Europe, 2007), comparing race and ethnicity data collection in four typical European countries.
3. George Yancy, *Black Bodies, White Gazes* (Lanham, Md.: Rowman and Littlefield, 2008), pp. 75, 156.
4. International Convention on the Elimination of All Forms of Racial Discrimination (1969), available at http://www2.ohchr.org/english/law/cerd.htm.
5. *Plessy v. Ferguson*, 163 U.S. 537 (1896); *Dred Scott v. Sandford*, 60 U.S. (19 How.) 393 (1857); *Korematsu v. United States*, 323 U.S. 214 (1944).
6. *Korematsu v. United States*, 323 U.S. 214 (1944), "all legal restrictions which curtail the civil rights of a single racial group are immediately suspect."
7. Johnson v. California, 543 U.S. 499 (2005).
8. "A Little Local Color," *New York Times*, September 19, 1982 p. 29.
9. Constitution of the State of Florida, Article I, section 12.
10. Constitution of the State of California, Article 1, section 1.
11. Constitution of the State of Washington, Article I, section 7.
12. Chris Goodman, "Redacting Race in the Quest for Colorblind Justice: How Racial Privacy Legislation Subverts Antidiscrimination Laws," *Marquette Law Review*. 88 (2004), pp. 299, 344.
13. Cf. *U.S. v. New Hampshire*, 539 F. 2d 277 (1st Cir. 1976).
14. Cf. *Caulfield v. Board of Education of the City of New York*, 583 F.2d 605, 611 (2nd Cir. 1978).
15. *Whalen v. Roe*, 429 U.S. 589 (1977).
16. Privacy Act of 1974, 5 U.S.C. § 552a; the Freedom of Information Act, 5 U.S.C. § 552, Exemption (b)(6); Health Insurance Portability and Accountability Act, 42 U.S.C.S. §§ 1320d-1329d-8; Financial Services Modernization Act, Title V,15 *U.S.C.* §§ 6801–6809; Fair Credit Reporting Act, 15 U.S.C. 1681 et seq.; Family Education and Right to Privacy Act, 20 U.S.C. § 1232g; Video Privacy Act, 18 U.S.C. § 2710 et seq., Children's Online Privacy Protection Act, 15 U.S.C. 6501 et seq.; Electronic Communications Privacy Act, 18 U.S.C. 2510 et seq.
17. American Law Institute, *Restatement (Second) of Torts 652A-E.*

18. *Cheesman v. Ameritítle*, Civil Case No. 07-3094 (USDC E.D. Wa 2010).
19. See generally Randall Kennedy, *Nigger: The Strange Career of a Troublesome Word* (New York: Vintage 2003).
20. See *Morales v. Daley*, 116 F. Supp. 2d 801 (S.D. Texas 2000).
21. See http://www.ftc.gov/bcp/edu/microsites/donotcall/psa.html, last visited August 18, 2010.
22. The Population Registration Act of 1950 classified every South African as either white, colored, (including Asian ancestry) or native (black African). The 1991 census in Bosnia-Herzegovnia counted Muslims, Serbians, and other ethnicities. The Brazilian census has become increasingly racialized, through color classifictions such as, in the 1980 census, white, black, yellow, and mixed colors. Cf. Richard Visek, *Creating the Ethnic Electorate Through Legal Restorationism: Citizenship Rights in Estonia, Harvard International Law Journal* 38 (1997), pp. 315–73.
23. See a discussion of the Florida firm's website at www.cmh.pitt.edu/newsdna.htm.
24. See Josephine Johnston, "Resisting a Genetic Identity: the Black Seminoles and Genetic Tests of Ancestry," *Journal of Law, Medicine & Ethics* 31 (Summer 2003), pp. 262–85. Johnston considers whether Black Seminole Freedman should play the race-gene card to establish membership in the main Seminole tribe.
25. "African-American Lives," hosted by Harvard professor Henry Louis Gates, was a four-hour documentary examining black American's ties to other racial and national groups. The series was aired on public television in 2006.
26. R. Richard Banks, "Introduction, Symposium: Border People and Anti-discrimination Law," 17 *Harvard Black Letter Journal*, 17 (Spring, 2001), pp. 23–32.
27. Had the initiative passed, the state constitution would have been amended as follows: Section 32 is added to Article I of the California Constitution as follows: Sec. 32. (a) The state shall not classify any individual by race, ethnicity, color or national origin in the operation of public education, public contracting or public employment. (b) The state shall not classify any individual by race, ethnicity, color or national origin in the operation of any other state operations, unless the legislature specifically determines that said classification serves a compelling state interest and approves said classification by a 2/3 majority in both houses of the legislature, and said classification is subsequently approved by the governor. (c) For purposes of this section, "classifying" by race, ethnicity, color or national origin shall be defined as the act of separating, sorting or organizing by race, ethnicity, color or national origin including, but not limited to, inquiring, profiling, or collecting such data on government forms. (d) For purposes of subsection (a), "individual" refers to current or prospective students, contractors or employees. For purposes of subsection (b), "individual" refers to persons subject to the state operations referred to in subsection (b). (e) The Department of Fair Employment and Housing (DFEH) shall be exempt from this section with respect to DFEH-conducted classifications in place as of March 5, 2002. (1) Unless specifically extended by the legislature, this exemption shall expire ten years after the effective date of this measure. (2) Notwithstanding DFEH's exemption from this section, DFEH shall not impute a race, color, ethnicity or national origin to any individual. (f) Otherwise lawful classification of medical research subjects and patients shall be exempt from this section. (g) Nothing in this section shall prevent law enforcement officers, while carrying out their law enforcement duties, from describing particular persons in otherwise lawful ways. Neither the governor, the legislature nor any statewide agency shall require law

enforcement officers to maintain records that track individuals on the basis of said classifications, nor shall the governor, the legislature or any statewide agency withhold funding to law enforcement agencies on the basis of the failure to maintain such records. (h) Otherwise lawful assignment of prisoners and undercover law enforcement officers shall be exempt from this section. (i) Nothing in this section shall be interpreted as prohibiting action which must be taken to comply with federal law, or establish or maintain eligibility for any federal program, where ineligibility would result in a loss of federal funds to the state. (j) Nothing in this section shall be interpreted as invalidating any valid consent decree or court order which is in force as of the effective date of this section. (k) For the purposes of this section, "state" shall include, but not necessarily be limited to, the state itself, any city, county, city and county, public university system, including the University of California, California State University, community college district, school district, special district, or any other political subdivision or governmental instrumentality of or within the state. (l) This section shall become effective January 1, 2005. (m) This section shall be self-executing. If any part or parts of this section are found to be in conflict with federal law or the United States Constitution, the section shall be implemented to the maximum extent that federal law and the United States Constitution permit. Any provision held invalid shall be severable from the remaining portions of this section.

28. After the failure of Proposition 54, Ward Connerly continued efforts to eliminate affirmation action based on race, ethnicity, sex, and national origin in higher education. See, e.g., "Effort To Ban Race, Gender Considerations Advances in Michigan," *Black Issues in Higher Education*, January 27, 2005, vol. 21, no. 25; pp. 8–9; Brian DeBose, "Group Seeks Affirmative Action Vote; Few in Michigan Back Bid to Abolish Policy," *The Washington Times*, May 28, 2006 Sunday, p. A2.
29. Adrienne M. Byers, "Closing Argument: Don't Turn Back the Clock on Civil Rights," *Los Angeles Lawyer* 24 October, 2001), p. 52.
30. Byers, 52.
31. Eva Jefferson Paterson, "Part 1: The Importance of Slavery Reparations: and Still We Rise," 6 *Berkeley Journal of African-American Law & Policy Report* 6 (2004), pp. 15–20. See also Laura Dudley Jenkins, "Symposium: Race, Caste and Justice: Social Science Categories and Antidiscrimination Policies in India and the United States," *Connecticut Law Review* 36 (Spring, 2004), pp. 747–85.
32. Cf. Maurice R. Dyson, "Multiracial Identity, Monoracial Autheticity & Racial Privacy: Towards an Adequate Theory of Multiracial Resistance," *Michigan Journal Race and Law* 9 (Spring 2004), pp. 387–420.
33. Deborah Kong, "NAACP Opposes California Initiative to Bar Racal Classifying," Associated Press State and Local Wire, July 9, 2002.
34. Banks, p. 25.
35. *N. H. Civil Liberties Union v. City of Manchester*, 821 A.2d 1014 (Sup. Ct. N.H. 2003).
36. New Hampshire Revised Statutes Annotated, RSA 91-A:1 et seq.
37. *N. H. Civil Liberties Union* at 1017.
38. *N. H. Civil Liberties Union* at 1018.
39. *N. H. Civil Liberties Union* at 1018.
40. *N. H. Civil Liberties Union* at 1018.
41. *Pavesich v. New England Life Insurance Co.*, 50 S.E. 68 (Ga. 1905).
42. *Pavesich* at 69.

43. *Pavesich* at 69.
44. Samuel Warren and Louis Brandeis, "The Right to Privacy," *Harvard Law Review* 4 (1890), p. 193.
45. See generally Dorothy J. Glancy, "Privacy and the Other Miss M" (Symposium on the Right to Privacy), *Northern Illinois University Law Review* 10 (1990), pp. 401–40.
46. *Roberson v. Rochester Folding Box Company*, 64 N.E. 442 (N.Y. 1902).
47. *Roberson* at 443.
48. *Roberson* at 558, Gray, dissenting.
49. *Pavesich* at 195, 70: "While neither Sir William Blackstone nor any of the other writers on the principles of the common law have referred in terms to the right of privacy, the illustrations given by them as to what would be a violation of the absolute rights of individuals are not to be taken as exhaustive, but the language should be allowed to include any instance of a violation of such rights which is clearly within the true meaning and intent of the words used to declare the principle."
50. *Pavesich* at 194, 69–70.
51. *Pavesich* 196; 70.
52. *Pavesich* 204; 74.
53. Cf. *Manola v. Stevens and Meyer* (N.Y. Sup. Ct. 1890 [unpublished opinion]), in which the court enjoined display of a photograph of a performer taken without her consent.
54. *Pavesich v. New England Life Insurance Co.* et al., 122 Ga. 190, 196; 50 S.E. 68, 70 (1905): "All will admit that the individual who desires to live a life of seclusion can not be compelled, against his consent, to exhibit his person in any public place, unless such exhibition is demanded by the law of the land. He may be required to come from his place of seclusion to perform public duties,—to serve as a juror and to testify as a witness, and the like; but when the public duty is once performed, if he exercises his liberty to go again into seclusion, no one can deny him the right. One who desires to live a life of partial seclusion has a right to choose the times, places, and manner in which and at which he will submit himself to the public gaze."
55. *Griswold v. Connecticut*, 381 *U.S.* 479 (1965).
56. The Privacy Act (1974), 5 U.S.C. § 552a.
57. William L. Prosser, "Privacy," *California Law Review* 48 (1960), p. 383–423. See also American Law Institute, *Restatement of Torts (Second)*, Sections 652 B-E.
58. See *Roberson v. Rochester Folding Box Co*, 171 NY 538 (NY 1902). The refusal of the New York's courts to recognize a right to privacy led its legislature to adopt privacy protection via statute. See *N.Y. Civil Rights Law Section* 50, 51 (McKinney 1992).
59. See, e.g., *Weil v. Johnson*, N.Y. Slip. Op. 50513(U), 2002 WL 31972157, at 4 (N.Y. Sup. Ct. September 27, 2002), explaining why reporting on newsworthy events does not violate New York's privacy statute. See generally Anita L. Allen, "Why Journalists Can't Protect Privacy," in *Journalism and the Debate Over Privacy*, Craig L. LaMay, ed. (New York: Routledge, 2003), p. 69. describing financial and other pressures that lead news media to intrude into personal lives.
60. See Kathleen Carroll, "Finding A Criminal in a Crowd of Faces," *New York Times*, November 11, 2001, at C2. See www.darkgovernment.com/news/long-distance-facial-recognition. Last visited June 4, 2011.
61. Adrea Uhde and Sharon Turco, "Ballpark Kiss was Parolee's Goodbye," *Cincinnati Enquirer*, May 30, 2003, p. D2.

62. I refer here to two fictional dystopias, envisioning futures marked by extremes of public and private surveillance of everyday life: George Orwell's 1984 (New York: Hart, Brace, Javanovich, 1949) and the film *The Minority Report* (20th Century Fox/Dreamworks, 2002, staring Tom Cruise and directed by, Steven Spielberg).
63. Video Voyeurism Prevention Act of 2004, 18 U.S.C.A. Sec. 1801.
64. Joshua Blackman, "Omniveillance, Google, Privacy in Public, and The Right to Your Digital Identity: A Tort for Recording and Disseminating an Individual's Image Over the Internet," *Santa Clara Law Review* 49 (2009), pp. 313–92.
65. See *CBS, Inc. v. Partee*, 556 N.E. 2d 648 (Ill. App. 1990).
66. Freedom of Information Act, 5 U.S. C. Sec 552.
67. *CBS, Inc., v. Cecil A. Partee, State's Attorney of Cook County*, Illinois, 198 Ill. App. 3d 936; 556 N.E.2d 648; 1990 Ill. App. ("In January 1989 the plaintiff requested the following information from the State's Attorney: (1) the names of all assistant State's Attorneys; (2) the race of each assistant State's Attorney; (3) the names of the 'First Chair' assistant State's Attorneys; (4) the names of the assistant State's Attorneys in supervisory positions to be identified by title and department; and (5) the most recent salaries of each assistant State's Attorney and the dates of hire. The defendant gave the plaintiff the names, titles, most recent salaries and the dates of hire of all assistant State's Attorneys but refused to identify any assistant State's Attorneys by race.")
68. *CBS*, at 940, 649. This case hinges on the interpretation of section 7 of the FOIA (Ill. Rev. Stat. 1987, ch. 116, par. 207), which provides, in part, as follows:

    The following shall be exempt from inspection and copying: . . .

    (b) Information which, if disclosed, would constitute a clearly unwarranted invasion of personal privacy, unless such disclosure is consented to in writing by the individual subjects [***4] of such information. The disclosure of information that bears on the public duties of public employees and officials shall not be considered an invasion of personal privacy. Information exempted under this subsection (b) shall include but is not limited to:

    . . .

    (ii) personnel files and personal information maintained with respect to employees, appointees or elected officials of any public body or applicants for such positions.

    Cf. *Bowie v. Evanston Community Consolidated School Dist.* No. 65, 128 Ill. 2d 373; 538 N.E.2d 557 (Ill. Sp. Ct. 1989). The court here permitted the release of pupil test scores sought under Illinois FOIA, but noted that release might not be permitted if the race of particular students could be inferred from redacted data because, for example, there were very few pupils of one race in a particular class.
69. *United States Department of Justice v. Reporters Committee for Freedom of the Press*, 489 U.S. 749 (1989).
70. *United States Department of Justice v. Reporters Committee for Freedom of the Press*, 489 U.S. 749 (1989), holding that criminals and suspects have a privacy interest in hard to access, practically obscure, public information.
71. Cf. *Department of Fair Employment & Housing v. Superior Court*, 99 *Cal. App.* 4th 896 99 Cal. App. 4th 896; 121 Cal. Rptr. 2d 615. (Ca. App. Ct. 5th Dist. 2002).
72. *Hicks v. Robeson County*, 187 FRD 232 232 (EDNC 1999).

73. *Hill v. Dillard's, Inc.*, 2002 U.S. Dist. LEXIS 981 and *Hill v. Dillard's, Inc.*, 2001 U.S. Dist. LEXIS 24450.
74. *Waters v. United States Capitol Police Bd.*, 216 F.R.D. 153 (D.D. C. 2003).
75. *Lissner v. United States Customs Service*, 241 F.3 1220 (9th Cir. 2001).
76. Adrian Piper, "Passing for White, Passing for Black," *Transition* 58 (1992), pp. 4–32.
77. See generally June Cross, *Secret Daughter: A Mix-Raced Daughter and the Mother Who Gave her Away*, (New York: Viking 2006).
78. See generally Gregory Howard Williams, *Life on the Color Line: The True Story of a White Boy Who Discovered He Was Black* (New York: Penguin, 1996).
79. The "one-drop" rule has also guided officials. See F. James Davis, *Who is Black?: One Nation's Definition* (Penn State University Press, 1991), pp.4-16, explaining a policy and social practice originating in the American south of defining any person with even one black ancestor as black.
80. The EEOC has assumed a committment to increasing race data collection and analysis between 2008 and 2013, with the hopes of reducing racial discrimination. See http://www.eeoc.gov/initiatives/e-race/goals.html#goal1, last visited February 21, 2009. The EEOC Compliance Manual (CCH) par. 5403,632.3(b)(2)(iii), at 4316 (March. 1987, superceded) offered advice on collecting race data: "Self-identification is the preferred method of obtaining information necessary to identify an individual by race, sex, or ethnic group. Where information is not provided by an individual that indicates affiliation with a race, sex, or ethnic group, the person requesting the information should, where possible, secure and record the information through observation." The same "self-identification" bias is reflected in current instructions for completing Employer Information Report form EEO-1, the form employers with work forces larger than 15 are required to submit on an annual basis. See http://www.eeoc.gov/eeo1survey/instructions_form.pdf, last visited February 21, 2009. Cf. Department of Labor guidelines for required race data collection by government contractors, http://www.dol.gov/esa/ofccp/regs/compliance/directives/dir265.htm, last visited February 21, 2009: "Self-identification is the most reliable method and the preferred method for compiling information about a person's gender, race or ethnicity. Contractors are encouraged to use tear off sheets, post cards, or short forms to request demographic information from applicants. The contractor's invitation to an applicant to self-identify his or her gender, race, or ethnicity should always clearly state that the provision of such information is voluntary. While self-identification is the preferred method, visual observation also can be an acceptable method for identifying the gender, race and ethnicity of applicants, although it may not be reliable in every instance. Visual observation may be used when the applicant appears in person and declines to self-identify his or her gender, race or ethnicity. Where, in response to an invitation from the contractor, the applicant declines to self-identify his or her gender, race or ethnicity, and visual observation is not feasible, there is nothing more for the contractor to do. OFCCP would not hold a contractor responsible for applicant data when the applicant declines to self-identify and there are no other acceptable methods of obtaining this information."
81. See generally, Jerry Kang, Cyber-Race, *Harvard Law Review* 113 (2000), pp. 1131–208 and "Trojan Horses of Race," *Harvard Law Review* 118 (2005), pp. 1489–593, arguing that "most of us have biases against minorities even though we may not recognize them.

82. See generally Lucy S. Dawidowicz, *The War Against the Jews: 1933–1945*, (New York: Holt, Rinehart and Winston, 1975), p. 59.
83. My source for the historical facts recited in this paragraph is Saul S. Friedman, *A History of the Holocaust* (London/Portland, OR: Vallentine Mitchell 2004), pp. 71, 109, 114, 121–22, 132, 135, 197, 242, 265, and 271–74.
84. The so-called "Race Directive" is officially known as the Council Directive 2000/43/EC of 29 June 2000 implementing the principle of equal treatment between persons irrespective of racial or ethnic origin. The Race Directive and two others, 2000/78/EC and 2004/113/EC, together prohibit discrimination on grounds of sex, racial or ethnic origin, age, disability, sexual orientation, religion or belief in employment, occupation and vocational training, as well as in non-employment areas such as social protection, health care, education and access to goods and services, including housing, which are available to the public. Discrimination based on sex is prohibited in the same range of areas, with the exception of education and media and advertising. However, discrimination based on age, religion and belief, sexual orientation and disability is prohibited only in employment, occupation and vocational training. In early 2011 the EU proposed an additional directive implementing the principle of equal treatment between persons irrespective of religion or belief, disability, age or sexual orientation outside the labour market. See Proposal for a Council Directive on implementing the principle of equal treatment between persons irrespective of religion or belief, disability, age or sexual orientation {SEC(2008) 2180} {SEC(2008) 2181} /* COM/2008/0426 final - CNS 2008/0140 */, http://eur-lex.europa.eu/LexUriServ/LexUriServ.do?uri=COM:2008:0426:FIN:EN:HTML.
85. An important example is the "Privacy Directive," Directive 95/46/EC of the European Parliament and of the Council of 24 October 24, 1995 on the protection of individuals with regard to the processing of personal data and on the free movement of such data, identifies certain data as sensitive.
86. Directive 95/46/EC of the European Parliament and of the Council of 24 October 24, 1995. Under Article 8 of the Privacy Directive, "The processing of special categories of data," Member States shall prohibit the processing of personal data revealing racial or ethnic origin, political opinions, religious or philosophical beliefs, trade-union membership, and the processing of data concerning health or sex life."

    1. Paragraph 1 shall not apply where:
        (a) the data subject has given his explicit consent to the processing of those data, except where the laws of the Member State provide that the prohibition referred to in paragraph 1 may not be lifted by the data subject's giving his consent; or
        (b) processing is necessary for the purposes of carrying out the obligations and specific rights of the controller in the field of employment law in so far as it is authorized by national law providing for adequate safeguards; or
        (c) processing is necessary to protect the vital interests of the data subject or of another person where the data subject is physically or legally incapable of giving his consent; or
        (d) processing is carried out in the course of its legitimate activities with appropriate guarantees by a foundation, association or any other non-profit-seeking body with a political, philosophical, religious or trade-union aim and on condition that the processing relates solely to the members of the body or to persons who have regular contact with it in connection with its purposes and that' the data are not disclosed to a third party without the consent of the data subjects; or

(e) the processing relates to data which are manifestly made public by the data subject or is necessary for the establishment, exercise or defence of legal claims.

2. Paragraph 1 shall not apply where processing of the data is required for the purposes of preventive medicine, medical diagnosis, the provision of care or treatment or the management of health-care services, and where those data are processed by a health professional subject under national law or rules established by national competent bodies to the obligation of professional secrecy or by another person also subject to an equivalent obligation of secrecy.
3. Subject to the provision of suitable safeguards, Member States may, for reasons of substantial public interest, lay down exemptions in addition to those laid down in paragraph 2 either by national law or by decision of the supervisory authority.
4. Processing of data relating to offences, criminal convictions or security measures may be carried out only under the control of official authority, or if suitable specific safeguards are provided under national law, subject to derogations which may be granted by the Member State under national provisions providing suitable specific safeguards. However, a complete register of criminal convictions may be kept only under the control of official authority. Member States may provide that data relating to administrative sanctions or judgements in civil cases shall also be processed under the control of official authority.
5. Derogations from paragraph I provided for in paragraphs 4 and 5 shall be notified to the Commission
6. Member States shall determine the conditions under which a national identification number or any other identifier of general application may be processed.

87. *Official Journal of the European Communities* of 23 November 1995 No L. 281 p. 3, *Directive 95/46/EC of the European Parliament and of the Council of 24 October 1995 on the protection of individuals with regard to the processing of personal data and on the free movement of such data.*
88. Article 8 (2)(a), *Directive 95/46/EC of the European Parliament and of the Council of 24 October* 1995.
89. Chuck Sudetic, *Blood and Vengeance: One Family's Story of the War in Bosnia* (New York: W.W. Norton & Company, 1998), p. 116:

    The gunfire became sporadic. Women and children from the nearest village combed the woods and the roadside, taking guns from the trucks and the Serb dead while there was still daylight. Some of the Serbs, afraid of being taken prisoner, threw away their identification cards and tried to mix in with the Muslims.

90. Gerard Prunier, *The Rwanda Crisis: History of a Genocide* (New York: Columbia University Press, 1997) p. 249:

    To be identified on one's card as a Tutsi or to pretend to have lost one's papers meant certain death. Yet to have a Hutu ethnic card was not automatically a ticket to safety. In Ruhengeri or Gisenyi and at times in Kigali, southern Hutu suspected of supporting the opposition parties were also killed. And people were often accused of having a false card, especially if they were tall and with a straight nose and thin lips. Frequent intermarriage had produced many Hutu-looking Tutsi and Tutsi-looking Hutu. In towns or along the highways, Hutu who looked like Tutsi were very often killed, their denials and proffered cards with the "right" ethnic mention being seen as a typical Tutsi deception.

See also Helen M. Hintjens, "Explaining the 1994 Genocide in Rwanda," in *The Journal of Modern African Studies* 37, no. 2 (June, 1999), pp. 241–86. See generally Christian P. Scherrer, *Genocide and Crisis in Central Africa: Conflict Roots, Mass Violence, and Regional War* (New York: Praeger, 2001); Linda Melvern, *Conspiracy to Murder: The Rwandan Genocide* (London: Verso, 2004).

91. See press reports, including J. Michael Kennedy and Borzou Daragahi, "Baghdad Jolted by Sectarian Killing Sprees and Bombings," *Los Angeles Times*, July 10, 2006, p. A1; Jonathan Steele, "Iraq violence: Shia massacre revives fears of civil war: Mahdi army blamed for Baghdad street slaughter: Shias killed as car bombs explode near mosque," *The Guardian*, July 10, 2006, http://www.guardian.co.uk/world/2006/jul/10/iraq.jonathansteele ("Witnesses said gunmen, some masked, set up roadblocks and stopped motorists in the mainly Sunni suburb of Jihad, near Baghdad airport, demanding to see identity cards. Those with Sunni names were shot dead; Shias were released."). Patrick Cockburn, "Dozens die as sectarian attacks escalate in Iraq," *The Independent*, July 10, 2006, p. 22 ("Four carloads of gunmen arrived at 10 am and started stopping vehicles. Those with identity cards showing they had Sunni names were shot. Bodies were dumped throughout the area.").
92. See generally Jack M. Balkin; Reva B. Siegel, "Principles, Practices, and Social Movements," *University of Pennsylvania Law Review* 154 (April 2006), pp. 927–49.
93. John Rawls, *Justice as Fairness: A Restatement*, Erin Kelly, ed. (Cambridge, Mass.: Belknap Press, 2001), sec. 6 at 14. See generally John Rawls, *A Theory of Justice* (Cambridge, Mass.: Harvard University Press, 1971); and *Political Liberalism* (New York: Columbia University Press, 1993).
94. Rawls, *Justice as Fairness* 6.2, p. 15.
95. Ibid. 13, p. 42.
96. Ibid. 13, p. 42.
97. Cf. Richa Amar, "Unequal Protection and the Racial Privacy Initiative," *UCLA Law Review* 52 (April 2005), pp. 1279–310.
98. Rawls, *Justice as Fairness* 13, pp. 42–43.
99. Ibid. 16, p. 55.
100. Ibid. 18.4, p. 64–65.
101. Ibid. 18.4, p. 65.
102. Ibid. 18.5, p. 65.
103. Ibid. 18.6, p. 66.
104. Ibid. 17.2, p. 59.
105. See, e.g., *Washington Post Co. v. Minority Business Opportunity Commission*, 560 A.2d 517, 523 (D.C. App. 1989), where defendants and two intervenors alleged disclosure of race would lead to competitive disadvantages, but the court of appeals held that it was "not persuaded that disclosure of the race, per se, of the principals of an enterprise would lead to competitive injury."
106. Anita L. Allen, "Data Control: Conceptual, Practical, and Moral Limits of the Paradigm," *Connecticut Law Review* 32 (2000), pp. 861–75.
107. NAACP at 458 ("We think that petitioner argues more appropriately the rights of its members, and that its nexus with them is sufficient to permit that it act as their representative before this Court"). The Court would argue in the reproductive privacy cases on the 1960s and 1970s that abortion providers have standing to assert the privacy interests of individuals and couples claiming constitutional rights of access to medical contraception or abortion services.

108. See http://www.naacp.org/about/history/mwo/ ("The NAACP was criticised by some members of the African American community. Booker T. Washington opposed the group because it proposed an outspoken condemnation of racist policies in contrast to his policy of quiet diplomacy behind the scenes. Members of the organization were physically attacked by white racists. John R. Shillady, executive secretary of the NAACP was badly beaten up when he visited Austin, Texas in 1919.").
109. See http://www.naacp.org/about/history/index.htm, last visited October 1, 2008. See also http://www.naacp.org/about/history/howbegan/index.htm, last visited October 1, 2008 quoting Mary White Ovington's 1914 recollection of the founding of the NAACP ("So I wrote to Mr. Walling, and after some time, for he was in the West, we met in New York in the first week of the year of 1909. With us was Dr. Henry Moskowitz, now prominent in the administration of John Purroy Mitchell, Mayor of New York. It was then that the National Association for the Advancement of Colored People was born. It was born in a little room of a New York apartment. It is to be regretted that there are no minutes of the first meeting, for they would make interesting if unparliamentary reading.").
110. *Brown v. Board of Education*, 348 U.S. 886 (1954).
111. Ala.Code, 1940, Tit. 10, §§ 192–98.
112. A series of four Supreme Court cases were necessary before Alabama dropped its bid to exclude the NAACP from its borders. See *NAACP v. Alabama ex rel. Flowers*, 377 U.S. 288 (1964); *NAACP v. Gallion*, 368 U.S. 16 (1961); *NAACP v. Alabama ex rel. Patterson*, 360 U.S. 240 (1959); *NAACP v. Alabama ex rel. Patterson*, 357 U.S. 449 (1958).
113. See, for example, *American Communications Assn. v. Douds*, 339 U.S. 382, 402 (1950). Cf. *NAACP*, at 462, citing Douds ("It is hardly a novel perception that compelled disclosure of affiliation with groups engaged in advocacy may constitute as effective a restraint on freedom of association as the forms of governmental action in the cases above were thought likely to produce upon the particular constitutional rights there involved.").
114. *NAACP* at 462–63.
115. See generally "Symposium, Left Out in the Cold? The Chilling of Speech, Association, and the Press in Post-9/11 America," *American University Law Review* 57 (2008), pp. 1203–547. See *United States v. U.S. Dist. Court* (Keith, J.), 407 U.S. 297 (1972).
116. *Bates v. City of Little Rock*, 361 U.S. 516 (1960).
117. NAACP at 466 ("And we conclude that Alabama has fallen short of showing a controlling justification for the deterrent effect on the free enjoyment of the right to associate which disclosure of membership lists is likely to have").
118. *NAACP* at 463: "Such a '... subordinating interest of the State must be compelling,' Sweezy v. New Hampshire, 354 U. S. 234,354 U. S. 265 (concurring opinion)."
119. *Bates v. City of Little Rock*, 361 U.S. 516 (1960).
120. *Wallace v. Brewer*, 315 F. Supp. 431 (M.D. Ala. 1970).
121. *NAACP* at 462.
122. Anil Kalhan, *The Fourth Amendment and Privacy: Implications of Interior Immigration Enforcement*, *U.C. Davis Law Review* 41 (2008), pp. 1137–218.
123. Kalhan, *The Fourth Amendment and Privacy*, 1183.
124. Ibid., 1183.
125. *Whalen v. Roe*, 429 U.S. 589 (1977).
126. *Uphaus v. Wyman*, 360 U.S. 72 (1959).
127. *Doe I and Doe II v. Individuals Whose True Names are Unknown*, 561 F.Supp.2d 249 (D.Ct. 2008).

128. Nicole Ozer, "Rights 'Chipped' Away: RFID and Identification Documents," *Stanford. Technology Law Review* (2008), pp. 1–76.
129. Ozer, 35.
130. See http://www.eeoc.gov/policy/docs/race-color.html, last visited February 21, 2009.
131. Kenneth Prewitt, "Racial Classification in America: Where Do We Go from Here?" *Daedalus* 1 (134), January 1, 2005, p. 5.

Chapter 7

1. Directive 95/46/EC of the European Parliament and of the Council of 24 October 1995 on the protection of individuals with regard to the processing of personal data and on the free movement of such data, OJL, 23.11. 1995, p. 31.
2. Directive 95/46/EC of the European Parliament and of the Council p. 31.
3. Cf. Paul Schwartz, "Preemption and Privacy," *Yale Law Journal* 118 (2009) pp. 902–947.
4. See http://ec.europa.eu/justice/policies/privacy/review/index_en.htm.
5. See http://europa.eu/legislation_summaries/justice_freedom_security/fight_against_terrorism/l33277_en.htm.
6. GLB includes provisions to protect consumers' personal financial information held by financial institutions. See Title V, Subtitle A of the Gramm-Leach-Bliley Act, Pub. L. No. 106–102, 113 Stat. 1338 (1999) (codified as amended at 15 U.S.C.A. § 6801 et seq. (2000)).
7. Federal Register, Federal Trade Commission, CFR Part 314, Standards for Safeguarding Customer Information, Final Rule, available at www.ftc.gov/os/2002/05/67fr36585.pdf.
8. Federal Trade Commission, About Identity Theft, available at http://www.ftc.gov/bcp/edu/microsites/idtheft/consumers/about-identity-theft.html.
9. See http://www.ftc.gov/bcp/conline/pubs/credit/pretext.htm\.
10. *Reporters Committee for Freedom of the Press*, 489 U.S. 749 (1989). Freedom of Information Act, 5 U.S.C. Section 552.
11. Grayson Barber Accord, "Personal Information in Government Records: Protecting the Public Interest in Privacy," *Saint Louis University Public Law Review* 25 (2006), pp. 63–122.
12. Public Law 109–13 (May 11, 2005).
13. See a useful web page at http://www.news.com/8301-10784_3-9848924-7.html?tag=newsmap.
14. A Nokia product, Lifeblog, archives cell phone messages and photographs. See Mark Ward, "Log Your Life via Your Phone," BBC News Online (2004), available at http://news.bbc.co.uk/2/hi/technology/3497596.stm (visited January 12, 2008). Weblog technology that enables users to record thoughts, photos, video, and audio is being marketed under the "lifelog" rubric. See, for example, Real Life Log, online at http://www.reallifelog.com (visited January 12, 2008).
15. Gordon Bell and Jim Gemmell, "A Digital Life," *Scientific American* 58 (March 2007), pp. 58–60 traces lifelogging from its origins in post-WWII technologies to the present and speculates about future inroads lifelogging may make into daily lives. See also Alec Wilkinson, "Remember This? A Project to Record Everything We Do In Life," *The New Yorker* (May 28, 2007), pp. 38–39.
16. The Warhol Collections/Archives (The Andy Warhol Museum 2007), online at http://www.warhol.org/collections/archives.html (visited January 12, 2008).

17. See http://www.defensetech.org/archives/002411.html, last visited September 12, 2008. DARPA, "LifeLog Proposer Information Pamphlet," SOL BAA 03-30 (2003), available online at http://web.archive.org/web/20030603173339/http//www.darpa.mil/ipto/Solicitations/PIP_03-30.html (visited January 12, 2008).
18. See Martin Dodge and Rob Kitchin, "Outlines of a World Coming into Existence: Pervasive Computing and the Ethics of Forgetting," *Envir & Planning B: Planning & Design* 34 (2007), pp. 431, 432–34 (2007).
19. See Martin Dodge and Rob Kitchin, "The Ethics of Forgetting in an Age of Pervasive Computing 1" (CASA Working Paper Series 92, March 2005), online at http://www.casa.ucl.ac.uk/working_papers/paper92.pdf (visited January 12, 2008), characterizing lifelogs, among other things, as "socio-spatial archives that document every action, every event, every conversation, and every material expression of an individual's life." See Steve Mann, "Equiveillance: The Equilibrium between Sur-veillance and Sous-veillance 2" (On the Identity Trail, May 2005), online at http://www.idtrail.org/files/Mann, Equiveillance.pdf (visited January 12, 2008); Steve Mann, Jason Nolan, and Barry Wellman, "Sousveillance: Inventing and Using Wearable Computing Devices for Data Collection in Surveillance Environments," *Surveillance and Society* 1 (2003), pp. 331, 332.
20. For an overview of the original all-American time capsule project, see 1939 "Westinghouse Time Capsule Complete List Contents," *New York Times Magazine* (1996), online at http://www.nytimes.com/specials/magazine3/items.html (visited January 12, 2008).
21. See, for example, Adam J. Kolber, "Therapeutic Forgetting: The Legal and Ethical Implications of Memory Dampening," *Vanderbilt Law Review* 59 (2006), pp. 1561, 1595–98 (2006), arguing that pharmacological memory dampening may be warranted as treatment for trauma victims and should not be avoided out of blind bias in favor of natural cognitive abilities. See also Ellen McGrath, "The Rumination Rut," *Psychology Today* (April 11, 2003), online at http://www.psychologytoday.com/articles/200304/the-rumination-rut (last accessed February 22, 2011), and Michael E. Addis and Kelly M. Carpenter, "Why, Why, Why?: Reason-giving and Rumination as Predictors of Response to Activation- and Insight-oriented Treatment Rationales," *Journal of Clinical Psychology* 55 (1999), pp. 881, 882–84 (1999), analyzing the connection between a patient's explanation for depression and the most effective treatment for that patient.
22. *Melvin v. Reid*, 297 P 91 (Cal Ct App 1931).
23. *Sidis v. F-R Publishing Corp*, 113 F2d 806 (2d Cir 1940).
24. *Briscoe v. Reader's Digest*, 483 P2d 34 (Cal 1971), overruled by *Gates v. Discovery Communications, Inc.*, 101 P3d 552 (Cal 2004), holding that a corporation was not liable to an offender for publishing facts obtained from public official records.
25. The court employed the concept of "practical obscurity" in *DOJ* v *Reporters Committee for Freedom of the Press*, 489 U.S. 749, 771 (1989).
26. The case for forgetting is laid out in Viktor Mayer-Schönberger, *The Virtue of Forgetting in the Digital Age* (Princeton, N.J.: Princeton University Press, 2009).
27. Anita L. Allen, "The Virtuous Spy: Privacy as an Ethical Limit," *The Monist: An International Quarterly Journal of General Philosophical Inquiry* 91 (1) (2008), pp. 1–22.
28. Charlotte Twight, "Watching You, Systematic Federal Surveillance of Ordinary Americans," The Independent Review 4 (1999), pp. 165–200.
29. See Electronic Communications Privacy Act of 1986, Pub L No 99–508, 100 Stat 1848, regulating but not blocking government access to phone and intent communications; Foreign Intelligence Surveillance Act of 1978, Pub L No 95–511, 92 Stat 1783, codified as amended at

50 U.S.C.A. § 1801 et seq (2007), regulating but not blocking access to private communications and homes.

A National Security Letter is a secret administrative subpoena used by the FBI to obtain information in private hands without obtaining a search warrant. As described by the FBI, "A National Security Letter (NSL) is a letter request for information from a third party that is issued by the FBI or by other government agencies with authority to conduct national security investigations." See FBI, "Press Release on National Security Letters," online at http://www.fbi.gov/pressrel/pressrel07/nsl_faqs030907.htm (visited January 12, 2008).

Communications Assistance for Law Enforcement Act, Pub L No 103–404, 108 Stat 4279 (1994). See also FCC, Communications Assistance for Law Enforcement Act (CALEA) (2007), online at http://www.fcc.gov/calea (visited January 12, 2008). In response to concerns that emerging technologies such as digital and wireless communications were making it increasingly difficult for law enforcement agencies to execute authorized surveillance, Congress enacted CALEA on October 25, 1994. CALEA was intended to preserve the ability of law enforcement agencies to conduct electronic surveillance by requiring that telecommunications carriers and manufacturers of telecommunications equipment modify and design their equipment, facilities, and services to ensure that they have the necessary surveillance capabilities. See "Second Report and Order and Memorandum Opinion and Order, In the Matter of Communications Assistance for Law Enforcement Act and Broadband Access and Services," No 04–295, *2 (May 3, 2006), online at http://fjallfoss.fcc.gov/edocs_public/attachmatch/FCC-06-56A1.pdf (visited January 12, 2008).

30. See William Cheng, Leana Golubchik, and David Kay, "Total Recall: Are Privacy Changes Inevitable?, Proceedings of the 1st ACM Workshop on Continuous Archival and Retrieval of Personal Experiences," 86 (October 15, 2004), proposing a complex encryption framework as a solution to privacy concerns in a lifelogging world, see http://bourbon.usc.edu/iml/recall/papers/carpe2k4-pub.pdf, last visited June 5, 2011. See also University of Southern California Multimedia Lab, "Total Recall: A Personal Information Management System" (2005), online at http://bourbon.usc.edu/iml/recall (visited January 12, 2008).
31. See Cheng, Golubchik and Kay, p. 2. But see Anita L. Allen, *Uneasy Access* (Rowman & Littlefield, 1988), pp. 125–28, noting courts' general unwillingness to recognize any broad right to privacy in public, but defending the concept. See also Helen Nissenbaum, "Protecting Privacy in an Information Age: The Problem of Privacy in Public," *Law & Philosophy* 17 (1998), pp. 559, 573–75, citing examples of courts' reluctance to allow one person's privacy rights to encroach on the freedom of others.
32. *Katz v. United States*, 389 U.S. 347 (1967).
33. See *Vermont v. Costin*, 720 A.2d 866, 168 Vt. 175, 180 (S. Ct. Vt. 1998). See also DHS Privacy Office Public Workshop CCTV: Developing Privacy Best Practices, "Legal and Policy Perspectives Panel," at 3-6, http://www.dhs.gov/xlibrary/assets/privacy/privacy_workshop_cctv_Transcript_Legal_and_Policy_Perspectives_Panel.pdf, last accessed 15 August 2009.
34. See Cheng, Golubchik and Kay, p. 3, arguing that "Indeed, in the current US environment of terrorist threats, the political climate supports access to information by law enforcement, even without judicial intervention, if that information is perceived to have national security implications.").
35. Compare Scott Carlson, "On the Record, All the Time," *Chronicle of Higher Education* (February 9, 2007), pp. A31, A33–35, examining practical social issues posed by audio and

video lifelogging). But see generally Gaia Bernstein, "When Technologies Are Still New: Windows of Opportunity for Privacy Protection," *Villanova Law Review* 51 (2006), p. 921, remarking that legal norms and technological protections of privacy may be inferior to aptly timed "social shaping" whereby privacy protecting practices and incentives are integrated into appropriate settings.

36. See, for example, *People v. Miller,* 60 Cal App 3d 849, 855 (1976): "Contrary to defendant's contention, evidentiary use of the diary did not violate the constitutional privilege against self-incrimination. The privilege does not prevent the otherwise lawful seizure of a document even when its contents are communicative." See also *Andresen v Maryland,* 427 U.S. 463, 465 (1976), holding that business records properly seized could be admitted into evidence without violating the "Fifth Amendment's command that '[n]o person shall be compelled in any criminal case to be a witness against himself"; *United States v. Dawson,* 516 F2d 796, 807 (9th Cir 1975), holding that the admission of a properly seized note from the defendant prisoner to another prisoner did not violate the defendant's protection against self-incrimination; *United States v. Bennett,* 409 F2d 888, 897 (2d Cir 1969), holding that a letter found during a lawful search, even though it was self-incriminating, could be admitted into evidence; *People v. Thayer,* 408 P2d 108, 110 (Cal 1965), noting that self-incriminating writings can be seized and admitted into evidence.
37. Carl Felsenfeld, "Unnecessary Privacy," *Transnational Suffolk Law Review* 25 (2002), pp. 365–88.
38. S. I. Benn, "Privacy, Freedom and Respect for Persons," in Pennock, J. R and Chapman, J. W., eds. (1971) *NOMOS XIII: Privacy*, 1.
39. R. C. Post, "The Social Foundations of Privacy: Community and Self in the Common Law Tort," *California Law Review* 77 (1989), p. 957; Jeffrey H. Reiman, "Privacy, Intimacy and Personhood," *Philosophy and Public Affairs* 6 (1976), pp. 26–44.
40. Compare Helen Nissenbaum, "Privacy as Contextual Integrity," *Washington Law Review* 79 (2004), pp. 119-158, 136, distinguishing norms of appropriateness and distribution norms for information disclosures. See generally Helen Nissenbaum, *Privacy in Context: Technology, Policy, and the Integrity of Social Life* (Palo Alto, Calif.: Stanford University Press 2009).
41. See Lior Jacob Strahilevitz, "A Social Networks Theory of Privacy," *University of Chicago Law Review* 72 (2005), pp. 919–88.
42. Reiman, "Privacy, Intimacy, and Personhood," 26–44.
43. Daniel J. Solove, "A Taxonomy of Privacy: Surveillance," *University of Pennsylvania* 154 (2006) 477–560, 498.
44. John Stuart Mill, *On Liberty* (1859), chapter IV: Of the Limits to the Authority of Society over the Individual (London: Longman, Roberts & Green, 1869).
45. Lisa Nelson, "Normative Dimensions of Paternalism and Security," *A Journal of Law and Policy for the Information Society* 2 (Winter 2005/2006), pp. 27–51.

Chapter 8

1. Class Action Complaint, filed February 11, 2010 at 23 in *Robbins v. Lower Merion School District,* No. 10-665 (E.D. Pa.).
2. Ballard Spahr, *Report of Independent Investigation Regarding the Monitoring of Student Laptop Computers by the Lower Merion School District,* prepared at the request of Lower Merion School District, May 3, 2010 at 58.

3. Blake Robbins, interview, WebcamGate Teen: "I Hope They're Not Watching Me," *NBC 10 News Philadelphia*, NBC, February 22, 2010. Accessed April 5, 2010. http://www.nbcphiladelphia.com/news/tech/WebcamGate-Teen-I-Hope-Theyre-Not-Watching-Me-84826357.html.
4. Defendants Memorandum of Law in Opposition to Plaintiffs' Motion for Class Certification, filed July 16, 2010 at 5-6, in *Robbins v. Lower Merion School District*, No. 10-665 (E.D. Pa.). In order to protect Robbins's privacy the school has remained silent on the content of the webchat. Ibid. at p. 5, n.4.
5. Jeff Schreiber, "Two Mike and Ikes and One Motion," *America's Right*, February 20, 2010. Accessed April 5, 2010. http://americasright.com/?p=3237; see also Robbins, "I Hope They're Not Watching Me."
6. Ballard, *Report of Independent Investigation* at 58.
7. *Robbins v. Lower Merion School District* at 24.
8. Lower Merion School District, "About LMSD." Accessed April 5, 2010. http://www.lmsd.org/sections/about/
9. *Robbins v. Lower Merion School District* at 22.
10. Ibid. at 26.
11. Dan Hardy and Bonnie Clark, "Student Claims School Spied On Him Via Computer Webcam," *The Philadelphia Inquirer*, February 19, 2010.
12. John P. Martin, "Lower Merion district's laptop saga ends with $610,000 settlement," *Philadelphia Inquirer*, October 12, 2010. Settlement Order filed October 15, 2010 at 1–2, in *Robbins, et al. v. Lower Merion School District, et al.*, No. 10-665 (E.D. Pa.).
13. Children's Online Privacy Protection Act of 1998, 15 U.S.C. 6501–506 (Supp. V 2000).
14. See the reports of the Center for Media Education, 2120 L Street, NW, Suite 200, Washington, DC, 20037, online at www.cme.org.
15. U.S. Privacy Protection Study Commision, *Personal Privacy in an Information Society* 3–6 (1977).
16. What are now termed "fair information practice principles" originated from a U.S. Department of Health, Education, and Welfare report, *Report of the Secretary's Advisory Committee on Automated Personal Data Systems* (1973), available at http://aspe.hhs.gov/DATACNCL/1973privacy/c3.htm. The principles are subject to interpretation and diverse elaboration, although some formulations have special legal significance, such as the formulation of the U.S. Federal Trade Commission, available at http://www.ftc.gov/reports/privacy3/fairinfo.shtm.
17. See http://www.ftc.gov/reports/privacy3/fairinfo.shtm.
18. See 15 U.S.C. 6502(a)(1) and 6501(2)(A). The term "operator" is defined as "any person who operates a website located on the Internet or an online service and who collects or maintains personal information from or about the users of or visitors to such website or online service, or on whose behalf such information is collected or maintained, where such website or online service is operated for commercial purposes, including any person offering products or services for sale through that website or online service, involving commerce."
19. See 15 U.S.C. 6502 (b)(1)(B)(i)–(iii).
20. See 15 U.S.C. 6502 (b)(1)(B)(i)–(iii).
21. See *Hodgson v. Minnesota*, 497 U.S. 417, 455 (1990), holding that a two-parent notification and consent requirement for minor women seeking abortions is unconstitutional, despite the availability of a judicial bypass that would allow minors to obtain abortions without the consent of either parent.
22. See COPPA, 6502(a)(1), (b)(1)(D).
23. See COPPA, 6502(b)(1)(C).

24. See http://www.ftc.gov/privacy/privacyinitiatives/childrens_shp.html, last visited February 8, 2009.
25. See http://www.ftc.gov/privacy/privacyinitiatives/childrens_educ.html, last visited February 8, 2009.
26. See Reuters, "Oops, Kids Must Be 13 to Log Onto Spears' Site," *Toronto Sun*, May 8, 2001, at 49.
27. See Press Release, FTC, "Internet Site Agrees to Settle FTC Charges of Deceptively Collecting Personal Information in Agency's First Internet Privacy Case" (August 13, 1998), charging GeoCities with misrepresenting the purposes for which it was collecting personally identifying information from children and adults. Available at http://www.ftc.gov/opa/1998/9808/geocitie.htm.
28. See Press Release, FTC, "Young Investor Website Settles FTC Charges" (May 6, 1999), available at http://www.ftc.gov/opa/1999/05/younginvestor.shtm.
29. See *FTC v. Toysmart.com*, No. 00-11341-RGS (D. Mass. filed July 21, 2000), available at http://www.ftc.gov/opa/2000/07/toysmart2.shtm.
30. See www.truste.org.
31. Press Release, FTC, "FTC Announces Settlement with Bankrupt Website, Toysmart.com, Regarding Alleged Privacy Policy Violations" (July 21, 2000), available at http://www.ftc.gov/opa/2000/07/toysmart2.shtm.
32. Press Release, FTC, "FTC Announces Settlements with Websites that Collected Children's Personal Data Without Parental Permission" (April. 19, 2001).
33. The Federal Trade Commission maintains a webpage on which all of its COPPA Enforcement Actions, including the Jolly Time Popcorn and Ohio Arts Company cases mentioned in this paragraph can be researched by name and date, http://www.ftc.gov/privacy/privacyinitiatives/childrens_enf.html. The Jolly Time subpage is available at http://www.ftc.gov/opa/2002/02/popcorn.shtm.
34. Press Release, "FTC Settlement with Ohio Arts Company," available at http://www.ftc.gov/opa/2002/04/coppaanniv.shtm.
35. Press Release, "FTC Settlement with Sony," available at http://www.ftc.gov/opa/2008/12/sonymusic.shtm.
36. See COPPA, section 1302(1).
37. See Joseph Turow and Lilach Nir, The Annenberg Public Policy Center, *The Internet and the Family 2000: The View from Parents, The View from Kids* 12 (May 2000), pp. 9, 29, reporting not only that teenagers (ages thirteen to seventeen) said they used the Web substantially more than "tweens" (ages ten to twelve), but also that more teenagers provided information to websites about themselves than tweens.
38. 5 U.S.C. 552a(h) (2001).
39. Family Educational Rights and Privacy Act, 20 U.S.C. 1232g (2001). See also 1232g(b)(1).
40. Family Educational Rights and Privacy Act, 20 U.S.C. 1232 g(a)(4)(B)(iv) (2001).
41. See, e.g., Mo Krochmal, "First Amendment Advocates Launch Watchdog Group," *TechWeb* (December 1, 1997), describing the formation of an alliance group designed to advocate for freedom of expression on the Internet; Brian Sullivan, "Sen. Kerry: Online Taxes, Privacy Changes Coming" (May 22, 2001), contending that traditional businesses get an unfair advantage over online businesses if online businesses are prevented from collecting information about consumer buying habits. See also Electronic Privacy Information Center, "Faulty Filters: How Content Filters Block Access to Kid-Friendly Information on the

Internet" (December 1997), reporting that filtering mechanisms prevented children from obtaining useful and appropriate information from the Internet.

42. See Joseph Turow and Lilach Nir, The Annenberg Public Policy Center, *The Internet and the Family 2000: The View from Parents, The View from Kids* 12 (May 2000), finding that many parents believe their children's exposure to the Internet might interfere with the values and beliefs they want to teach them. But the influence of the Internet on families is not all bad. The Internet may improve communication in some families who use e-mail to keep in close contact. See The Pew Internet & American Life Project, *Tracking Online Life: How Women Use the Internet to Cultivate Relationships with Family and Friends* 7 (2000).
43. Michael Lewis, "Jonathan Lebed's Extracurricular Activities," *New York Times Magazine,* February 25, 2001, pp. 6, 26.
44. See Joseph Turow & Lilach Nir, *The Internet and the Family 2000: The View from Parents, The View from Kids,* p. 4 ("American parents and youngsters are often of very different minds when it comes to giving personal information to websites. Kids' release of information to the Web could well become a new arena for family discord"). See also Center for Media Education, 4–5 ("The advertising industry is learning how to exploit young computer users more effectively.... The sooner marketers can reach children, the more products they can sell to them over the years"). See Turow and Nir p. 35 (finding that children are substantially more likely than parents to give up personal information to a website when free gifts are offered).
45. See Press Release, FTC, "New Rule Will Protect Privacy of Children Online" (October. 20, 1999, explaining the goals of COPPA, and also explaining that the rule "is flexible enough to accommodate the many business practices and technological changes occurring on the Internet," and that there are "several exceptions to the requirement of prior parental consent."
46. Tyler Prochnow, "Software to Help Facilitate COPPA Compliance, E-commerce," May 2000 ("To be truly good corporate citizens, sites that do not want visitors under the age of 13 should encourage the use of filtering software by parents"). Filtering software is more responsive to the policy concerns that led to the enactment of the highly controversial COPA statute than COPPA. COPA, the Children's Online Protection Act, went into law October 21, 1998. 47 U.S.C.A. 231 (West Supp. 2000). COPA requires commercial sites that include materials harmful to minors (such as hard pornography) to ensure that minors do not access such materials. See *ACLU v. Reno,* 217 F.3d 162, 166 (3d Cir. 2000), holding that the COPA "imposes an impermissible burden on constitutionally protected First Amendment speech."
47. Anecdotally, this was the case in my household (which included two children under 13) following COPPA's implementation.
48. In response to the FTC's notice of proposed rulemaking for the Children's Online Privacy Protection Rule, many parents expressed opposition to the rule, stating that the rule is paternalistic, parents should be responsible for protecting their children, and websites would pass on increased administrative costs to consumers. See, e.g., FTC, Public Comments, supra note 7, at cmts. 12, 24, 31.
49. See http://www.ftc.gov/opa/2005/04/coppacomments.htm.
50. See http://www.ftc.gov/opa/2006/06/socialnetworking.htm: "The Federal Trade Commission today called on social networking sites to make sure children visiting their sites can stay safe and their parents can protect them. Testifying for the FTC, Commissioner Pamela Jones

Harbour told the House Committee on Energy and Commerce Subcommittee on Oversight and Investigation that there is a 'need for social networking websites—individually, collectively, and, most importantly, expeditiously—to develop and implement safety features to protect children who visit their sites and empower parents to protect their children when they do so." Harbour also emphasized that "the Federal Trade Commission is committed to helping create a safer online experience for children."

51. See generally Health Insurance Portability and Accountability Act of 1996, 110 Stat. 1936; Gramm-Leach-Bliley Act of 1999, 113 Stat. 1338.
52. Turow and Nir, p. 35 (finding that children are substantially more likely than parents to give up personal information to a website when free gifts are offered).
53. See Center for Media Education, *Web of Deception: Threats to Children from Online Marketing,* explaining how online prizes, games, surveys, and advertising invade children's privacy and constitute unfair and deceptive advertising. Available at http://www.cme.org/children/marketing/deception.pdf. at 7.
54. Center for Media Education, at 7.
55. Carl S. Kaplan, "Suit Considers Computer Files, Cyber Law," *New York Times,* September 29, 2000, available at http://www.nytimes.com/2000/09/29/technology/29CYBERLAW.html. Gramm-Leach-Bliley Act of 1999, supra note 120, at tit. 5 (to be codified in relevant part at 15 U.S.C. 6801–809).
56. *Wisconsin v. Yoder,* 406 U.S. 205 (1972).
57. Video Privacy Act of 1988, 18 U.S.C. 2710 (2000); Gramm-Leach-Bliley Act of 1999, 15 U.S.C. 6801–809).
58. Privacy Act of 1974, 5 U.S.C. 552a (2000).
59. The definition of "person," "individual," "consumer," "customer," or "employee" includes minors under the Fair Credit Reporting Act, 15 U.S.C. 1681a(b) (2000), the Privacy Act, 5 U.S.C. 552a(a)(2) (2000), the Right to Financial Privacy Act, 12 U.S.C. 3401(4) (2000), the Video Privacy Protection Act, 18 U.S.C. 2710(a)(1) (2000) and the Employee Polygraph Protection Act, 29 U.S.C. 2001(2) (2000), respectively.
60. See *New Jersey v. T.L.O.,* 469 U.S. 325, 330–33 (1985); see also *Veronica School District v. Acton,* 515 U.S. 646, 655–56 (1995).
61. See David L. Sobel, "Statement before the Commission on Online Child Protection" (June 9, 2000), available at http://epic.org/free_speech/copa/statement_6_00.html. Press release, ACLU, "Is Cyberspace Burning? ACLU Says Internet Ratings May Torch Free Speech on the Net" (August. 7, 1997), available at http://www.aclu.org/news/n080797a.html. According to the ACLU, the notion of self-rating is "no less offensive to the First Amendment than a proposal that publishers of books and magazines rate each and every article or story, or a proposal that everyone engaged in a street corner conversation rate his or her comments." See *ACLU v. Reno,* 217 F.3d 162, 166 (3d Cir. 2000), holding that the Child Online Protection Act "imposes an impermissible burden on constitutionally protected First Amendment speech."
62. See http://www.aclu.org/technology-and-liberty/cyberspace-burning (last accessed Febraury 20, 2011).
63. Margie K. Shields and Richard E. Behrman, "Children and Computer Technology: Analysis and Recommendations," *Future of Children* 10 (2000), pp. 4, 6 (2000), available at http://www.futureofchildren.org/cct/index.htm (last visited January 22, 2001).
64. Michael Lewis, "Jonathan Lebed's Extracurricular Activities," pp. 6, 26.

65. Alexander Baldinger, "Candidate Profiles Pop Up on Facebook; Web Effort Aimed at Md. Students," *Washington Post*, June 19, 2006: "Facebook tallied upwards of 7 billion page views during April 2006, making it the seventh-most visited site on the Web."
66. See, e.g., "All The Cool People Are Irish" (Loyola Maryland) http://wesleyan.facebook.com/group.php?gid=2201145609 (accessed August 1, 2006); "Damn Right I Like The Life I Live" (University of Princeton) http://wesleyan.facebook.com/group.php?gid=2200094981 (accessed August 1, 2006); "Oooh, Was That Mean? I'm Sorry, I Didn't Mean it. Oh Wait, Yes I Did" (Vassar College)

    http://wesleyan.facebook.com/group.php?gid=2200078323 (accessed August 1, 2006); "I Go To Michigan and Therefore am Better Than You" (University of Michigan) http://weslevan.facebook.com/group.php?gid=2200918558 (accessed August 1, 2006); "Everybody Hates Us Because We're Cooler Than You" (Tufts University) http://weslevan.facebook.com/group.php?gid=2200139948 (accessed August 1., 2006); and "Cal Sucks" (University of Stanford)

    http://wesleyan.facebook.com/group.php?gid=2200060819, accessed August 1, 2006).
67. See http://www.nytimes.com/2006/06/26/technology/26link.html, visited June 5, 2011..
68. Dareh Gregorian, "XXXtortion Rap for Cyber 'Perv'—Scammed Coeds for Nudie Pix: DA," *New York Post*, June 19, 2006.
69. See, e.g., *CNN Saturday Morning News*, CNN, June 17, 2006: "The prospective employer decided to go online to MySpace to see what they could find about the student before they scheduled that interview. Well on this page, the student listed one of his interests smoking blunts which is a cigar filled with marijuana. Now needless to say here, that entry on the Web site lost the student any chance of getting hired with that company."
70. See e.g., L. Van Zoonen, "Feminist Internet Studies," *Feminist Media Studies*, 1 (1) (March 1, 2001), pp. 67–72(6).
71. *Remsburg v. Docusearch*, 816 A.2d 1001 (NH 2003).
72. For possible reasons why people are more willing to expose themselves on the Internet, see Adam Joinson, "Causes and Implications of Disinhibited Behavior on the Internet," *Psychology and the Internet: Intrapersonal, Interpersonal, and Transpersonal Implications*, ed. Jayne Gackenbach (San Diego: Academic Press, 1998), 43–60. Joinson argues (pp. 43–44) that "there is a growing acceptance that the Internet somehow leads people to behave in ways they do not in 'real life.'" One possible explanation for this is the phenomenon of "disinhibition" which "c[an] be summarized as behavior that is less inhibited than comparative behavior in real life. Thus disinhibition on the Internet is... seen as any behavior that is characterized by an apparent reduction in concerns for self-presentation and the judgment of others."

    See also Patricia Wallace, *Psychology of the Internet* (Cambridge: Cambridge University Press, 2001), 169, explaining that "the nature of the Internet is likely to trigger that disinhibition we see so often in other aspects of online behavior. People may feel freer to read erotic stories and view explicit messages online when they might never have entered an adult motive theater or visited a live sex show. They may also feel freer to explore the fetishes, alternative subcultures, and the deviant in ways that have not really been feasible in the past." Wallace also argues that Internet can be "hyperpersonal" as well, as when using the Internet, "you sit at a computer screen feeling relatively anonymous, distant, and physically safe, and you sometimes feel closer to the people on the other side of your screen whom you have never seen than to the people in the next room" (p. 151).
73. According to *The Independent*, Ms. Ringley had to remove JenniCAM "under pressure from the online payment service Paypal because of concerns over the scenes of nudity." See "Unlikely Hits of the Internet," *Independent*, May 4, 2006.

74. Rachel Spencer and Matthew Acton, "Web & Wild; Exclusive; Real Life Sex Stories," *News of the World*, May 28, 2006.
75. Ibid.
76. Dave Krager, "Virtual Voyeurism: Webcams, Which Let Regular Folks Exhibit Their Lives on the Net, Have Made Viewers of Us All," *Time*, June 29, 1998, international edition, p. 58.
77. See, e.g., Danny Bradbury, "Science & Technology: Smile! You're on Webcam; A Man is Attacked in Bournemouth. The Crime is Reported by a Teenager," *Independent*, April 13, 2005 ("In many cases, people out and about in public are not aware that they are being looked at").
78. Ibid.
79. 9 N.W. 146 (Mich. 1881).
80. Ibid., at 148.
81. See, e.g., *Knight v. Penobscot Bay Med. Ctr.*, 420 A.2d 915, 917–08 (Me. 1980), in which the court upheld the lower court's determination that a man who had watched a woman give birth, erroneously believing that his observation was authorized, did not commit a tortuous invasion of privacy.
82. Ellen Goodman, "Internet Intimacy?" *Boston Globe*, June 21, 1998.
83. Anita L. Allen, *Uneasy Access: Privacy for Women in a Free Society* (Totown, N.J.: Rowman & Littlefield, 1988).
84. See Susan Ferraro, "The Anguished Politics of Breast Cancer," *New York Times*, August 15, 1993.
85. Aimee Heckel, "A Not-So-Private Part Vaginal Surgeries Take Center Stage on Popular Show–But is Their Starring Role Just Hollywood Hype?" *Boulder Daily Camera*, March 28, 2006.
86. See http://secondlife.com/.
87. Compare Daniel J. Solove and Chris J. Hoofnagle, "A Model Regime of Privacy Protection," *Illinois Law Review* 357 (2006), pp. 242, 265, 271–74.

Afterword

1. Anita L. Allen, "Driven Into Society: Philosophies of Surveillance Take to the Streets of New York," *Amsterdam Law Forum*, vol. 1, no 4. (2009). This is an online journal article, available at http://ojs.ubvu.vu.nl/alf/article/view/92/166.
2. Bible (Revised Standard Version), Matthew 6:1–6, 16–21.
3. *Pavesich v New England Life Insurance Co*, 50 SE 68 (GA 1905).

INDEX